Agriculture, biodiversity and markets

Livelihoods and agroecology in comparative perspective

Edited by

Stewart Lockie and David Carpenter

publishing for a sustainable future

London • New York

First published in paperback 2011

Earthscan

2 Park Square, Milton Park, Abingdon, Oxon OX14 4RN
Simultaneously published in the USA and Canada by Earthscan
711 Third Avenue, New York, NY 10017
Earthscan is an imprint of the Taylor & Francis Group, an informa business

First issued in paperback 2011

ISBN: 978-1-84407-776-2 hardback
ISBN: 978-0-415-50735-6 paperback

Cover design by Susanne Harris

A catalogue record for this book is available from the British Library

Library of Congress Cataloging-in-Publication Data has been applied for.

At Earthscan we strive to minimize our environmental impacts and carbon footprint
through reducing waste, recycling and offsetting our CO_2 emissions, including
those created through publication of this book. For more details of our
environmental policy, see www.earthscan.co.uk.

Contents

Tables, Figures and Boxes

Tables

Figures

Boxes

Appendices

Acronyms

4C	Common Code for the Coffee Community
AMF	arbuscular-mycorrhizal fungi
ANAPQUI	Asociación Nacional de Productores de Quinua, Bolivia
API	Agricultural Price Index
BDS	Business Development Services
BWI	Biodiversity and Wine Initiative, South Africa
CAFÉ	Starbucks Coffee and Farmer Equity Program
CAP	EU Common Agricultural Policy
CAR	WTO Corrective Action Request
CBD	Convention on Biological Diversity
CDBC	Community Development and Biodiversity Conservation
CDM	Clean Development Mechanism of the Kyoto Protocol
CFPRA	Campagao Farmers Production and Research Association, the Philippines
CGIAR	Consultative Group on International Agricultural Research
CITES	Convention on International Trade in Endangered Species
COAG	FAO Committee on Agriculture
CRP	US Conservation Reserve Program
CVSCAFT	Central Visayan State College of Agriculture, Forestry and Technology, the Philippines
Defra	UK Department for Environment, Food and Rural Affairs
DSB	WTO Dispute Settlement Body
EBI	CRP Environmental Benefits Index
ESS	Environmental Stewardship Scheme, UK
EU	European Union
FAO	United Nations Food and Agriculture Organization
FAO	Food and Agriculture Organization of the United Nations
FBA	Fitzroy Basin Association, Australia
FSC	Forest Stewardship Council
FV	Farmer Variety
GATT	General Agreement on Tariffs and Trade
GI	Geographical Indication
GlobalGAP	Global Partnership for Good Agricultural Practice
GMO	Genetically-modified organism
HCVF	High Conservation Value Forest
IBPGR	International Board for Plant Genetic Resources
IPPC	International Plant Protection Convention
IPR	Intellectual property right
IRRI	International Rice Research Institute
ISO	International Organization for Standardization
ISPM	International Standards for Phytosanitary Measures

ITCPGR	International Technical Conference on Plant Genetic Resources
MAO	Municipal Agricultural Office, the Philippines
MASIPAG	Farmer-Scientist Partnership for Development
MBI	Market-based incentive /Market-based instrument
MEA	Millennium Ecosystem Assessment
MSSRF	MS Swaminathan Research Foundation, India
MV	Modern Variety
NAFTA	North American Free Trade Area
NASAA	National Association for Sustainable Agriculture, Australia
NGO	non-governmental organization
NOP	USDA National Organic Program
NQ Dry Tropics	North Queensland Dry Tropics Natural Resource Management Group, Australia
NTFP	non-timber forest product
OECD	Organisation for Economic Co-operation and Development
OIE	World Organisation for Animal Health
PBR	plant breeders' rights
PDO	Protected Designation of Origin
PES	payments for environmental services/payments for ecosystem services
PGI	Protected Geographical Indication
PGRFA	plant genetic resources for food and agriculture
PO	people's organization
PPB	Participatory Plant Breeding
PPM	production and processing method
PRA	pest risk analysis
PRONAA	Programa Nacional de Apoyo Alimentaria (Peru)
PVCA	participatory value chain analysis
PVP	Plant Variety Protection
SEARICE	South East Asian Regional Initiative for Community Empowerment
SMTA	Standard Material Transfer Agreement
SPF	stochastic production frontier
SPS Agreement	Agreement on The Application of Sanitary and Phytosanitary Measures
TE	technical efficiency
TRIPS	WTO Agreement on Trade-Related Aspects of Intellectual Property Rights
TV	Traditional Variety
UNEP	United Nations Environment Program
UPOV	International Union for the Protection of New Varieties of Plant
UPOV Convention	International Convention for the Protection of New Varieties of Plant

US	United States
USDA	United States Department of Agriculture
WIPO	World Intellectual Property Organization
WTO	World Trade Organization
WWF	World Wide Fund for Nature

Contributors

Miguel A Altieri is Professor of Agroecology at the University of California, Berkeley. He is a member of the Steering Committee of the United Nations Food and Agriculture Organization's Globally Important Agricultural Heritage Systems program, the goal of which is to dynamically conserve the world's remaining traditional farming systems. He is also President of the Latin American Scientific Society of Agroecology and Coordinator of the International Agroecology Program at the Centre for the Study of the Americas in Berkeley. His research aims to elucidate basic ecological principles for the design and management of sustainable agroecosystems with a particular focus on the ways in which biodiversity can contribute to the design of pest-stable systems.

Bustanul Arifin is an agricultural economist from Lampung University, Indonesia, whose research focus includes national agricultural policy development and resource economics.

Robert Black is a lawyer and regulatory scientist now working as an independent consultant in biosecurity law, regulation and risk assessment. Previously he was Principal Scientist, and then Reader in Law, at the University of Greenwich, United Kingdom.

David Carpenter holds a PhD in Human Ecology from the Australian National University. His thesis focused on the agroecological adaptations of resource poor rice farmers in the Philippines. David currently works for the Australian Agency for International Development (AusAID) in the Asia Regional Branch. Prior to joining AusAID, Dr Carpenter worked as a Senior Research Officer at Central Queensland University conducting research into the livelihoods of Filipino farmers.

David Dumaresq lectures in agroecology and sustainable systems and convenes the Australian National University's Human Ecology Program. He has operated commercial organic farms and served on the National Executive of the National Association for Sustainable Agriculture, Australia. David's research and teaching focuses on the environmental, economic and social sustainability of farm systems and alternative management practices; agroecological interactions between farming operations, plant growth and soil ecological function; transdisciplinary research methodologies and their application to postnormal science and policy development; and environmental philosophy.

Girigan Gopi is an economist engaged in research on agrobiodiversity, landuse patterns, tribal livelihoods and gender. For over ten years he has been involved in studies focused on paddy ecosystems. He works with the M.S. Swaminathan Research Foundation's Community Agrobiodiversity Centre (CAbC) in Kerala,

India. The CAbC was established in 1997 with a mission to promote socially inclusive and gender perceptive development processes and research-driven technology dissemination that inculcates ethical values in biodiversity conservation to achieve rural prosperity.

C.P. Gracy is an agricultural economist from the University of Agricultural Sciences Bangalore, India. Her current research interests include contract farming and the integration of small farmers with supermarkets.

Jon Hellin works at the International Maize and Wheat Improvement Center (CIMMYT). He has a PhD in Geography from Oxford Brookes University, where he is also an Honorary Research Associate, an MSc in Forestry and its Relation to Land Use and a BA (Hons) in Modern History from Oxford University. He has nineteen years' agricultural research and rural development experience from Latin America, South Asia and East Africa. Since completing a cross-disciplinary PhD on land management in Central America, his research has focused on farmers' livelihood security and access to markets.

Sophie Higman is a science writer and editor with Green Ink, a publishing services company that specializes in communicating research and development to eradicate hunger, poverty and environmental degradation worldwide. She has a background in forestry and rural livelihoods with a BA (Hons) in Zoology and an MSc in Forestry and its Relation to Land Use from Oxford University. She worked in Latin America for over 10 years and has written two books, one on sustainable forest management and the other on farmers' access to markets in Latin America.

Alder Keleman is a social scientist specializing in the study of crop diversity in Latin America. She was supported at the International Maize and Wheat Improvement Center (CIMMYT) in Mexico, and subsequently at the Food and Agriculture Organization (FAO) in Rome, Italy, by a Congressional Hunger Fellowship. She holds a Master of Environmental Science and a Master of Arts in International Relations, and is currently a PhD student at Yale University's School of Forestry and Environmental Studies.

Tran Ngoc Kham is a resource economist at Tay Nguyen University, Vietnam, whose area of interest includes natural resource management in the Central Highlands of Vietnam.

Irina Kireeva graduated in law and qualified as a lawyer at Moscow State University (Russian Federation) in 1997 with the highest honours. In 1997-98 she took the degree of Master in Laws at Leuven University (Belgium). Since joining O'Connor and Company in March 2002 Irina has been dealing with a variety of international and European trade issues (including WTO law in the areas of agriculture, sanitary and phytosanitary measures, technical barriers, intellectual property and regional integration). She has extensive expertise and knowledge of EU food safety and quality policy law as well as animal welfare.

Dan Klooster is Associate Professor of Latin American Studies at the University of Redlands, California. His work examines community forestry policy, the ways globalization creates transnational rural livelihoods and affects possibilities for forest conservation, and forest certification as an emerging form of governance with critical implications for sustainable community development in Latin America. He recently held a Fulbright-Garcia Robles Scholarship to study the role of forest certification in conservation and development in Oaxaca, Mexico. He obtained a PhD in Geography from the University of California, Los Angeles.

Nadesapanicker Anil Kumar is a systematic botanist working with the M.S. Swaminathan Research Foundation's Community Agrobiodiversity Centre. In 2007, he was a participant in the Watson International Scholars of the Environment Program. His most recent research includes a regional survey of wild edible plant species and rare, endemic, and threatened plant species of the Western Ghats region in India. He is also involved in a series of initiatives that facilitate sustainable agricultural and rural development in the Malabar region of Kerala, India. As a scientist in biodiversity, he has published many research papers, books, extension publications and popular articles on subjects including biodiversity, conservation, ethnobotany, and floristics/taxonomy.

Stewart Lockie is Professor of Sociology in the Research School of Social Sciences at the Australian National University, and Adjunct Professor of Environmental Sociology at CQUniversity Australia. His research addresses natural resource management policy, the incorporation of environmental and social values in markets for agricultural commodities, cultures of food consumption, and social impact assessment. He is co-author of *Going Organic: Mobilizing Networks for Environmentally Responsible Food Consumption* (CABI, 2006).

Jeffrey C. Milder is Research Associate at Ecoagriculture Partners (Washington, DC, USA) and a PhD Candidate in the Department of Natural Resources at Cornell University (Ithaca, New York, USA). His research focuses on integrating biodiversity conservation with human well-being in farming regions and other human-dominated landscapes in Central America and the United States.

Gerald Moore is currently an Honorary Fellow with Bioversity International, dealing primarily with the implementation of the International Treaty on Plant Genetic Resources for Food and Agriculture. Prior to that he was Legal Counsel of FAO from 1988 to 2000 and as such was closely involved in facilitating the Treaty negotiations. Since retiring from FAO he has been a regular member of CGIAR observer delegations to the Treaty negotiations and sessions of the Governing Body of the Treaty. He is a barrister-at-law and has law degrees from Cambridge University and the University of California at Berkeley.

Tad Mutersbaugh is Associate Professor of Geography and Director of Latin American Studies at the University of Kentucky. Drawing on fieldwork with coffee growers in Oaxaca, Mexico, his research is focused on the political economy of certification and the relationships between certification, international markets, rural development, the organization of work within households and villages, and local conservation ecologies.

Jeff Neilson is a geographer at the University of Sydney, Australia, with interests in rural development and natural resource management across South and Southeast Asia.

Amani Omer is an environmental economist in the School of Social Sciences, the University of Manchester. She has worked on the economics of biodiversity and agricultural and environmental sustainability. Her work focuses on applied theory and empirical research on the interactions between agrobiodiversity and modern intensive agriculture. Her current research interests include sustainable consumption, sustainable intensification and environmental management.

Unai Pascual is a lecturer in ecological economics at the Department of Land Economy, University of Cambridge, UK. He carries out research on landuse change including biodiversity economics. Among other positions, with regard to agrobiodiversity, he is a member of the Agrobiodiversity Science Committee of Diversitas and an honorary fellow of Bioversity International.

Parameswaran Prajeesh is a botanist with the M.S. Swaminathan Research Foundation's Community Agrobiodiversity Centre. His research focuses on rice genetic diversity in the wetland rice fields of Wayanad district of Kerala, India. He also has a research interest in laws and policies related to the environment and to the resource access and rights of rural and tribal communities.

Bill Pritchard is an economic geographer at the University of Sydney, Australia. His research addresses the ways that economic, social and cultural processes intermesh with one another to create the specificities of place and space.

Paul Rogé is a graduate researcher at UC Berkeley where he studies the resilience of traditional farming systems in Mexico to climate change. Paul is keenly interested in community-based rural development. He has collaborated as a researcher and volunteer with several organizations in the United States and Latin America, including the Agriculture and Land-Based Training Association and el Centro de Desarrollo Integral Campesino de La Mixteca. Paul is knowledgeable in ecologically-based pest management, organic farming, and composting methods.

Noel Russell is Senior Lecturer in Environmental and Agricultural Economics in the School of Social Sciences, University of Manchester. He has previously studied and worked at University College Dublin, University College Galway and Cornell University. Noel's current research includes investigations into the economics of biodiversity and ecological services, the economics of sustainable intensification in agricultural production, and the role of commercial and economic criteria in assessing the sustainability of farming.

Sara J. Scherr is an agricultural and natural resource economist whose career has focused on agricultural and forest policy and land management in tropical developing countries. She is founder and President of Ecoagriculture Partners, an NGO that supports agricultural communities who manage landscapes both to increase production and incomes, and to enhance wild biodiversity and ecosystem services. She is a member of the United Nations Environment Program Advisory Panel on Food Security and a member of the Board of Directors of The Katoomba Group and REBRAF-USA. Dr Scherr has published numerous articles and books including *Farming with Nature: The Science and Practice of Ecoagriculture* (Island Press, 2007, co-edited with Jeff McNeely).

Seth Shames is a project manager at Ecoagriculture Partners (EP). He leads the Payments for Ecosystem Services in Agriculture Landscapes project and manages EP's international and domestic policy engagement. In this capacity, he has organized a coalition of groups to engage on agricultural issues at the UN Convention on Biological Diversity, conducted research on environment and development policies in East Africa, and advised on policy options to link environmental management and food security. Other research topics have included ecoagriculture in protected areas, sustainable biofuels production, and agriculture and climate change. In addition to his work at EP, Seth has studied conservation tillage schemes for small farmers in Ethiopia, agroforestry systems in Peru and, and organized Community Supported Agriculture groups in New York City. He holds a MESc from the Yale School of Forestry and Environmental Studies and a BA from Columbia in Anthropology and Environmental Science.

Rosemarie Siebert is a senior researcher at the Institute of Socio-Economics at the Leibniz Centre for Agricultural Landscape Research (ZALF) in Müncheberg, Germany. Dr Siebert's research covers acceptance of landuse change, farmers' attitudes towards environmental issues, rural development and rural restructuring in East Germany. She has extensive experience in inter- and transdisciplinary research work and in project management and evaluation. Dr Siebert works as an independent evaluator for the European Commission and is Associate Editor of the journal *Rural Sociology*.

Lindsay Soutar is a geographer at the University of Sydney, Australia, with research interests in environmental management in Southeast Asia.

Dr C.S. Srinivasan is a lecturer in the Department of Agricultural and Food Economics at the University of Reading, UK. His main research interest is in the economic impacts of intellectual property rights (IPR) regimes as applied to innovations in agriculture. His research has focused on the potential impacts of plant variety protection regimes in developing countries. His research has also examined genetic resource policy issues and the impact of IPRs on agricultural biotechnology innovations. Prior to joining academia, Dr Srinivasan was a civil servant in India with extensive experience of administration and implementation of agricultural and rural development programs.

Edward Stone is a doctoral student and Robert Johnson fellow in the Department of Agriculture and Resource Economics at Oregon State University. His primary field of study is natural resource and environmental economics. His interests include the economics of ecosystem service provision, spatial economics of natural resources, and land use change.

Rebeka Tennent is a PhD candidate in the Research School of Social Sciences at the Australian National University and is currently completing a dissertation on the relationships between private food standards, food security and international donor policy. Rebeka recently completed her Masters dissertation on the social impacts of GlobalGAP for Australian horticultural producers at CQUniversity Australia. Her research interests include natural resource management, private regulation, agricultural biodiversity, food security, and development aid.

Erik Thévenod-Mottet is a geographer by training. Between 2001 and 2009, he was a researcher at AGRIDEA in Lausanne, Switzerland, with a focus on agro-food quality policies. Previously, he worked for a wine interprofessional organization and a certification body specializing in Geographical Indications (GIs). He works now for the Swiss Institute for Intellectual Property as an expert on GIs, and pursues his scientific activities on the links between origin products and environmental and cultural issues, in particular through the legal and institutional formalization of the related production systems.

JunJie Wu is Professor in the Department of Agriculture and Resource Economics at Oregon State University. He also holds the Emery N. Castle Professorship in Resource and Rural Economics at Oregon State University. He is a University Fellow at Resources for the Future. He has studied a variety of economic and policy issues related to agricultural production, resource conservation, and environmental management. His recent projects have focused on optimal design of conservation policies for the provision of ecosystem services, spatial modeling of land use change and environmental impacts, interactions between agricultural production and water quality, and spatial disparities in economic development. He is coeditor of *Frontiers in Resource and Rural Economics* (RFF Press, 2006).

Acknowledgements and Disclaimer

Many people contribute in largely unseen ways to an undertaking as large and as international in scope as this book. The idea for the book was conceived when both editors were employed through Central Queensland University (CQU) and engaged in research supported by the Australian Research Council (Project No. DP0664599). Our subsequent career moves have only added to the transaction costs for other participants in the project and we are grateful for their patience and cooperation. We are particularly grateful to Tim Hardwick, Commissioning Editor at Earthscan, and to Yvonne Holbeck and James Douglas from the Institute for Health and Social Science Research at CQU, for their assistance in bringing this to completion.

As the parents of young children, we are acutely aware both of our responsibility to care for the world they will inherit, and of how understanding our families have been in our pursuit of this and other projects.

Importantly, this work is solely that of the editors and the respective chapter authors and does not reflect the opinion of AusAID or the Australian Government.

Stewart Lockie
David Carpenter

1

Agriculture, Biodiversity and Markets

Stewart Lockie and David Carpenter

It is widely accepted that the sustainability of the global ecosystem in general, and of agriculture in particular, is dependent on the preservation, enhancement, and exploitation of biological diversity. Biological diversity—both wild and cultivated—underwrites the sustainability of agricultural production through the provision of the raw genetic material needed to drive innovation and adaptation, and through the provision of ecosystem processes and services that play important functional roles in agricultural systems. Agricultural biodiversity—or agrobiodiversity—plays a pivotal role in the livelihoods of all farmers regardless of resource endowment or geographical location. It provides the basic resources farmers need to adapt to varying conditions in marginal environments and the resources required to increase productivity in favourable areas. Clearly, there is a very close relationship between biodiversity and the livelihoods and well-being of agricultural communities. The need to protect and enhance agricultural biodiversity seems obvious. But what exactly does it mean to protect or enhance agricultural biodiversity? And how is this best achieved? As compelling as the case for agrobiodiversity may appear, these seemingly simple and straightforward questions demand complex and wide-ranging answers.

In introducing the topic of agriculture, biodiversity and markets this chapter will therefore attempt two, seemingly contradictory, things. On the one hand, it will 'muddy the waters' by problematizing the notion of biodiversity as it is applied to agricultural systems and their sustainability. On the other, the chapter will seek to restore some clarity by highlighting the conceptual issues, research questions, and policy dilemmas that must be addressed if we are to use biodiversity to make significant improvements to the livelihoods and sustainability of agricultural communities. The argument will be put that the case for promoting biological diversity within agricultural systems is not as obvious as may first appear. Scale effects, species interactions and migration, temporal variability, human values and activities, market relationships, and a host of other factors, conspire to render absolute measures of on-farm species diversity potentially misleading. By itself, in

1

other words, the notion of biological diversity provides only a partial insight into the health and likely resilience of agroecosystems. This does not mean that biodiversity is unimportant in either a material or conceptual sense. What it does suggest is the need to get a much better handle on the ecosystem services and other benefits that biodiversity provides to agriculture and the respective roles played by organisms, communities of organisms, and farming communities alike, in the co-production of valued ecosystem processes and services.

The need, we would argue, to take a more sophisticated and comparative approach to the understanding and management of biodiversity is underscored by the controversy that has surrounded a number of major international attempts at biodiversity preservation. Biodiversity preservation has been used to justify restricting farmers' rights by placing controls over production processes or by forced removal from designated biosphere reserves. Conversely, biodiversity preservation has been used to defend farmers' intellectual property against bioprospecting and to argue their rights to access the 'public' intellectual property encapsulated in cultivars and landraces bred on government research stations. Reflecting this, social scientists have produced an array of literature arguing for an understanding of the interconnectedness of social justice and ecosystem health; the negative impacts of trade liberalization and other economic imperatives on biodiversity; the potential exploitation of people's understanding of biodiversity through inaccessible intellectual property regimes; and the positive roles that often marginalized groups such as indigenous peoples and women might play in the preservation of biodiversity through traditional livelihood strategies. Agroecologists and others have provided support for these arguments by documenting the contribution that farmers make to maintaining and increasing crop diversity, the various selection and breeding mechanisms they employ to do so, and the tangible benefits these practices bring to local communities. This research has demonstrated that agrobiodiversity cannot be divorced from the rich cultural diversity and local knowledge that underpins livelihood systems. However, the services provided by biodiversity to agriculture and to agricultural communities remain, at best, partially understood and in need of substantial elaboration. For example:

- Comparatively few studies have been able to articulate in detail the specific contribution of biodiversity to agricultural community livelihoods, and vice versa. While it is almost universally accepted that biodiversity is essential for long-term sustainability, food security and so on, our understanding of how biodiversity contributes to farmers' short-term economic well-being is relatively poor. It is no great surprise that in the absence of this sort of information many farmers trade biodiversity off in order to pursue other goals.
- While many authors have critiqued the role of global capitalism in establishing an environmentally destructive treadmill of technology, little attention has been paid to the specific ways in which actors such as agribusiness firms and food retailers influence on-farm biodiversity management, the potential for market relationships in general to internalize the costs of biodiversity protection, or the

strategies that farmers use to maintain their own agency, or influence, over the management of agrobiodiversity assets.

- Similarly, the evolution of private systems of food quality regulation that exist outside of international governance structures such as the Convention on Biodiversity and the World Trade Organization have not been examined rigorously in relation to agricultural biodiversity. With private regulatory systems increasingly integrating environmental and social standards within their definitions of food quality, it has become essential to understand not only how food quality standards are changing, but which farmers are included or excluded from the markets regulated by these standards and the ensuing social and environmental affects.

- The concentration of genetic resources in the tropical countries of the so-called developing world has led to a predominant focus on the activities of resource-poor farmers from these countries. Not only has this seen the relationships between biodiversity and farm livelihoods elsewhere relatively under-researched, it has also led to a lack of analysis of how measures designed to protect agricultural biodiversity in one part of the world might impact—positively or negatively—on biodiversity elsewhere.

To address these gaps, this book brings together a range of case studies from around the world that examine relationships between biodiversity and agricultural livelihoods in specific spatial and social settings. However, accepting that the vast majority of the world's farmers are now integrated, to at least some extent, in global networks of governance and exchange, this book also explicitly addresses the ways in which farm livelihoods and biodiversity are influenced by public and private systems of regulation, market-based incentives and intellectual, biological and physical property rights regimes. The remaining sections of this chapter will introduce the main thematic issues of the book and will emphasize the interrelationships between agriculture, biodiversity and markets, with particular emphasis on the importance of biodiversity to agricultural production and sustainable livelihoods, the different types of market-based mechanisms that are employed to conserve and enhance agrobiodiversity, and the main multilateral mechanisms that influence agricultural biodiversity management at a global level.

Biodiversity, agricultural production and livelihoods

The Convention on Biological Diversity (CBD) defines biodiversity as 'the variability among living organisms from all sources ... and the ecological complexes of which they are part: this includes diversity within species, between species and of ecosystems' (UNEP, 1992). It is useful to think of biodiversity as having three main levels: genetic diversity (e.g. infraspecific diversity, genetic variance etc), species diversity (interspecific diversity), and ecosystem diversity (Wilson, 1988; Heywood, 1995).

Human societies benefit directly from a variety of ecosystem services provided by biodiversity. These services may be categorized as supporting, provisioning, regulating and cultural services. To define these in a little more detail:

- *Supporting services* include primary productivity, the formation of soil and the recycling of nutrients, which, in themselves, provide the basis for all other ecosystem services;
- *Provisioning services* include the tangible products that can be sourced from ecosystems including food, fibre, water and fuel;
- *Regulating services* include the processes which act to regulate climate and disease, mitigate floods, purify water etc; and
- *Cultural services* include the provision of nonmaterial benefits that human societies derive from ecosystems such as aesthetic, recreational, educational and spiritual values (see MEA, 2005).

Subsumed under the general category of biodiversity is agrobiodiversity, which 'encompasses the variety of plants and animals and micro-organisms at genetic, species and ecosystems level which are necessary to sustain key functions in the agroecosystem, its structures and processes for, and in support of, food [and fibre] production and food security' (Cromwell, 1999, p11). The biological resources that underpin agrobiodiversity and the agroecological services they provide include genetic resources, edible plants and crops, livestock, freshwater fish, soil organisms, naturally occurring insects, bacteria and fungi that control insect pests and diseases, agroecosystem components and types, and wild resources of natural habitat and landscapes (Thrupp, 2000).

It is important to emphasize that agrobiodiversity is not just the sum of agricultural or wild resources necessary for production (crop varieties, pollinators etc). Reflecting the argument made in the introduction to this chapter, two dimensions of complexity will be considered here: first, the co-production of agrobiodiversity by human and non-human communities; and second, the functional relationships between specific communities of organisms and desired ecosystem services.

In addition then to agricultural and wild genetic resources, agrobiodiversity must be seen to include the practices and food production systems employed by farmers throughout the world to dynamically manage those resources (Brookfield and Padoch, 1994). It is these myriad local practices that maintain and expand (in situ) the genetic diversity that underpins agricultural production. The role of resource poor farmers in the developing world is particularly important as these farmers manage by far the largest stock of agricultural genetic resources in the most diverse agroecosystems. A number of factors influence this tendency towards diversity. These include:

- The need to farm in complex and heterogeneous environments characterized by variation in soil qualities, topography, microclimate, photoperiods etc;

- The need to cope with production risks and uncertainties such as climatic variability, pest and pathogens etc;
- The need manage resources in order to comply with economic constraints, avoid or minimize labour shortages etc; and,
- The need to satisfy social needs and preferences such as forging social ties and providing for special consumption items, gastronomic choice and ritual obligations (Bellon, 1996).

The management of agrobiodiversity is thus an active anthropogenic enterprise that cannot be divorced from the rich cultural diversity and local knowledge embodied in livelihood systems (Prain et al, 1999; Thrupp, 2000). The reproduction of agrobiodiversity—particularly crop diversity—is socially and culturally mediated within vastly different human-ecological systems. Crop genetic diversity is a fundamental resource for the development of new crop varieties (Andersen, 2006); it is essential for food security and poverty alleviation (Cromwell, 1999; Thrupp, 2000); and it provides an important nutritional basis for subsistence farmers (Frei and Becker, 2004). It is, therefore, possible to argue that the greatest threat to agrobiodiversity comes not from its exploitation or explicit destruction (as is the case with 'wild' biodiversity) but from its non-use as farming systems become more homogenized and specialized.

In attempting to understand the ways in which biodiversity supports those ecological services essential to food and fibre production, it is important to recognize that all agroecosystems may be described as ecosystems that have been modified to promote enhanced productivity among a limited number of desired species. This suggests a need to focus particular attention on the specific functions that each species performs within that system. Functional biodiversity, therefore, is defined according to the relationships between groups of organisms (such as bacteria and fungi), the ecosystem-level functions they perform (such as decomposition), and the ecosystem goods or services these functions provide (such as nutrient cycling and the detoxification of chemical or biological hazards) (Swift et al, 2004). The absolute number of species present within an agroecosystem does not necessarily provide a useful indicator of functional biodiversity because the number of species required to provide essential ecosystem processes and services may be relatively small, in the short-term, provided that all essential ecosystem processes are covered (Swift et al, 2004). Further, biodiversity at the micro scale tends to be variable across both time and space due to the dynamic nature of environmental conditions that influence species behaviour and to the ability of many species to move and colonize new ecological niches (Zimmerer, 1994). Again, none of this is to say that high levels of absolute biodiversity within agroecosystems are redundant; nor that reductions in global biodiversity are insignificant provided essential local functions are maintained. The point is, rather, that changes in absolute biodiversity are highly scale dependent and can be misleading when applied exclusively at the field scale (Zimmerer, 1994). The implications of functional biodiversity for agriculture and farm livelihoods will be taken up further in Chapters 2 and 3.

The multilateral regulation of agricultural biodiversity

The Convention on Biological Diversity is the principle multilateral framework to address the issue of agricultural biodiversity. While the CBD does not provide a specific definition of agricultural biodiversity, related documents and decisions promote an expansive understanding of agrobiodiversity that embraces the social and ecological hybridity of agricultural landscapes. Decision III/11 of the United Nations Environment Program Conference of the Parties to the CBD (the key decision-making body) (UNEP/CBD/COP/3/38, no date, pp81-82) argues that agrobiodiversity is the foundation of food security and poverty alleviation. Agrobiodiversity presents opportunities to reduce synthetic input use while maintaining yields through natural pest control and fertilization. It is seen both as 'the essential source of genetic variability for responding to biotic and abiotic stress through genetic adaptation' and as a source of 'protection against uncertainties in the market'. Similarly, at the same time that the living organisms comprising agrobiodiversity function at the most fundamental level as agents of nitrogen, carbon, energy and water cycling, they must simultaneously be understood as the products of human management of ecosystems. Such management may, however, degrade biodiversity at the ecosystem, species and genetic levels just as easily as it may enhance it. In particular, excessive land clearing, monoculture, over-mechanization, and the misuse of agricultural chemicals have diminished the diversity of fauna, flora and micro-organisms, simplifying the environment and undermining the stability of production systems. As a consequence, Decision III/11,15e (UNEP/CBD/COP/3/38, no date, p77):

> Encourage[s] the development of technologies and farming practices that not only increase productivity, but also restore and enhance biological diversity and monitor adverse effects on sustainable agricultural diversity. These could include *inter alia,* organic farming, integrated pest management, biological control, no-till agriculture, multi-cropping, intercropping, crop rotation and agricultural forestry.

In addition to the promotion of such biodiversity-friendly agricultural practices among farmers, the Convention encourages signatory governments to utilize and build on the indigenous knowledge systems of local communities, to broaden the base of genetic material available to farmers, to conserve farm animal genetic resources, and to implement the Global Plan of Action for the Conservation and Sustainable Utilization of Plant Genetic Resources. This latter agreement seeks to ensure the conservation of plant genetic resources for food and agriculture, to promote sustainable utilization and thus to reduce poverty and food insecurity, to promote equitable benefit sharing from the exploitation of traditional knowledge and recent innovation alike, and to assist in national planning and capacity building (FAO, 1996).

According to McGraw (2002), one of the most innovative aspects of the CBD is its application of the concept of sustainable development to move biodiversity discourse beyond species conservation per se to include the management of biological resources for human benefit. However, while the CBD obliges signatories to monitor and regulate activities that threaten significant adverse impacts on biodiversity, it does not 'provide binding standards of behaviour' nor specify how parties must act to ensure 'sustainable use of their own biological resources' (Jacquemont and Caparros, 2002, p176). This lack of enforceability has been attributed both to the emphasis within the document on protecting national sovereignty (Jacquemont and Caparros, 2002) and to the myriad complexities and uncertainties associated with biodiversity as a topic of scientific and governmental interest (McGraw, 2002). As argued in the previous section, the need to provide for a variety of essential ecosystem services in the modified environments of agroecosystems requires some understanding of the functional relationships between organisms. However, as Swift et al (2004) point out, the definition of biodiversity provided by the CBD is so broad and inclusive as to provide little guidance on how to move beyond the use of 'diversity' as a useful abstraction and towards an understanding of the specific attributes of communities of organisms in particular locations and ecosystems.

The CBD has attempted to deal with this complexity and uncertainty in at least two ways. First, in 2000 the Conference of the Parties adopted an 'ecosystems approach' intended to enable integrated and adaptive management based on scientific assessment of all levels of biological organization including the structure, processes, functions and interactions among organisms (including humans) and their environments (Herkenrath, 2002). Second, the International Treaty on Plant Genetic Resources for Food and Agriculture—which came into effect in November 2001—established binding rules and institutional mechanisms to facilitate access to plant genetic material for major food crop and forage species and to guarantee the sharing of benefits arising from research and plant breeding. Additionally, the Treaty recognizes and provides some protection for farmers' own conservation and management of plant genetic resources and requires parties to develop policy and legal measures that promote diversity at all levels within farming systems (Cooper, 2002). Nevertheless, the primary focus of the Treaty remains the establishment of a multilateral system for access and benefit sharing that—while not inconsistent with the ecosystem focus of the CBD—provides clarity and legally binding rules only in relation to the transfer and use of genetic materials derived from a limited number of crop and forage species. Application of the ecosystems approach to agriculture is, therefore, dependent on national regimes of biodiversity governance, leaving considerable scope for multiple and conflicting interpretations of what this might mean and how it might relate to other international agreements concerning trade, intellectual property and so on.

Aside from those multilateral arrangements that directly target agrobiodiversity such as those mentioned above, it is also important to analyse the impact that other multilateral agreements have on agrobiodiversity—either directly or indirectly. Of particular importance in this regard is the impact international property rights law is having on plant genetic diversity. The effects that the World Trade Organization's

(WTO) Agreement on Trade Related Aspects of Intellectual Property Rights (TRIPS) are having on the in situ conservation of agrobiodiversity in the developing world will be discussed at length in Part 1.

Market-based mechanisms to conserve and enhance agrobiodiversity

One of the most pressing problems in relation to the maintenance and enhancement of agrobiodiversity involves finding ways that the ecosystem services provided by agrobiodiversity can be effectively valued by market mechanisms. This is particularly important when considering the reach of the global agricultural market and the corresponding decrease in subsistence and diverse farming systems (see Part 2). Agrobiodiversity continues to be depleted through rapid landuse change as biodiverse farming practices are replaced with less biodiverse practices. These changes arise due to a lack of market acknowledgement of biodiverse farming practices and are further influenced by macroeconomic policies that provide perverse incentives for non-biodiverse agriculture. These incentives include tax concessions, subsidies and price controls for certain crops (see Pascual and Perrings, 2007).

It is important to acknowledge that farmers are, by preserving biodiverse agricultural practices and landscapes, providing the fundamental resources necessary for future agricultural production across the globe. These resources include the genetic material that resides in the thousands of plant and animal species managed intentionally and unintentionally by farmers, as well as the other ecological services that biodiverse agricultural systems provide. At present, one could argue that farmers in general, and farmers in developing countries in particular, are not sufficiently rewarded for the provision of this public good (i.e. the maintenance and enhancement of agrobiodiversity for future exploitation). As individual farmers are the agents who decide how much, and what, agrobiodiversity to conserve based on their personal objectives, it is important to use whatever mechanisms are available to reconcile private with social values with regard to agrobiodiversity (Jackson et al, 2007).

While the development of market-based mechanisms designed to encourage sustainable landuse in general has been slow (Koziell and Swingland, 2002), recent years have seen some progress. Part 3 of this book will present case studies of farmers' experiences of mechanisms which seek to place a direct monetary value on agricultural biodiversity. These will include mechanisms such as organic, fair trade and bird friendly certification schemes. Some of these schemes aim to reward producers for environmentally and/or socially beneficial practices with price premiums over those received for uncertified or 'conventional' produce, while others pay no premiums but are used instead by downstream actors such as retailers to exclude those suppliers who cannot demonstrate environmentally responsible production practices from the market. Part 3 will also examine value chain coordination activities that also provide no explicit price premiums but which are oriented instead towards supporting biodiversity protection and exploitation through the development of markets for underutilized plant products.

Part 4 will examine market mechanisms that focus on the conservation of agricultural biodiversity as an ecosystem service that provides benefits to the wider community and for which, on that basis, the wider community should pay. These schemes, often referred to as payments for environmental services or payments for ecosystem services (PES) are market-based, voluntary transactions where buyers and sellers come together to trade environmental services such as carbon sequestration, watershed protection, biodiversity conservation or landscape/seascape beauty (see Padilla et al, 2005). Around the world, these schemes are adding support to the more traditional conservation and environmental management initiatives undertaken by governments and donor agencies. Schemes in which payments are made to conserve biodiversity in agricultural and forest landscapes by providing compensation to farmers and land managers who either retain biodiversity or who engage in more ecologically sound agricultural or land management practices are increasing in popularity—particularly, it seems, in Latin America (see Ferraro, 2001; Ferraro and Kiss, 2002; Landell-Mills and Porras, 2002; Pagiola et al, 2002, 2004; World Bank, 2003). Such mechanisms conceptualize biodiversity—or at least aspects of biodiversity—as a public good that lies outside the market and for which farmers have no direct responsibility. As such, these raise important questions about how much different aspects of biodiversity contribute to farm productivity, the extent to which farmers ought to be expected to protect biodiversity and other environmental values as a condition of resource access, farmers' capacity to provide desired ecosystem services and so on. The case studies presented in Part 4 will examine the contribution of PES to biodiversity conservation in the short-term, as well as the influence of such schemes over the ways in which farmers understand biodiversity and their long-term responsibilities towards it.

Conclusion

The erosion of agricultural biodiversity exhibits many characteristics of market failure; the quite fundamental role of biological resources and processes in supporting food and fibre production and trade appearing both to be poorly understood and generally under-valued. Of course, there is no one way to 'fix' a market and chapters in this book analyse a variety of approaches including information provision, national and multilateral regulation, and the use of market-based instruments. The evidence presented throughout the book supports a number of broad conclusions about the relationships between agricultural biodiversity, livelihoods and markets (these are discussed in more detail in Chapter 18).

- Ecosystem services provided by biodiversity to agriculture do provide tangible economic benefits to farmers as well as helping them to manage risk and underwriting the sustainability of their farms in the longer-term. All farms derive benefits from the genetic diversity of domesticated plants and animals whether they are involved in in situ conservation and breeding or not. There is some evidence that managing to maximize species and endemic biodiversity is more likely to be profitable in marginal agricultural environments. However, even modern intensive agricultural systems derive measurable economic benefits from native and landscape biodiversity.

- However, simply informing farmers and other stakeholders of the financial benefits of biodiversity-friendly farming practices is unlikely to have a significant impact on their uptake. This is especially the case when such practices are complex, labour or capital intensive, inconsistent with personal and cultural values, unsupported by mainstream research and extension agencies, and/or not clearly connected with ecosystem services of value to farmers.

- It is not diversity per se that delivers ecosystem services but the functional relationships between groups of organisms. Promoting biodiversity-friendly practices without consideration of these functional relationships and what they mean for agriculture may lead to sub-optimal sustainability outcomes and undermine farmer interest and commitment.

- There is a pressing need to balance regulatory systems that protect native biodiversity *from* agriculture with systems that focus on what native biodiversity can do *for* agriculture. Currently, there is an enormous regulatory blindspot at both the national and multilateral levels in relation to functional relationships between landscape diversity, the role of agriculture in maintaining that diversity, and the services it provides to agriculture.

- Given that species exhibit highly variable levels of spatial and temporal mobility, the delivery of specific ecosystem services through biodiversity is very much scale-dependent.

- At the genetic level, critical agroecological principles focus on utilization of more than one variety of important plants and animals—or of genetically heterogeneous landraces—in order to provide insurance against pests, diseases and climatic variability while also providing for more varied dietary and livelihood opportunities.

- However, farmers are not, on the whole, interested in polarized debates over the merits of in situ conservation of traditional varieties versus ex situ conservation and modern breeding techniques. They are interested in equitable access to different kinds of genetic material and recognition of their own conservation and breeding efforts.

- At the species level, agroecological principles focus on the development of farming systems that both capitalize on the functional relationships between species (planned biodiversity) and which feed and protect biological activity more generally (associated biodiversity). In practical terms, this means more complex agroecologies, more use of perennial plants, and reduced use of tillage and agrochemicals.

- Yet with so many potential combinations of species, research is needed both in the design and evaluation of various spatial and temporal combinations and in the documentation and testing of species combinations used in traditional farming systems.

- At the landscape level, agroecological principles focus on mosaics of agroecosystems and relatively natural ecosystems. Connectivity between habitat types provides for species migration and increases the capacity of predator populations to respond to increases in pest numbers.
- Much is unknown, however, about the optimal mix of farmed agroecologies relative to comparatively natural ecosystems within a landscape. More research is needed into the contribution of relatively natural ecosystem components within predominantly agricultural landscapes and the degree to which endemic biodiversity may purposefully be built into those landscapes without compromising productivity or, in fact, while lifting it.
- At the same time, the complex mix of stakeholders and property rights implicated in landscape-scale management means that research into ecosystem processes needs to be backed up with the development of robust and participative planning institutions and processes.
- Institutional development is also needed to manage biodiversity at the genetic level. Despite polarized debates over international intellectual property rights frameworks (e.g. the TRIPS Agreement), the impact of these frameworks on genetic diversity is dependent on how they are utilized within national regulatory regimes. At the present time, lack of legal and scientific capacity and infrastructure is hampering the development of effective national regulatory systems.
- The most advanced market-based approaches to biodiversity conservation are arguably standards systems including eco-labels (organic, bird-friendly etc) and Geographical Indications. While these provide a mechanism to generate higher economic returns in recognition of particular practices or product qualities, standardized compliance checklists are not, by themselves, sufficiently sophisticated to address complex sustainability issues. They are particularly bad at linking the activities of individual producers or groups of producers with landscape-scale biodiversity management strategies.
- Continued government intervention (albeit not always regulatory intervention) is needed to promote landscape-level planning and monitor ecosystem health, on the one hand, and to facilitate market information, regulate transactions, provide infrastructure and clarify property rights, on the other.
- Payments for ecosystem service offer another market-based approach that, in theory, offers potential to allocate government and private expenditure more efficiently. However, targeting is essential to ensure that the focus of exploitative activities does not simply shift from newly protected to previously unused resources and to ensure that those resources which are protected are concentrated enough to provide a critical mass of interconnected activities.
- At the same time, planners need to be careful not to target PES schemes too tightly. The more sophisticated the targeting criteria for payments, the less freedom resource users have to make their own decisions about whether and under what conditions to provide a particular service. The reality is that PES schemes seldom offer incentives that fully cover the cost of service provision

and are most often taken up by farmers who are particularly interested in the environmental goals of these schemes.

- Market-based approaches are not a panacea for biodiversity management but a useful tool that must be carefully targeted and complemented by measures to build the capacity of farmers, NGOs and governments alike to plan and manage natural resources to achieve environmental and production goals.

References

Andersen, R. (2006) 'Governing agrobiodiversity: The emerging tragedy of the anti-commons in the South', *47th Annual Convention of the International Studies Association,* San Diego, CA, 22–25 March

Bellon, M.R. (1996) 'The dynamics of crop infraspecific diversity: A conceptual framework at the farmers' level', *Economic Botany*, vol 50, no 1, pp26–39

Brookfield, H. and Padoch, C. (1994) 'Appreciating agrobiodiversity: A look at the dynamism and diversity of indigenous farming practices', *Environment*, vol 36, no 5, pp6–11 and 37–44

Cooper, H. (2002) 'The International Treaty on Plant Genetic Resources for Food and Agriculture', *Review of European Community and International Law*, vol 11, no 1, pp1–16

Cromwell, E. (1999) *Agriculture, Biodiversity and Livelihoods: Issues and Entry Points*, Overseas Development Institute, London

Ferraro, P.J. (2001) 'Global habitat protection: Limitations of development interventions and a role for conservation performance payments', *Conservation Biology*, vol 15, no 4, pp1–12

Ferraro, P.J. and Kiss, A. (2002) 'Direct payments for biodiversity conservation', *Science*, vol 298, pp1718–1719

Food and Agriculture Organization of the United Nations (FAO) (1996) *Global Plan of Action for the Conservation and Sustainable Utilization of Plant Genetic Resources*, FAO, Rome

Frei, M. and Becker, K. (2004) 'Agro-biodiversity in subsistence-orientated farming systems in a Philippine upland: Nutritional considerations', *Biodiversity and Conservation*, vol 13, pp1591–1610

Herkenrath, P. (2002) 'The implementation of the Convention on Biological Diversity: A non-government perspective ten years on', *Review of European Community and International Law*, vol 11, no 1, pp29–37

Heywood, V.H. (1995) *Global Biodiversity Assessment*, Cambridge University Press, Cambridge

Jackson, L.E., Pascual, V. and Hodgkin, T. (2007) 'Utilizing and conserving agricultural biodiversity in agricultural landscapes', *Agriculture, Ecosystems and Environment*, vol 121, pp196–210

Jacquemont, F. and Caparrós, A. (2002) 'The Convention on Biological Diversity and the Climate Change Convention 10 years after Rio: Towards a synergy of the two regimes?', *Review of European Community and International Law*, vol 11, no 2, pp169–180

Koziell, I. and Swingland, I.R. (2002) 'Collateral biodiversity benefits associated with "free-market" approaches to sustainable land use and forestry activities', *Philosophical Transactions: Mathematical, Physical and Engineering Science,* vol 360, no 1797, pp1807–1816

Landell-Mills, N. and Porras, I. (2002) *Silver Bullets or Fools Gold? A Global Review of Markets for Forest Environment Services and Their Impact on the Poor,* IIED, London

McGraw, D. (2002) 'The CBD: Key characteristics and implications for implementation', *Review of European Community and International Law,* vol 11, no 1, pp17–28

Millennium Ecosystem Assessment (MEA) (2005) *Ecosystems and Human Well-Being: Current State and Trends: Findings of the Condition and Trends Working Group,* Island Press, Washington, DC

Padilla, J.E., Bennagen, M.E.C., Tongson, E., Lasco, E. and Tolosa, M. (2005) 'Conference—workshop summary', *Proceedings from the National Conference—Workshop on Payments for Environmental Services: Direct Incentives for Biodiversity Conservation and Poverty Alleviation,* Manila, 1–2 March

Pagiola, S., Agostini, P., Gobbi, J., de Haan, C., Ibrahim, M., Murguetio, E., Ramirez, E., Rosales, M. and Ruiz, J.P. (2004) *Paying for Biodiversity Conservation Services in Agricultural Landscapes,* World Bank Environment Department Paper No 96, Washington, DC

Pagiola, S., Bishop, J. and Landell-Mills, N. (eds) (2002) *Selling Forest Environmental Services: Market-based Mechanisms for Conservation and Development,* Earthscan, London

Pascual, U. and Perrings, C. (2007) 'Developing incentives and economic mechanisms for insitu biodiversity conservation in agricultural landscapes', *Agriculture, Ecosystems and Environment,* vol 121, pp256–268

Prain, G., Fujisaka, S. and Warren, M.D. (eds) (1999) *Biological and Cultural Diversity: The Role of Indigenous Agricultural Experimentation in Development,* Intermediate Technology Publications, London

Swift, M., Izac, A. and van Noordwijk, M. (2004) 'Biodiversity and ecosystem services in agricultural landscapes: Are we asking the right questions?', *Agriculture, Ecosystems and Environment,* vol 104, pp113–134

Thrupp, L.A. (2000) 'Linking agricultural biodiversity and food security: The valuable role of agrobiodiversity for sustainable agriculture', *International Affairs,* vol 76, no 2, pp265–281

United Nations Environment Program (UNEP) (1992) *Convention on Biological Diversity. Concluded at Rio de Janeiro on 5 June 1992.* UNEP, Nairobi

United Nations Environment Program, Convention on Biological Diversity Conference of the Parties (UNEP/CBD/COP/3/38) (no date) *Pending Issues Arising From the Second Meeting of the Conference of the Parties: Rome,* UNEP, Rome

Wilson, E.O. (1988) *Biodiversity,* National Academic Press, Washington, DC

World Bank (2003) *Guatemala Western Altiplano Natural Resources Management Project: Project Appraisal Document*, World Bank Report No. 25660-GUA, Washington, DC

Zimmerer, K. (1994) 'Human geography and the "new ecology": The prospect and promise of integration', *Annals of the American Association of Geographers*, vol 84, no 1, pp108–125

2

The Ecological Role and Enhancement Of Biodiversity in Agriculture

Miguel A. Altieri and Paul Rogé

Biodiversity in agriculture, or agrobiodiversity, refers to all crops and animal breeds, their wild relatives, and other species (e.g. pollinators, symbionts, pests, parasites, predators, decomposers, and competitors) that co-exist and interact within crop lands and/or their surrounding environments (Altieri, 1999). It includes populations of variable and adaptable landraces, as well as wild and weedy relatives, from which the entire range of domestic crops is derived (Harlan, 1975). Components of agrobiodiversity include genes, populations, species, communities, and ecosystems, as well as the landscapes in which agroecosystems are embedded.

Most components of agrobiodiversity perform ecological functions and deliver services that sustain ecosystem processes and the natural resource base upon which agriculture depends. Ecosystem services beyond the production of food, fibre, fuel, and income include the recycling of nutrients, control of microclimates, regulation of hydrological processes, pollination, regulation of undesirable organisms, and detoxification of noxious chemicals. All renewal processes and ecosystem services performed by agrobiodiversity are largely biological. Therefore, their persistence depends upon the maintenance of biological diversity (Altieri and Nicholls, 2004a). When these natural services are lost due to biological simplification, the economic and environmental costs can be significant. For example when agroecosystems, deprived of their basic functional components, lack the capacity to sponsor their own soil fertility and pest regulation, external inputs are needed to supply crops with these services. This can have negative economic consequences and create a suite of environmental problems.

Biodiversity simplification in agriculture results in an artificial ecosystem that requires constant human intervention. While, in natural ecosystems, the internal regulation of function is a product of plant biodiversity through flows of energy and nutrients, under agricultural intensification this form of control is progressively lost (Swift and Anderson, 1993). Thus commercial seedbed preparation and mechanized planting replace natural methods of seed dispersal; chemical pesticides replace natural controls on populations of weeds, insects, and pathogens; and genetic manipulation replaces natural processes of plant evolution and selection. Even decomposition is altered since plant growth is harvested and soil fertility maintained, not through nutrient recycling, but with fertilizers (Cox and Atkins, 1974).

A growing number of scientists, farmers, and private citizens fear for the long-term sustainability of ecologically simplified and highly input-dependent food production systems. Questions are being raised about the loss of biodiversity, the loss of productive capacity through soil erosion, the growing dependence of modern agriculture on non-renewable resources, the heavy reliance on chemical fertilizers and pesticides, and the vulnerability of large-scale monocultures to climate change and pest-disease outbreaks.

These concerns have gained renewed attention with the expansion of transgenic crops and agrofuel plantations which, by 2007, covered 115 million hectares worldwide—mostly with monocultures of soybean and maize (Altieri, 2007). The expansion of these technologies into developing countries may not be wise or desirable, especially if the promotion of these monocultures results in serious social and environmental problems. These countries are rich in agricultural diversity; traditional and small farmers have historically used mixed farming systems with high degrees of plant diversity, in the form of polycultures, agroforestry, and animal integration patterns, providing a strong ecological foundation to sustain small farm productivity and to design agroecological models that benefit the rural poor under varying climatic conditions and marginal environments (Altieri, 1995). Furthermore, large numbers of farmers in developing countries have limited access to the synthetic inputs that substitute for ecological services in intensified agricultural systems and may particularly benefit from the maintenance and enhancement of biodiversity (Francis, 1986).

Worldwide, experimental evidence suggests that biodiversity can be used to enhance soil fertility and improve pest management while sustaining acceptable yields without dependence on external inputs (Altieri and Letourneau, 1984; Andow, 1991). For example, several studies have shown that it is possible to stabilize insect communities in agroecosystems by promoting vegetational infrastructures that support natural enemy populations (Landis et al, 2000; Schellhorn et al, 2008; Lundgren et al, 2009) and to enhance soil biota—which play important roles in organic matter decomposition, nutrient cycling and soil-borne disease suppression—through the use of antagonists (Magdoff and van Es, 2000).

After exploring the key roles and functions of biodiversity in agroecosystem function, this chapter analyses the various options of agroecosystem design which, based on current agroecological theory, should provide for the optimal use and enhancement of functional biodiversity in crop fields.

Modern agriculture and biodiversity

Modern agriculture has led to the simplification of environmental structure over vast areas, replacing nature's diversity with a small number of cultivated plants and domesticated animals. In fact, the majority of the world's agricultural landscapes are planted with some 12 species of grain crops, 23 vegetable crop species, and about 35 fruit and nut crop species (Fowler and Mooney, 1990); that is, no more than 70 plant species spread over approximately 1,440 million hectares of presently cultivated land. Added to this problem is the genetic homogeneity that exists within some of the most commonly planted crops. For example, in the United States, 60 to 70 percent of the total bean acreage is planted with two to three bean varieties, 72 percent of the potato acreage with four varieties, and 53 percent of the cotton acreage with three varieties (NAS, 1972) Researchers have repeatedly warned about the extreme vulnerability associated with this genetic uniformity (Tripp, 1996; Brush et al, 2003; Gepts, 2006).

Cultivated plants grown in genetically homogeneous monocultures often do not possess the necessary ecological defence mechanisms to tolerate outbreaks of pests or disease. Modern agriculturalists have selected crops for high yields and high profitability, sacrificing natural resistance to pests and disease for productivity (Robinson, 1996). While significant amounts of toxic secondary compounds remain in many edible crops, the general trend has been the gradual reduction of the chemical and morphological (physical) features that protect plants. This is coupled with the simplification of the production environment inherent in monoculture agriculture. Not only are fewer species present in monocultures—reducing adaptive capacity—ecological niches are left unoccupied and open to colonization by pest species. As a result, crop plants are usually more vulnerable than their wild relatives to pest and disease attack and agroecosystems are subject to more frequent insect outbreaks than are natural ecosystems, despite intensive human inputs (Altieri and Nicholls, 2007).

Modern agricultural practices such as pesticide application also negatively affect natural enemies (predators and parasites) and key soil biota components, which do not thrive well in toxic environments. Further, a new wave of environmental effects may be associated with the massive deployment of transgenic crops whose effects are not limited to pest resistance and the creation of new weeds or virus strains (Marvier, 2001). Transgenic crops can produce environmental toxins with potential to move through the food chain and precipitate a series of unintended consequences for key ecological processes. These toxins may negatively affect biocontrol agents such as invertebrate populations which, in turn, can affect nutrient cycling. These toxins can also persist in the soil profile by binding to colloids. It is not yet possible to determine the specific long-term impacts of transgenic crops on agrobiodiversity and the ecological processes it mediates (Altieri, 2007). However, as long as monocultures remain the structural foundation of modern agricultural systems, agroecological research suggests that pest problems will persist (Altieri and Nicholls, 2007; Figure 2.1).

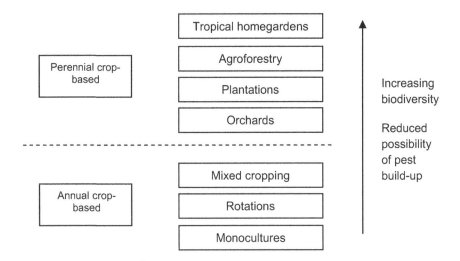

Figure 2.1. A classification of dominant agricultural agroecosystems on a gradient of diversity and vulnerability to pest outbreak.

One of the major challenges for those advocating ecological forms of agricultural production is to develop strategies to overcome the ecological limits imposed by biodiversity-poor monocultures. The promotion of biodiversity within agricultural systems is the cornerstone strategy for overcoming such limits. Associated with this is the redesign of agroecosystems at multiple scales with a view to improving the diversity of associated biota, which in turn generally leads to more effective pest control, pollination and tighter nutrient cycling (Altieri, 1995; Gliessman, 1998). As more information about the specific relationships between biodiversity, ecosystem processes, and productivity in a variety of agricultural systems is accumulated, guidelines for design can be developed further and used to improve agroecosystem sustainability and resource conservation.

Biodiversity in traditional farming systems

A conspicuous feature of traditional farming systems is the degree of plant diversity in the form of polycultures and/or agroforestry patterns (Altieri, 2000). Traditional cropping systems are also genetically diverse, containing numerous varieties of domesticated crop species as well as their wild relatives. Maintaining genetic diversity appears to be of even greater importance as land becomes more marginal and hence farming more risky. For example in Peru, where farmers plant up to 50 varieties of potato, the number of potato varieties cultivated increases with the altitude of the land farmed. Genetic diversity confers at least partial resistance to diseases that are specific to particular strains of crops and allows farmers to exploit different soil types and microclimates for a variety of nutritional and other uses (Brush, 1982).

These diversified agroecosystems have emerged over centuries of cultural and biological co-evolution and represent the accumulated experiences of peasants interacting with the environment with limited access to external inputs, capital, or scientific knowledge (Wilken, 1987). Using inventive self-reliance, experiential knowledge, and locally available resources, peasants have often developed farming systems adapted to local conditions that generate sustained yields and meet subsistence needs, despite marginal land endowments and the low use of external inputs (Altieri, 2002). Interactions between crops, animals and trees result in beneficial synergisms that allow biodiverse agroecosystems to sponsor their own soil fertility, pest control and productivity (Marten, 1986; Wilken, 1987; Altieri, 1995; Vandermeer et al, 1998), such as:

- Interplanting crops that enrich the soil with organic matter counteracts the tendency of certain crops to deplete the soil;
- Intercropping diverse plant species provides habitat for the natural enemies of insect pests as well as alternative host plants for pests;
- Mixing different crop species or varieties can delay the onset of diseases, reduce the spread of disease-carrying spores and modify environmental conditions such as humidity, light, temperature and air movement, so that they are less favourable to the spread of certain diseases; and
- Many intercropping systems prevent competition from weeds by creating complex canopies that block sunlight from reaching sensitive weed species, or by allelopathic inhibition of germination and growth of weeds.

The sustainability of intercropping, agroforestry, shifting cultivation and other traditional farming methods derives, in part, from their mimicry of natural ecological processes. This use of natural analogies suggests principles for the design of agricultural systems that make effective use of sunlight, soil nutrients, rainfall, and biological resources (Ewell, 1986). Much of the anthropological and ecological research conducted on traditional agriculture has shown that when not disrupted by economic or political forces, most indigenous modes of production have a strong ecological basis and lead to the regeneration and preservation of biodiversity and natural resources. Several scientists now recognize that traditional farming systems can be models of efficiency as these systems incorporate careful management of soil, water, nutrients, and biological resources. By studying these systems, ecologists can enhance their understanding of the dynamics of complex systems, especially the relationship between biodiversity and ecosystem functioning, thus enriching ecological theory. Moreover, principles can be derived for practical application in the design of more sustainable farming systems appropriate to small farmers in the developing world. In fact, several advances in modern agroecology have resulted from the study of traditional agroecosystems and a series of novel agroecosystem designs have been modelled after successful traditional farming systems (Altieri, 2004).

Organic agriculture and biodiversity

Most practitioners and supporters of organic agriculture believe that organic farms have positive impacts on biodiversity, and that farmland under organic agriculture does not exhibit the same dramatic decline in biodiversity that occurs in conventional agricultural farmland. These biodiversity benefits are likely to derive from the specific environmental features and management practices employed within organic systems, which are either absent or rarely utilized in the majority of conventional systems (Lampkin, 1992). The use of biological and management practices by organic farmers to manage fertility and pests, such as green manuring, composting, intercropping, and rotation, encourage habitat heterogeneity and floral diversity. These are known to benefit invertebrate and vertebrate biodiversity across a range of taxa.

Clearly, the benefits to biodiversity of organic farming may vary according to factors such as location, climate, crop-type and species, and are likely to be strongly influenced by the specific management practices adopted. One European study, for example, found 9 to 11 weed species in organically managed wheat plots compared with one species in conventional plots (Mader et al, 2002). It also found between 28 and 34 carabid species in organic systems as opposed to 22 to 26 species in conventional systems. Some specialized and endangered species were present only in the organic systems. This difference can largely be explained by the effects of pesticides. A particularly remarkable finding was a significant increase in soil microbial diversity in the organic systems, which in turn mediated soil fertility in low-input fields.

One of the most complete analyses of the effects of organic agriculture on biodiversity, which included the review of 76 published studies, found that species abundance and/or richness, across a wide range of taxa, was higher on organic farms than on locally representative conventional farms (Hole et al, 2005). The majority of these studies recorded higher weed abundance and species richness in fields under organic management, regardless of the arable crop being grown. Although differences in microbial (bacteria and fungi) communities between organic and conventional systems were less dramatic, there was evidence of a general trend towards elevated bacterial and fungal biomass and activity under organic systems. Comparative studies also indicated a general trend for higher earthworm abundance and species diversity in the organic systems.

The review by Hole et al (2005) indicates that the biodiversity benefits of organic management are likely to accrue through the provision of a greater quantity and quality of both crop and non-crop habitat than on conventional farms. Three broad organic management options seem to be particularly beneficial to farmland biodiversity: (1) prohibition/reduced use of chemical pesticides and synthetic fertilizers; (2) sympathetic management of non-crop habitats and field margins; and (3) preservation of mixed farming. While these three biodiversity friendly management options are characteristic of most organic farming operations they are certainly not ubiquitous or unique. Some organic farms are highly specialized, large-scale and monocultural operations managed with the same input-substitution approach that characterizes conventional agriculture, merely replacing the use of disallowed synthetic inputs with bacteriological herbicides, sulphur-based fungicides and naturally-derived fertilizers (Lockie et al, 2006). Such farms usually contain low levels of plant, arthropod and microbial biodiversity despite their compliance with organic certification standards (Altieri, 2002). At the same time, a variety of approaches to agricultural sustainability that are not specifically organic incorporate, to varying degrees, the three key practices mentioned above. These include Integrated Pest Management, Whole Farm Planning, Fair Trade etc (Lockie et al, 2006).

Managing planned and associated biodiversity

Two distinct components of biodiversity can be recognized in agroecosystems. The first, planned biodiversity, includes the crops and livestock purposely included in an agroecosystem. The second component, associated biodiversity, includes all the soil flora and fauna, herbivores, carnivores, decomposers etc that colonize the agroecosystem from surrounding environments. The functional relationship between these components and the ecosystems of which they are a part is illustrated in Figure 2.2. Both planned and associated biodiversity have direct functions in the provision of ecosystem services as illustrated by the bold arrows. However, planned biodiversity also has an indirect function, illustrated by the dotted arrow in the figure, which is realized through its influence on associated biodiversity (Vandermeer and Perfecto, 1995).

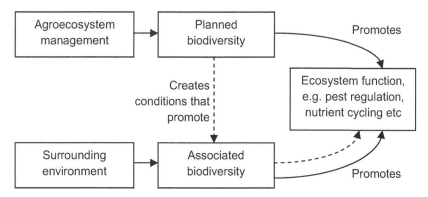

Figure 2.2. The relationship between planned and associated biodiversity in promotion of ecosystem function (adapted from Vandermeer and Perfecto, 1995).

Complementary interactions between the various biotic components of agroecosystems can be of a multiple nature. Some of these interactions can be used to induce positive and direct synergisms and effects on the biological control of specific crop pests and plant diseases, soil fertility regeneration and soil conservation. The exploitation of these interactions in real situations involves agroecosystem design and management and requires an understanding of the numerous relationships between soils, microorganisms, plants, insect herbivores, and natural enemies (Altieri and Nicholls, 2004b). According to agroecological theory, the optimal behaviour of agroecosystems depends on the level of interaction between the various biotic and abiotic components. By assembling a functional biodiversity it is possible to initiate synergisms which subsidize agroecosystem processes by providing ecological services such as the activation of soil biology, the recycling of nutrients, the enhancement of beneficial arthropods and antagonists, and so on (Altieri, 1995; Gliessman, 1998).

Agroecology aims to exploit the complementarity and synergisms that result from combining different components of both planned and associated biodiversity including crops, trees, and animals in spatial and temporal arrangements such as polycultures, agroforestry systems, and crop-livestock mixtures. Agroecologists encourage agricultural practices which increase the abundance and diversity of above and below-ground organisms and which in turn provide key ecological services to agroecosystems (Reijntjes et al, 1992).

Agroecosystem biodiversity components and their ecological function

Beneficial insects: predators and parasitoids

Increasing the richness of a particular guild of predators or parasitoids, or both, can reduce the density of a widespread group of herbivorous pests and, in turn, increase the yield of economically important crops. Experience with biological control suggests that when enemy species act together, the population density of specific pests is suppressed more than could be predicted from the summed impact of each enemy species alone (Debach and Rosen, 1991). Experience also suggests that this is more likely to occur in polycultural than in monocultural agroecosystems (Andow, 1991). Although most research has documented insect population trends in single versus complex crop habitats, a few have concentrated on elucidating the nature and dynamics of the relationships between plants and herbivores—and between herbivores and their natural enemies—in diversified agroecosystems. Several lines of research have developed (Altieri and Letourneau, 1982, 1984; Altieri, 1994, 1995):

- Crop–weed–insect interaction studies: evidence indicates that weeds influence the diversity and abundance of insect herbivores and associated natural enemies in crop systems. Certain weeds (mostly Umbelliferae, Leguminosae and Compositae) harbour beneficial arthropods that suppress pest populations.
- Insect dynamics in annual polycultures: overwhelming evidence suggests that polycultures support a lower herbivore load than do monocultures. Relatively more stable natural enemy populations persist in polycultures due to the more continuous availability of food sources and micro-habitats, while specialized

herbivores are more likely to find and remain on pure crop stands that provide concentrated resources and monotonous physical conditions.

- Herbivores in complex perennial crop systems: orchards with rich floral undergrowth exhibit a lower incidence of insect pests than clean cultivated orchards due to the increased abundance and efficiency of predators and parasitoids. In some cases, ground cover directly affects herbivore species, which discriminate between trees with and without cover beneath.
- Pest management in agroforestry systems: like other polycultures, insect populations are more stable in complex agroforestry systems because a diverse and more permanent habitat can maintain an adequate population of the pest and its enemies at critical times (van den Bosch and Telford, 1964).
- The effects of adjacent vegetation: one way to re-introduce biodiversity into large-scale monocultures is by establishing diverse vegetation along field margins and/or hedgerows which may serve as biological corridors allowing the movement and distribution of useful arthropod biodiversity within agroecosystems (Boaltman, 1994).

The available literature suggests that the design of vegetation management strategies must include knowledge and consideration of: (1) crop arrangement in time and space; (2) the composition and abundance of non-crop vegetation within and around fields; (3) the soil type; (4) the surrounding environment; and (5) the type and intensity of management. The response of insect populations to environmental manipulations depends upon their degree of association with one or more of the vegetational components of the system. Extension of the cropping period or planning temporal or spatial cropping sequences may allow naturally occurring biological control agents to sustain higher population levels on alternate hosts or prey and to persist in the agricultural environment throughout the year.

Since farming systems in a region are managed over a range of energy inputs, levels of crop diversity, and successional stages, variations in insect dynamics are likely to occur and may be difficult to predict. Planning of a vegetation management strategy in agroecosystems must therefore take into account local variations in climate, geography, crops, local vegetation, inputs, pest complexes etc, which might increase or decrease the potential for pest development under some vegetation management conditions. The selection of component plant species can also be critical. Systematic studies on the quality of plant diversification with respect to the abundance and efficiency of natural enemies are needed. As pointed out by Southwood and Way (1970), what seems to matter is functional diversity and not diversity per se. These effects of diversification can only be determined experimentally across a wide range of agroecosystems. The task is formidable since enhancement techniques must necessarily be site specific.

Beneficial insects: pollinators

Pollination is critical to the overall maintenance of biodiversity, as over 200,000 flowering plant species depend on pollination. In agroecosystems, pollinators are essential for orchard, horticultural and forage production, as well as the production of seed for many root and fibre crops. Data from 200 countries revealed that fruit, vegetable or seed production from 87 of the leading global food crops is dependent upon animal pollination (Klein et al, 2007).

As farm fields have become larger, and the use of agricultural chemicals has increased, mounting evidence points to a potentially serious decline in populations of pollinators. In agroecosystems, pollinator diversity and abundance is critically dependent on the availability of natural habitat in proximity to the farm site. Farm management may also influence the diversity and abundance of native bees found on farms (Kremen et al, 2008). On organic farms near natural habitat, native bee communities were found to be capable of providing full pollination services even for crops with heavy pollination requirements (e.g. watermelon, *Citrullus lanatus*), without the intervention of managed honeybees. Conventional farms experienced greatly reduced diversity and abundance of native bees, resulting in insufficient pollination services from native bees alone.

Agricultural intensification simultaneously reduces the richness, abundance and biomass of bees, and promotes local extinction of the most efficient bee pollinators. Pollinator populations have been adversely affected by increased pesticide use and much of their natural habitats, which includes hedgerows, dead trees and old fence posts, have been destroyed to make room for more farmland. There is ample evidence to suggest that pollinator populations are in decline and that such declines are affecting agricultural productivity (Ricketts et al, 2008). A global shortage of bees and other insect pollinators is reducing crop yields around the world and could lead to far higher prices for fruits and vegetables (Kevan et al, 1990).

The ecological role of weeds

Although weeds may compete with crop species, research shows that weeds play an important role in supporting biodiversity within agroecosystems. Several studies have demonstrated that the presence of weeds within or around crop fields influences the dynamics of the crop and associated biotic communities (Fiedler et al, 2008; Hyvonen and Huusela-Veistola, 2008). The manipulation of a specific weed species, a particular weed control practice, or the level of weediness of a cropping system can affect the ecology of insect pests and associated natural enemies (Altieri and Letourneau, 1982).

Weeds also positively affect the biology and dynamics of beneficial insects, and offer many important requisites for natural enemies such as alternative prey/hosts, pollen, or nectar as well as microhabitats that are not available in weed-free monocultures (Altieri and Letourneau, 1984). As insect pests are not always present in annual crops the provision of resources such as alternate host locations and pollen-nectar can contribute to the persistence of viable natural enemy populations in the absence of pests.

Research has shown that outbreaks of certain types of crop pests are less likely to occur in weed-diversified crop systems than in weed-free fields, mainly due to the increased mortality imposed by natural enemies. Crop fields with a dense weed cover and high diversity usually have more predacious arthropods than weed-free fields. The successful establishment of parasitoid populations usually depends on the presence of weeds that provide nectar for adult female wasps. Examples of cropping systems in which the presence of specific weeds has enhanced the biological control of particular pests have been reviewed by Altieri and Nicholls (2004). A literature survey by Baliddawa (1985) showed that population densities of 27 insect pest species were reduced in weedy crops compared to weed-free crops.

Research also suggests that interactions of weeds with arbuscular-mycorrhizal fungi (AMF) can increase the beneficial effects of weeds on the functioning of agroecosystems. Through a variety of mechanisms, weed-AMF interactions may reduce crop yield losses to weeds, limit weed species shifts, and increase positive effects of weeds on soil quality and beneficial organisms (Jordan et al, 2000).

Soil biota

Soil provides habitat for a diverse array of organisms—microbes (fungi, bacteria and actinomycetes) and animals such as nematodes, mites, collembola, diplopoda, earthworms and arthropods (Davies, 1973), which contribute to the maintenance and productivity of agroecosystems. The rhizosphere, which is the interface between plant roots and the soil environment, is the location of much soil biological activity and plant-microbe interactions including symbioses, pathogenic infection, and competition. A square metre of an organic temperate agricultural soil may contain 1000 species of organisms with population densities in the order of 106 per square metre for nematodes, 105 per square metre for micro arthropods, and 104 per square metre for other invertebrate groups. One gram of soil may contain over a thousand fungal hyphae and up to a million or more individual bacterial colonies. Energy, carbon, nitrogen and other nutrient fluxes through the soil's decomposing subsystem are dominated by fungi and bacteria, although invertebrates play a certain role in nitrogen flux (Swift and Anderson, 1993). The types of species present and their level of activity depends on micro-environmental conditions including temperature, moisture, aeration, pH, pore size, and types of food sources.

The community of soil organisms incorporates plant and animal residues and wastes into the soil and digests them, creating soil humus, which is a vital constituent for good physical and chemical soil conditions, and the recycling of carbon and mineral nutrients. This decomposition process includes the release of carbon dioxide to the atmosphere where it can be recycled through higher plants, and the release of essential plant nutrients in inorganic forms that can be absorbed by plants. Also, since the microbial biomass itself is a relatively labile fraction of the soil organic matter, nutrients in the biomass become available as live microbes digest dead microbial cells.

There is evidence that soil microbial diversity confers protection against soil-borne disease, but crop and soil type and management also play a role. Studies show that mycorrhizal diversity positively contributes to nutrient and, possibly, water use efficiency. The effects of soil fauna on nutrient and water use efficiencies are also apparent, but diversity effects may be indirect, through effects on soil structure (Giller et al, 1997).

There is no doubt that soil organisms are fundamentally important to the functioning of agroecosystems. Various functional groups of soil biota have been proposed such as: roots, ecosystem engineers, litter transformers, phytophages and parasites, micro-predators and microflora. In their role as regulators of soil ecosystem processes, soil organisms perform a number of vital functions in support of soil physical structure and chemical fertility including:

- Decomposition of plant residues, manures, and organic wastes;
- Humus synthesis;
- Improvement of soil structure;
- Mineralization of organic N, S, and P;
- Increase in the availability of plant nutrients; for example, P, Mn, Fe, Zn, Cu;
- Biological nitrogen fixation;
- Plant growth promotion: growth hormones, changes in seed germination, floral development, root and shoot biomass;
- Altering soil structure and aggregation;
- Suppressing pathogenic organisms;
- Breakdown of toxic compounds;
- Biological control of weeds for example, biological herbicides; and
- Enhanced drought tolerance of plants (Hendrix et al, 1990; see also Magdoff and van Es, 2000).

Given the ecological services provided by soil biodiversity, soil organisms are crucial for the sustainability of agroecosystems. Therefore, it is important to define and encourage agricultural practices that increase the abundance and diversity of soil organisms by enhancing habitat conditions, soil organic matter content and resource availability, and to avoid practices that reduce soil biodiversity. Sustained agricultural productivity may depend on the selection of management practices that enhance soil biological function in the fixation of atmospheric nitrogen, recycling of carbon and nutrients, and suppression of soil pathogens.

The types of agricultural management practices that influence soil biological activity are those that enhance nutrient cycling, add carbon and nitrogen inputs, improve the soil physical environment, and avoid synthetic chemicals that can harm soil microbial and faunal activity. Such practices include the use of cover crops and/or green manures, inclusion of a high-residue crop or perennial sod, applications of manure or compost, and reduced tillage and lower use of nitrogen fertilizers.

Reduced tillage (with surface placement of residues) creates a relatively more stable environment and encourages development of more diverse decomposer communities and slower nutrient turnover. Evidence suggests that conditions in no-till systems favour a higher ratio of fungi to bacteria, whereas in conventionally tilled systems bacterial decomposers may predominate (Hendrix et al, 1990). Residue has an important effect on organic substrate availability and soil micro-climatic characteristics. Soils with residues chopped and left as mulch generally support higher populations of surface feeding earthworms. Soil unprotected by surface mulch will freeze much faster than mulched soil and earthworm mortality increases in the absence of a gradual period of adjustment to decreasing temperatures (Davies, 1973).

Soil biotic populations can also be increased through direct introduction of organisms. Earthworms have been commonly introduced in a number of instances for soil conditioning and enhanced soil structure and fertility. Inoculation of seeds or roots with rhizobia, mycorrhizae, and Trichoderma are examples of direct manipulations of microflora to enhance plant performance (Miller, 1990). A major problem to overcome in the use of inoculations and introductions is ensuring the establishment of the introduced organisms. Competition from a diverse indigenous soil biota may overwhelm introduced organisms. Additionally, limited availability of food resources may result in extinction or emigration. It may be necessary to add food supplies or organic amendments along with inocula to aid establishment (Miller, 1990).

Most agricultural plants are colonized by mycorrhizal fungi, which have a substantial impact on crop productivity. Many studies have demonstrated the dramatic plant growth response achieved following inoculation with mycorrhizal fungi in low-fertility soils. These organisms can be used as bio-fertilizers but responses are often disappointing, especially in high-input agricultural systems. Management practices such as pesticides, tillage, crop rotation, and fallowing may adversely affect populations of mycorrhizal fungi in the field.

The literature on soil management practices to enhance existing microbial antagonists is voluminous. Organic amendments are recognized as initiators of two important disease-control processes: increase in dormancy of propagules and their digestion by soil microorganisms (Palti, 1981). Organic additions increase the general level of microbial activity and the more microbes that are active, the greater the chances that some of them will be antagonistic to pathogens (Fry, 1982).

Leguminous residues are rich in available nitrogen and carbon compounds, and they also supply vitamins and more complex substrates. Biological activity becomes very intense in response to amendments of this kind and may increase fungistasis and propagule lysis.

Conclusion

This chapter presents some ideas and principles on how to design and manage biodiverse farms that are rich in beneficial insect fauna and soil biota. Diversity—both agricultural and biological—becomes one of the integral foundations of such farming systems. Polycultures are typically favoured over monocultures and perennial, reduced-till systems with high species diversity are emphasized to reduce negative impacts resulting from intensive annual cropping systems. Rather than subsidizing soils, overdrafting groundwater, or relying on high-input fertilizers and pest control chemicals, practitioners work with planned and associated biodiversity and their synergisms to boost biological efficiency. Wild habitats may be incorporated to establish populations of beneficial insects and pollinators. Cover cropping and/or animals provide on-site sources of organic matter and nutrients.

Locally adapted varieties and species can create regionally specific genetic resilience. In this approach, the use of local biodiversity should be prioritized.

Clearly, a key strategy in sustainable agriculture is to reincorporate diversity into the agricultural landscape through various cropping designs. Emergent ecological properties develop in diversified farms, which allow the system to function in ways that maintain soil fertility, crop production, and pest regulation. The main approach is to use management methods that increase agroecosystem diversity and complexity (in space and time) as a foundation for establishing beneficial interactions that keep pest populations in check and maintain soil quality.

Different options to diversify cropping systems are available depending on whether the current monoculture systems that will be modified are based on annual or perennial crops. Diversification can also take place outside the farm. For example, field boundaries can be diversified with windbreaks, shelterbelts, and living fences to improve habitat for wildlife and beneficial insects. Additional benefits of these strategies include providing resources of wood, organic matter, resources for pollinating bees, and, in addition, modify wind speed and microclimate. Plant diversification can be considered a form of conservation biological control with the goal of creating a suitable ecological infrastructure within the agricultural landscape to provide resources such as pollen and nectar for adult natural enemies, alternative prey or hosts, and shelter from adverse conditions. These resources must be integrated into the landscape in a way that is spatially and temporally favourable to natural enemies and practical for producers to implement.

In summary, key ecological principles for the design of diversified and sustainable agroecosystems include:

- Increasing species diversity as this promotes fuller use of resources (nutrients, radiation, water etc), pest protection and compensatory growth. Many researchers have highlighted the importance of various spatial and temporal plant combinations to facilitate complementary resource use or to provide intercrop advantage such as in the case of legumes facilitating the growth of cereals by supplying extra nitrogen. Compensatory growth is another desirable trait as if one species succumbs to pests, weather or harvest, another species fills the void maintaining full use of available resources.

- Enhance longevity through the addition of perennials that contain a thick canopy thus providing continual cover that can also protect the soil. Constant leaf fall builds organic matter and allows uninterrupted nutrition circulation. Dense, deep root systems of long-lived woody plants are an effective mechanism for nutrient capture offsetting the negative losses through leaching. Perennial vegetation also provides more habitat permanence and contributes to pest-enemy complexes.

- Introduce fallow periods to restore soil fertility through biologically mediated mechanisms, and to reduce agricultural pest populations as life cycles are interrupted with forest regrowth or legume-based rotations.

- Enhance additions of organic matter by including high biomass-producing plants. Accumulation of both 'active' and 'slow fraction' organic matter is key for activating soil biology, improving soil structure and macroporosity and elevating the nutrient status of soils. Moreover, organic matter forms the foundation of complex food webs, which influence the abundance and diversity of natural enemies.

- Increase landscape diversity by promoting a mosaic of agroecosystems representative of various stages of succession. Risk of complete failure is spread among, as well as within, the various cropping systems. Improved pest control is also linked to spatial heterogeneity at the landscape level.

When properly implemented, diversification strategies lead to the establishment of the desired type of plant, insect and soil biodiversity and the ecological infrastructure necessary for attaining optimal pest control and soil fertility. As emphasized in this chapter, it is important to ensure that above ground diversification schemes are complemented by soil organic management, as both above and below ground biodiversity together form the pillars of agroecosystem health.

References

Altieri, M.A. (1994) *Biodiversity and Pest Management in Agroecosystems*, Haworth Press, New York, NY

Altieri, M.A. (1995) *Agroecology: The Science of Sustainable Agriculture*, Westview Press, Boulder, CO

Altieri, M.A. (1999) 'The ecological role of biodiversity in agroecosystems', *Agriculture, Ecosystems and Environment*, vol 74, pp19–31

Altieri, M.A. (2000) 'Multifunctional dimensions of ecologically based agriculture in Latin America', *International Journal of Sustainable Development and World Ecology*, vol 7, pp62–75

Altieri, M.A. (2002) 'Agroecology: The science of natural resource management for poor farmers in marginal environments', *Agricultural Ecosystems and Environment*, vol 93, pp1–24

Altieri, M.A. (2004) 'Linking ecologists and traditional farmers in the search for sustainable agriculture', *Frontiers in Ecology and Environment*, vol 2, pp35–42

Altieri, M.A. (2007) 'Transgenic crops, agrobiodiversity and agroecosystem function', in I.E.P. Taylor (ed) *Genetically Engineered Crops: Interim Policies, Uncertain Legislation*, Haworth Press, New York, NY

Altieri, M.A. and Letourneau, D.K. (1982) 'Vegetation management and biological control in agroecosystems', *Crop Protection*, vol 1, pp405–430

Altieri, M.A. and Letourneau, D.K. (1984) 'Vegetation diversity and insect pest outbreaks', *CRC Critical Reviews in Plant Sciences*, vol 2, pp131–169

Altieri, M.A. and Nicholls, C.I. (2004a) *Biodiversity and Pest Management in Agroecosystems*, Haworth Press, New York, NY

Altieri, M.A. and Nicholls, C.I. (2004b) 'Designing species rich pest suppressive agroecosystems through habitat management', in D. Rickerl, C. Francis, R. Aiken, C.W. Honeycutt, F. Magdoff and R. Salvador (eds) *Agroecosystem*

Analysis, Agronomy Monograph 43, American Society of Agronomy, Crop Science Association of America and Soil Science Society of America, Madison, WI, pp49–61

Altieri, M.A. and Nicholls, C.I. (2007) 'Agroecology: Contributions towards a renewed ecological foundation for pest management', in M. Kogan and P. Jepson (eds) *Perspectives on Ecological Theory and Pest Management*, University Press, Cambridge

Andow, D.A. (1991) 'Vegetational diversity and arthropod population response', *Annual Review of Entomology*, vol 36, pp561–586

Baliddawa, C. (1985) 'Plant-Species diversity and crop pest-control: An analytical review', *Insect Science and its Application*, vol 6, pp479–487

Boaltman, N. (1994) *Field Margins: Integrating Agriculture and Conservation*, Monograph No. 58, British Crop Protection Council, Thornton Heath, Surrey

Brush, S.B. (1982) 'The natural and human environment in the central Andes', *Mountain Research and Development*, vol 2, pp14–38

Brush, S.B., Tadesse, D. and van Dusen, E. (2003) 'Crop Diversity in Peasant and Industrialized Agriculture: Mexico and California', *Society and Natural Resources*, vol 16, pp123–141

Cox, G.W. and Atkins, M.D. (1974) *Agricultural Ecology*, W. H. Freeman and Sons, San Francisco, CA

Davies, N. (1973) *A Guide to the Study of Soil Ecology*, Prentice Hall, NJ

DeBach, P. and Rosen, D. (1991) *Biological Control by Natural Enemies*, Cambridge University Press, Cambridge

Ewell, J.J. (1986) 'Designing agricultural ecosystems for the humid tropics', *Annual Review of Ecological Systems*, vol 17, pp245–71

Fiedler, A.K., Landis, D.A. and Wratten, S.D. (2008) 'Maximizing ecosystem services from conservation biological control: The role of habitat management', *Biological Control*, vol 45, pp254–271

Fowler, C. and Mooney, P. (1990) *Shattering: Food, Politics and the Loss of Genetic Diversity*, University of Arizona Press, Tucson, AZ

Francis, C.A. (1986) *Multiple Cropping Systems*, MacMillan, New York, NY

Fry, W.E. (1982) *Principles of Plant Disease Management*, Academic Press, New York, NY

Gepts, P. (2006) 'Plant genetic resources conservation and utilization: The accomplishments and future of a societal insurance policy', *Crop Science*, vol 46, pp2262–2278

Giller, K.E., Beare, M.H., Lavelle, P., Izac, M.N.I. and Swift, M.J. (1997) 'Agricultural intensification, soil biodiversity and agroecosystem function', *Applied Soil Ecology*, vol 6, pp3–16

Gliessman, S.R. (1998) *Agroecology: Ecological Processes in Sustainable Agriculture*, Ann Arbor Press, Chelsea, MI

Harlan, J.R. (1975) 'Our vanishing genetic resources', *Science*, vol 188, pp618–622

Hendrix, P.F., Crossley, D.A. Jr., Blair, J.M. and Coleman, D.C. (1990) 'Soil biota as components of sustainable agroecosystems', in C.A. Edwards, R. Lal, P. Madden, R.H. Miller and G. House (eds) *Sustainable Agricultural Systems*, Soil and Water Conservation Society, Ankeny, IA, pp637–654

Hole, D.G., Perkins, A.J., Wilson, J.D., Alexander, I.H., Grice, P.V., and Evans, A.D. (2005) 'Does organic farming benefit biodiversity?', *Biological Conservation*, vol 122, pp113–130

Jordan, N.R., Zhang, J. and Huerd, S. (2000) 'Arbuscular-mycorrhizal fungi: potential roles in weed management', *Weed Research*, vol 40, pp397–410

Hyvonen, T. and Huusela-Veistola, E. (2008) 'Arable weeds as indicators of agricultural intensity: A case study from Finland', *Biological Conservation*, vol 141, no 11, pp2857–2864

Kevan, P.G., Clark, E.A. and Thomas, V.G. (1990) 'Insect pollinators and sustainable agriculture', *American Journal of Alternative Agriculture*, vol 5, pp13–22

Klein, A.M., Vaissiere, B.E., Cane J.H., Steffan-Dewenter, I., Cunningham, S.A., Kremen, C. and Tscharntke, T. (2007) 'Importance of pollinators in changing landscapes for world crops', *Proceedings of the Royal Society B*, vol 274, pp303–313

Kremen, C., Williams, N.M., Bugg, R.L., Fay, J.P. and Thorp, R.W. (2008) 'The area requirements of an ecosystem service: Crop pollination by native bee communities in California', *Ecology Letters*, vol 7, pp1109–1119

Lampkin, N. (1992) *Organic Farming*, Farming Press, Ipswich

Landis, D.A., Wratten, S.D. and Gurr, G.A. (2000) 'Habitat management to conserve natural enemies of arthropod pests in agriculture', *Annual Review of Entomology*, vol 45, pp175–201

Lockie, S., Lyons, K., Lawrence, G. and Halpin, D. (2006) *Going Organic: Mobilizing Networks for Environmentally Responsible Food Production.* CABI Publishing, Wallingford

Lundgren, J.G., Wyckhuys, K.A.G. and Desneux, N. (2009) 'Population responses by *Orius insidiosus* to vegetational diversity', *Biocontrol*, vol 54, no 1, pp.135–142

Mader, P., Fliebbach, A., Dubois, D., Gunst, L., Fried, P. and Niggli, U. (2002) 'Soil fertility and biodiversity in organic farming', *Science*, vol 296, pp1694–1697

Magdoff, F. and van Es, H. (2000) *Building Soils for Better Crops*, SARE, Washington, DC

Marten, G.G. (1986) *Traditional Agriculture in Southeast Asia: A Human Ecology Perspective*, Westview Press, Boulder, CO

Marvier, M. (2001) 'Ecology of transgenic crops', *American Scientist*, vol 89, pp160–167

Miller, R.H. (1990) 'Soil microbiological inputs for sustainable agriculture', in C.A. Edwards, R. Lal, P. Madden, R.H. Miller and G. House (eds) *Sustainable Agricultural Systems*, Soil and Water Conservation Society, Ankeny, IA

NAS (National Academy of Sciences) (1972) *Genetic Vulnerability of Major Crops*, National Academy of Sciences, Washington, DC

Palti, J. (1981) *Cultural Practices and Infectious Crop Diseases*, Springer-Verlag, New York, NY

Reijntjes, C., Haverkort B. and Waters-Bayer, W. (1992) *Farming for the Future: An Introduction to Low External-Input and Sustainable Agriculture*, MacMillan, London

Ricketts, T.H., Regetz, J., Steffan-Dewenter, I., Cunningham, S.A., Kremen, C., Bogdanski, A., Gemmill-Herren, B., Greenleaf, S.S., Klein, A.M., Mayfield, M.M., Morandin, L.A., OchiengÕ, A. and Viana B.F. (2008) 'Landscape effects on crop pollination services: Are there general patterns?', *Ecology Letters*, vol 11, pp449–515

Robinson, R.A. (1996) *Return to Resistance: Breeding Crops to Reduce Pesticide Dependence*, International Development and Research Centre, Ottawa, Canada

Schellhorn, N.A., Bellatib, J., Paull, C.A. and Maratos, L. (2008) 'Parasitoid and moth movement from refuge to crop', *Basic and Applied Ecology*, vol 9, pp691–700

Southwood, R.E. and Way, M.J. (1970) 'Ecological background to pest management', in R.C. Rabb and F.E. Guthrie (eds) *Concepts of Pest Management*, North Carolina State University, Raleigh, NC

Swift, M.J. and Anderson, J.M. (1993) 'Biodiversity and ecosystem function in agroecosystems', in E. Schultze and H.A. Nooney (eds) *Biodiversity and Ecosystem Function*, Spinger-Verlag, New York, NY

Tripp, R. (1996) 'Biodiversity and modern crop varieties: sharpening the debate', *Agriculture and Human Values*, vol 13, no 4, pp48–63

Van den Bosch, R., and Telford, A.D. (1964) 'Environmental modification and biological control', in P. de Bach (ed) *Biological Control Of Insect Pests and Weeds*, Reinhold, New York, NY, pp459–488

Vandermeer, J. and Perfecto, I. (1995) *Breakfast of Biodiversity: The Political Ecology of Rain Forest Destruction*, Food First Books, Oakland, CA

Vandermeer, J., van Noordwijk, M., Anderson, J., Ong, C. and Perfecto, I. (1998) 'Global change and multi-species agroecosystems: Concepts and issues', *Agriculture, Ecosystems and Environment*, vol 67, pp1–22

Wilken, G.C. (1987) *Good Farmers: Traditional Agricultural Resource Management in Mexico and Guatemala*, University of California Press, Berkeley, CA

3

The Human Ecology of Agrobiodiversity

David Dumaresq, David Carpenter and Stewart Lockie

In coming to deal with the place of food production in industrial societies we face a set of strong tensions. There is the productivist view of agriculture as a technical problem of how best to exploit particular biophysical structures and functions to produce the maximum amount of useable food and fibre. Set against this is a spectrum of views of agriculture as a socio-cultural activity that all but defines a particular society or nation, farming as a way of life, through to it being seen as a key agent of economic development. Riding uneasily with all these is the growing understanding of the place of agriculture as the dominant form of human land management on the planet that must account for many landscape functions and processes other than just providing for human needs. We need a framework for understanding agriculture in all its complex roles of providing human sustenance and cultural meanings, as well as delivering ecosystems services.

To quote the noted American agricultural essayist Wendell Berry (1977), 'the problem with agriculture is a problem with culture'. Fundamentally, agriculture is a human cultural activity that only exists as a major form of landscape process because there are humans doing it. The purpose of this chapter, therefore, is to contextualize the problem of biodiversity decline within a human ecological understanding of agriculture and related ecosystem processes. In basic terms, human ecology encompasses the relationships we, as a species, have with the fundamental biophysical processes of the planet, mediated through the understandings that we generate of those processes through human action and interaction.

From this perspective, agrobiodiversity is seen not just as the sum of agricultural or wild resources necessary for food and fibre production (i.e. crop varieties, pollinators etc). It also includes the practices and food production systems employed by farmers throughout the world to dynamically manage those resources (see Brookfield and Padoch, 1994). It is these myriad local practices that continue to maintain and expand in situ the genetic diversity that underpins agricultural production. As such, agrobiodiversity cannot be divorced from the rich cultural diversity and local knowledge that underpins livelihood systems (Thrupp, 2000).

The human ecology of agriculture

Human ecology may be described as the interrelationships between humans, their cultures and the ecosystems within which they are embedded. These are summarized in Table 3.1. However, the science of human ecology goes beyond the recognition of multiple social and biophysical drivers of agricultural productivity. It adopts a holistic approach to these interrelated parts and seeks to understand them as parts of a single, complex interacting system. It is concerned with the processes (both natural and anthropogenic) that limit and change this system over time, including whether or not current arrangements are sustainable.

Table 3.1. Physical, biological, socio-economic and cultural determinants of agricultural productivity (after Altieri 1995)

Determinant	Factor
Physical	solar radiation, temperature, rainfall, water supply (moisture stress), soil conditions, slope, land availability
Biological	insect pests and natural enemies, weed communities, plant and animal diseases, soil biota, background natural vegetation, photosynthetic efficiency, cropping patterns, crop rotation
Socio-economic	population density, social organization, economics (prices, markets, capital, and credit availability), technical assistance, cultivation implements, degree of commercialization, labour availability
Cultural	traditional knowledge, beliefs, ideology, gender issues, historical events

In order to assess the sustainability of human ecologies it is necessary to build on approaches such as agroecology as introduced in Chapter 2. Within the agroecological conception, the ecological processes that are found under natural conditions (e.g. nutrient cycling, predator/prey interactions, competition among species, symbiosis and succession), are also seen to occur in the agricultural field/landscape (Altieri, 2002). While agroecosystems may have relatively low species diversity when compared to natural systems (Odum, 1984) and rely upon human inputs as substitutes for ecosystem services (Conway, 1987), ecological processes nonetheless play a vitally important role in maintaining the productivity, stability and sustainability of these systems (Altieri, 1995; Gliessman, 1998). The goal of the agroecological approach is to optimize and enhance these ecological processes with a view to producing agricultural commodities in a more sustainable way, and with fewer negative environmental and social impacts (Altieri, 2002).

What role then do humans play in the evolution of agroecologies? If we think of agriculture as a form of ecosystem management then two basic farming processes are recognizable as fundamental to driving what ecosystems services are available. These are photosynthesis and population dynamics. Farming may then be described—in simple ecological terms—as human management of a landscape in order to optimize the amount of photosynthesis that humans can capture via a mix of species that humans desire for consumption. In creating the most space, both spatially and temporally, for our desired crop and stock species we remove the species we do not want. This removal of undesired species has two phases: first, initial land clearance and the subsequent continuing occupation of this space by crops and pasture; and second, the continual management across time and space of pest, weeds and diseases—all undesired species.

For an agricultural activity to start there is an underlying human desire and motivation to do that activity. In this sense, human desires are the fundamental drivers that shape any agricultural activity. Different human desires will initiate and drive different agricultural activities. Differing agricultural activities will use differing sets of landscape components. A brief schema is set out below:

- Human desires giving rise to:
- Human activity in the landscape (e.g. food production) giving rise to:
- Landuse patterns (e.g. agriculture, cereal cropping etc) giving rise to:
- Characteristic land covers associated with different human communities.

In turn, these components will draw on underlying sets of ecosystem functions. These functions will be called upon by farmers to provide a range of ecosystem services. This act of calling upon ecosystem services is rarely a consciously planned act of management. Rather, ecosystem services are called upon simply by doing a particular activity in a particular place. We tend only to notice the ability of a landscape to provide such services when they fail. In part, this may be because we tend to overlook the fundamental ecosystem functions performed by plants. As Diaz et al (2004, p295) state:

> The photosynthetic activities of green plants provide the mechanism whereby resources enter ecosystems, and there has been gradual acceptance that in this process plants are not acting as a simple conduit. It is now widely accepted that differences between plants in the way they acquire, process and invest resources can have very large effects on the species composition and functioning of ecosystems.

Of issue here is that we tend not to think of agriculture driving ecosystem function in this way, but rather as changes of plant cover embedded in wider landscapes. As Altieri and Rogé indicate in the previous chapter, agricultural management crucially depends on ecosystem services, but agricultural activity also largely determines the provisioning of ecosystem services in farmed landscapes. Thus, we can extend our schema from culturally driven landuse settings giving that community its land cover and its characteristic vegetation mix. Land cover may be described as:

- A dominant suite of vegetation of human desired species that determine:
- Ecosystem functions providing:
- Ecosystem services that deliver:
- Landscape processes.

These processes, in turn, shape human perceptions of land productivity and beliefs about how particular landscapes can be used to fulfil human desires. Agriculture is both dependent upon ecosystem services and a major driver of what services are available. Figure 3.1 illustrates the dynamic relationships between anthropogenic and non-anthropogenic drivers of biodiversity outcomes.

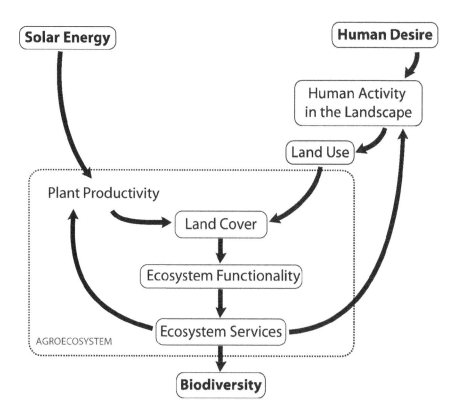

Figure 3.1. The human ecology of agroecosystems and agrobiodiversity.

In short, agriculture actively manages both the biodiversity of any farming landscape and the ecosystem functions and services that derive from that landscape. Biodiversity management of the landscape is a fundamental part of agriculture whether we like it or not. Given this, it would seem a simple step to move from viewing biodiversity and ecosystem services as having a casual, even happenstance benefit to agriculture, to viewing the integration of ecosystem functionality into the core of farming practice. While this approach may seem very far from the mainstream of modern industrial agriculture, it is at the heart of many recent developments for both cropping and grazing systems (see below). An all too obvious question is why such developments are not far more widespread?

It is important to note that solutions to declining biodiversity are as rooted in social, cultural and economic change as they are in material and technological change. Important questions, therefore, emerge around community acceptance of change, not to mention their capacity to change in light of markets that do not reward better environmental practice; government promotion of and incentives to increase external input use; rural poverty and pressures to migrate in search of employment; the associated loss of local and traditional knowledge; and so on. As Gliessman rightly states 'it is one thing to gain an understanding of what makes an agroecosystem function, yet it is quite another to apply such knowledge to solving the everyday problems faced by farmers around the world' (Gliessman, 1990, p3). What is required is an interface between our understanding of ecosystems theory as it relates to agriculture, and the much more complex social, economic and political systems through which agricultural production is mediated (Hart, 1986; Pretty, 1995).

Human ecology and scale: the political economy of species biodiversity

The purpose of this section is to emphasize that the human ecology of agrobiodiversity warrants consideration at a number of spatial and temporal scales. Human interactions with the species and ecosystems processes that comprise biodiversity are simultaneously local—rooted in individual decisions and face-to-face interactions within farming communities—and regional, national and global—rooted in regulatory frameworks, commodity flows, scientific institutions and exchanges, migration patterns, and so on.

The services provided by biodiversity are as important to the global economy as they are to the healthy functioning of ecosystems (Costanza et al, 1997). In fact, it has been estimated that the genetic resources provided by biodiversity to the global economy contribute between US$500 billion and US$800 billion every year in the areas of pharmaceuticals, botanical medicines, agricultural produce, horticultural products, crop protection products, non agricultural biotechnologies and personal care and cosmetics (Ten Kate and Laird, 2000). Services provided to agriculture by biodiversity include the decomposition of waste material, soil formation, nitrogen fixation, bioremediation of chemical pollution, the provision of crop and animal genetic resources, the biological control of pests, pest resistance, carbon sequestration and the harvesting of food and drugs from wild biota etc (Pimentel et al, 1997).

However, the real value of these services to agriculture is generally poorly understood and is certainly not internalized to any great degree within agricultural commodity markets. Instead, agriculture has followed an increasingly industrialized model in which services that could be provided by ecosystem processes are substituted wherever possible with synthetic and mechanized inputs (see Chapter 2). In the process, it has been argued, farmers have been forced to cede much of their control over production to the agribusiness firms that supply them with inputs and/or control down-stream commodity trade, processing and retailing (Goodman et al, 1987). While it is important not to paint farmers as passive victims of industrialization, it is telling that in relation to biodiversity some of the world's largest agribusiness companies have made very overt attempts to assert ownership, and then place strict regulatory controls over, farmers' access to genetic resources (RAFI, 1996).

International debate over the political economy of agrobiodiversity has focused largely on two main issues: (1) the destruction of diverse natural habitats such as tropical rainforests for the expansion of agriculture; and (2) intellectual property rights as these are applied to the genetic diversity of important food and fibre crops. Both these debates raise important issues about the respective rights and responsibilities of farmers, governments, agribusiness firms and others based primarily in the developing versus the developed worlds. While the developed world has by far the largest ex situ concentrations of biodiversity (approximately 75%) in seed banks, zoological gardens, botanical gardens and microbe, bacteria and fungi collections, some 83 percent of all the world's in situ genetic resources are located in the South (RAFI, 1996). The role of resource poor farmers in the developing world is particularly important in maintaining agrobiodiversity as these farmers manage by far the largest stock of agricultural genetic resources (i.e. infra or within-species biodiversity) in the most diverse agroecosystems (i.e. inter-species and landscape biodiversity).

A number of factors influence the tendency towards diversity among resource poor farmers including the need to farm in a range of different environments, the need to cope with production risks, the presence of pest and pathogens, avoiding or minimizing labour shortages, economic constraints, gastronomic choices, providing for special consumption items, as well as fulfilling rituals and forging social ties (Bellon, 1996). Thus, the developing world remains a reservoir for genetic resources (although the total stock is ever decreasing) while the world's developed countries—who have largely eroded their indigenous genetic resources—typically reap the financial rewards that biodiversity offers.

If markets, by themselves, do little to internalize biodiversity values or to promote equitable access to them, what impact have regulatory regimes had? As argued in Chapter 1, despite the inclusion of many positive provisions in mechanisms such as the Convention for Biological Diversity and the International Treaty on Plant Genetic Resources for Food and Agriculture to protect farmers' interests and promote an adaptive ecosystems approach to management, binding rules are largely restricted to matters such as access to plant genetic material for major food crop and forage species. According to Escobar (1998), the coupling of biodiversity management to the notion of sustainable development is used to define human benefit through the CBD and related documents in ways that emphasize economic use of, and intellectual property rights over, genetic resources. Further, as

Lockie (2009) argues, provisions for the protection of farmers' traditional rights must be seen in context of the legally binding nature of, and sanctions associated with, the free trade agenda of the World Trade Organization and its Agreement on Trade-Related Intellectual Property Rights. These regulatory issues will be taken up in more detail in Chapters 4 and 5.

The human ecology of landscape processes and biodiversity: the case of cell grazing

To illustrate the importance of understanding agrobiodiversity from a human ecological perspective, this section will consider the case of cell, or controlled-time, grazing. While cell grazing has been applied in numerous rangeland settings around the world we will examine its application in Australia. This will serve to emphasize that biodiversity management is a matter for all farmers irrespective of the cultural, economic and ecological characteristics of the locales in which they farm.

Cell grazing was introduced to Australia about 20 years ago. The key technocratic element of this management approach is to control not only the numbers of animals per unit area of land (which we might crudely think of as carrying capacity) but to also control the amount of time any one group of animals graze an area of pasture. This time control element is designed to achieve two management goals. The first is to allow the pasture plants sufficient time to recover between grazing episodes; thus allowing the plants to maximize growth of leaf, shoot and root mass to make best use of available water and nutrients. The second is to prevent animals constantly returning to re-graze the most desirable plants; thus preventing them being over-grazed, and less desirable species being under-grazed and becoming dominant.

Cell grazing is obviously very different to what is called 'set stocking'; an approach to management that, based on an assessment of the carrying capacity of a paddock (field) or farm, leaves much the same number of animals enclosed within the boundary fence of that paddock or farm year round. Most Australian graziers would now regard set stocking as poor management practice. Unrestricted, livestock will follow their natural instinct to graze preferred pasture species, to shelter in familiar locations, to stay close to water, and so on. At best, this leads to poor utilization of available feed and other resources. However, it also tends to lead to soil and water quality degradation in areas favoured by livestock and to declining pasture quality as more desirable species are effectively over-grazed while the growth of less palatable pasture species and weeds is largely unchecked. The constant presence of livestock also promotes high populations of internal and external animal parasites. It is now standard practice, therefore, to follow some variant of what are commonly referred to as rotational grazing or periodic spelling, both of which remove livestock entirely from pastures for a significant period of time each year to allow plants to recover and to break the life-cycles of parasites and other pests.

Cell grazing goes beyond rotational grazing and period spelling, however, in at least two key ways: first, it adopts a far more intensive approach to management;

and second, that management is based on a more clearly articulated set of agroecological principles. In the first instance, farms and paddocks are subdivided into smaller units based on features such as soil type, vegetation and topography. Management of those units is based on the principles of using short graze periods and long rests; maximizing stock density on each land parcel for the minimum time; controlling rest to suit the growth rate of plants; constantly adjusting stocking rates to match carrying capacity; planning, monitoring and controlling grazing; using a diversity of plants and animals to improve ecological health; and using large mob (herd) sizes to encourage natural herding behaviour (McCosker, 2000, p208). This is not, according to McCosker (2000, p8), 'for the faint hearted to those unwilling to invest in training'.

Farmers involved in cell grazing have experienced some impressive results. Robin Sparke of Moura in Central Queensland reported that after five years of cell grazing, and no re-sowing of pastures, the number of species, including palatable native grasses and legumes, within the pasture was increasing (Sparke, 2000). At the same time, both the total estimated pasture yield and the yield per 100mm of rainfall doubled. Not surprisingly, this led to higher beef production at lower cost. Shane Joyce of Theodore, also in Central Queensland, reported similar increases in pasture diversity, carrying capacity and overall farm productivity and profitability over a seven year period while also noting that the number of trees on the farm had increased substantially at no apparent cost to production, water quality had improved, weed burdens were reduced and wildlife was more abundant (Joyce, 2000). He notes that paddocks containing strips of timber regrowth (up to 40% of available land) offered habitat to pest insect predators such as orb-weaving spiders and birds, and higher levels of productivity than paddocks that had been completely cleared of trees. Improvements were noted in numerous indicators of soil health such as structure, nutrient availability, organic matter etc.

Both of these farmers clearly derived significant financial benefit from the introduction of management practices designed specifically to enhance the ecosystem services potentially offered by biodiversity. Despite this, some controversy has been generated over whether cell grazing offers genuine benefits over its less management-intensive alternatives. McCosker (2000) puts this controversy down to poor understanding of the cell grazing system and inappropriate selection, on that basis, of study sites. Dorrough et al's (2004) review of studies concludes that while much is still not known about the relative implications of different grazing strategies the financial benefits of managing grazing specifically to maximize pasture and landscape biodiversity are likely to be greatest in low productivity (i.e. fragile) landscapes best suited to low-input extensive grazing systems. This is certainly consistent with the reported experience of graziers such as Robin Sparke and Shane Joyce who have employed cell grazing methods in the low rainfall rangelands of Central Queensland. However, cell grazing is also increasing in popularity in south east Australia where the financial returns from investment in synthetic inputs are greater but the costs—in terms of soil acidification, salinization, weed and pest control etc—continue to grow.

Adoption of cell grazing has been estimated to be as low as 0.5 percent (McCosker, 2000). Considerably more have heard of cell grazing, attended training and/or implemented less intensive systems, such as rotational grazing, that certainly will have reduced problems such as over-grazing and associated soil erosion. In some respects, this should not be considered surprising. Management complexity has frequently been identified as a major barrier to the adoption of novel farming systems even where they have been proven profitable (Lockie et al, 1995). Even so, the dramatic improvements in productivity, profitability and *lifestyle* that have been reported by farmers managing specifically to enhance ecosystem services from biodiversity still begs the question as to why more farmers have not followed their lead.

Richards and Lawrence (2009; see also Richards et al, 2005) found that those Central Queensland producers who had adopted cell grazing had also adopted distinctive identities, management philosophies and social networks. These producers distanced themselves from traditional occupational signifiers such as 'cattlemen' or 'graziers' (signifiers their peers remained proud to identify with); some because they were no longer comfortable with their elitist connotations and others because they thought such terms provided only a partial insight into their multiple roles as beef producers, business people and environmental managers. Shane Joyce (2000, p229) expressed a similar sentiment, stating that: 'By putting our focus on the soil and not the cow we have been able to start a change for the better'. It would be easy to misinterpret this statement to suggest that animal welfare and performance were secondary to cell graziers, or that soil health did not figure in their decision-making prior to cell grazing. Neither conclusion would be true. The point is rather that in contradistinction with industry norms, which for two centuries have privileged animal genetics (measured by growth rates, feed conversion ratios, fertility etc) as the primary indicators of farm performance and management skill, cell graziers have consciously sought to shift their focus in the belief that a more holistic approach to resource management will deliver more benefits in terms of animal performance.

A key cultural shift for the managers of cell grazing systems is in moving from seeing themselves as, say, sheep or cattle farmers, to seeing themselves as natural resource managers using stock animals as a vegetation management tool. A further step that some farmers take is to see themselves as capturers of solar energy through the management of photosynthesis. David Marsh (2004, p2), a grazier from Boorowa in south west New South Wales, thus writes:

Rather than viewing our core business as producing agricultural commodities, we now see ourselves as managers of sunlight and time for an increasingly diverse biotic community of which we are a part.

The distancing from traditional occupational identities evident among Central Queensland cell graziers involved in Richards' research was reflected in a marginal status in local social networks that often pre-dated the adoption of cell grazing (Richards and Lawrence, 2009). Implementation of cell grazing often attracted criticism from neighbours; especially in the early years before benefits were apparent. Further, this criticism was not only directed at the principal farm manager but at children and other members of the family. Cell graziers thus developed and relied on their own peer groups with whom they shared information and benchmarked performance.

Cell grazing is not the only practice being implemented in Australia to improve the environmental performance of pastoral and other agricultural industries with potentially positive biodiversity outcomes. Property management planning (also called whole farm planning), for example, has been implemented on a wide scale and has contributed to more diverse agricultural landscapes in which annual crops are interspersed with patchworks of woodland, shelter belts (windbreaks), perennial pastures etc; areas sensitive to degradation such as waterways are fenced to exclude livestock; and so on. However, even though property management planning attempts to improve the efficacy of ecosystem processes and services, it does so mainly from the point of view of minimizing the environmental damage caused by agriculture and the costs that this might impose: (1) on production; and (2) on the wider community. Significant changes are made to field margins and unproductive areas, but what goes on inside the paddock, the site of production, remains largely unchanged (see Lockie, 1999, 2006). Biodiversity enters this picture in the guise of remnant native ecosystems that the wider community seeks to protect from agriculture, and as a limited number of native species that have proven useful on field margins (e.g. eucalypt shelter belts) or in the rehabilitation of degraded areas (e.g. saltbush pastures on salinized soils). Property management planning does not, therefore, represent a fundamental challenge to established farming practices or to the self-identities of Australian farmers. Cell grazing has much in common with property management planning but represents a conscious attempt to change what goes on inside the site of production; that is, to understand, enhance and capitalize on ecosystem services specifically derived from biodiversity and other natural resources. The key goal is to maximize the functional value of biodiversity, not the conservation of native species or ecosystem diversity for their own sake.

A similar trend can be seen in many cropping systems where farmers move from viewing soil as a growing medium for plants to access water and nutrients, to a system where plants are managed to optimize soil health which in turn supports greater crop returns. The key cultural shift here comes again with farmers seeing that what they are doing at core is capturing solar energy via plant cultivation and management that maintains and enhances soil fertility as well as producing harvestable material. One farmer from south east Australia described himself as someone who 'feeds the soil ecology'. That he grew a range of cereal crops for commercial market was a secondary consideration. A further step that some farmers take is to see themselves as capturers of solar energy by a range of methods including photosynthesis.

Conclusion

The management of agrobiodiversity is an active anthropogenic enterprise. The reproduction of agrobiodiversity is socially and culturally mediated, and takes place within vastly different human-ecological systems. As a consequence, it is possible to argue that some of the greatest threats to agrobiodiversity come not from exploitation or explicit destruction but from non-use, as farming systems become more specialized and homogenized. This is especially evident in relation to the infraspecific genetic diversity of cultivated plants and animals. As Chapters 5 and 7 show, diversity within cultivated species has co-evolved with human communities and depends for its continued viability on a range of strategies including: preservation in ex situ collections; continued use in traditional cultural practices; and continuing evolution through use within new social networks and norms among farmers as they negotiate the transition to sustainable modern agroecologies. Non-use of biodiversity also represents a threat, however, to the abundance and diversity of native or 'wild' species within agricultural landscapes. Such landscapes represent significantly modified (and usually simplified) agroecosystems that if left unmanaged are vulnerable to colonization by a limited number of exotic and/or pest species. As the case study of cell grazing demonstrates, *intentional* management of biodiversity at a number of levels (irrespective of whether species are cultivated or domesticated) is a key factor in the optimization of ecosystem functions and services.

References

Altieri, M. (1995) *Agroecology: The Science of Sustainable Agriculture,* 2nd edition, Westview Press, Boulder, CO

Altieri, M.A. (2002) 'Agroecology: The science of natural resource management for poor farmers in marginal environments', *Agricultural Ecosystems and Environment*, vol 93, pp1–24

Bellon, M.R. (1996) 'The dynamics of crop infraspecific diversity: A conceptual framework at the farmers' level', *Economic Botany*, vol 50, no 1, pp26–39

Berry, W. (1977) *The Unsettling of America: Culture and Agriculture*, Sierra Club Books, San Francisco, CA

Brookfield, H. and Padoch, C. (1994) 'Appreciating agrobiodiversity: A look at the dynamism and diversity of indigenous farming practices', *Environment*, vol 36, no 5, pp6–11 and 37–44

Costanza, R., d'Arge, R., de Groot, R., Farber, S., Grasso, M., Hannon, B., Naeem, S., Limburg, K., Paruelo, J., O'Neill, R.V., Raskin, R., Sutton, P. and van den Belt, M. (1997) 'The value of the world's ecosystem services and natural capital', *Nature*, vol 387, pp253–260

Conway, G. (1987) 'The properties of agroecosystems', *Agricultural Systems*, vol 24, pp95–117

Díaz, S., Hodgson, J., Thompson, K., Cabido, M., Cornelissen, J., Jalili, A., Montserrat-Martí, G., Grime, J., Zarrinkamar, F., Asri, Y., Band, S., Basconcelo, S., Castro-Díez, P., Funes, G., Hamzehee, B., Khoshnevi, M., Pérez-Harguindeguy, N., Pérez-Rontomé, M., Shirvany, A., Vendramini, F., Yazdani, S., Abbas-Azimi, R., Bogaard, A., Boustani, S., Charles, M., Dehghan, M., de Torres-Espuny, L., Falczuk, V., Guerrero-Campo, J., Hynd, A., Jones, G., Kowsary, E., Kazemi-Saeed, F., Maestro-Martínez, M., Romo-Díez, A. Shaw, S., Siavash, B., Villar-Salvador, P. and Zak, M. (2004) 'The plant traits that drive ecosystems: Evidence from three continents', *Journal of Vegetation Science*, vol 15, pp295–304

Dorrough, J., Yen, A., Turner, V., Clark, G., Crosthwaite, J. and Hirth, J. (2004) 'Livestock grazing management and biodiversity conservation in Australian temperate grassy landscapes', *Australian Journal of Agricultural Research*, vol 55, pp279–295

Escobar, A. (1998) 'Whose knowledge, whose nature? Biodiversity, conservation and the political ecology of social movements', *Journal of Political Ecology*, vol 5, pp53–82

Gliessman, S.R. (1990) 'Agroecology: Researching the ecological basis for sustainable agriculture', in S.R. Gliessman, (ed) *Agroecology: Researching the Ecological Basis for Sustainable Agriculture*, Springer-Verlag, New York, NY, pp3–10

Gliessman, S.R. (1998) *Agroecology: Ecological Processes in Sustainable Agriculture*, Ann Arbour Press, Chelsea, MI

Goodman, D., Sorj, B. and Wilkinson, I. (1987) *From Farming to Biotechnology: A Theory of Agro-Industrial Development.* Basil Blackwell, Oxford, UK

Hart, G. (1986) 'Interlocking transactions: Obstacles, precursors, or instruments of agrarian capitalism? *Journal of Development Economics*, vol 23, pp177–203

Joyce, S. (2000) 'Change the management and what happens: A producer's perspective', *Tropical Grasslands*, vol 34, pp223–229

Lockie, S. (1999) 'The state, rural environments and globalization: "Action at a distance" via the Australian Landcare Program', *Environment and Planning A*, vol 31, no 4, pp597–611

Lockie, S. (2006) 'Networks of agri-environmental action: Temporality, spatiality and identity within agricultural environments', *Sociologia Ruralis*, vol 46, no 1, pp22–39

Lockie, S. (2009) 'Agricultural biodiversity and neoliberal regimes of agri-environmental governance in Australia', *Current Sociology*, vol 57, no 3, pp407–426

Lockie, S., Mead, A., Vanclay, F. and Butler, B. (1995) 'Factors encouraging the adoption of more sustainable cropping systems in south-east Australia: Profit, sustainability, risk and stability', *Journal of Sustainable Agriculture*, vol 6, no 1, 61–79

Marsh, D. (2004) 'Farming: The holistic way', *The National Parks Association of New South Wales Journal*, December, pp1–4, http://holisticmanagement.org.au/PDF/Farming%20-%20the%20holistic%20way%20-%20David%20Marsh.pdf, accessed 9 September 2009

McCosker, T. (2000) 'Cell grazing: The first ten years in Australia', *Tropical Grasslands*, vol 34, pp207–218

Odum, E.P. (1984) Properties of agroecosystems, in R. Lowrance, B.R. Stinner and G.J. House (eds) *Agricultural Ecosystems*, John Wiley and Sons, New York, NY, pp8–11

Pimentel, D., Wilson, C., McCullum, C., Huang, R., Owen, P., Flack, J; Tran, Q., Saltman, T., and B. Cliff (1997) "Economic and Environmental Benefits of Biodiversity" BioScience, vol 47, no 11, pp747–757

Pretty, J. (1995) *Regenerating Agriculture: Policies and Practice for Sustainability and Self-Reliance*, Earthscan, London

Rural Advancement Foundation International (RAFI) (1996) 'The geopolitics of biodiversity: A biodiversity balance sheet, crucial decisions in 1996', *RAFI Communiqué*, 30th January 1996

Richards, C. and Lawrence, G. (2009) 'Adaptation and change in Queensland's rangelands: Cell grazing as an emerging ideology of pastoral ecology', *Land Use Policy*, vol 26, pp630–639

Richards, C., Lawrence, G. and Kelly, N. (2005) 'Beef production and the environment: Is it really "hard to be green when you are in the red"?', *Rural Society*, vol 15, no 2, pp192–209

Sparke, R. (2000) 'Cell grazing: A producer's perspective', *Tropical Grasslands*, vol 34, pp219–222

Ten Kate, K. and Laird, S.A. (2000) *The Commercial use of Biodiversity: Access to Genetic Resources and Benefit Sharing*, Earthscan, London

Thrupp, L.A. (2000) 'Linking agricultural biodiversity and food security: The valuable role of agrobiodiversity for sustainable agriculture', *International Affairs*, vol 76, no 2, pp265–281

4

Multilateral and National Regulatory Regimes for Agrobiodiversity

Gerald Moore

The growth of regulatory regimes for agrobiodiversity at both the global and national levels is relatively recent. Indeed it is only a short while ago that the importance of biodiversity for agriculture, and the dangers of genetic erosion, was first realized at the international level. This chapter will describe the growth of this awareness and the regulatory machinery that has been developed in response. It will also describe the regulatory initiatives that have been taken at the international level to protect the intellectual property interests of breeders and the impact that this has had on agrobiodiversity. It will then look briefly at the ways in which these international regulatory regimes have been implemented at the national level.

The development of regulatory regimes at the global level

Farmers have always been conscious of the importance of genetic diversity in increasing and maintaining yields and in protecting against fluctuations in those yields because of disease or drought. What is important is not so much inter species diversity as intra species (or infraspecific) diversity. This means the degree of genetic variation in a particular species, such as wheat (*Triticum*) rather than the diversity between species. It was partly in order to maintain that genetic diversity that farmers traditionally exchanged seeds of the same crops amongst themselves.

Soon after the Second World War there was growing concern that the world's food resources would be insufficient to meet the needs of a fast growing population. The response of the international community was to establish a number of international agricultural research centres bringing together agricultural scientists and plant breeders, such as Norman Borlaug of the International Maize and Wheat Improvement Centre, to develop new high-yielding varieties as a means of increasing food production. The so-called Green Revolution had spectacular results. At the same time, the introduction of the new and improved high yielding varieties tended to displace traditional farmers' varieties and hence to result in erosion of the very genetic resources on which the Green Revolution was based. To counter this new threat, the newly established Consultative Group on International Agricultural Research (CGIAR)—which drew together the original international agricultural research centres together with a number of new centres—mounted a systematic campaign to collect and conserve existing crop diversity. The campaign was coordinated by the International Board for Plant Genetic Resources (IBPGR) hosted by the Food and Agriculture Organization of the United Nations (FAO). Over the period 1974–1980, IBPGR collected and conserved more than 65,000 accessions from over 70 countries. The collected crop diversity was stored partly in the CGIAR centres and partly in national and regional gene banks.

Interdependence among farmers for crop diversity was not limited to the local level. The history of agriculture has been one of the exchange of crops from one region of the world to another (Harlan, 1992). Potatoes, for example, came originally from the Andean region of South America, but now form a mainstay of agricultural production in Europe, North America and many other regions of the world. Wheat, which originated in the Middle East, is now grown throughout the world, as is maize, which came from Central America. As these crops were transferred across the world, so they developed new characteristics adapted to the climatic needs and consumer preferences of their new locations. Indeed, in many instances the crops fared better in their new locations, freed from the pests and diseases prevalent in their original centres of origin. But once new diseases strike, it is often necessary to return to the centres of origin to find resistant traits to combat them. The Irish potato blight of the mid-19th century and the resultant famine is a striking historical example of this. The blight (caused by the fungus *phytophthora infestans)* appears to have originated in the mountains of Mexico and to have spread to Europe through the importation of a consignment of infected seed potatoes into Belgium. In the centre of origin of potatoes there are many varieties that were resistant to the disease. Had some of these resistant varieties been introduced along with the more vulnerable varieties, then the magnitude of the blight and its disastrous consequences could have been averted. A more recent example has been the taro leaf blight that has destroyed the staple taro harvest in Samoa and other Pacific Island States. Samoa had to turn to the Philippines and Palau to find resistant varieties. The Pacific Islands are now in the process of broadening the genetic bases of taro in the region in order to avoid the spread of the disease in the future (Brunt et al, 2001).

The world is dependent on a relatively small number of commercially grown crops for its food security. The cultivation of these crops is spread around the world and every region, and every country is dependent on plant genetic resources from other parts of the world to maintain the productivity of those crops and their resistance to disease and environmental challenges. A recent study prepared for the negotiations of the International Treaty on Plant Genetic Resources for Food and Agriculture (the Treaty) in the FAO placed the degree of interdependence of most regions for the major crops at over 50 percent. No one country or region was self sufficient from the point of view of plant genetic resources required for food and agriculture (Palacios, 1998).

It is these two factors, the importance of infraspecific genetic diversity for sustainable agriculture and food security and the interdependence of all countries on plant genetic resources, that are key to understanding the development of regulatory regimes for agrobiodiversity at the international level.

The International Undertaking on Plant Genetic Resources

The International Undertaking on Plant Genetic Resources was the first international instrument on plant genetic resources. As its name suggests, the International Undertaking is a voluntary, i.e. non-legally binding instrument, adopted by the FAO Conference in 1983. While the International Undertaking has largely been superseded by the Convention on Biological Diversity and the International Treaty, it is important to understand the concepts underlying it in order to comprehend further developments in the international regulatory regime.

The Undertaking dealt with problems posed by the erosion of agrobiodiversity by providing for the exploration of plant genetic resources, and for their preservation, evaluation and documentation. In particular, it called on adhering governments to take measures to ensure the protection and preservation of plant genetic resources of plants growing in areas of their natural habitat in the major centres of diversity (in situ conservation). It also called on them to ensure the scientific collection and safeguarding of important plant genetic resources in areas in which they were in danger of extinction on account of agricultural and other development (ex situ conservation). In this connection, the Undertaking called for the development of an internationally coordinated network of ex situ collections. These would be national, regional, and international centres that assumed responsibility to hold collections of plant genetic resources of particular plant species for the benefit of the international community.

The Undertaking addressed the issue of countries' interdependence by providing for the free availability of plant genetic resources for breeding and research. Article 1 records that the Undertaking was based on the 'universally accepted principle that plant genetic resources are a heritage of mankind and consequently should be available without restriction'. Article 5 of the Undertaking provides that it:

> will be the policy of adhering Governments and Institutions to allow access to samples of plant genetic resources under their control for the purpose of scientific research, plant breeding and genetic resources conservation (FAO Conference, 1983, p4).

The samples should 'be made available free of charge, on the basis of mutual exchange or on mutually agreed terms'.

The Undertaking provided in general terms for international cooperation to support the conservation and sustainable use of plant genetic resources, including through capacity building for developing countries and the intensification of international activities such as those carried out by the FAO and those supported by the CGIAR. It also called for the strengthening or establishment of funding mechanisms to support the practical implementation of the Undertaking.

While the governments of 113 countries announced that they were adhering to the International Undertaking, it never received universal acceptance. Some countries expressed reservations that the requirement of free availability of all plant genetic resources, including cultivated varieties, did not take full account of plant breeders' rights. Other reservations arose out of the concept that plant genetic resources should be considered to be a 'common heritage of mankind', which they considered to be in conflict with the sovereign rights of countries over their own natural resources.

These concerns were addressed in a series of three Agreed Interpretations of the International Undertaking adopted by the FAO Conference over the period 1989-91. The first agreed interpretation (Resolution 4/89), adopted in 1989, provided that Plant Breeders' Rights, as provided for under the International Convention for the Protection of New Varieties of Plant (UPOV Convention), were not incompatible with the International Undertaking (FAO Conference, 1989). The UPOV Convention gives protection to plant breeders' rights over new varieties they have developed that are new, distinct, uniform and stable, but requires that those new varieties remain freely available for further research and breeding.

To balance the notion of rewarding the formal breeding efforts of plant breeders, the first agreed interpretation launched the concept of Farmers' Rights in recognition of the enormous contribution made by famers of all regions to the conservation and development of plant genetic resources. The rationale was that farmers over the centuries have domesticated and developed plant genetic resources from their wild state into resources that form the basis of modern agriculture, and continue to develop and conserve agrobiodiversity. Wild ancestors often bear little resemblance to modern crops. Teocinte, for example, the wild ancestor of maize, has small hard ears that are easily shatterable. Breeding out characteristics such as the shattering of seed-heads prior to maturity or seed dormancy, all of which allowed plants to survive in the wild but which made them ill adapted to the needs of modern agriculture, was one of the main contributions of farmers to the development of modern agriculture. Farmers have not, however, been rewarded for their efforts. Nor are their continuing efforts supported. The products of formal breeding, on the other hand, which build on these past efforts of farmers, are protected under modern intellectual property systems.

The concept of Farmers' Rights was further elaborated in the Second Agreed Interpretation, although the precise legal nature of those rights was left intentionally vague. Indeed the concept was presented more as a political than a legal concept, and implementation was to be ensured through an international fund to be used to support plant genetic resources conservation, management and utilization programs.

The Third Agreed Interpretation dealt with the issue of sovereignty, providing that the concept of mankind's heritage is subject to the sovereignty of states over their plant genetic resources.

The Convention on Biological Diversity

While the International Undertaking was based on the notion of free availability of plant genetic resources in view of their importance for sustainable agriculture and food security, the Convention on Biological Diversity (CBD), which was adopted and opened for signature at the United Nations Conference on Environment and Development in 1992, stressed the element of state sovereignty over genetic resources. Access to genetic resources should be under the control of the state possessing those resources. The state and its local populations, whose efforts and traditional knowledge contribute much to the value of those resources, should be entitled to share fairly and equitably in the benefits to be derived from the use of those resources (UNEP, 1992).

The CBD is a framework convention in the sense that it sets out certain basic principles but leaves it to individual states to implement them in the way they choose. As one commentator has put it, 'its provisions are mostly expressed as shared goals and policies, rather than as hard and precise obligations' (Moore and Tymowski, 2005, p12). It is also a framework instrument in that it takes for the first time a comprehensive approach to the conservation and sustainable use of the earth's biodiversity. The CBD covers all genetic resources including plant genetic resources. It is oriented around three basic principles: the conservation of biodiversity, sustainable use of its components, and equitable sharing of the benefits arising from its utilization. Contracting Parties are required to develop national strategies, plans and programs for the conservation and sustainable use of biodiversity. They are also required to adopt measures for in situ conservation of biodiversity and for preserving and maintaining traditional knowledge, as well as measures for ex situ conservation.

Insofar as the availability of genetic resources is concerned, the Contracting Parties are required to create conditions that facilitate access to those resources for environmentally sound purposes by other Contracting Parties and undertake not to impose restrictions that run counter to the objectives of the Convention. However, in accordance with their sovereign rights over natural resources, the authority to determine access rests with national governments and is subject to national legislation. Access, where it is granted, is to be on mutually agreed terms and subject to prior informed consent of the Contracting Party providing the resources. All Contracting Parties, including both providers and users, are to take measures with the aim of sharing in a fair and equitable way the results of research and development and the benefits arising from the commercial and other utilization of the genetic resources with the Contracting Party providing the resources. In this connection, the CBD contains general provisions aimed at bringing about access to and transfer of technology, exchange of information, and technical and scientific cooperation, including participation in biotechnological research.

The CBD recognizes that the extent to which developing countries can effectively implement their commitments under the Convention will depend on provision of financial resources and provides for a financial mechanism that will provide new and additional financial resources to enable them to fulfill their obligations. The Convention also provides for a subsidiary body on scientific and technological advice and periodical meetings of the Conference of Parties.

In view of the framework nature of the CBD, provision is made in the Convention for the adoption of protocols by the Conference of Parties. One such protocol has already been adopted in 2000 on the movement of living modified organisms from one country to another (the so-called Cartagena Protocol on Biosafety). A series of non-binding guidelines have also been adopted on access and benefit sharing under the convention (the Bonn Guidelines) in 2002, and work is now progressing on the negotiation of an international regime on access and benefit sharing.

Given that the CBD covers all genetic resources, including plant genetic resources for food and agriculture, and that the Convention has almost universal coverage, the question arises as to why countries considered that it was necessary to negotiate yet another international treaty to cover plant genetic resources for food and agriculture.

The answer lies partly in the nature of plant genetic resources for food and agriculture as discussed above, their importance for sustainable agriculture and food security, and the interdependence of countries on those resources. While the CBD does not expressly so require, the access and benefit sharing regime of the CBD has tended to be implemented on a bilateral basis between the country or institution seeking access and the country of origin of the genetic resources. This means the negotiation of a series of individual bilateral agreements to secure access and set out the terms of benefit sharing. Such a web of bilateral agreements is simply not feasible for plant genetic resources for food and agriculture. This is because of the sheer magnitude of transfers that need to be effected and the excessive transaction costs that would be involved in the negotiation of such bilateral deals. Depending on the crop, breeders commonly work with up to 60 or so different landraces originating from 20 to 30 different countries (Moore and Tymowski, 2005). The concept of benefit sharing linked to the country of origin also poses difficulties for plant genetic resources for food and agriculture. The concept is easy to understand and apply where medicinal plants are found in rainforests; particularly where the value of those medicinal plants is enhanced by traditional knowledge. It is less easy to apply where the plant genetic resources of major crops have been transferred and developed throughout the world over the course of centuries.

The answer also lies in the fact that the CBD failed to deal with the issue of the ex situ collections acquired before the entry into force of the Convention and, in particular, with the large and important collections held by the CGIAR centres (Moore and Tymowski, 2005), or indeed with the specific question of the realization of Farmers' Rights.

It was for these reasons that the Nairobi Conference that adopted the text of the CBD also adopted a resolution recognizing the need to seek solutions to outstanding matters concerning plant genetic resources for food and agriculture within the FAO Global System for the Conservation and Sustainable Use of Plant Genetic Resources for Food and Agriculture. It called, in particular, for solutions to be found for the questions of access to ex situ collections acquired before the entry into force of the Convention and the realization of Farmers' Rights.

The invitation was taken up in 1993 by the FAO Conference, which requested (Resolution 7/93) the FAO Director-General to provide a forum for negotiations for the adaptation of the International Undertaking to bring it into harmony with the CBD. It also called for consideration of the issue of access on mutually agreed terms to plant genetic resources for food and agriculture, including those contained in the ex situ collections acquired before the entry into force of the CBD, as well as the realization of Farmers' Rights (FAO Conference, 1993).

International Treaty on Plant Genetic Resources for Food and Agriculture

The International Treaty on Plant Genetic Resources for Food and Agriculture was adopted in November 2001 after seven years of hard negotiations (FAO Conference, 2001; FAO, 2009). Its objectives follow very much those of the CBD, but applied to the narrower scope of plant genetic resources for food and agriculture (PGRFA). Thus it provides for the conservation and sustainable use of PGRFA and the fair and equitable sharing of benefits arising out of their use for sustainable agriculture and food security (Article 1.1). The Treaty is expressed as being in harmony with the CBD and is, in fact, an implementation of the principles of the CBD for one specific sector, that of plant genetic resources for food and agriculture.

Several of the early articles of the Treaty deal with the types of measures that the Contracting Parties are required to take to ensure the conservation, exploration, collection, characterization, evaluation and documentation of PGRFA and reflect the same principles of the CBD but with a specific application to agrobiodiversity. They also draw very much on a Global Plan of Action for the Conservation and Sustainable Utilization of Plant Genetic Resources for Food and Agriculture adopted by a Technical Conference in Leipzig in 1996 (ITCPGR, 1996). These general articles apply to all plant genetic resources for food and agriculture, defined as being any genetic material of plant origin that is of actual or potential value for food and agriculture. The Multilateral System of Access and Benefit-Sharing set up by the Treaty, on the other hand, applies only to a subset of PGRFA chosen by the negotiators of the Treaty (and subsequently the Contracting Parties who have the power to amend the list as set out in Annex 1 to the Treaty) on the basis of their importance for food security and the degree of interdependence of countries on them (Article 11.1). The Multilateral System blends the principles of the CBD with the particular needs of the agricultural sector, as originally expressed in the International Undertaking, to maintain the flow of PGRFA for research and breeding purposes with minimal transaction costs. Transfers of Annex 1 PGRFA are to be on standard terms and conditions, mutually agreed by all the Contracting Parties to the Treaty and set out in a Standard Material Transfer Agreement (SMTA) adopted by the Governing Body at its first session in 2006 (FAO, 2006). The prior informed consent of the Contracting Parties, as required by the CBD, is considered to have been given by Contracting Parties in becoming parties to the

Treaty and further prior informed consent requirements are waived, at least for access to material held in ex situ conditions (Article 11.1) Since the terms and conditions of access are standard there is no longer any need to negotiate on a bilateral basis, nor indeed is it possible to do so for material covered by the Multilateral System. The Multilateral System covers automatically all PGRFA of Annex 1 crops and forages that are 'under the management and control of the Contracting Parties and in the public domain' (Article 11.2). The exact meaning of this criterion is not entirely clear in all countries, but would appear to mean material that is physically and legally controlled by the governments concerned and free of intellectual and other property rights. Other holders of PGRFA are invited to include their materials in the Multilateral System, though each Contracting Party agrees to take measures to encourage them to do so. The Secretariat of the International Treaty has asked Contracting Parties to indicate the material that has been included in the Multilateral System in their jurisdictions, either automatically or voluntarily.

In effect, the Multilateral System creates a common pool of genetic resources available to all other Contracting Parties for research and breeding. The benefits arising from the use of those genetic resources are also shared on a multilateral or pooled basis. One of the main benefits is facilitated access to those resources in the first place, so essential are they to sustainable agriculture and food security in all countries. Other benefits, as covered by the Treaty, include the exchange of information, including information on technologies, results of technical, scientific and socio-economic research, characterization, evaluation and utilization regarding PGRFA under the Multilateral System. This information is to be made available through a global information system to be set up under Article 17 of the Treaty. The benefits include access to and transfer of technology, and various measures are set out in the Treaty to encourage such access and transfer. They also include capacity building and the sharing of monetary and other benefits arising from commercialization. In this connection, the Treaty establishes an innovative system of monetary benefit sharing that is linked to the goal of the Treaty of promoting availability of PGRFA under the Multilateral System for research and development. Under the Treaty a share of the benefits arising from the sale of PGRFA products that incorporate material accessed from the Multilateral System is to be paid into the Multilateral System. The payment is mandatory where availability of the product for further research and breeding is restricted. Where future availability is not so restricted, then the payment is encouraged but not mandatory. In the SMTA adopted by the Governing Body at its Second Session in 2007, the payment was set at 0.77 percent (the actual figures set out in the SMTA are 1.1% less 30%) of the gross sales generated by the product (FAO, 2007).

Benefits from monetary and other benefit sharing under the Multilateral System flow not to the individual provider of the resources but to the Multilateral System itself to be shared out for the benefits of farmers in all countries; especially farmers in developing countries and countries in transition who conserve and sustainably utilize PGRFA. This multilateral pooling of benefits raises interesting issues with respect to the enforceability of the SMTA. Given that benefits under the SMTA flow to the Multilateral System and not to the providers of resources, such providers have a proportionately limited interest in enforcing the terms and conditions of the SMTA relative to the immediate and subsequent recipients of the material. The Multilateral System is itself, in effect, a third party beneficiary to the SMTA. Recognizing this, the Governing Body resolved in June 2006 for the FAO to represent the interests of the Multilateral System as third party beneficiary and give it certain rights to initiate dispute settlement proceedings in the event of a violation of the terms and conditions of the SMTA (FAO, 2006).

Another important issue left open under the CBD but settled under the Treaty was the status of ex situ collections acquired before the entry into force of the CBD. Between them, the ex situ collections held in trust by the CGIAR centres amount to over 650,000 accessions, including landraces and wild relatives important as a source of genetic diversity when seeking new traits including resistance to disease and the effects of climate change. Article 15 of the Treaty deals with the status of these collections and how material in those collections will be maintained and distributed in the future. PGRFA of Annex 1 crops and forages will be brought into the Multilateral System and made available through the SMTA under the same terms and conditions as material under the management and control of Contracting Parties. Non-Annex 1 material collected before the entry into force of the Treaty will also be made available under the terms and conditions of the SMTA. Non-Annex 1 material acquired after the entry into force of the Treaty is to be made available under terms and conditions consistent with those set by the country of origin of the PGRFA. The Treaty calls on the CGIAR centres, all of which have their own international legal personality, but which cannot be Parties to the Treaty since they are not states, to sign agreements with the Governing Body placing their collections within the purview of the Treaty. All eleven CGIAR centres holding ex situ collections have signed such agreements, as have a number of other international institutions holding international collections.

The Treaty also dealt with the other issue left unsettled under the CBD, namely Farmers' Rights. Article 9 of the Treaty repeats the recognition accorded by the International Undertaking of the enormous contribution that local and indigenous communities and farmers of all regions of the world, particularly those in the centres of origin and crop diversity, have made and will continue to make for the conservation and development of plant genetic resources for food and agriculture. It then recognizes that the responsibility for realizing Farmers' Rights rests with national governments. Without being prescriptive as to the measures that governments should take, the Treaty offers some examples of the types of rights that Contracting Parties should protect as appropriate and subject to their own national legislation. These include the protection of traditional knowledge relevant to PGRFA, the right to participate equitably in sharing benefits arising from the utilization of PGRFA and the right to participate in decision-making at the national level on matters related to the conservation and sustainable use of PGRFA.

One of the major points under negotiation was the issue of Farmers' Rights with respect to the use and exchange of farm-saved seed—the so-called 'farmers' privilege' under UPOV type legislation (see below). The Treaty is neutral on this point, Article 9.3 stating that:

> Nothing in this Article shall be interpreted to limit any rights that farmers may have to save, use, exchange and sell farm-saved seed/propagating material, subject to national law and as appropriate.

TRIPS and UPOV

A review of international regulatory regimes affecting agrobiodiversity would not be complete without some mention of the Agreement on Trade-Related Aspects of Intellectual Property Rights (TRIPS) and the International Convention for the Protection of New Varieties of Plants (UPOV Convention).

The TRIPS Agreement was concluded as part of the Uruguay Round that established the World Trade Organization, and sets certain minimum requirements for the protection of intellectual property (WTO, 1994). In particular, Article 27.3 of the TRIPS Agreement allows WTO Members to exclude from patentability plants and animals other than micro-organisms, and essentially biological processes for the production of plants and animals. However, WTO Members are required to provide for the protection of plant varieties either by patents or by an effective sui generis system or by any combination of both. The operation of this provision, and indeed the whole of the TRIPS Agreement, has been a great source of contention in recent years, with a number of countries calling for changes to the TRIPS Agreement to avoid what are perceived to be negative impacts on biodiversity. Indeed, express provision is made for the review of Article 27.3 four years after the entry into force of the WTO Agreement. A focal point of the review process, which the TRIPS Council was mandated to take up in 2001 in Doha was the interaction between the TRIPS Agreement and the CBD along with the protection of traditional knowledge and folklore.

While the TRIPS Agreement does not make any express reference to the UPOV Convention, UPOV is clearly a sui generis system of plant varieties protection that would meet the requirements of Article 27.3. Indeed, it provides a ready-made model that an increasing number of countries are happy to take up, although WTO Members are not obliged to accept that model if it does not fit their own national requirements.

The UPOV Convention was originally concluded in 1961 and subsequently revised in 1972, 1978 and 1991. Of these, the Acts of 1978 and 1991 are most salient. UPOV basically requires members to provide for the registration and protection of plant breeders' rights over new varieties in their national jurisdictions. The basic requirement for registration of new varieties is that the varieties should be new, distinct, uniform and stable. Much discussion on the impact of the UPOV system on agrobiodiversity has focused on the criterion of uniformity and, to a lesser degree, that of stability.

The scope of breeders' rights was somewhat expanded in the 1991 UPOV Act to bring it more in line with patent protection as the result of pressures from breeders in developed countries (UPOV, 1991). The 1991 UPOV Act provided for exclusive rights for production or reproduction (multiplication), conditioning for the purpose of propagation, offering for sale, selling or other marketing, exporting, importing and stocking for any of the above purposes. Exclusive rights were to be granted for a period of at least 20 years. The 1978 UPOV Act allowed farmers to save, use and exchange farm-saved seed since these were not considered to be covered in the original formulation of the exclusive rights of breeders, which focused on commercial exploitation (UPOV, 1978). This was always referred to as the 'farmers' privilege'. The 1991 revisions closed this loophole. The so-called farmers' privilege was given express sanction in the 1991 Act, but only as an option that members may provide for in their national legislation, and with greatly tightened wording that would exclude the sale or exchange of farm-saved seed. Article 15(2) of the 1991 Act allowed Contracting Parties, within reasonable limits and subject to the safeguarding of the legitimate interests of the breeder, to restrict the rights of the breeder to allow farmers to plant farm-saved seeds of protected varieties on their own holdings. This strengthened protection of breeders' rights is viewed by a number of countries, particularly those in Africa, as encroaching on farmers' traditional practices of exchanging seed. Such countries have resisted adhering to the 1991 UPOV Act or using it as a model for their own plant variety protection laws (see Helfer, 2004; Srinivasan, this volume).

The development of regulatory regimes at the national level

As it is not possible to cover the entire range of regulatory regimes relevant to agrobiodiversity in this chapter, this section will focus on broad issues shaping the development of national regulatory regimes. The development of such regimes is complicated by the intangible nature of genetic resources and uncertainty governing their status and ownership.

National legal systems tend to recognize two types of legal ownership; that over physical tangible property such as plants, animals or houses, and that over intangible property such as intellectual property. Intellectual property is the product of some act of creation, and intellectual property rights derive from that act of creation. Genetic resources, other than protected varieties, do not fall neatly into either of these two categories. The essential element of genetic resources is the intangible information contained in those resources, although access to this information may be through the acquisition of tangible expressions of that information (see Young, 2004). Traditionally, ownership of genetic resources, insofar as any such ownership has been recognized, has been linked to ownership of the biological resources such as the wheat in farmers' fields or the material held in ex situ genebanks. Ownership of the genetic resources per se (i.e. the intangible element) has been recognized only where they are the product of some act of creation, as for example through the granting of intellectual property rights over new plant varieties. National sovereignty over genetic resources means that countries have the power to manage those resources and to regulate access to them.

But the recognition of national sovereignty does not solve the issue of ownership. This is a matter that needs to be resolved in each national legal system. In many countries, legal ownership of genetic resources still follows the ownership of land and the biological resources on that land. But an increasing number of countries are now recognizing the separate ownership of genetic resources by the state.

Other obstacles include the lack of multidisciplinary scientific, institutional and legal capacity to develop satisfactory regulatory systems for agrobiodiversity at the national level, and the overlapping competences of different ministries responsible for agrobiodiversity, such as environment and agriculture. In the case of federal states, additional difficulties may be caused by the allocation of responsibilities between the federal government and the individual states.

National regulatory regimes specifically targeted at the protection of agrobiodiversity tend to focus, for the most part, on implementation of the CBD through national legislation dealing generally with environment protection or with genetic resources. National legislation dealing with national parks, wildlife protection, protected species, forests and agricultural land are also relevant.

Few countries have national legislation dealing specifically with the implementation of the International Treaty. Most are dealing with the implementation of the Treaty through administrative measures. The only need for legislation arises when legal regimes are already in place for the implementation of the CBD and there is a consequent need to carve out legal space for the simplified procedures envisaged under the Multilateral System created by the Treaty.

With respect to intellectual property rights, an increasing number of countries are providing for the protection of new plant varieties either through patents or through sui generis systems based mostly, but not exclusively, on the UPOV model. But the impact of agrobiodiversity concerns can be seen in some of the new legislation. Norway is one example, where concerns over the implications of joining the 1991 UPOV Act for traditional practices of farmers in exchanging farm saved seeds led to the decision to remain with the 1978 Act (Andersen and Winge, 2008). A more comprehensive approach to the protection of Farmers' Rights has been adopted through India's Protection of Plant Varieties and Farmers' Rights Act of 2001. This Act protects the rights of farmers to use, sow, re-sow, exchange, share and sell farm-saved seed, including seed of a variety protected by breeders' rights, provided that the farmer does not sell branded seed packaged and labeled as a seed variety protected under the Act (see Srinivasan, Chapter 5). It also allows for the registration of farmers' varieties and protects tribal or rural families from the misappropriation of genetic material they have conserved and developed by plant breeders.

Conclusion

Agrobiodiversity is essential for sustainable agriculture and food security. Its importance will increase in the future given the pressures of climate change and the consequent need for all countries to develop new varieties that can respond to new environmental challenges. Recent studies on the effects of climate change on agriculture indicate that over the next 50 years there will be little overlap in average temperatures during the growing season when compared with those evident over the last 50 years. In other words, the hottest summers in the past will be the coolest in the future. New regulatory regimes are now in place at the global level that will help the world to conserve and sustainably use agrobiodiversity. To be effective, these regimes need to be implemented fully at the national level.

References

Andersen, R. and Winge, T. (2008) 'Success stories from the realization of farmers' rights related to plant genetic resources for food and agriculture', FNI Report 4/2008, The Fridtjof Nansen Institute, Lysaker, Norway

Brunt, J., Hunter, D. and Delp, C. (2001) *A Bibliography of Taro Leaf Blight*, Secretariat of the Pacific Community, Noumea, New Caledonia

Food and Agriculture Organization of the United Nations (FAO) (2006) *IT/GB-1/06/Report: First Session of the Governing Body of the International Treaty on Plant Genetic Resources for Food and Agriculture, Madrid*, FAO, Rome

Food and Agriculture Organization of the United Nations (FAO) (2007) *IT/GB-2/07/Report: Second Session of the Governing Body of the International Treaty on Plant Genetic Resources for Food and Agriculture, Rome*, FAO, Rome

Food and Agriculture Organization of the United Nations (FAO) (2009) *Resolution 3/2001: Adoption of the International Treaty on Plant Genetic Resources for Food and Agriculture and Interim Arrangements for its Implemetation*, FAO, Rome

Food and Agriculture Organization of the United Nations Conference (FAO Conference) (1983) *International Undertaking on Plant Genetic Resources: Extracted from Resolution 8/83 of the Twenty-second Session of the FAO Conference*, FAO, Rome

Food and Agriculture Organization of the United Nations Conference (FAO Conference) (1989) *Resolution 4/89: Agreed Interpretation of the International Undertaking*, FAO, Rome

Food and Agriculture Organization of the United Nations Conference (FAO Conference) (1993) *Resolution 7/93: Revision of the International Undertaking on Plant Genetic Resources*, FAO, Rome

Food and Agriculture Organization of the United Nations Conference (FAO Conference) (2001) *Resolution 3/2001: Adoption of the International Treaty on Plant Genetic Resources for Food and Agriculture and Interim Arrangements for its Implemetation*, FAO, Rome

Harlan, J.R. (1992) *Crops and Man*, 2nd ed, American Society of Agronomy Inc., Crop Science Society of America Inc., Madison, WI

Helfer, L. (2004) 'Intellectual property rights in plant varieties International legal regimes and policy options for national governments', Food and Agriculture Organization of the United Nations, Rome

International Technical Conference on Plant Genetic Resources (ITCPGR) (1996) *Global Plan of Action for the Conservation and Sustainable Utilization of Plant Genetic Resources for Food and Agriculture*, ITCPGR, Leipzig

Moore, G. and Tymowski, W. (2005) *Explanatory Guide to the International Treaty on Plant Genetic Resources for Food and Agriculture*, IUCN, Gland, Switzerland and Cambridge

Palacios, X.F. (1998) 'Contribution to the estimation of countries' interdependence in the area of plant genetic resources', FAO Commission on Genetic Resources for Food and Agriculture, Background Study Paper No. 7, Rev 1

Young, T. (2004) 'Legal issues regarding the international regime: Objectives, options and outlook', in S. Carriosa, S. Brush, B. Wright and P. McGuire, (eds), *Accessing Biodiversity and Sharing the Benefits: Lessons from Implementing the Convention on Biological Diversity*, IUCN Environmental Policy and Law Paper No. 54, IUCN

United Nations Environment Program (UNEP) (1992) *Convention on Biological Diversity. Concluded at Rio de Janeiro on 5 June 1992.* UNEP, Nairobi

World Trade Organization (WTO) (1994) *Agreement on Trade-Related Aspects of Intellectual Property Rights*, WTO, Geneva

International Union for the Protection of New Varieties of Plant (UPOV) (1978) *International Convention for the Protection of New Varieties of Plants of December 2, 1961, as Revised at Geneva on November 19, 1972, and on October 23, 1978*, UPOV, Geneva

International Union for the Protection of New Varieties of Plant (UPOV) (1991) *International Convention for the Protection of New Varieties of Plants of December 2, 1961, as Revised at Geneva on November 19, 1972, on October 23, 1978, and on March 19, 1991*, UPOV, Geneva

5

Plant Breeders' Rights and On-Farm Seed Saving

C.S. Srinivasan

This chapter examines the impact of plant breeders' rights (PBR) regimes on the ability of farmers to save seed and engage in the conservation and enhancement of plant genetic resources that provide the raw genetic material for new crop varieties. In developed countries, intellectual property regimes for plant variety innovations have become well established over the last four decades. By circumscribing farmers' ability to save seed from protected varieties for use from one harvest to the next, such regimes are believed to strengthen incentives for private investment in plant breeding. Over the last decade, several developing countries have also adopted PBR protection systems in compliance with the Agreement on Trade-related Aspects of Intellectual Property Rights (TRIPS). Restrictions on the use of farm-saved seed are of major concern due to the adverse implications these could have for farm livelihoods—especially for subsistence farmers and smallholders. For this reason, attempts have been made in some developing counties to balance the monopoly rights that PBR regimes confer on institutional breeders with Farmers' Rights provisions that seek to reward farming communities for conservation of plant genetic resources and encourage on-farm innovation. In contrast with developed countries, therefore, it is possible that PBR regimes in developing countries may have only a limited impact on the ability of farmers to save seed and engage in on-farm innovation. However, this chapter will argue that the legal frameworks emerging in developing countries provide ineffectual intellectual property protection, significantly diluting incentives for institutional breeders while providing few rewards for on-farm conservation or innovation.

Evolution of plant variety protection in developed countries

The history of intellectual property rights stretches back some 700 years. The comparatively late emergence of plant variety protection (PVP) as a form of intellectual property right (IPR) is attributable, in part, to the nature of institutional arrangements required to apply IPRs to a self-reproducing innovation and the difficulties that breeders have in appropriating returns from such innovations. The emergence of plant variety protection had also to be preceded by paradigm shifts regarding the applicability of IPRs to living material and the adaptation of patent law concepts to plant variety innovations. Box 5.1 explains how patent law concepts have been adapted over a period of time to give rise to a sui generis system of protection for new plant varieties, the key criteria being: inventive step, utility, novelty and disclosure.

The adaptations of patent law concepts played only a facilitating role in the application of IPRs to plant varieties. Given the public good characteristics of plant variety innovations, it was the public sector that was dominant in plant breeding in developed countries for a long period. Increasing private sector participation in plant breeding, initially in the development of hybrid corn varieties in the United States, provided the impetus for an IPR framework for plant varieties for encouraging innovation and private sector investment (Kloppenburg, 1988). In Europe, the real impetus for a system of plant breeders' rights came from efforts to regulate the seed trade in European countries from the early years of the 20th century. Growth of the seed trade created a need for regulation to prevent the exploitation of farmers through unscrupulous trade practices. Regulation of the seed trade involved one or more of the following elements:

- Registration regulations: which stipulated that only seeds of registered varieties could be offered for sale;
- Denominational regulations: which stipulated that seeds be sold under the proper variety names, labelled by variety and producer. The breeder of the variety became the owner of the variety name, which was registered;
- Certification regulations: which controlled the quality (physical and genetic purity) of seed flowing to farmers through field inspections at different stages of seed production (certification eventually became mandatory in most European countries).

If farmers had to be provided with quality seed, then it was necessary to give breeders some degree of control over the multiplication of varieties bred by them. Though these regulations were intended to prevent malpractice in the production and marketing of seed, it was a short step from here to a system of plant breeders' rights. In fact, it has been argued that registration and certification conferred de facto IPRs on breeders in European countries even before formal PVP systems were introduced (Berlan and Lewontin, 1986).

Early PVP systems included the US Plant Patent Act 1930 which provided protection to varieties of plants that reproduced themselves asexually. In the Netherlands, the Breeders' Ordinance of 1941 granted a very limited exclusive right for breeders of agriculturally important species to market the first generation of certified seed. In Germany in 1953, the Law on the Protection of Varieties and the Seeds of Cultivated Plants gave breeders the exclusive right to produce seed of their varieties for the purposes of the seed trade and to offer for sale and market such seed. In the period prior to 1961, while a number of governments provided limited rights to plant breeders, the criteria for granting of rights differed from country to country and even the concept of 'variety' was not treated uniformly across all jurisdictions. There was no guarantee that the rights that governments were prepared to grant their own nationals would be extended to citizens of other countries. Where varieties were protected in one country but not in another, several distortions could result. It was the adoption of the International Convention for the Protection of New Varieties of Plants (UPOV) in 1961 that provided, for the first time, recognition of the rights of plant breeders on an international basis (UPOV, 1987). The Convention has undergone two major revisions in 1978 and 1991.

The UPOV Convention attempted to harmonize the PVP legislation of member countries. It specified uniform criteria for the protection of new varieties as distinctness, uniformity and stability. These criteria reflected the need for identifiability of a variety as a prerequisite for the application of IPRs. The Convention required member states to accord the same treatment to nationals of other states as they accorded to their own nationals. It also provided for certain elements of reciprocity. Importantly, it defined the scope of breeders' rights, which extended to *production for purposes of commercial marketing of the propagating material of the new plant variety*. The UPOV Convention of 1978 (UPOV, 1994a) and the PVP legislation of most member countries had two important features which distinguished the protection of plant varieties from patents. These were:

- Farmers' privilege: which acknowledged the right of farmers to use farm-saved seed. The breeders' right extended only to the production of seed for commercial marketing and consequently the use of farm-saved seed was outside the purview of the breeders' right.
- Research exemption: which provided that the use of a new (protected) variety as the initial source of variation for creating other new varieties and marketing them was free; that is, it did not require the breeder's authorization.

There were both practical and political reasons for protecting farmers' privilege. The practical reason concerned the difficulty for breeders to effectively monitor or seek to control what was happening on individual farms, while farmers expressed a strong interest politically in maintaining their traditional practice of saving seed. Seed saving by farmers is a centuries old tradition that is regarded a fundamental right by most farmers. Any attempt to do away with this practice would not only have been unacceptable for a large number of UPOV member states, it may have made PVP simply unworkable.

Box 5.1. Adaptations of patent law to plant variety protection

Inventive Step

Under patent law, an invention must encompass more than an obvious extension of what was previously known. Where varieties have been developed though conventional plant breeding (i.e. crossing followed by selection), inventiveness is recognized in the identification of further crosses for development. This process is in many ways similar to the one used in the development of traditional varieties in farmers' fields (Eyzaguirre and Iwanaga, 1996). The inventive step requirement in PVP, therefore, also requires that a variety be distinctive with respect to important characteristics (UPOV, 1994a). This is readily established for genera and species for which reference varieties are already known. But in the case of a previously unknown wild relative or other discovery, evidence of human effort and intervention must also be shown; the right under PVP accruing to the breeder who has bred or *discovered and developed* a variety.

The distinctness criterion leads to two other criteria for protection of plant varieties—uniformity and stability. Uniformity implies that a group of plants of a given variety exhibit only a limited amount of variation in their distinguishing characteristics. Stability requires that these distinguishing characteristics remain unchanged following repeated cycles of propagation. Without uniformity and stability, varieties are not distinguishable over time, making a protection system inoperative.

Utility

Patent law requires some use for the invention to be identified in the application. In the case of plant varieties, utility may be judged along several dimensions such as yield, resistance to biotic and abiotic stresses and adaptation to specific locations (or aesthetic value). As with industrial inventions, it may not always be possible to specify the incremental utility accruing from a variety. While evaluation of varieties for value in cultivation and use is routinely undertaken in a number of countries, it has been argued that, for plant varieties capable of being used in agriculture and horticulture, or even indirectly used as lines for subsequent breeding, utility should be deemed to be self-evident. Even materials discovered in the wild may contain useful resistance or other beneficial traits. The utility criterion has, therefore, been dispensed with in PVP law and a variety can be protected as long as it is distinct, uniform and stable.

Novelty

Patent law requires that an invention must be new to ensure that society does not grant privileges for materials already in the public domain. Some systems specify absolute novelty (no prior disclosure) while others allow a period after initial announcement within which protection can be granted. In the case of plant varieties (especially when new varieties are the result of selection), absolute novelty may be difficult to establish. Moreover, unlike inventions, which can be accessed by a written description, plant varieties become available only when physical material is accessed. Accordingly, novelty is deemed to be lost only when physical material of a variety is freely available. This will usually occur when a variety is commercialized. Therefore, in the case of plant varieties, it is the concept of 'commercial novelty' which is applied; i.e. the variety should not have been offered for sale for more than a prescribed period.

Disclosure

Patent disclosures serve multiple functions including: revealing the invention; providing information (allowing the patent to be duplicated on expiration of the patent); and contributing to the storehouse of technical information. Disclosure must enable a person skilled in the art to recreate the invention. This poses problems in the context of plant varieties because new varieties may be the result of spontaneous mutations occurring in nature or simply because the information on the derivative history of a variety may be lacking. A written description of the variety does not enable it to be replicated. The disclosure requirement in PVP law has been handled by requiring a deposit of a sample of seeds of the protected variety and also by requiring the breeder to maintain his or her variety (so that the PVP Authority can verify that the variety still exists). The deposited sample also serves as a reference sample.

The research exemption recognized the dependence of new varieties on existing varieties. In the absence of such an exemption, the grant of protection to a variety could completely foreclose the development of more varieties based on the protected variety. This would go against the basic objective of stimulating innovation. The research exemption meant that a protected variety could be freely used in the development of other new varieties. Moreover, the intention behind PVP (at least in the initial years of UPOV) was to stimulate the creation of new varieties, not to confer ownership of the underlying genetic resources on breeders. Accordingly, the protection under the 1978 Convention did not to give the plant breeder any rights in the genes, the underlying genetic resource, contained in the new variety.

While there is a clear rationale for farmers' privilege and researchers' exemption in PVP law, these provisions have also significantly diminished the returns that breeders of new varieties are able to appropriate from their innovations. The researchers' exemption enabled varieties which were only marginally different from already protected varieties to qualify for protection as new varieties and deprive the original breeders of potentially substantial royalties. Similarly, farmers' privileges were estimated to deprive breeders of up to 70 percent of the returns that would have been appropriated from Plant Breeders' Rights were farmers unable to use farm-saved seed of protected varieties for replanting or exchange and had to buy fresh seed for every round of sowing (Srinivasan, 2001, 2003). Researchers' exemption, farmers' privilege and the additional problem of enforcing rights against a widely dispersed group of users (who could all easily reproduce the innovation) meant that PVP came to be regarded as a weak IPR instrument providing only limited incentives for innovation (Perrin et al, 1983; Bulter and Marion, 1985; Kalton et al, 1989; Jaffe and Van Wijk, 1995; Frey, 1996; Alston and Venner, 2002).

In developed countries, the limited appropriability of returns afforded by PVP has led to concerted efforts (strongly advocated by the private seed industry) to improve appropriability through: changes to existing PVP laws such as the extension of breeders' rights from the propagating material to the harvested material and the recognition that some varieties are 'essentially derived' from existing varieties; the introduction of stronger IPR regimes for plant varieties including, in the US, patent protection; seed industry practices designed to improve returns accruing to breeders, such as contracts controlling the use of harvested material; and technological solutions that limit the reproductive capacity of harvested material.

The revision of the UPOV Convention in 1991 was designed to strengthen protection to breeders under PVP laws. This chapter will focus on how efforts to improve the appropriability of returns have circumscribed farmers' privilege. Specifically, Article 5(1) of the 1978 UPOV Convention stipulated that the prior authorization of the breeder was necessary for the production of protected material for commercial purposes but not for purposes such as re-sowing on the farmer's own land. While this was a minimum stipulation which left stronger forms of protection open to signatory governments the vast majority of UPOV member states did limit, in one way or another, the exercise of the breeders' right over material that was harvested and re-sown on the same farm. Such material did not include only seeds of the kinds that farmers normally save. It also applied to fruit and plantation crops and to cut flowers. A person could buy one fruit tree, propagate it and plant a vast orchard with no remuneration to the breeder, claiming to be exercising farmers' privilege. Modern techniques of tissue culture multiplied opportunities for circumventing breeders' rights.

Accordingly, when the Convention was revised in 1991 (UPOV, 1994b), the minimum right of the breeder in relation to propagating material was extended to all production or reproduction (multiplication) without the specification that this be for the purposes of commercial marketing only [Article 14(1)]. If this were all, the effect would have been to eliminate in their entirety the rights of farmers to save seed from protected varieties for re-sowing on their own farms. This would have been unacceptable for the great majority of UPOV member states. Therefore, Article 15(2) permits member states to restrict breeders' rights within 'reasonable limits' in order to permit farmers to save or re-sow seed on their farms provided that, in doing so, they take steps to safeguard the legitimate interests of breeders. The 1991 Convention thus replaced a provision in which the breeders' right did not cover seed saved on the farm with a provision which did cover such seed but left each member state free to make exceptions in light of national circumstances. Farmers' Rights to save seeds from harvest remain only as an exception to breeders' rights.

Different UPOV member countries have applied the revised provisions differently. Prior to the revision of the UPOV Convention in 1991, US legislation accorded an unconditional farmers' privilege to all growers of sexually propagated species. However, in response to seed industry concerns about the extensive prevalence of brown-bagging (i.e. the sale or exchange by farmers of protected material without explicit use of proprietary brand/variety names) farmers' privilege was restricted through a series of judicial decisions. The post-UPOV 1991 amendments to US legislation have reinforced the case-law led restrictions on the scope of farmers' privilege. US PVP law now allows the use of farm-saved seed only for the purpose of replanting the farmer's own land and farmers are not required to pay a royalty on the use of farm-saved seed. Exchange of farm-saved seed of protected varieties is no longer permitted. The European Union, on the other hand, has chosen to limit the privilege to certain species only, to give an unqualified privilege only to small farmers, and to give big farmers a privilege to save seed provided they pay appropriately for that privilege. Despite resistance from farmer groups in countries like France and Spain (GRAIN, 2007), most national legislation in the EU requires the majority of farmers to pay royalties on the use of farm-saved seed of protected varieties. In developed countries, therefore, efforts to improve the appropriability of returns for institutional breeders have ensured that farmers no longer have unfettered rights over the use of farm-saved seeds.

Developing country context

Developing countries have tended to rely heavily on public research systems for plant breeding research. This has been influenced not only by the public good characteristics of plant breeding and the market failure argument, but also by the fact that in many developing countries there may not have been any significant research capability in the private sector. In the absence of pre-existing research capability in the private sector, incentive measures like PVP could evoke only a very limited research and development response from the private sector. In many developing countries, the private sector was either completely excluded from the seed industry and plant variety research or its participation was highly regulated (Jaffee and Srivastava, 1994). The limited size of commercial seed markets in many developing countries may have also dampened incentives for private investment in plant breeding. Moreover, many of the varietal breakthroughs in developing countries (such as those that were responsible for the Green Revolution in South Asia and elsewhere) resulted from collaboration between their National Agricultural Research Systems and International Agricultural Research Centres, in which IPRs played no role at all. In fact, the absence of an IPR regime may have facilitated freer exchange of germplasm and breeding material than might have been otherwise possible. Consequently, PVP was not an important issue on the policy agenda for developing countries. Prior to the mid-1990s, very few developing countries adopted PVP and, of those that did, little was done to enforce it (Jaffe and Van Wijk, 1995).

The inclusion of IPRs as a trade-related issue in the Uruguay Round of the General Agreement on Tariffs and Trade negotiations, culminating in the TRIPS Agreement as part of the Agreement establishing the World Trade Organization (WTO), dramatically altered the priority accorded to plant variety protection in developing countries. Article 27(3) of the TRIPS Agreement requires Members to implement PVP either through patents, an effective sui generis system, or a combination of the two. The Agreement does not specify what the constituents of a sui generis system of protection should be. Nor does it specify how effectiveness should be evaluated. But in allowing the option of a sui generis system the Agreement recognizes the difficulties involved in applying patent law concepts to plant varieties and the reservations that many countries have about the appropriateness of patent systems for living organisms. TRIPS provides some flexibility to Member countries in fashioning PVP systems best suited to their needs. Transition periods of five to ten years from the date of the WTO Agreement (1-1-1995) were allowed to developing countries of different categories to implement the provisions of the Agreement.

The adoption of PVP legislation as a consequence of obligations imposed by an international agreement (rather than being demand led) has led to a divisive debate in many developing countries about the fundamental desirability of extending IPRs to agriculture and the potential adverse impact of a protection regime on smallholders and resource-poor farmers. Concerns about the adverse impacts of protection on farmers' livelihoods and the domestic seed industry have strongly influenced the design and implementation of PVP in developing countries. In the PVP debate in developing countries, the precise mechanisms by which the adverse impacts of PVP are likely to be felt are often not articulated, nor are they clearly distinguished from adverse impacts associated with other policy measures (e.g. removal of agricultural input subsidies, liberalization of imports of agricultural products or inputs etc. Very often, the criticism of PVP is subsumed under the more general criticism of globalization, liberalization and market-oriented policies. It then becomes difficult to disentangle the criticisms of a specific measure like PVP from criticisms of a package of policy measures designed to open the economy to foreign trade and investment, reduce state control of the economy and increase private sector participation in economic activity. Nevertheless, several important concerns about the adverse impacts of PVP can be distilled from the PVP debate in India and other developing countries (see Shiva, 1991; Jaffe and Van Wijk, 1995; Sahai, 1996; RAFI, 1996; GRAIN, 1999). The key concern is that farmers could face restrictions on their traditional and fundamental right to use farm-saved seed. Varieties protected by IPRs are likely to be more expensive than non-protected varieties. This may exclude poor farmers from the use of new (protected) varieties and increase the productivity/income gap between rich and poor farmers. Such trends are likely to be amplified should PVP facilitate the concentration of market share in the seed industry among multinational companies better placed than domestic suppliers to manage international IPR portfolios. Dependence on multinational firms raises related concerns about national food security, the incentives such firms have to develop varieties that meet the needs of smallholders and resource-poor farmers, and the displacement of public research from plant breeding. PVP may also generate pressures for the development of genetically uniform varieties. The adoption of genetically uniform varieties over large areas may contribute to the erosion of genetic diversity on farmers' fields.

A major set of concerns about PVP stems from the view that an IPR regime on plant varieties must necessarily be linked with measures to promote the conservation and sustainable use of agricultural biodiversity. These arguments are summarized below:

- All modern varieties bred by institutional breeders and afforded protection under PVP law are derived from plant genetic resources that have been conserved and enhanced over generations by rural and farming communities. The grant of an exclusive right to a breeder for a new variety represents unfair appropriation of the efforts of these communities. Such a view can lead to two positions. The first is outright rejection of the legitimacy of breeders' rights. The second, more prevalent position is that a breeder who is granted protection must be forced to share the benefits derived from protection with the communities that were the source of parental material. This position would call for appropriate benefit sharing mechanisms to be an integral part of any PVP legislation.
- The unfair appropriation of plant genetic resources by plant breeders is often international in scope. The Convention on Biological Diversity (CBD) recognizes the sovereign rights of nations over their biological resources and encourages them to regulate the exchange of biological resources with other countries. An important objective of CBD provisions is that the country which is the source of a biological resource should be able to share in the benefits when that resource is used in the development of commercially useful products elsewhere. It is therefore argued that a PBR legislation by itself is inequitable unless it is simultaneously supplemented by, or contains, measures that regulate the international transfer of plant genetic resources and assure reasonable remuneration for the use of such resources. This is said to be particularly important for developing countries like India and Brazil that are considered to be major centres of genetic diversity and the centre of origin for some important crops (Vavilov, 1951).
- A related argument is that the application of IPRs to the final products of plant breeding will inevitably serve as a trigger for institutional change that will restrict the free flow of plant genetic material (including those not currently subject to IPRs) between countries and between the public and private sectors. This will eventually disrupt the progress of plant breeding which has hitherto been critically dependent on the free, unrestricted exchange of such material.

It must be noted that many of the above concerns are not mutually consistent and involve very different assumptions about the likely impact of PVP. For instance, the view that denies the legitimacy of IPRs over living material (including plant varieties) is inconsistent with the view that such IPRs should be extended to farmers, communities and even to countries over all their biological resources.

Similarly, fears about the displacement of the public research system are inconsistent with the view that the private sector will not respond to PVP incentives.

Moreover, many of the arguments need to be carefully qualified. The criticism that PVP could lead to restrictions on the use of farm-saved seed ignores the fact that most developing country legislation provides an almost unfettered right to farmers to use farm-saved seed. Any IPR regime that confers a monopoly right on an innovator will probably lead to an increase in the price of the product and this may well be true of plant varieties as well. However, given that the objective of PVP is to stimulate innovations that may otherwise not be available to farmers, the important question is whether the rise in prices will be disproportionate to the benefits offered by the new variety (this may depend on the degree of competition in the market and the stringency with which breeders' rights are enforced). It is the additional social surplus created by the innovation and its distribution between farmers, seed suppliers and consumers that should be the central concern.

The concern regarding the influx of foreign varieties as a consequence of PVP ignores the fact that the grant of a PVP certificate does not authorize the titleholder to market the protected variety in a country. The introduction of new varieties in a country is generally governed by marketing regulations that are independent of PVP (e.g. India's New Policy on Seed Development, 1988). While the availability of PVP may affect the incentives of multinational companies to invest in a developing country, their entry into the domestic seed industry is governed by the policy on industrial investment, including the policy on foreign direct investment. In many developing countries (e.g. India, Brazil), the seed industry has witnessed the entry of a number of multinationals in the last ten years following the liberalization of investment policy, even in the complete absence of an IPR regime. Similarly, the concerns relating to the adverse impact of PVP on genetic diversity ignore the fact that the adoption of a limited number of high-yielding varieties on large areas is a trend witnessed dating back (at the very minimum) to the Green Revolution in the 1960s and 70s in many developing countries when PVP was not even contemplated.

Developing country approach to PVP legislation

A number of developing countries have enacted PVP legislation over the last decade, while several others are reported to be in the process of doing so. Thirty one developing countries were signatories to the UPOV Convention in 2007 (out of 67 total members). Other developing countries, including India, implemented PVP legislation despite remaining outside the UPOV Convention. The design of PVP legislation in developing countries has been dominated by the perceived need to mitigate the potential adverse effects on farm livelihoods that could arise from the grant of monopoly rights to institutional breeders rather than on the goal of providing strong incentives for private sector innovation and investment. A key feature of PVP legislation in developing countries, almost without exception, is the explicit recognition of Farmers' Rights to *save, use* and *exchange* seeds of protected varieties without payment of royalties to IPR holders. Some legislation (like India's

PVP Act) allows farmers to exchange and even sell seeds of protected varieties saved on the farm. The only restriction placed on farmers is that they should not use the protected variety denomination or brand name in the course of exchange or other transactions. In most developing countries, where commercial seed accounts for less than 20 percent of seed use, informal seed exchange is dominant and there are millions of farmers dispersed over a very large number of holdings, the enforcement of any restriction on the use of farm-saved seed would probably not be possible. Monitoring the use of brand names or variety denominations in informal seed exchanges in rural areas is also an unrealistic proposition. Unfettered rights for on-farm seed saving, have, therefore, been embedded in the PVP legislation of developing countries. This may have been a pragmatic choice, but it also underlines the political economy of PVP legislation in developing countries—PVP legislation would have been politically unacceptable (and a non-starter) unless it respected farmers' seed saving tradition.

Explicit recognition of Farmers' Rights to use farm-saved seed of protected varieties is not the only protection afforded to farmers in developing country PVP legislation. Many developing countries have inserted a range of Farmers' Rights provisions which attempt to strike a balance between the incentives provided to institutional breeders and the need to reward and encourage on-farm conservation and enhancement of plant genetic resources. These measures are also intended to mitigate the perceived deleterious effects of conventional PVP regimes on farming communities and include:

- *Benefit sharing*: these provisions are generally designed to force institutional breeders who apply for protection of new varieties to share their economic returns with farming communities that may have been the source of parental materials used by the breeders. Different models for benefit sharing may be envisaged. Breeders may be required to share a portion of their royalties on protected varieties with identified farmers or farming communities. This may be facilitated by allowing farmers, farming communities or their representatives to make benefit sharing claims when an application for protection is made. Alternatively, breeders may be required to contribute a portion of their PVP royalties to a common conservation or gene-fund which is then used to promote on-farm conservation activity. The PVP Authority may not only have to examine applications for protection in terms of the distinctness, uniformity and stability criteria but may also have to adjudicate claims for benefit sharing and set the terms of benefit sharing.
- *Prior informed consent*: these provisions require breeders applying for protection to disclose the pedigree of the new varieties and the source of parental materials used in their development. Some legislation also requires breeders to show that they have obtained prior-informed consent from farming communities where parental material has been sourced. These provisions are designed to ensure that the contribution of farming communities to the development of new varieties is recognized and facilitates the enforcement of benefit sharing provisions.

- *Recognition of farmers' varieties*: some developing country legislation allows for protection to be granted to farmers' traditional varieties even though such varieties may have been in the public domain for a long period and may not strictly meet the criteria of distinctiveness, uniformity and stability. The intention behind these provisions is not only to recognize the role of farming communities in the conservation and development of traditional varieties but also to prevent the appropriation of IPRs over these varieties by institutional breeders or seed companies. Protection for farmers' varieties may also assist in the enforcement of benefit sharing provisions when these varieties are used in the development of other new varieties.

In some developing countries, the above provisions are not incorporated in PVP legislation but in regulations concerning biodiversity rights flowing from the CBD that govern access to biological resources. Therefore, PVP legislation has to be examined along with biodiversity rights legislation in order to understand the scope of Farmers' Rights provisions. Several regional bodies have developed model legislation on plant variety protection and/or access and benefit sharing in the context of the exchange of biological resources. These include the African Union Model Law on Rights of Local Communities, Farmers, Breeders and Access; the ASEAN Framework Agreement on Access to Biological and Genetic Resources; and the Andean Community Decision 391: Common Regime on Access to Genetic Resources (for a compendium of relevant legislation and regulations, refer to www.upov.int and www.grain.org).

In order to assess the potential impact of PVP legislation in developing countries, it is necessary to consider the administrative, technical and legal infrastructure available for its implementation. However, political debate in many developing countries over the desirability of having PVP has taken the focus away from the infrastructure that needs to be put in place and the preparatory work that needs to be done before PVP implementation can commence. PVP requires technical expertise and administrative infrastructure to test varietal distinctness, uniformity and stability for a range of agricultural and horticultural crops. Even in countries with large national agricultural research systems (e.g. India, Brazil, China), that have built up substantial capabilities in the public sector for variety testing, it is still necessary to develop independent and credible arrangements for testing—preferably at arms-length from the public research institutions involved directly in plant breeding. Large reference collections need to be established to examine the novelty of varieties submitted for protection. Developing countries also need to establish agreements that will enable them to search the reference collections of other countries in order to assess the novelty of foreign varieties submitted for protection. Systems need to be put in place to ensure the security of seeds and other reproductive materials as they pass through the testing system. Effective implementation of PVP also requires a judicial system that can provide reasonably quick remedies against infringement without imposing excessive transaction costs on IPR holders.

The infrastructure and processes required for implementing Farmers' Rights provisions are still more extensive and complex. Giving effect to Farmers' Rights requires comprehensive documentation of existing agrobiodiversity in the country and its geographical distribution—which even developed countries are yet to accomplish. It also requires processes by which ownership of traditional varieties or landraces can be attributed to farmers and farming communities—a challenging task in the context of material that has long been in the public domain, is constantly evolving and has been exchanged between communities for generations. The complex pedigree of modern varieties (which may include a good proportion of material sourced from foreign countries) makes it difficult to determine the contribution of specific parental varieties in the development of any new variety. Adjudication of benefit sharing claims at the stage of grant protection can pose difficulties as the commercial potential of new varieties cannot be accurately predicted. Monitoring the countrywide sales of protected varieties at the level of individual protected varieties for enforcing benefit sharing provisions calls for substantial investment in seed industry regulation.

In light of the institutional capacity and infrastructure required to implement PVP systems, it is perhaps not surprising that there is little evidence of effective implementation of PVP legislation in developing countries. A recent World Bank study of PVP implementation in five developing countries thus found that in two (India and Uganda) implementation was yet to commence; in another two (Colombia and Kenya) implementation was limited; and in one (China) a steady increase was evident in the number of PVP certificates issued since PVP was implemented through a decree in 1999 (Tripp et al, 2007). In India, no PVP certificates had been issued even though the legislation had been on the statute books since 2001.

It is important to note that the issue of a large number of PVP certificates does not, by itself, constitute evidence of effective implementation. Effective implementation depends upon the extent to which institutional breeding programs (in the public and private sectors) protect their innovations using the PVP system, the returns they are able to appropriate as a result of protection, and the extent to which IPR holders find it worthwhile to enforce protection and guard against infringements. The price premium enjoyed by protected varieties over non-protected varieties is often used as an indirect indicator of the effect of protection. Empirical analysis of protected varieties in China (Hu et al, 2006) suggests that price premiums for protected rice varieties are positive but modest. There is no information available on the extent to which IPR holders in developing countries attempt to enforce protection through litigation. However, the absence of even anecdotal evidence may indicate that IPR holders in developing countries do not find such enforcement cost-effective. Where PVP certificates are issued, they appear to be used mainly as a marketing tool or as a branding device to prevent copying by competitors, not as a means through which to prevent unauthorized multiplication by farmers or the unorganized seed sector.

Many developing countries have seen major structural change in the seed sector over the last decade. Domestic firms have been consolidated—resulting in rising levels of concentration in the industry—while foreign seed companies have acquired an increasing presence through foreign direct investment, mergers and acquisitions, and collaborations. However, none of these changes appear to have been induced or mediated by changes in the IPR regime. Developing countries that have not complied with TRIPS (e.g. by not putting in place a PVP system) have not faced sanctions and little headway appears to have been made in TRIPS' review of the effectiveness of IPR provision in WTO Member countries. Interestingly, multinational seed companies also no longer appear to be clamouring for the strong implementation of IPR regimes in developing countries. This, perhaps, reflects the realization that appropriation of returns from the introduction of new varieties depends critically on several (non-IPR) elements of the regulatory framework including policy on foreign direct investment in the seed sector, marketing approval and quality control systems and the control that seed companies can exercise over seed production and distribution networks. The non-implementation of IPRs may evoke little concern from the private sector if they are not seen as being central to private investment by foreign or domestic companies.

There is, as yet, very little information on the implementation of Farmers' Rights provisions. But even if developing countries were to find a way of implementing these provisions, it is clear that these would increase transaction costs for breeders and reduce the economic returns that breeders can appropriate from PVP. This underlines the fundamental contrast between developed and developing countries. The evolution of PVP in developed countries has been oriented toward improving the appropriability of returns for IPR holders, whereas in developing countries the design of the legislation has been oriented to restricting returns that can be appropriated by institutional breeders. The slow development of infrastructure required for implementation, limited prospects of prompt judicial enforcement of rights, the complexities and transaction costs of obtaining protection as a consequence of Farmers' Rights provisions and the underlying philosophy that IPR legislation must seek to restrict appropriation of monopoly profits by IPR holders all point in the direction of weakly implemented PVP regimes in developing countries. The weak stimulus for innovation and investment is likely to leave the private sector unenthusiastic about the PVP system.

Conclusion

The evolution of plant variety protection in developed countries has been driven primarily by the objective of providing improved incentives for private innovation and investment in plant breeding. The quest for better appropriability of private returns for plant breeders has, over time, severely restricted farmers' privilege for on-farm seed saving. The restriction of farmers' privilege and the resulting consequences for farming livelihoods have been major concerns in developing countries as they design and implement plant variety protection regimes. But the experience of developed countries may not be an accurate guide to potential impacts in developing countries. The design of PVP legislation in developing countries has been influenced by a diversity of concerns and has been oriented to addressing the perceived inequities in a system that grants monopoly rights to institutional innovators. This has led to legislation that not only explicitly safeguards farmers' on-farm seed saving practices, but also attempts to reward farmers for their contribution to the conservation and enhancement of agricultural biodiversity. The complexity of legislation in developing countries and the limited availability of infrastructure for implementation portend the emergence of rather ineffectual property regimes, which are unlikely to pose any significant threat to on-farm seed saving traditions in developing countries for the foreseeable future.

References

Alston, J.M. and Venner, R.J. (2002) 'The effects of the Plant Variety Protection Act on wheat genetic improvement', *Research Policy*, vol 31, no 4, pp527–542

Berlan, J.P. and Lewontin, R. (1986) 'Breeders' rights and patenting life forms', *Nature*, vol 322, pp785–788

Butler, L. and Marion, B. (1985) *The Impact of Patent Protection on the U.S. Seed Industry and Public Plant Breeding*, Food Systems Research Group Monograph 16, University of Wisconsin Madison, Madison, WI

Eyzaguirre, P. and Iwanaga, M. (1996) *Participatory Plant Breeding*, International Plant Genetic Resources Institute, Rome.

Frey, K.J. (1996) *National Plant Breeding Study-I: Human and Financial Resources Devoted to Plant Breeding Research and Development in the United States in 1994*, Special Report 98, Iowa Agriculture and Home Economics Experiment Station, Iowa State University, IA

GRAIN (1999) 'Plant variety protection to feed Africa?', *Seedling*, vol 7, no 4, pp1–4, www.grain.org/seedling/?id=32, accessed 11 August 2009

GRAIN (2007) 'The end of farm-saved seed? Industry's wish list for the next revision of UPOV', GRAIN Briefing, www.grain.org/briefings_files/upov-2007-en.pdf, accessed 5 August 2009

Hu, R., Huang, J., Pray, C. and Huang, J. (2006) 'The impact of Plant Breeders' Rights on technology availability in China', Poster paper presented at the International Conference of Agricultural Economists, Gold Coast, Australia, August 12–18

Jaffe, W. and Van Wijk, J. (1995) *The Impact of Plant Breeders' Rights in Developing Countries: Debate and Experience in Argentina, Chile, Colombia, Mexico and Uruguay*, Inter-American Institute for Co-operation in Agriculture and University of Amsterdam, Amsterdam

Jaffee, S. and Srivastava, J. (1994) 'The roles of the public and private sectors in enhancing the performance of seed systems', *The World Bank Research Observer*, vol 9, no 1, pp97–117

Kalton, R.R., Richardson, P.A. and Frey, N.M. (1989) 'Inputs in private sector plant breeding and biotechnology research programs in the United States', *Diversity*, vol 5, no 4, pp22–25

Kloppenburg Jr., J.R. (1988) *First the Seed: The Political Economy of Plant Biotechnology 1492–2000*, Cambridge University Press, Cambridge

Perrin, R.K., Kunnings, K.A. and Ihnen, L.A. (1983) *Some Effects of the U.S. Plant Variety Protection Act of 1970*, Economics Research Report No. 46, Department of Economics and Business, North Carolina State University, NC

RAFI (1996) *Enclosures of the Mind: Intellectual monopolies. A resource kit on community knowledge, biodiversity and intellectual property*, RAFI, Ottawa, Canada

Sahai, S. (1996) 'Protecting plant varieties: UPOV should not be our model', *Economic and Political Weekly*, vol 31, no 41/42, pp2788–2789

Shiva, V. (1991) *The Violence of the Green Revolution: Third World Agriculture, Ecology and Politics,* Zed Books, London

Srinivasan, C.S. (2001) 'International experience of Plant Variety Protection: Lessons for India', PhD thesis, University of Reading, Reading

Srinivasan, C.S. (2003) 'Exploring the Feasibility of Farmers' Rights', *Development Policy Review*, vol 21, pp419–447

Tripp, R., Louwaars, N. and Eaton, D. (2007) 'Plant Variety Protection in developing countries. A report from the field', *Food Policy,* vol 32, no 3, pp354–371

UPOV (1987) *The First Twenty-Five Years of the International Convention for the Protection of New Varieties of Plants*, International Union for the Protection of New Varieties of Plants, Geneva

UPOV (1994a) *International Convention for the Protection of New Varieties of Plants of December 2, 1961 as Revised at Geneva on November 10, 1972, and on October 23, 1978*, International Union for the Protection of New Varieties of Plants, Geneva

UPOV (1994b) *International Convention for the Protection of New Varieties of Plants of December 2, 1961 as Revised at Geneva on November 10, 1972, and on October 23, 1978, and on March 19, 1991*, International Union for the Protection of New Varieties of Plants, Geneva

Vavilov, N.I. (1951) 'The origin, variation, immunity and breeding of cultivated plants', *Chronica Botanica*, vol 13, pp1–364

6

International Biosecurity Frameworks to Protect Biodiversity with Emphasis on Science and Risk Assessment

Robert Black and Irina Kireeva

If the country were open on its borders, new forms would certainly immigrate, and this would also seriously disturb the relations of some of the former inhabitants. Let it be remembered how powerful the influence of a single introduced tree or mammal has been shown to be (Charles Darwin, 1859, p81).

Regulatory frameworks for biosecurity have traditionally focused on the protection of agriculture and forestry through quarantine. More recently, these frameworks have expanded in two directions. First, concerns with the protection of trade and markets have brought greater emphasis on the assessment of risk in decision-making. Second, consideration of risk has itself expanded to include environmental and habitat protection. In this chapter, the authors elaborate on biosecurity frameworks that contribute to the protection and conservation of biodiversity with the objective of emphasizing linkages between biosecurity, biodiversity, markets for farmers and international trade. While not discussed in detail, it is important to note that biosecurity-related threats to biodiversity, agricultural markets and farmer livelihoods are likely to become significantly more acute as a consequence of climate change. Climate change may influence biodiversity by damaging habitats and by promoting the spread of pests and pathogens. It has already been observed that some plant pests are increasing their range as a wider geographical area provides favourable climatic and environmental conditions (Biological Diversity Advisory Committee, 2006).

Regulatory frameworks considered here include the World Trade Organization (WTO) Agreement on The Application of Sanitary and Phytosanitary Measures (SPS Agreement) and Agreement on Trade-Related Aspects on Intellectual

Property Rights (TRIPS), the Cartagena Protocol on Biosafety, and animal health frameworks under the World Organisation for Animal Health (OIE). These are in addition to the Convention on Biological Diversity (CBD) and the International Plant Protection Convention (IPPC) already introduced in earlier chapters of the book. Particular attention will be regulation of the movement of plants and animals provided for by the IPPC and CBD in protecting habitats and the linkages and possible conflicts with the WTO Agreements.

Meaning of biosecurity

The United Nations Food and Agriculture Organization (FAO) defines biosecurity as:

> a strategic and integrated approach that encompasses the policy and regulatory frameworks (including instruments and activities) that analyse and manage risks in the sectors of food safety, animal life and health, and plant life and health, including associated environmental risk (COAG, 2003, p1).

> [biosecurity] is composed of three sectors, namely food safety, plant health and life, and animal life and health. These sectors include food production in relation to food safety, the introduction of plant pests, animal pests and diseases, and zoonoses, the introduction and release of Genetically Modified Organisms (GMOs) and their products, and the introduction and safe management of invasive alien species and genotypes (COAG, 2001, p1).

Biosecurity, therefore, encompasses border controls for plant, animal and human health and environmental protection as well as supporting measures such as eradication of outbreaks and containment of introduced organisms under quarantine for experimental purposes. Biosecurity covers all policy, laws and regulatory frameworks to manage risks associated with food and agriculture in the broad sense (including fisheries and forestry). The risks mainly come from the introduction into an area or territory of organisms that are harmful to people, animals (domesticated and wild) and plants (pests, disease organisms or pathogens and invasive species), as well as contamination of food and other products with harmful substances such as pesticides and food additives. Biosecurity includes the protection of biodiversity because the environment is made up of plant and animal life as well as of human culture.

Biosecurity has become recognized as a necessary umbrella concept for the various regulatory frameworks identified above because of the profound impact of trade globalization. On the one hand, international agreements protecting animal and plant life and biodiversity—such as the CBD and the Convention on International Trade in Endangered Species (CITES)—reflect widely held concerns about the future of the planet's natural resources. On the other, WTO agreements— most notably the SPS Agreement—provide an enforceable international legal framework for ensuring that measures to protect human, animal and plant life and the environment are consistent with free trade, as opposed to measures designed principally to protect domestic production from competition (Barker and Mander, 1999).

The revised texts of the IPPC of 1997 and the Cartagena Protocol on Biosafety (adopted by the Conference of the Parties to the CBD in 2000 to protect biological diversity from the potential risks posed by living modified organisms resulting from modern biotechnology) reflect the need to balance biosecurity with free trade. However, there are significant differences in the traditional approach to plant and animal health and WTO's rules. As mentioned above, the traditional approach to biosecurity has been protection of agriculture—conceived as plant and animal health—from pests through the use of quarantine. The IPPC targets pests and pathogens of plants while the OIE targets animal diseases and zoonoses (animal diseases transmissible to humans). However, the environmental dimension of biosecurity is such that IPPC should not only be seen as protecting agriculture and economic forestry but also natural vegetation, because damage to plants by harmful organisms such as pests, in the narrow sense, and invasive species more generally, impacts negatively on the environment.

In the animal health frameworks of the OIE, there is corresponding recognition that animal diseases introduced with imported livestock can infect wildlife as well as farm animals (and wildlife are an important source of animal disease and zoonoses) (see, for example, Sainsbury, 1998). This is exemplified by current concerns over such animal diseases as rinderpest, foot and mouth disease and avian influenza. There is grave concern over aquatic organisms because diseases can spread very rapidly in water and introduced fish, crustacea etc can become seriously invasive:

> So-called invasive wild and domestic animal species or non-indigenous plants threaten many ecosystems, for example by introducing alien species into some ecological niches, with growing negative environmental consequences worldwide. When natural ecosystems are threatened by invasive wild animal populations or by domestic animal populations that have become wild or semi-wild, it is important to control the demography of such populations which can also serve as highly effective disease reservoirs for numerous pathogens. In this respect, the OIE is seeking to develop standards for the humane control of these undesirable categories of animal populations where necessary (OIE, 2008a).

In this respect it is noteworthy that the OIE is a partner of the CBD on invasive alien species.

Risk analysis under the SPS Agreement

The SPS Agreement has a two-fold objective: first, it aims to recognize the sovereign right of Members to provide the level of health protection they deem appropriate; and second, it aims to ensure that SPS measures do not represent unnecessary, arbitrary, scientifically unjustifiable, or disguised restrictions on international trade.

With respect to the first objective, the SPS Agreement allows Member countries to set their own food safety and animal and plant health standards but encourages use of international standards, guidelines and recommendations where they exist. International standards are said to be justified by definition and do not require additional scientific justification. Members may adopt SPS measures which result in higher levels of health protection—or measures for health concerns for which international standards do not exist—provided these measures are scientifically justified. Alternatively, under the Agreement, Members may adopt measures that are less stringent than existing international standards, even where these allow products that are less protective or even harmful to health to enter its market.

In relation to the second objective, Article 5 of the SPS Agreement mandates that SPS measures which are restrictive to trade must be based on assessment of the actual risks involved. Article 2.2 states that SPS measures should be based on science, not maintained without sufficient scientific information and only applied to the extent necessary (proportionality requirement). Further, if requested by another WTO Member, an explanation of the reasons for restrictive measures must be provided.

In order to establish whether an SPS measure is based on risk assessment as required by Article 5.1, it is important to determine what is meant by *risk assessment*. Annex A(4) of the SPS Agreement recognizes two distinct types of risk assessment. The first applies to SPS measures whose aim is to protect against the establishment or spread of a pest or disease. It is defined as:

> the evaluation of the likelihood of entry, establishment or spread of a pest or disease within the territory of an importing WTO Member according to the sanitary or phytosanitary measures which might be applied, and of the associated potential biological and economic consequences.

The second type of risk assessment applies to any measures designed to protect humans and animals from so-called 'food-borne' risks. It is defined as:

> the evaluation of the potential for adverse effects on human or animal health arising from the presence of additives, contaminants, toxins or disease causing organisms in food, beverages or feedstuffs.

The international standards-setting organizations referenced in the SPS Agreement contextualize risk assessment within a wider process of *risk analysis*. Risk analysis is a systematic way of gathering, evaluating, recording and disseminating information leading to recommendations for a position or action in response to an identified hazard (WTO, undated a). It involves four steps:

- *Hazard Identification*: specification of the adverse event which is of concern;
- *Risk Assessment*: estimation of the probability (i.e. the actual likelihood and not just the possibility) of the hazard occurring, the consequences of that hazard occurring, and the degree of uncertainty involved;
- *Risk Management*: identification and implementation of the best option for reducing or eliminating the likelihood of the hazard occurring; and
- *Risk Communication*: open exchange of explanatory information and opinions that lead to better understanding and decisions (WTO, undated a, Section 2.5).

In the *Australia-Salmon* dispute—which concerned an SPS measure designed to protect against 'pest or disease' risks—the Appellate Body noted that the language in the definition of risk assessment was different for the two types of risk. However, the Appellate Body clarified the standard to some extent by saying that some of the evidence contained in the risk assessment for one type of product may be useful for the risk assessment of another. For an assessment of pest and disease risk to be valid, it must evaluate the likelihood (*viz*, the probability) of the entry, establishment or spread of disease and the associated biological and economic consequences. This *likelihood* must also be measured according to the SPS measures which might be applied. However, it was found that this evaluation of likelihood can be expressed either quantitatively or qualitatively. A cumulative three part test has, therefore, developed from the case law on the proper way to conduct a risk assessment for 'disease or pest related' risks:

- WTO Members should identify the specific diseases or pests that they want to keep out, as well as the potential biological and economic risks involved;
- WTO Members should evaluate the likelihood of entry, establishment or spread of these diseases, along with the potential economic and biological cost; and
- WTO Members should evaluate the likelihood of entry, establishment or spread of pests or diseases according to the SPS measures which might be applied.

This test is largely consistent with the process of risk analysis described above.

How the WTO's SPS Agreement influences international biosecurity frameworks

The main international biosecurity frameworks covering live plants and animals respectively (and propagating material, sperm, eggs etc) are the International Plant Protection Convention, originating in 1951, and codes and standards under the World Organisation for Animal Health (OIE) that was created in 1924. Both the Secretariat of the IPPC and the OIE are recognized as International Standard Setting Bodies (hereinafter referred as 'ISSB') in the SPS Agreement. The third ISSB is the

Codex Alimentarius Commission convened by the FAO and the World Health Organization.

Before the SPS Agreement came into force, prospective importers of plants or planting material were required to show that these materials constituted no danger to plants already in the destination country; the so-called precautionary approach. Export certification was broadly along the line of freedom from pests on a cursory examination. Since 1995, and appearance of the SPS Agreement, a change of attitude in official services (and profound changes in the regulatory framework) became necessary. In consequence, the IPPC was substantially revised in 1997 to accommodate the SPS principles and approaches to risk assessment; the current version coming into force on 2 October 2005. Now, irrespective of whether or not a country is a Member of the WTO, if it has adopted the IPPC, that Member is obligated to allow prospective importers of plant material to proceed with importation unless it is able to demonstrate a meaningful risk. Further, import permits of any kind are falling out of favour as the imposition of additional bureaucracy may itself be construed as a potential trade barrier (Black, 2003a).

The two approaches, precautionary (applying the 'Precautionary Principle' or risk aversion), on the one hand, and a risk assessment-based approach on the other, have fuelled debate about the relative enforceability of WTO's trade agreements and the Multilateral Environmental Agreements under the United Nations including the CBD (Stilwell and Tarasofsky, 2001; Mann and Porter 2003)

The OIE's Terrestrial Animal Health Code and the Aquatic Animal Health Code provide parallel provisions for animal diseases to the IPPC's provisions for (plant) pests. The IPPC and the OIE Codes differ in the nature of their respective standards. Whereas the OIE standards include international lists of animal diseases and zoonoses as well as standard procedures, the multiplicity of host plants and potential pests means that there are no internationally recognized plant pests. Therefore, the IPPC standards refer to standards for phytosanitary measures against these pests (International Standards for Phytosanitary Measures or ISPMs). This has consequences for the way the scientific evidence provision of the SPS Agreement is applied under the two frameworks.

Under the OIE, a listed animal disease or zoonosis does not have to be justified as a basis for measures to prevent its introduction or spread. Instead, only the actual measures taken against one of these diseases require justification. Under the IPPC, the pest itself must be justified as a quarantine pest; defined as:

> a pest of potential economic importance to the area endangered thereby and not yet present there, or present but not widely distributed and being officially controlled.

In turn this impacts on how risk analysis is used for biosecurity, as discussed in the next section.

Risk analysis and decision-making for biodiversity protection

It was explained above that risk analysis has special significance in implementation of the IPPC because there are no standard plant pests that compare with the internationally recognized animal diseases and zoonoses listed by the OIE. Instead, International Standards for Phytosanitary Measures address the processes that must be undertaken to develop phytosanitary measures. One of the first ISPMs, ISPM No. 02 was the *Framework for Pest Risk Analysis*. Pest risk analysis (PRA) was developed in the late 1980s for plant health (Griffin, 2002). ISPM No. 02 has largely been superseded by the fuller elaboration provided in ISPM No. 11, the title of which—*Pest risk analysis for quarantine pests including analysis of environmental risks and living modified organisms*—was adopted after successive expansions of the document firstly to incorporate analysis of environmental risks and then living modified organisms (FAO terminology for genetically modified organisms).

Expansion of the PRA framework was undertaken in collaboration with the Secretariat of the CBD. As well as providing details for the conduct of pest risk analysis, the standard:

> also includes details regarding the analysis of risks of plant pests to the environment and biological diversity, including those risks affecting uncultivated/unmanaged plants, wild flora, habitats and ecosystems contained in the PRA area [i.e. the area being considered as vulnerable to the introduction of the pest]. [It also includes] guidance on evaluating potential phytosanitary risks to plants and plant products posed by living modified organisms (IPPC, 2004).

As for other aspects of risk analysis, the PRA includes both risk assessment and risk management (IPPC, 2004). We would argue that ISPM No. 11 does not provide a practical scheme for PRA. Nevertheless, the standard does demonstrate the importance of PRA as the basis for most measures concerning international movement of plants and plant products and any type of organisms that might damage the environment. Such measures include official designation of pests as quarantine pests, all phytosanitary import requirements and approval or rejection of applications for import permits. Applying the expansion provided by the 2004 revision beyond the traditional agricultural sphere for quarantine, the standard covers a potentially wide range of organisms that might impact on habitats and biodiversity. This is not to say that the National Plant Protection Organization (the Competent Authority for plant health in SPS terms) is necessarily the official organization responsible for making import decisions on 'environmental matters'. Rather there should only be a single risk analysis framework for both agricultural and environmental decision-making on imports.

Furthermore, it should only be necessary for prospective importers to apply to one authority since it would be considered a trade barrier if two or more agencies undertook risk analysis and issued permits separately. The implications of this for legislation and permits are considered below. The OIE has equivalent risk analysis frameworks in Chapter 2 of the Terrestrial Animal Code (OIE, 2008b) and in Chapter 1.4 of the Aquatic Animal Health Code (OIE, 2008c). The components of risk analysis described in the Terrestrial Code are hazard identification, risk assessment, risk management and risk communication, consistent with international norms as described above. However, risk analysis on animal diseases starts from the premise that the diseases are mostly already recognized internationally.

At this point, it important to consider whether there are accidental or deliberate introductions under discussion. Traditional quarantine was mainly concerned with unintentional introductions or with introductions through deliberate, but illegal, actions (smuggling) that were not usually intended to do harm. However, alien species have been introduced deliberately on countless occasions with often disastrous consequences for agriculture and the environment. Table 6.1 provides examples of the ill-effects of deliberate introductions across most of the taxonomic categories of plants and animals. Vertebrates may be introduced as livestock (goats, rabbits), pets, for game and fur, and for biological control. Invertebrates have been introduced as food animals, as beneficial organisms (e.g. bees, silkworm) and for biological control. Plants may be introduced as ornamental and amenity species, and for commercial exploitation (agriculture, horticulture, forestry, firewood, biofuel etc).

Introduction of alien species for biological control is potentially risky because the intention is to impact on a pest species but the introduced organism may affect non-target species. The FAO has introduced guidelines for the safe introduction and use of such agents (FAO, 1995). The authors do not know of any examples of microorganisms (fungi, bacteria, viruses) introduced as biological control agents that have attacked non-target or beneficial species (although a fungus used for control of thistles, *Phomopsis cirsii*, is said to be a threat to artichokes; Landcare Research, 2000). However, many plant pathogens, particularly fungi, have caused immense destruction to natural vegetation when introduced accidentally on deliberately introduced goods; for example Dutch elm disease.

Given the potential impact of invasive alien species on habitats and biodiversity it is critical that proposed introductions be risk assessed against objective criteria before a decision is made. Implementation of risk analysis in specific jurisdictions is considered in more detail below, with particular reference to introduced aquatic organisms.

Table 6.1. Deliberate introductions of alien species that have invaded habitats and reduced biodiversity

Taxonomic category	Examples	Reason for introduction and impact on biodiversity
Vertebrates		
Fish	Zander	Introduced as game fish; out-competes native species as a predator
Amphibians	Cane toad in Australia	Introduced to control pests in sugarcane; highly poisonous to mammals, including humans
Reptiles	Monitor lizards in Florida	Escaped or unwanted pets hunting native fauna
Birds	Barn owl in Seychelles	Introduced to control rodents; hunts native birds
Mammals	Mongoose in many countries	Introduced as pet and to control snakes, now considered as pests, eating eggs, chickens
	Goat in St Helena	Destroyed virtually all native plant species and habitats
	Mink in United Kingdom	Escaped from fur farms, voracious predator of native fauna
Invertebrates		
Insects	Gypsy moth (*Lymantria dispar*) for silk production	Became serious pests of hardwood trees when introduced to North America
	Asian lady beetle (*Harmona axyridis*)	Introduced to control aphids, outcompetes native species (and taints wine!)
Molluscs	Giant African land snail in many countries	Introduced as pet or food resource, regarded as pest in many countries and further introduction prohibited
Crustacea	Red signal crayfish in United Kingdom	Introduced for restaurant trade; escapees endangering native crayfish and other species

Plants			
	Angiosperms	Water hyacinth throughout tropics and subtropics	Introduced apparently as an ornamental; is one of most notoriously invasive plants
		Paper mulberry (Broussonetia papyrifera) in Ghana	Introduced for paper making (handicrafts) as in Asia; became seriously invasive through lack of resources and know-how for exploitation
	Gymnosperms	Invasive conifer species world-wide (for forestry)	There are proportionally more invasive species of conifers than flowering plants.
	Pteridophytes	Giant Salvinia (*Salvinia molesta*)	A giant form of the floating form; native to South America and invasive elsewhere in warm climates when introduced.
	Bryophytes	Tree ferns	Introduced Australian tree ferns are considered invasive in Hawaii.
		Campylopus introflexus	This moss native to the Southern Hemisphere is invasive in Europe.
	Algae	Many species of seaweeds and freshwater algae	Algae are considered to be seriously invasive in freshwater and marine habitats but it is not clear whether they are intentional or accidental introductions.

Genetically-modified organisms (GMOs) also warrant consideration as alien species. Potential for biodiversity damage stems primarily from the spread of pollen from GMO crops to other plants; thereby spreading the modified genes. This has been demonstrated in Mexico where traditional maize varieties or landraces have been contaminated by GM maize (Anonymous, 2009). The threat from the spread of herbicide resistance to wild plants and thereby the creation of 'super-weeds' is as yet not supported. While these instances are seized upon by fundamental opponents of biotechnology as ammunition to oppose GMOs outright, an alternative more consistent with biosecurity frameworks would be to apply risk analysis on a case-by-case basis even though uncertainty, as with the introduction of other alien species, always remains in practice.

As well as enabling more objective decisions to be made on individual cases, there is also an element of 'horizon scanning' to PRA in relation to predictions about what possible risks might emerge in the future. The most important element here is probably climate change. With signs that, generally, the earth is getting warmer (with some areas predicted to become cooler nonetheless), there will be profound changes to the distribution of plants and animals and habitats (Lovejoy and Hanna, 2005). Patterns of agriculture will also change. For example, it is predicted that the main zone of olive growing will move to mid-France while the Sahel and East Africa will become even drier. This will affect pest distribution with pest organisms having the potential to affect a wider range of hosts, including natural species. The effects are not limited to primary influence on plants. The likely extinction of forest birds in Hawaii due to climate change mediated through avian malaria has been documented (LaPointe et al, 2005), as well as the impact of change on aquatic animals (Allan et al, 2005).

In spite of the objective of risk analysis being a scientific exercise carried out objectively in order to provide a sound basis for decision-making, there are serious elements of controversy in risk analysis, especially relating to biodiversity protection. These come primarily from tension between application of the precautionary principle advocated in multilateral environmental agreements and the approach of almost exclusive resort to risk assessment provided for in the SPS Agreement. Controversy in risk assessment also comes from the role of uncertainty and from the use of 'expert judgment' in risk analysis. These tensions have manifested themselves in several controversial issues.

Whereas, in the agricultural sphere, the involvement of PRA in phytosanitary measures is largely settled, there is perhaps an intrinsic difficulty when it comes to the extension to environmental protection because the CBD (and some other multilateral environmental agreements such as the Framework Convention of Climate Change) deliberately take a precautionary approach. The preamble to the CBD (p144) re-phrases Principle 15 of the Rio Declaration which is taken as the source of the Precautionary Principle:

> Noting also that where there is a threat of significant reduction or loss of biological diversity, lack of full scientific certainty should not be used as a reason for postponing measures to avoid or minimize such a threat.

Conversely, the SPS Agreement, article 5.7 states that:

> In cases where relevant scientific evidence is insufficient, a Member may provisionally adopt sanitary or phytosanitary measures on the basis of available pertinent information, including that from the relevant international organizations as well as from sanitary or phytosanitary measures applied by other Members. In such circumstances, Members shall seek to obtain the additional information necessary for a more objective assessment of risk and

review the sanitary or phytosanitary measure accordingly within a reasonable period of time.

It is clear that this is only a temporary approach in contrast to the full precautionary approach of the CBD. Nowhere is the tension seen more acutely than in the controversies on importation and use of GMO crop varieties (discussed in more detail in the next section). The Cartagena Protocol on Biosafety to the CBD was intended to form a bridge between the SPS Agreement and the CBD. The Cartagena Protocol applies a 'prior-informed consent approach' but many argue that the key clause providing a deliberate attempt at compromise fails to address adequately the key issue; others argue that precaution is unnecessary because no serious risks of GM cropping have emerged and the public is no longer interested (SciDev Net, 2006). The United States has not signed the Cartagena Protocol, which was one factor cited in its success over the EU in the trade dispute over the alleged EU moratorium on GM seed.

The second element in these controversies—uncertainty—equates with 'lack of full scientific certainty' in the Rio Declaration/CBD. Paradoxically, however, risk analysis recognizes that virtually all risk assessments will have elements of uncertainty and requires the assessors to state the sources of uncertainty as precisely as possible. For example in ISPM No. 11, at the conclusion to the risk assessment phase of PRA (section 2.4), we find:

> Estimation of the probability of introduction of a pest and of its economic consequences involves many uncertainties. In particular, this estimation is an extrapolation from the situation where the pest occurs to the hypothetical situation in the PRA area. It is important to document the areas of uncertainty and the degree of uncertainty in the assessment, and to indicate where expert judgement has been used. This is necessary for transparency and may also be useful for identifying and prioritizing research needs.

Furthermore, the added guidance on environmental pests notes:

> It should be noted that the assessment of the probability and consequences of environmental hazards of pests of uncultivated and unmanaged plants often involves greater uncertainty than for pests of cultivated or managed plants. This is due to the lack of information, additional complexity associated with ecosystems, and variability associated with pests, hosts or habitats.

In the fields we are considering, the most frequent source of uncertainty is having data on the properties and behaviour of the organism in its native area but not knowing whether the organism will respond similarly to the new environment into which it has been introduced. Statements of uncertainty are often used by decision-makers or politicians to justify claims that assessments are invalid or that the assessors are incompetent (Holt, et al, 2006). Current approaches to overcome this difficulty are to quantify the uncertainty (determine the degree of uncertainty in ISPM No. 11).

The related issues of precaution and uncertainty are particularly acute for policy makers in the European Union because the former is one of the pillars of environmental protection in the EC Treaty (Article 174) and hence brings the EU into conflict with some trading partners. An important policy document from the European Commission provides guidance on when and how the precautionary principle may be used (Commission of the European Communities, 2000). The trigger is when uncertainty reaches such a level (by quantitative or semi-quantitative assessment) that risk assessment is not meaningful. This has been tested and applied in the European Courts (the *Pfizer case* and others; see Van Asselt and Vos, 2006) and there are signs that other jurisdictions are adopting this approach as seen in the landmark Australian case, *Telstra Corporation Limited v Hornsby Shire Council* (LECNSW, 2006). The following section will discuss the impact of the precaution/risk analysis debate on international trade in living organisms and products from them.

Trade, biosecurity and biodiversity

We have already seen how the WTO's SPS Agreement shifted the focus of biosecurity from a precautionary approach to one based on risk analysis. Another important difference between the CBD and the SPS Agreement is that only the latter is enforceable. Dispute settlement procedures provided for under the CBD have never been used and, even if they were, the losing party would not necessarily face economic sanctions if they did not comply with the ruling. The treatment of environmentally-based restrictions on trade by the WTO is thus critical in shaping biosecurity and biodiversity outcomes related to trade.

One of the critical questions in this regard has been the extent to which nations may attempt to safeguard natural resources and biodiversity in other countries by taking actions to prevent the importation of sensitive articles and thus limit the commercial benefits of exploitation. There are two elements to these actions, direct and indirect. For direct controls, the key international instrument is the CITES, under which international trade in certain live species, and products derived from them, is prohibited (Black, 2003b). Additionally, there may be attempts to limit imports of natural products whose production or harvesting endangers species other than those traded. Whereas it is accepted that there can be voluntary controls exercised through, for example, eco-labelling and sustainability certification (e.g. 'dolphin friendly tuna'), is it actually possible to prohibit the import of items linked with environmental damage in the production area?

This has been the subject matter of a number of cases brought before the WTO Dispute Settlement Body (DSB). Perhaps most well known of such environmental disputes was the *Mexico etc versus US: 'tuna-dolphin'* case through which US restrictions on the importation of yellow fin tuna caught using methods that also resulted in the deaths of large numbers of dolphins was successfully challenged by Mexico in 1991 through the General Agreement on Tariffs and Trade (GATT) (WTO, undated b). The GATT ruled that the US could not restrict the import of Mexican tuna 'simply because Mexican regulation on *the way tuna was produced* did not satisfy US regulations'. Neither could it impose its own domestic laws on another country (WTO, undated b). While the US did not initially comply with the GATT ruling, the threat of similar action following the formation of the WTO in 1995 was sufficient for the US to remove its restrictions. While the Appellate Body of the DSB has declined in this and similar cases to make definitive rulings on the central issue of which, between trade and environment, is more important, it has challenged what are referred to as extra-territorial measures and attempts to regulate production and processing methods (PPMs) as opposed to product quality or content.

In a case more directly related to biosecurity, the USA, Canada and Argentina launched the *EC: Approval and marketing of biotech products* dispute (WTO, undated c) in response to the EU's moratorium on release of GMO seed into the environment for commercial crop production until completion of farm-scale trials to assess environmental risks. A major issue contested was the EU's precautionary approach provided for under Article 174 of the EC Treaty and the Cartagena Protocol. The WTO, however, found that because none of the three complainants were contracting parties to the Cartagena Protocol (and the USA was not a contracting party to the CBD), the Protocol had limited effect in this dispute. Again, the issue of the precautionary principle was side-stepped by the DSB. Another important factor that was not considered was whether GMO products and non-GMO equivalents are considered to be 'like' or 'unlike'. If they are considered 'unlike', the production of crops and food from GMO seed would be a PPM that could legitimately, under WTO rules, be tested for adverse environmental effects. It would follow that restrictions on the importation of GMO seed would be a territorial, rather than an extra-territorial, measure if such testing determined that introduced GMOs presented a biosecurity threat to domestic ecosystems and industries such as organic agriculture, which is considered in more detail below (Gene Watch, UK, 2006).

The complainants in this dispute also threatened to add the EU's compulsory labelling regime for food derived from GMOs (Regulation (EC) 1829/2003 and Regulation (EC) 1830/2003) to the matters in dispute. These require that foods containing more than 0.9 percent GM content must be labeled as such. Calls for a lower threshold of 0.1 percent specifically for organic food have not yet been addressed. Labelling has not yet been added to the dispute. However, the US and Canada object to compulsory labeling on the basis that unless such labeling has a demonstrable basis in health risks it may be considered a Technical Barrier to Trade. It is interesting to note that the Cartagena Protocol, in requiring states to take a precautionary approach to biosafety, does allow them to take socio-economic issues into account in their risk assessments. However, as noted above, the WTO is unlikely to regard this provision as applicable to this particular dispute.

Impact of biosecurity on farmers' livelihoods

Traditional agriculture-based quarantine, as provided by governments through official bodies, is seen as an equitable 'public good' based on the principle that 'prevention is better than cure' (Black and Sweetmore, 1995; Outhwaite et al, 2007). In the changed regulatory environment, biodiversity-related biosecurity can be seen to impact on farmers in several ways:

- Pest or invasive species damaging the habitat from where the harvested product comes as well as direct attack on the species harvested;
- Imported plants introducing pests but not natural enemies of the pest;
- Deliberately introduced plants and animals becoming invasive in their new home because of lack of natural enemies;
- Extra-territorial conservation measures—such as prohibition or licensing—applied against imports;
- Recognition of biodiversity through voluntary green labelling etc;
- Issues of who owns or has the right to exploit natural resources—i.e. issues of intellectual property;
- Consumer resistance to products they believe to have been produced in ways that negatively impact on biodiversity and biosecurity;
- Consumer resistance to products they believe to be of poor quality or risky to consume as a consequence of biosecurity breaches;
- Increased production costs associated with the control of pests and diseases;
- Increased compliance costs associated with public and private regulatory schemes for biosecurity.

Cultivation of GM crops, for example, raises issues regarding farmers' access to markets that require GM food to be labelled or, conversely, where there is potential for farmers to exploit premium prices in the market for organic and/or GM-free products. A general approach to organic production creates market opportunities and reduces pollution from pesticides and fertilizers. It is irrelevant in a biosecurity or biodiversity sense whether organic food is healthier than conventional food for those who consume it. However, reduced agrochemical use will mean less pollution and less damage to habitats and biodiversity.

In Europe, outbreaks of foot and mouth disease have brought the word 'biosecurity' into common use (Black, 2003b; Outhwaite et al, 2007). However, farmers may not be aware of successful biosecurity activities, especially those directed at environmental protection rather than agriculture. Attitudes to biosecurity among farmers and other people in the agricultural industries were investigated by socio-legal research in Belize (Outhwaite et al, 2007, 2008). It was found that farmers were preoccupied with protecting their crops and livestock from everyday problems rather than responding to the biosecurity agenda of regulatory bodies, and resented cost-recovery approaches to charging for public services like inspections and issuing of health certificates.

Of all the issues potentially affecting farmers, however, intellectual property (IP) is the most controversial (Dasgupta, 1999; Blakeney and Drahos, 2001; Dutfield, 2002). The preamble to the CBD makes it clear that states have sovereign rights over their natural resources and it is understood that communities own such things as local landraces of rice and other crops. Great controversy was introduced when the WTO's TRIPS Agreement on came into force in 1995. For the first time, the provisions under Article 27 allowed and encouraged life forms and genes to be patented (see Chapters 4 and 5). This provision prompted accusations that TRIPS was encouraging 'biopiracy' in those developing countries which had not adopted systems for plant variety registration (O'Connor, 2003). It also exposed problems over the protection of genetically heterogeneous landraces that cannot be classified as varieties (O'Connor, 2003). That this has happened is evidenced by the now notorious basmati rice scandal and similar attempts to put a patent on Thai jasmine rice. WTO must have known that TRIPS would become the most controversial of its 'biological' agreements and hence the provision for review of Article 27.3(b):

> Paragraph 19 of the 2001 Doha Declaration has broadened the discussion. It says the TRIPS Council should also look at the relationship between the TRIPS Agreement and the UN Convention on Biological Diversity, the protection of traditional knowledge and folklore. It adds that the TRIPS Council's work on these topics is to be guided by the TRIPS Agreement's objectives (Article 7) and principles (Article 8), and must take development issues fully into account.

There has been some debate but no resolution of these issues, which clearly are vital for conservation of biodiversity and the implementation of the CBD (Ruiz, 2000). One might ask, 'What is the biosecurity perspective on this?' It is argued here that exploitation of a country's natural resources without the authority of the sovereign owners should be regarded as *reverse breach of biosecurity*.

Towards integration of biosecurity and biodiversity protection

This chapter will now consider how biosecurity and biodiversity measures can be integrated in practice, using mainly the EU as an example. Two aspects are developed: the regulatory frameworks, and approaches to assessment of environmental impact of alien species.

The relationships between the EU's phytosanitary systems and invasive species control are reviewed by Schrader and Unger (2004), while both animal health and phytosanitary controls in the UK against the EU and international background of habitat protection are considered by Black (2003b). The starting point for IPPC-based controls is Directive 2000/29/EC of the Council of the European Union. Schrader and Unger (2004) note that:

> This framework includes ... some specific obligations to limit the spread or to eradicate certain organisms that are not yet widespread in the community and are harmful to plants and plant products. Thus, the EU phytosanitary system provides an excellent framework for the implementation of measures against invasive alien species that are harmful to plants, plant communities and plants in any ecosystem ... The Guiding Principles on measures against

invasive alien species (mitigation of impacts, eradication, containment and control) of the Convention on Biological Diversity are widely covered regarding the plant sector. However, the systems, including monitoring and research, need some adaptation concerning indirect plant pests in particular invasive plants and impacts on the uncultivated environment.

Once again making the distinction between intentional and unintentional introductions, there is an added distinction between officially harmful organisms and non-harmful organisms in Directive 2000/29/EC, *viz*, derogations are necessary through permits or licences to import harmful organisms for research and development purposes. However, more significant for biodiversity is Council Directive 2002/89/EC of 28 November 2002 amending directive 2000/29/EC. Article 3(7) of the revised directive now authorizes member states and the European Commission to apply the provisions of the Directive's framework of protective measures to those organisms 'which are suspected of being harmful to plants or plant products but are not listed in Annexes I and II'.

Thus, Article 3(7) provides the legal basis to regulate on the EU level (and within EU member states) the intentional introduction of invasive alien species within the scope of the IPPC. This includes at least weeds and invasive alien plants. It is expected that measures will be taken on intentional imports of invasive alien species after the procedures and methods for risk analysis are implemented for this purpose.

In this context, the UK Department for Environment, Food and Rural Affairs (Defra) commissioned a project to develop a comprehensive process for risk assessment of any kind of 'non-native' (alien) species that posed a threat to the environment (Baker et al, 2007). The starting point was the PRA schemes of the European and Mediterranean Plant Protection Organization and the Regional Plant Protection Organization for Europe and Trans-Asia. This basic framework was adopted so that any non-species in any taxonomic category could be examined, not just pests or harmful organisms in the plant health sense. Specialist modules permit selection of relevant 'pathways' for entry (which are more numerous than for pests) and their relative importance, the vulnerability of 'receptors' (habitats and host species) and the consequences of policies to be assessed and appropriate risk management options to be selected. The scheme covers both intentional and unintentional introductions. By means of spreadsheets that summarize the level of risk and invasive attributes and economic impact, new methods for quantifying economic impact and summarising risk and uncertainty were explored. Although designed for the UK, the scheme can readily be applied elsewhere. The treatment of invasiveness relied heavily on the weed risk assessment scheme developed by Pheloung et al (1999) in Australia and adopted elsewhere. The question of 'quantifying uncertainty' in invasions is now receiving increased attention (e.g. Sikder et al, 2006).

It is appropriate to conclude this section with some remarks about achieving consistency in biosecurity legislation that addresses protection of biodiversity. Given that the primary focus of biosecurity is border controls, the first question is 'which official body or bodies should be regulating border controls and under what laws should they be doing so, environmental or agricultural?' It has been explained that ISPM No. 11 on PRA covers 'environmental pests' but it could be implemented either by plant health bodies or by the national environmental authority. Whichever body is given competency, and whatever governing law is used as the basis for implementing rules, it is important that there is cross-referencing between plant health and environmental legislation to ensure that there is one consistently applied framework for risk analysis and that procedures and permits are not duplicated.

As part of the drive towards consistency, definitions for such concepts as 'pests', 'invasive species', and 'risk assessment' in different legislative instruments must be brought into alignment. In some jurisdictions, this can be done easily through such phrases as 'risk assessment takes the same meaning as in the Plant Health Act'. However, in some jurisdictions, cross-referencing in this manner either is not allowed or is allowed only in very vague terms. This may also apply to references to international legal sources such as multilateral environmental agreements and agreements of the WTO because of constraints imposed by the Constitution or by rules in a 'Law on Laws' that exists in some jurisdictions. Because of such constraints imposed on drafting appropriate legislation, many jurisdictions are plagued by overlapping or contradictory legal provisions implemented by different government departments or ministries such as agriculture, environment and health. Indeed, rivalry between different bodies may encourage such legislative absurdities.

Conclusion

The conservation of biodiversity has its own fundamental international legal framework in the CBD. However, in practical terms this is not enforceable. The IPPC provides a means to implement border controls to prevent the intentional or accidental introduction of organisms that might damage habitats and reduce biodiversity. This is through the expanded pest risk analysis framework of ISPM No. 11. The IPPC, in general, and ISPM No. 11, more specifically, are compatible with the WTO's SPS Agreement by providing objective means of assessing risks and measures to reduce risk. Steps are being taken to implement this general framework specifically for potentially invasive species and other alien organisms that might be environmentally damaging. The OIE is beginning a similar approach to the potential danger to wildlife from cross-boundary movement of live animals and eggs and sperm.

Unfortunately, the prevailing ambiguity in WTO's policies on environmental protection trade rules, and in apparent WTO jurisprudence on these matters, seem to discourage more indirect action such as restricting trade on products whose harvesting or production endangers species or habitats. This is seen in the debate over the place of the precautionary principle in trade decision-making and in WTO jurisprudence on 'like' and 'unlike' products and production and processing methods. However, resolution over the risk assessment/precautionary divide may be emerging with greater understanding of the role of uncertainty in risk assessment and criteria for quantifying uncertainty.

Border controls are applied to imports and to exports. Under the CBD, states have sovereign rights over their natural resources and they should be allowed to regulate the exportation of products as well as encouraging sustainable agriculture and sustainable utilization of natural products. CITES has been implemented successfully by many countries desiring to take action to prevent the extinction of endangered species by prohibiting imports of endangered live species or products there from that evade export controls (or in cases where export controls are non-existent). The authors suggest that export of goods from endangered species or that result from habitat damage should be regarded as a reverse breach of biosecurity. This concept would help put this activity in an appropriate context and perhaps help to highlight the dangers of biopiracy.

GMOs are a special category of organisms that are regarded as potentially damaging to the environment and to biodiversity in some quarters. The debate surrounding this aspect of the impact of GMOs exemplifies some of the more general issues in the 'CBD vs. WTO' controversy. The Cartagena Protocol on Biosafety (as a Protocol to the CBD) was an attempt to bridge the divide but is not generally regarded as effective or useful in providing transparent regulation of the international movement of GMOs in relation to the objectives of the CBD.

Acknowledgements

The authors wish to thank Mr Isra Black for his helpful comments and suggestions on the manuscript.

References

Allan, J.D., Palmer, M. and Poff, L. (2005) 'Climate change and freshwater ecosystems', in T.E. Lovejoy and L. Hannah (eds) *Climate Change and Biodiversity*, Yale University Press, New Haven, USA

Anonymous (2009) 'Mexico: traces of GM maize concerned', in 'GMO Safety', 11 March 2009, www.gmo-safety.eu/en/news/680.docu.html, accessed 20 April 2009

Baker, R.H.A., Black, R., Copp, G.H., Haysom, K.A., Hulme, P.E., Thomas, M.B., Brown, A., Brown, M., Ray J.C., Cannon, R.J.C., Ellis, J., Ellis, M., Ferris, R., Glaves, P., Gozlan, R.E., Holt, J., Howe, E., Knight, J.D., MacLeod, A., Moore, N.P., Mumford, J.D., Murphy, S.T., Parrott, D., Sansford, C.E., Smith, G.C., St-Hilaire, S. and Ward, N.L. (2007) 'The UK risk assessment scheme for all non-native species', in W. Rabitsch, F. Essl and F. Klingenstein (eds) *Biological Invasions—from Ecology to Conservation (Neobiota, vol 7)*, Berlin

Barker, D. and Mander, D. (1999) 'Invisible government. The World Trade Organization: Global government for the new millennium?' International Forum on Globalization, San Francisco, October, p18., www.ifg.org/aboutwto.html, accessed 20 April 2009

Biological Diversity Advisory Committee (2006) *Climate Change and Invasive Species: A Review of Interactions*, www.environment.gov.au/biodiversity/pub lications/interactions-cc-invasive.html, accessed 20 April 2009

Black, R. (2003a) 'Can phytosanitary services in African countries meet the challenges of globalization?', *Proceedings of BCPC Pests and Diseases Conference 2000*, pp1167–1174

Black, R. (2003b) 'The legal basis for controls on importation of animal and plant material into the United Kingdom', *Environmental Law Review*, vol 5, pp179–192

Black, R., Sweetmore A. (1995) *Plant Quarantine. A Primer for Development Workers*, Natural Resources Institute, Chatham Maritime, UK

Blakeney, M. and Drahos, P. (2001) *IP in Biodiversity and Agriculture: Regulating the Biosphere*, Sweet and Maxwell, London

Commission of the European Communities (2000) 'Communication from the Commission on the precautionary principle', COM (2000) 1, Brussels 2 February 2000, http://eur-lex.europa.eu/smartapi/cgi/sga_doc?smartapi!celexp lus!prod!DocNumber&lg=en&type_doc=COMfinal&an_doc=2000&nu_doc=1, accessed 21 April 2009

Committee on Agriculture (COAG) (2001) *Biosecurity in Food and Agriculture Discussion Paper*, Committee on Agriculture 16th Session, Rome, 26–30 March 2001, www.fao.org/docrep/meeting/003/x9181e.htm#P50_367, accessed 7 May 2009

Committee on Agriculture (COAG) (2003) *Biosecurity in Food and Agriculture Discussion Paper*, Committee on Agriculture 17th Session, Rome 31 March–4 April 2003, www.fao.org/biosecurity/, accessed 5 June 2009

Darwin, C. (1859) *On the Origin of Species by Means of Natural Selection, or the Preservation of Favoured Races in the Struggle for Life*, John Murray, London http://darwin-online.org.uk/content/frameset?itemID=F373&viewtype=text&pageseq=1, accessed 5 August 2009

Dasgupta, B. (1999) 'Patent lies and latent danger: A study of the political economy of patents in India', *Economic and Political Weekly*, vol 4. pp979–993

Dutfield, G. (2002) *Intellectual Property Rights, Trade and Biodiversity*, Earthscan, London

Food and Agriculture Organization of the United Nations (FAO) (1995) *Code of Conduct for the Import and Release of Exotic Biological Control Agents*, Report of the Conference of FAO, 28th Session, www.fao.org/docrep/x5585E/x5585 e0i.htm, accessed 20 April 2009

Gene Watch UK (2006) *The WTO GMO Dispute: The Interim Report of the Dispute Panel*, Briefing note from GeneWatch UK, March 31, 2006, www.genewatch.org/uploads/f03c6d66a9b354535738483c1c3d49e4/Interim_re port_short_note.pdf, accessed 21 April 2009

Griffin, R. (2002) *PRA: A Global Perspective, Present and Future*, NAPPO PRA Symposium, Puerto Vallarta, Mexico.

Holt, J., Black, R. and Roshan Abdallah (2006) 'A rigorous yet simple quantitative risk assessment method for quarantine pests and alien invasive species' *Annals of Applied Biology*, vol 149, pp167–173

IPPC (2004) 'International Standards for Phytosanitary Measures (ISPMs)', www.ippc.int/servlet/CDSServlet?status=ND0xMzM5OSY2PWVuJjMzPSom Mzc9a29z, accessed 20 April 2009

Land and Environment Court of New South Wales (LECNSW) (2006) *Telstra Corporation Limited v Hornsby Shire Council* NSWLEC 133, Reported decision (2006) 146 LGERA; (2006) 67 NSWLR 256.

Landcare Research (2000) 'What's new in biological control' May 2000, no 15, www.landcareresearch.co.nz/publications/newsletters/weeds/wtsnew15.pdf, accessed 20 April 2009

LaPointe, D., Benning, T.L. and Atkinson, C. (2005) 'Avian malaria, climate change, and native birds of Hawaii', in T.E. Lovejoy and L. Hannah (eds) 'Climate Change and Biodiversity', Yale University Press, New Haven, USA

Lovejoy, T.E. and Hannah, L. (eds) (2005) *Climate Change and Biodiversity*, Yale University Press, New Haven, CT

Mann, H., Porter, S. (2003) *The State of Trade and Environmental Law 2003: Implications for Doha and Beyond*, International Institute for Sustainable Development/Center for International Environmental Law, Winnipeg, Canada

O'Connor, B. (2003) 'Protecting traditional knowledge: An overview of a developing area of intellectual property law', *Journal of World Intellectual Property*, vol 6, no 5, pp677–698

Outhwaite, O.M., Black, R. and Laycock, A.M. (2007) 'The pursuit of grounded theory in agricultural and environmental regulation: A suggested approach to empirical legal study in biosecurity', *Law and Policy*, vol 24, pp493–528

Outhwaite, O., Black, R. and Laycock, A. (2008) 'The significance of cost recovery for the regulation of agricultural health: A case study in pursuing grounded theory', *Journal of Law and Society*, vol 35, pp126–148

Pheloung, P.C., Williams, P.A. and Halloy, S.R. (1999) 'A weed risk assessment model for use as a biosecurity tool evaluating plant introductions', *Journal of Environmental Management*, vol 57, pp239–251

Ruiz, M. (2000) *The International Debate on Traditional Knowledge as Prior Art in The Patent System: Issues and Options for Developing Countries*, CIEL, www.ciel.org/Publications/PriorArt_ManuelRuiz_Oct02.pdf, accessed 5 August 2009

Sainsbury, D. (1998) *Animal Health*, 2nd ed, Blackwell, Malden, MA

SciDev Net (2006) 'The Cartagena Protocol: A waste of time and money?', Opinion, 28 April 2006, www.scidev.net/en/opinions/the-cartagena-protocol-a-waste-of-time-and-money.html, accessed 21 April 2009

Schrader, G. and Unger, J-G. (2004) 'Plant quarantine as a measure against invasive alien species: The framework of the International Plant Protection Convention and the plant health regulations in the European Union, *Biological Invasions*, vol 5, pp1387–1464

Sikder, I.U., Mal-Sarkar, S. and Mal, T.K. (2006) 'Knowledge-based risk assessment under uncertainty for species invasion', *Risk Analysis*, vol 26, pp239–252

Stilwell, M., and Tarasofsky, R. (2001) *Towards Coherent Environmental and Economic Governance: Legal and Practical Approaches to MEA-WTO Linkages*, WWF-CIEL Discussion Paper, Worldwide Fund for Nature, Gland, Switzerland

Van Asselt, M.B.A. and Vos, E. (2006) 'Precautionary principle and the uncertainty paradox', *Journal of Risk Research*, vol 9, no 4, pp313–336

World Organisation for Animal Health (OIE) (2008a) 'Improving wildlife surveillance for its protection while protecting us from the diseases it transmits' (Editorials from the Director General, 16 October 2008)', www.oie.int/eng/ed ito/en_edito_juil08.htm, accessed 20 April 2009

World Organisation for Animal Health (OIE) (2008b) 'Risk analysis in Terrestrial Animal Health Code', www.oie.int/eng/normes/mcode/en_titre_1.2.htm, accessed 20 April 2009

World Organisation for Animal Health (OIE) (2008c) 'Risk analysis in Aquatic Animal Health Code', www.oie.int/eng/normes/fcode/en_titre_1.4.htm, accessed 20 April 2009

World Trade Organization (WTO) (undated a) 'SPS Agreement Training Module', World Trade Organization, Geneva, www.wto.org/english/tratop_e/sps_e/sps _agreement_cbt_e/intro1_e.htm, accessed 5 June 2009

World Trade Organization (WTO) (undated b) 'Environment Disputes 4: Mexico etc versus US: "tuna-dolphin"', World Trade Organization, Geneva, www.wto.org/english/tratop_e/envir_e/edis04_e.htm, accessed 6 June 2009

World Trade Organization (WTO) (undated c) 'Dispute Settlement: Dispute DS291—European Communities: Measures affecting the approval and marketing of biotech products', World Trade Organization, Geneva,. www.wto.org/english/tratop_e/dispu_e/cases_e/ds291_e.htm, accessed 6 June 2009

7

Complementarity in the Conservation of Traditional and Modern Rice Genetic Resources on the Philippine Island of Bohol

David Carpenter

For thousands of years prior to the discovery and proliferation of modern plant breeding techniques, rice farmers throughout the world utilized locally adaptable traditional varieties (TVs) in the reproduction of agriculture. These varieties are still used throughout the developing world—usually in marginal rice farming environments where modern varieties (MVs) are either unsuitable or unavailable. These genetically heterogeneous varieties or 'landraces' formed the foundation of traditional rice farming systems and provided farmers with the means to adapt to variable environmental stresses and economic pressures. With the advent of modern plant breeding techniques and through large scale interventions such as the Green Revolution, these relatively adaptable but often low yielding varieties were gradually replaced with higher yielding and photoperiod insensitive MVs—particularly in favourable rice growing environments. While this process has no doubt helped increase agricultural production at aggregate levels worldwide it has also, according to some authors, led to widespread genetic erosion as genetically heterogeneous TVs are substituted for more genetically homogenous MVs (Thrupp, 2000).

It has been argued that the genetic homogeneity which has accompanied the spread of MVs is also having adverse impacts on food security and, ultimately, on the sustainability of modern agriculture because a 'reduction in diversity often increases vulnerability to climatic and other stresses, raises the risks for individual farmers, and can undermine the stability of agriculture' (Thrupp, 2000). The conservation of TVs thus supports the development of more sustainable modes of agricultural production by providing the genetic diversity necessary for the development of plants better adapted to marginal conditions, evolving pests, changing climates and soils (Cleveland and Murray, 1997).

Strategies to conserve the genetic diversity of crops include 'on farm' or in situ conservation (Altieri and Merrick, 1987; Brush, 1991; Bellon, 1997) and 'off farm' or ex situ conservation (FAO, 1996). The ex situ conservation of plant genetic resources is effected in international, national, and local gene banks. Here, genetic material gathered by governments, NGOs, and farmer groups is maintained as seed, vegetative or whole plant material on a short, medium, or long-term basis using a variety of techniques. The in situ conservation of genetic resources is an important complement to ex situ conservation because it is a dynamic process through which varieties are subjected to evolutionary pressures that continue to shape their genetic makeup (Bellon, 1997). However, our knowledge of in situ conservation options is limited (FAO, 1996; Bellon, 1997; Zhu et al, 2003). According to Zhu et al (2003: 159), the myriad of biophysical, socioeconomic, and cultural variables that influence farmers' decisions to conserve varietal diversity lead to questions regarding whether in situ conservation is 'economically feasible and sustainable in the context of modern agriculture or whether it must be relegated to areas of the world where subsistence farming, low yields, and low economic returns favour TVs'.

While the importance of conserving TVs to the sustainability of agriculture is clear, this chapter will argue that adopting an overly static view of their conservation is problematic. As the forthcoming case study will demonstrate, contemporary post-Green Revolution farmers—particularly those in marginal areas—adopt a dynamic approach to the management of plant genetic material that encompasses both traditional and modern elements, and that places importance on the acquisition and on-farm trialling of previously unavailable varieties whether they be from traditional or modern sources. This extends to the breeding of new varieties with mixed genetic heritage and to the 'creolization' of MVs due to artificial or natural selection. The Farmer Varieties (FVs) that often result from this experimentation, and from the ongoing process of natural selection, play an important role in the livelihoods of resource poor farmers, and are often a significant proportion of the plant genetic resources available to them. It follows from this that it is important also to move away from any simplistic dichotomy between traditional and modern varieties (particularly those that assume 'traditional is good, modern is bad' or vice versa) to a more sophisticated approach that focuses on providing farmers with new rice varieties from a multiplicity of sources which they can subject to local experimentation. To do this, the channels of access to rice plant genetic material need to be opened, new social networks need to be developed, and two types of complementarity need to be encouraged: complementarity between farmers, NGOs and formal breeders; and complementarity between in situ and ex situ conservation efforts.

This chapter will begin with a discussion of the state of rice plant genetic diversity in the Philippines, and in situ and ex situ conservation efforts there, before moving on to document the in situ conservation practices witnessed during one rice growing season in the village of Campagao on the island of Bohol. The chapter will conclude with a discussion of a number of important issues arising from the research including the importance of appropriation, the paradox of varietal favouritism, the need to foster complementarity, and the impact plant variety protection legislation may have on the in situ conservation practices of rice farmers in the Philippines.

The state of rice plant genetic diversity in the Philippines

Since the advent of the Green Revolution, TVs have largely been displaced in the Philippines by MVs in favourable rice growing environments—a phenomenon witnessed throughout the world and one that has led to significant increases in global food production. It has been estimated that prior to the Green Revolution up to 3500 traditional rice varieties existed in the Philippines (Pelagrina, 2000; CDBC, 2001), and that at least 300 of these varieties have been displaced since the introduction of MVs in the 1960s (Thrupp, 2000; Wood et al, 2000). By 1986, 97 percent of the Philippines' irrigated rice land was planted to MVs (David et al, 1994) comprising just five to six sister lines released by the Philippine Seed Board (Borromeo and Hernandez, 1987). By 2000, 44 so-called High Yielding Varieties (HYVs) and three hybrid rice varieties were available to Filipino farmers (Tabien, 2000).

Despite the primacy of MVs, pockets of TVs continue to persist in the Philippines (David et al, 1994). Fujisaka (1999), for example, has documented the widespread use of TVs in some upland and lowland rainfed areas of northern Mindanao and northern Luzon. Magnifico (1997) has documented the collection of 300 TVs in the mainly upland regions of north Cotabato province, and, according to Leibig et al (2002), a conservation and breeding project carried out by the South East Asian Regional Initiative for Community Empowerment (SEARICE) identified 298 different rice landraces in a survey occupying only 1/25th of the land area of Mindanao. Thus, while the substitution of traditional with modern varieties has certainly led to a substantial reduction in rice plant genetic diversity in the Philippines, such substitution has occurred predominantly in favourable rice growing environments. In marginal areas, a number of other factors influence rice plant genetic diversity. Fujisaka (1999), for example, argues that the adoption of a limited number of successful TVs can also lead to a reduction in local rice plant genetic diversity in upland and rainfed lowland areas. His study of upland rice farmers in Mindanao and lowland rice farmers in Luzon tracked the increased use of a select few preferred varieties that performed particularly well in their respective environments and came to dominate over time. In the upland areas, TVs with characteristics such as high yield, early maturation, disease resistance, and good eating quality persisted. In the flood-prone, rainfed areas, by contrast, those varieties with tall stature, flood tolerance, good eating quality, and low input requirements tended to persist (Fujisaka, 1999). The evidence from the forthcoming study also suggests that farmers tend to prefer a few select varieties that perform well under certain conditions.

The full impact of farmer decision-making on genetic diversity, however, can only be assessed when considered in relation to a host of other factors that influence both the nature and outcomes of those decisions. Morin et al (2002), for example, examined the erosion of rice plant genetic diversity in northern Luzon following the 1997–1998 El Nino (a climatic event associated with unusually dry conditions on the western edge of the Pacific Rim) and two subsequent typhoons in 1998. While these may be understood as natural and somewhat indiscriminate phenomena, their effect on genetic diversity was highly variable across the villages studied. Mediating these climatic events were a range of factors such as: (1) the preference of farmers to plant TVs in drought susceptible rainfed areas; (2) the limitations of local seed supply infrastructure; (3) the location of individual farms in relation to seed supply; (4) the policies and programs of the Department of Agriculture, which promoted MVs over TVs; and (5) the characteristics of the available TVs themselves, which were late maturing and, therefore, replaced by the shorter duration MVs as farmers tried to ameliorate the risk of water stress late in the season.

A complex array of structural, biophysical and behavioural factors thus combine to affect the rate and type of genetic erosion witnessed in marginal rice growing areas in the Philippines (see Fujisaka, 1999; Morin et al, 2002). Such erosion is not a simple matter of MVs replacing TVs. In fact, MVs may play their own role in enriching the genetic diversity of traditional systems through their direct use, provision of genetic material to local breeding efforts, and 'creolization' (Wood and Lenne, 1997). This will be highlighted in the forthcoming case study.

Ex situ and in situ conservation strategies

Because of its fundamental significance to agriculture, rice plant genetic diversity has been the focus of coordinated national and international ex situ conservation efforts. In 1996, there were approximately 420,500 rice plant accessions worldwide (FAO, 1996). Around the same time, there were some 86,800 rice varieties stored in the gene bank at the International Rice Research Institute at Los Banos in the Philippines (IRRI, 2003), and nearly 46,000 accessions stored in the Philippine National Germplasm Collection (Leibig et al, 2002). Yet it is doubtful that the country's rice plant genetic diversity is adequately represented in ex situ collections. For example, IRRI holds only 137 accessions for the entire island of Mindanao, whereas the aforementioned study by Magnifico (1997) identified 300 TVs in just one of Mindanao's 18 provinces. There are also concerns about the viability of ex situ germplasm and the lack of access farmers have to varieties stored ex situ (Zhu et al, 2003).

The foundation of long-term ex situ conservation strategies is the frozen storage of seeds. Views are polarized on the merits of this relative to in situ conservation. Some argue, for example, that frozen storage may subject seed to artificial evolutionary pressures (Vaughan and Chang, 1992) and should not, therefore, even be considered a form of conservation (Witcombe and Joshi, 1997). Yet as Wood and Lenne (1997) point out, ex situ and in situ conservation achieve different goals and there is no reason to necessarily regard the two strategies as mutually exclusive. Ex situ conservation is a low cost way to store thousands of accessions without loss of viability—the absence of insect and fungal infestation being particularly important in this regard. The problems with ex situ conservation stem from the fact that varieties require constant multiplication in order to provide sufficient material for use. Unfortunately, this material is not easily accessed by farmers.

This chapter will return to the possibility of greater synergy between ex situ and in situ conservation systems. It is worth noting, however, that a number of projects have been initiated within the Philippines that do seek some level of integration of in situ and ex situ conservation strategies, particularly in relation to the conservation of Farmer Varieties (FVs); that is, of landraces and TVs selected by farmers, as well as MVs which have adapted to farmers' environments by deliberate or natural selection (Cleveland and Soleri, 2007). One of these projects is the Community Development and Biodiversity Conservation (CDBC) project which will be discussed in the case study section. Another major initiative is the MASIPAG (Farmer-Scientist Partnership for Development) program, which involves developing farmer-selected and bred varieties for dissemination, in conjunction with the adoption of organic farming practices (Yap, 2000). MASIPAG has conserved 668 TVs and developed 539 FVs since its inception in 1986 (GRAIN, 2000).

While both in situ and ex situ conservation strategies help conserve agricultural biodiversity, their success with regard to development goals can only be measured by the extent to which they improve the welfare of resource-poor farmers. In this regard, the conservation of in situ and ex situ genetic resources cannot be divorced from other aspects of the agricultural system. It is important to remember that while diversity of plant genetic material is a necessary condition for sustainable agriculture it is by no means a sufficient one. Land tenure and agrarian reform (Hirtz, 1998; Borras, 2001), the declining productivity of rice farming (Pingali et al, 1997), the impact of abiotic stresses (Hossain et al, 1996; Lansigan et al, 2000), and informal local credit markets (Nagarajan et al, 1995; Fukui and Hara, 1996) all continue to shape the fate of resource-poor farmers in the Philippines, and all need to be addressed alongside the conservation of rice plant genetic material.

Management of rice biodiversity in Campagao, Bohol

Data for this case study were collected between May and December 2002 with the cooperation of 51 farmers from the village of Campagao, a small agricultural community in southern Bohol (see Figure 1). Twenty-six of the farmers involved in the research were members of the local farmers' association, the Campagao Farmers' Production and Research Association (CFPRA), which, since 1996, had been involved in the aforementioned CDBC project with SEARICE. This project was focused on empowering farmers by giving them the knowledge and skills to develop their own locally adapted rice varieties using varietal selection, varietal trials, and rice breeding techniques.

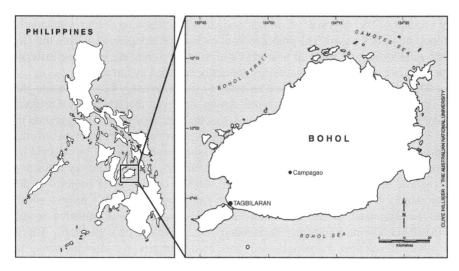

Figure 7.1. The Philippine archipelago, Bohol and Campagao

In Campagao, rice production takes place on alkaline soils in irrigated and rainfed lowland valleys. Land holdings range between 0.125 and four hectares (with an average of 0.9 ha) and rice yields vary between 1.25 and 3.3 tonnes per hectare. Of the farmers interviewed, 72 percent were tenants or held leases over all their land with the remainder owning some or all of the land they cultivated. Despite the karst topography and presence of many natural springs, access to water for the purposes of irrigation is variable. Eighty percent of farmers have access to some type of irrigation, typically from permanent or semi-permanent springs, or riverine sources. The quality of the canals that feed the rice paddies is also variable. The majority of canals are made of clay or stone and require constant maintenance during the rice growing season, a process managed by a cooperative labour association called a *kanaway*, which consists of all the farmers who share an irrigation canal.

Table 7.1. Seasonal rice cropping calendar: Campagao

Season	Jan	Feb	Mar	Apr	May	Jun	Jul	Aug	Sep	Oct	Nov	Dec
Panuig					S, LP	T	T, W	W	H	H		
Panolilang	W	H	H							S, LP	T, W	W

S, LP- Seedling and Land Preparation; T- Transplanting; W-Weeding; H-Harvesting.

The farmers of Campagao plant rice twice each year, first during *panuig* or the wet season (June–October), and second during *panolilang* or the dry season (November–March). The seasonal rice-cropping calendar is summarized in Table 7.1.

Varietal trials, varietal selection, and farmer breeding (1996–2002)

The CDBC project had two primary aims: the first being to increase the diversity of rice plant genetic resources available to farmer partners; and the second to empower farmers by helping them develop the knowledge needed to select (and in some cases breed) rice varieties suited to local environments. With respect to the former, SEARICE began by collecting 52 rice varieties (MVs, TVs, and FVs) from 10 towns around Bohol in 1996. These varieties were distributed to 69 farmers in three villages where SEARICE had carried out farmer field schools, including Campagao. During the first season, the CFPRA farmers were exposed to a variety of field assessment methods that included making both qualitative and quantitative observations. Farmers were subsequently encouraged to carry out on-farm field trials by themselves and SEARICE coordinators worked with farmers to assess these trials each season. Between *panolilang* 1996 and *panuig* 2002, the farmers of CFPRA carried out 583 individual varietal trials. During this time, trials were conducted for a total of 233 different rice varieties in lowland rainfed and lowland irrigated paddies throughout Campagao. SEARICE and the farmers of CFPRA also worked closely with a neighbouring agricultural college—the Central Visayan State College of Agriculture, Forestry and Technology (CVSCAFT), which maintains a large ex situ seed bank, multiplies seeds each year, and conducts varietal trials as part of student training.

Eighty-seven percent of the trials were of FVs. These included farmer varieties acquired from non-local sources (64% of FVs), those developed by CFPRA farmers through selection (20%) and breeding (12%), and those bred by a farmer from a neighbouring village and a CDBC project partner (4%). The non-local FVs were obtained by CFPRA farmers through field schools they attended throughout Bohol and in other parts of the Philippines; especially Mindanao and Negros. FVs were also obtained by SEARICE coordinators from other farmer groups they were working with in Bohol and Mindanao, as well as from locations overseas, most notably Thailand and Vietnam. These varieties typically have local names that may describe the origin of the variety, its characteristics, or its parentage. Of the 129 non-local FVs trialled between 1996 and 2002, about 20 were subsequently used in production on an ongoing basis. These varieties have also proved useful as material for off-type selection and breeding by local farmers.

As the CFPRA varietal trials progressed, the farmers became more comfortable with their assessment of rice characteristics, and many farmers who had no previous experience with varietal selection began selecting their own varieties. In total, 40 selections were developed by CFPRA farmers between 1996 and 2002. Most of these varieties were selected from off-types of non-local FVs or off types of IR66 (a very popular MV introduced in the 1980s), using panicle selection for the development of characteristics, alternating with positive mass selection to increase the volume of seed supply. This cycle would often be repeated several times until the requisite characteristics and uniformity were established.

The 26 CFPRA bred varieties developed between1996 and 2002 were bred by one farmer who had a particular interest in breeding and off-type selection. Mang Cicenio Salces, the president of CFPRA, learned to breed rice while attending a farmers' field school on rice breeding in Cotabato, northern Mindanao, in 1996. On his return to Campagao, he began breeding varieties that would adapt to his low input, organic system of farming. For a long time, Mang Cicenio recognized traits that he wanted to replicate in four varieties (two MVs and two FVs) from which he was determined to create new varieties. He used a process of panicle selection alternating with positive and negative mass selection to develop traits and stabilize his varieties over seven generations. To date, Mang Cicenio's low input organic system remains one of the most viable, highest yielding and stable rice production systems in Campagao, only surpassed in terms of yield by one other farmer (a large landowner who uses significant quantities of inorganic and organic fertilizer each year). Economic analysis, however, demonstrates that Mang Cicenio's system produces the highest net return per kilo of rice produced of all the farmers studied (Carpenter, 2005).

The trials of MVs conducted between 1996 and 2002 included formally released varieties (i.e. PSBRC4, 10, 12, 14, 22, 24, 30, and 32) as well as varieties developed by IRRI (i.e. IR24, 36, 42, 64, and 74). These varieties were discarded for a number of reasons including poor pest and disease resistance, drought intolerance, and an inability to adapt to the local alkaline soils. They disappeared from later trials altogether. Despite the availability of alternative MVs, IR66 continued to be the most popular MV planted during the 1996–2002 period.

Panuig 2002

During the *panuig* season of 2002 (June–October), the author documented the use of rice plant genetic resources among the 51 participating farmers. During this period, the Campagao farmers planted 33 different varieties of rice; 25 of which were FVs, six MVs, and two TVs. In relation to production, varietal diversity was much higher for the 26 CFPRA members (26 varieties) than for the 25 non-CFPRA farmers (14 varieties). Table 7.2 lists the eight most popular varieties planted by Campagao's farmers and their frequency of planting as well as the percentage of land area planted to each variety (i.e. as a percentage of the total land area planted to rice by the 51 farmers). By far the most popular variety used during this period was the variety known locally as 'Vietnam'. This variety was introduced to Campagao by a SEARICE coordinator after a trip to Vietnam in 1998. The original 100 grams of seed was given to one CFPRA farmer to trial and the variety became so popular that demand for it soon outstripped supply.

Many Campagao farmers prefer 'Vietnam' because of its early maturation (85–90 days from sowing), its palatability, its ability to adapt to varying landscapes, and its response to minimal amounts of fertilizer. During *panuig* 2002, 18.7 tonnes of 'Vietnam' were produced by the 25 farmers who grew the variety. For some, 'Vietnam' surpassed IR66 as the most preferred variety in the village. Many of the 51 farmers interviewed had already planted the variety for three seasons in a row and were looking for another variety to plant in *panolilang* 2002 before planting 'Vietnam' again in 2003. IR66 continued to be a popular variety and was described by many farmers as the best variety available in Campagao. *Pilit* varieties (glutinous TVs) also remained popular due to their use in local sweet delicacies.

Despite their popularity, however, they occupied a small land area. Mang Cicenio's CS1 variety was being planted by CFPRA farmers who wanted to exploit its pest and disease resistance and its response to organic inputs. Interestingly, the use of MVs such as PSBRC18 and PSBRC82 was low despite the government's subsidization scheme and the volume planted by some of the larger landowners. The lack of local adoption was partly due to the perception that RC82 is a sickly variety that is susceptible to a wide array of pests and diseases, and is not tolerant to drought conditions. In addition, RC18 matures later than many other varieties.

Table 7.2. Most popular rice varieties planted in Campagao, 2002

Variety	Frequency (n=51)	% Total land area
Vietnam	25	29.0
IR66	11	10.0
Pilit (puwa/puti)	10	1.7
CS1	6	7.0
MB	6	5.3
RC82	5	7.0
Japan Red	5	5.1
RC18	3	12.5
Total		77.6

Other varieties such as MB and Japan Red, both red-seed-coated varieties, are becoming increasingly popular due primarily to their palatability, drought tolerance, and early maturation. These varieties are popular with farmers who cultivate rainfed paddies. Of the varietal classes planted by Campagao's farmers in 2002, FVs continued to be the most widely planted. Of the 25 planted, 18 were from non-local sources and 7 were farmer selections or breeds developed by CFPRA farmers. Of the 51 farmers surveyed, 41 planted at least one FV, seven planted at least one farmer-bred variety, 10 planted at least one TV (usually glutinous), and 18 planted MVs. Every one of the 25 FVs planted in Campagao in *panuig* 2002 was unavailable to Campagao's farmers before the CDBC project began in 1996. All but two of the varieties planted during *panuig* 2002 had been trialled at some stage by CFPRA's farmers.

Varietal trials during panuig 2002

During *panuig* 2002, 17 CFPRA farmers conducted trials with 27 different varieties of rice. Of the 27 varieties planted, 24 were FVs and 11 of these were varieties bred locally by either Mang Cicenio or a farmer from a neighbouring village with an interest in rice breeding. Only four local selections were planted for trial, and only two farmers planted them. CFPRA farmers undertaking these trials could be differentiated into two broad groups. First, there were those farmers who, like Mang

Cicenio, were developing new varieties and using panicle and mass selection techniques to stabilize their selections. These trials were usually long-term as it takes quite a few seasons to build up the necessary seed supply for production-level planting. Second, there were those farmers who acquired small amounts of seed from varieties they had observed and planted them in their paddies to assess the adaptability of that variety to their own paddy environment. These were usually much shorter-term trials and did not necessarily lead to any increase in diversity. The former, larger-scale trials are particularly important for increasing rice plant genetic diversity and thus the choices available to farmers. These trials, however, are substantially more demanding of time and resources and, therefore, were usually undertaken by farmers both with a keen interest in varietal development and with sufficient land and water resources (including drainage control to avoid the washing out of trial plots).

Seed acquisition and supply

The process of exchanging seed between farmers is the most popular method of seed acquisition in Campagao. This is locally referred to as *balo-balo*. Table 7.3 summarizes the methods of seed supply adopted by participating farmers for the *panuig* 2002 season. As this shows, farmers exchanged seeds with relatives and friends from the local area, from other parts of Bohol, and from other provinces such as Mindanao. Farmers seem to take any opportunity they can to exchange seeds with friends and relatives when they observe a good variety. Problems do arise, however, especially if a farmer waits too long before asking another farmer to exchange, if a seedbed is washed away, or if the seedlings are destroyed by pests such as the Golden Kuhol snail. When this occurs, farmers are often forced to rely on any seeds that are available, and these seeds may not be suited to a particular paddy environment.

Table 7.3. Methods of seed supply, *panuig* 2002

Method of seed supply	Frequency
Balo-Balo (exchange)	39
Purchase from MAO	7
From own trials	5
Pito-Pito	5

Two farmers who were particularly important to the seed supply system in Campagao were Mang Cicenio, who developed the CS and Red Japan varieties, and Mang Felicio Omac, who was the first farmer to conduct trials of the very popular 'Vietnam' variety. These two farmers participated in 30 percent of the exchanges that took place before the 2002 *panuig* season. Apart from supplying their immediate relatives with high quality seeds, as many farmers do, these men were responsible for a significant number of exchanges with non-relatives. They also participated in exchanges with many non-CFPRA farmers.

The purchase of seeds from the Municipal Agricultural Office (MAO) continued to be a method of supply favoured by those farmers with larger farms and non-agricultural sources of income. All of the farmers who purchased seeds from the MAO said they do so every season to access high quality seeds. *Pito-pito* (wherein harvesters receive $1/7^{th}$ of the gross rice harvest for harvesting and threshing) was a source of seed for those farmers who also laboured in others farmers' paddies, but as many *pito-pito* labourers are landless, they tend to sell or consume the fruits of their labour. Only five farmers planted varieties straight from the previous season's trials; all but one of which were off-type selections or locally bred varieties.

Discussion

The importance of appropriation

One of the most important aspects of the CDBC project has been the extent to which the benefits of the CFPRA varietal trials have been appropriated by non-CFPRA farmers. For example, in *panuig* 2002, all but 2 of the 33 varieties planted by the 51 CFPRA and non-CFPRA farmers had been trialled at some stage since 1996 in a variety of landscapes and soils in Campagao. Non-CFPRA farmers were using many of the varieties developed by CFPRA farmers and many were purposely seeking out these varieties and using the traditional seed distribution methods to access them (e.g. *pito-pito* and *balo-balo)*. The widespread use of 'Vietnam' and the demands on the farmer who originally conducted trials of this variety demonstrate this. The extended kin networks of the village facilitated seed distribution. So, despite not participating in conservation programs themselves, and indeed having no knowledge of in situ conservation practices at all in many cases, farmers were able to appropriate the benefits of many years of local experimentation. This suggests that it may not be necessary to undertake village-wide programs in order to develop and disseminate new genetic material. Rather, it may be more important to focus attention on a group of committed farmers and a few individuals who demonstrate the ability to select and breed locally adaptable varieties. The traditional seed distribution methods and other forms of social capital can then be relied upon to disseminate the new FVs.

The importance of empowerment and establishing linkages

Despite the decrease in rice plant genetic diversity that occurred during the Green Revolution, the above case study demonstrates that local in situ conservation programs can substantially increase the genetic resources available to resource-poor farmers. This diversity benefits farmers by expanding the choices they have available and increasing the probability they will find varieties adaptable to their specific paddy environments and economic circumstances. In the case of the Campagao CDBC project, this increase in diversity was the direct result of empowering farmers with the knowledge to conduct varietal trials, varietal selection, and varietal breeding. This has not only given farmers the confidence to conduct trials and select varieties suited to their paddy conditions, it has empowered them to develop their own varieties from a large selection of previously unavailable genetic material.

The importance of local ex situ conservation partners, such as the Central Visayan State College of Agriculture, Forestry and Technology, has also proved important as the limited resources of the local farmers' association restricts the number of varieties they can actively conserve ex situ. The success of the CDBC project can be attributed to two factors. The first of these is the access to resources in the form of seeds and seed conservation capacity that has arisen through forming links with other farmers and organizations such as SEARICE and CVSCAFT. The second is the increase in the human capital or intellectual resources of the farmers' association, which has given farmers the knowledge they require to make more informed decisions about what are appropriate rice varieties for their paddy environments and economic circumstances. Equally important, this new knowledge has helped instil in the CFPRA farmers a disposition towards critical thinking. This has helped the farmers assess a suite of possible alternatives in all aspects of their farming systems.

The paradox of varietal favouritism

As the data from the case study have suggested, there was a significant increase in the overall quantum of rice plant genetic material available to Campagao's farmers following the initiation of the CDBC project in 1996. Over 200 varieties were trialled between 1996 and 2002 in varying environments, many of which were subsequently used in production. Despite this, farmers favour a limited number of broadly adaptable (and one assumes genetically heterogeneous varieties) over a larger number of less adaptable varieties. The cases of IR66 and 'Vietnam' demonstrate this. IR66 has been one of the dominant varieties since the 1990s; the red seed coated off-types it produces being very important in the production of FVs. More recently, 'Vietnam' has come to dominate the fields of Campagao in much the same way as certain MVs have come to dominate more favourable rice growing environments.

Therefore, while the intention of the CDBC project has been to foster rice plant genetic diversity through the provision of new genetic material, and while they have also attempted to increase field level varietal diversity each season, it seems that for farmers the primary goal is not diversity per se, but discovery—discovery of another IR66 or another 'Vietnam'. Conservation of genetic diversity is just one component within farmers' dynamic approach to varietal management. And for most farmers, it is a small component as they turn over, or churn through, varieties and conserve, for a time, only those that meet their needs. Once these varieties are no longer useful they are also discarded (though their genetic heritage may live on in other FVs).

The case for complementarity

The popularity of widely adaptable FVs should be recognized by national agricultural and breeding institutions. Instead of their exclusive focus on genetically uniform varieties adapted to particularly favourable environments and conditions, these institutions might better concentrate on producing genetically heterogeneous varieties that are adaptable both to more marginal environments and to variable growing conditions. The dissemination of these varieties should be accompanied by farmer selection and breeding initiatives that enable farmers to further develop FVs suited to their local environments. FVs with particular adaptations could then be disseminated through the indigenous seed supply networks that already exist (e.g. the *balo-balo* system). This Participatory Plant Breeding (PPB) is seen as crucially important for resource poor farmers in marginal environments (Ceccarelli and Grando, 2002; Cleveland and Soleri, 2002).

This is obviously a challenge for both formal breeding agencies and NGOs. Formal breeding agencies and government agricultural workers often discount the contribution farmers can make to selection and breeding initiatives, and some actively contest the ability of farmers to undertake such scientific procedures. During this research the author encountered at least three very senior agricultural workers in the Philippines who flatly denied that farmers were breeding rice varieties and then using these varieties in production. Two of these officers claimed the author was confusing breeding with selection, and one suggested that farmers were incapable of understanding the complexities of plant genetics because, to quote, 'genetics was the hardest thing I studied at university' (see Carpenter 2005).

Any collaboration between NGOs and institutional breeders will also be difficult for NGOs who work directly with farmers in the area of in situ conservation, many of whom see institutional breeders and the MVs they produce as direct threats to the types of low input, biodiverse farming systems they promote. As the data in this case study suggest, farmers are more interested in genes and characteristics than they are in agricultural heritage. Therefore, what is important is the provision of new, viable genetic material whether that is from traditional, mixed, or modern sources. Locally adaptable MVs that produce off-types farmers can use in the development of FVs can play an important role in rice production in marginal environments.

In order to ensure this new material can be accessed there will need to be enhanced complementarity between formal ex situ conservation programs and informal in situ programs. What is required is a type of dynamic, iterative relationship between ex situ and in situ conservation where new, viable and disease free seed is made available for farmers to trial in situ; the circumstances of successful trials (e.g. landscape types, water management regime, soil characteristics, disease resistance etc) can then be documented with the information stored in a central database for subsequent use by other farmers and NGOs. New FVs can also be stored safely ex situ. Further complementarity could be encouraged between farmers, NGOs and genetic researchers who could assess the genetic characteristics of preferred varieties and the potential they might have for producing favourable off-types.

The Plant Variety Protection Act (2002)

One impediment to the development of FVs and the complementarity agenda outlined above is the Philippine government's Plant Variety Protection (PVP) Act 2002. This Act provides for the protection of new plant varieties and establishes a Plant Variety Protection Board whose members guide the implementation of the Act and decide on some of its more ambiguous provisions. For example, the Act offers some protection for small farmers, allowing them to continue to exchange, use, sell, and save seeds, provided that these seeds will be used only for reproduction and replanting on their own land. However, it is unclear what a small farmer is in the context of rice production. While the Act may be ambiguous about the rights of small farmers, it is much more explicit about the rights of private and public plant breeders who, under the Act, can apply for exclusive rights over new varieties they claim to have developed or discovered. The sale, exchange, or use for breeding or selection purposes of these protected varieties is classified as a criminal offence.

The Act also extends to varieties that are 'essentially derived' from protected varieties. These provisions will make it illegal for farmers to develop and disseminate FVs from protected material. While it is possible under the Act for farmers to claim exclusive rights over varieties they have developed, the limited resources of farmers will, for all intents and purposes, preclude them from claiming protection over the FVs they have developed. In the absence of such protection, and relying on the discovery provisions under the Act, plant breeders may be able to claim rights over varieties developed by farmers if farmers or farmers' associations have not registered these varieties or included them in a local inventory. The provisions contained in this Act indicate a failure of the Philippine government to adequately acknowledge the important role that local seed supply systems play in the lives of resource-poor farmers and the role farmers play in varietal selection and breeding. The type of partnerships and complementarity mentioned in the foregoing section will be impossible, and indeed illegal, under the provisions of this Act.

Since the passing of the PVP Act, SEARICE, CFPRA, and many other Bohol-based NGOs and people's organizations (POs) have actively opposed the legislation through awareness-raising activities, community protest, and legal means. In Bohol, pamphlets have been produced in the local dialect informing Boholano farmers of the probable impact of the PVP legislation. Farmers from CFPRA and many other POs have held workshops with their fellow farmers informing them of the impact of the PVP Act. Affidavits outlining farmers' concerns have been drafted and signed by hundreds of farmers, and thousands of Boholano farmers have signed the Bohol Farmers Network Declaration in opposition to PVP legislation. Aside from this, farmers have organized protest plantings of varieties that may be threatened by the legislation. They have also developed community registries that document all the FVs within a community, and they have physically protested against the law in the provincial capital. SEARICE and other NGOs are also examining legal options, including appeals to provincial law making bodies for support and attempts to repeal the legislation through the Philippine Supreme Court. Filipino farmers and the NGOs who work with them realize how important it is to protect Farmers'

Rights to freely develop and exchange local varieties. The scale and intensity of opposition to the PVP Act suggest that until this right is secured, protests against the Act will continue.

Conclusion

The foregoing discussion highlights the important role farmers play in the conservation of rice plant genetic diversity and in the development of Farmer Varieties. It has demonstrated the preference farmers have for genetically heterogeneous varieties adapted to a variety of local growing conditions and local cultural preferences, as well as the capacity farmers have for innovation through experimental trials, varietal selection, and varietal breeding. This is a vitally important survival strategy for resource-poor farmers in marginal areas who, while lacking physical and financial capital, can use social and human capital to access one of the remaining 'free' resources available to them—rice plant genetic diversity. This chapter has argued that the innovation demonstrated by farmers should be supported through the development of two types of complementarity: complementarity between formal and informal selection and breeding programs; and complementarity between ex situ and in situ conservation efforts. This will help ensure that farmer scientists are provided with new, viable genetic material to trial in local environments. However, with the passing of the PVP Act (2002), access to this vital resource may be restricted and this will place an even heavier burden on the already over-burdened Filipino farmer.

References

Altieri, M. and Merrick, L. (1987) 'In situ conservation of crop genetic resources through maintenance of traditional farming systems', *Economic Botany*, vol 41, no 1, pp86–96

Bellon, M.R. (1997) 'On-farm conservation as a process: An analysis of its components', in L. Sperling and M. Loevinsohn (eds) *Using Diversity: Enhancing and Maintaining Genetic Resources On-Farm*, International Development Research Centre, www.idrc.ca/ library/document/104582/bellon. html, accessed 17 June, 2003

Borras Jr., S.M. (2001) 'State-society relations in land reform implementation in the Philippines', *Development and Change*, vol 32, pp531–561

Borromeo, T. and Hernandez, J. (1987) 'Philippine rice genetic resources: Status, problems and prospects', *Philippine National Conference on Genetic Resources and Development*, September 1987, Tagaytay, Philippines

Brush, S. (1991) 'A farmer-based approach to conserving crop germplasm,' *Economic Botany*, vol 45, no 2, pp153–165

Carpenter, D.B. (2005) 'An agroecological analysis of the adaptations of resource poor rice farmers from a Philippine barangay', PhD thesis, School of Resources, Environment and Society, Australian National University, Canberra

CDBC (Community Development and Biodiversity Conservation Program) (2001) *A Study on Plant Genetic Resources, Diversity and Seed Supply System of Bohol Island, Philippines*, Technical Report No. 1, Southeast Asian Regional Initiative for Community Empowerment, Quezon City, Philippines

Ceccarelli, S. and Grando, S. (2002) 'Plant breeding with farmers involves testing the assumptions of conventional plant breeding: Lessons from the ICEARD barley program', in D.A. Cleveland, and D. Soleri (eds) *Farmers, Scientists and Plant Breeding: Integrating Knowledge and Practice,* CABI Publishing, Wallingford

Cleveland, D.A. and Murray, S.C. (1997) 'The world's crop genetic resources and the rights of indigenous farmers', *Current Anthropology*, vol 38, no 4, pp477–515

Cleveland, D.A and Soleri, D. (2002) 'Farmers, scientists and plant breeding: Knowledge, practice and the possibilities for collaboration', in D.A. Cleveland and D. Soleri (eds) *Farmers, Scientists and Plant Breeding: Integrating Knowledge and Practice,* CABI Publishing, Wallingford

Cleveland, D.A. and Soleri, D. (2007) 'Extending Darwin's analogy: Bridging differences in concepts of selection between farmers, biologists and plant breeders', *Economic Botany,* vol 61, no 12, pp121-136

David, C., Cordova, V. and Otsuka, K. (1994) 'Technological change, land reform, and income distribution in the Philippines', in C. David and K. Otsuka (eds) *Modern Rice Technology and Income Distribution in Asia,*   Reinner, Boulder, CO

FAO (Food and Agriculture Organization of the United Nations) (1996), *Report on the State of the World's Genetic Resources for Food and Agriculture,* Technical Conference on Plant Genetic Resources, Leipzig Germany, June 17–23, 1996, Rome, Italy: Plant Production and Protection Division, Food and Agriculture Organization of the United Nations.

Fujisaka, S. (1999) 'Side-stepped by the green revolution: Farmers traditional rice cultivars in the uplands and rainfed lowlands', in G.S. Prain Fujisaka and M.D. Warren (eds) *Biological and Cultural Diversity: The Role of Indigenous Agricultural Experimentation in Development,* Intermediate Technology Publications, London

Fukui, S. and Hara, Y. (1996) 'An economic analysis of rural informal credit market with reciprocity', in S. Fukui and Y. Hara (eds) *Social and Institutional Changes in the Rural Philippines*, Global Area Studies Report No. 25, The Southeast Asian Way for Development, Organizing Committee for Global Area Studies, Kyoto

GRAIN (2000) 'Growing diversity-Asia,' www.grain.org/gd/en/case-studies/cases/doc-word/as-abstract-philippines-masipag-en.doc, accessed June 23 2003

Hirtz, F. (1998) 'The discourse that silences: Beneficiaries' ambivalence towards redistributive land reform in the Philippines,' *Development and Change*, vol 29, pp247–275

Hossain, M., Gascon, I.B. and Revilla, I.M. (1996) 'Constraints to growth in rice production in the Philippines', in R.E. Evenson, R.W. Herdt and M. Hossain (eds) *Rice Production in Asia: Progress and Priorities*, CABI Publishing, Wallingford

IRRI (International Rice Research Institute) (2003) 'Rice biodiversity.' www.irri.org/irriintra/IRRI/textonly/science/genetics%20resources/rice %20biodiversity/rice20%biodiversity.htm, accessed 30 June 2003.

Lansigan, F.P., los Santos, W.L. and Coladilla, J.O. (2000), 'Agronomic impacts of climate variability on rice production in the Philippines', *Agriculture, Ecosystems and Environment*, vol 82, pp129–137

Leibig, K., Alker, D., ould Chih, K., Horn, D., Illi, H. and Wolf, J. (2002) *Governing Biodiversity: Access to Genetic Resources and Approaches to Obtaining Benefits from their Use: the Case of the Philippines*, German Development Institute, Bonn

Magnifico, F. A. (1997) 'Community-based resource management: CONSERVE (Philippines) experience', www.idrec.ca/books/focus/833/magnific.html accessed 17 June 2003

Morin, S. R., Calibo, M., Garcia-Belen, M., Pham, J. L. and Palis, F. (2002) 'Natural hazards and genetic diversity in rice', *Agriculture and Human Values*, vol 19, pp133–149

Nagarajan, G., Meyer, R.L. and Hushak, L.J. (1995) 'Segmentation in the informal credit markets: The case of the Philippines', *Agricultural Economics*, vol 12, pp171–181

Pelagrina W. (2000) 'Biodiversity and the sustainability of rice farming systems', in IIRR and ILEIA, *Enhancing Sustainability of the Rice Economy in the Philippines*, Workshop Proceedings. Leusden, The Netherlands: International Institute for Rural Reconstruction, James Y.C. Yen Centre, Silang, Cavite, Philippines, and Centre for Information on Low External Input and Sustainable Agriculture, pp81–83

Pingali, P. L., Hossain, M. and Gerpacio, R.V. (1997), *Asian Rice Bowls: The Returning Crisis*, CABI Publishing, Wallingford

Tabien R. (2000) 'High-yield rice production technologies,' in IIRR and ILEIA, *Enhancing Sustainability of the Rice Economy in the Philippines*, Workshop Proceedings, Leusden, The Netherlands: International Institute for Rural Reconstruction, Y.C. James Yen Centre, Silang, Cavite, Philippines, and Centre for Information on Low External Input and Sustainable Agriculture, pp. 30–33

Thrupp, L.A. (2000) 'Linking agricultural biodiversity and food security: The valuable role of agrobiodiversity for sustainable agriculture', *International Affairs*, vol 76 no 2, pp265–281

Vaughan, D.A. and Chang, T.T. (1992), 'In situ conservation of rice genetic resources', *Economic Botany*, vol 46, no 4, pp368–383

Witcombe, J.R. and Joshi, A. (1997) 'The impact of farmers participatory research on biodiversity of crops', www.idrc.ca/books/focus/833/ witcombe.html, accessed 17 June 2003

Wood, D. and Lenne, J.M. (1997) 'The conservation of agrobiodiversity on farm: Questioning the merging paradigm', *Biodiversity and Conservation*, vol 6, pp109-129

Wood, S., Sebastian, K. and Scherr, S.J. (2000) 'Pilot analysis of global agroecosystems', www.wri.org/wri/wr2000/agroecosystems_page.html, accessed 17 June 2003

Yap, E. (2000) 'Farmer-led seed breeding technologies', in IIRR and ILEIA, Enhancing *Sustainability of the Rice Economy in the Philippines*, Workshop Proceedings, Leusden, The Netherlands: International Institute for Rural Reconstruction, Y.C. James Yen Centre, Silang, Cavite, Philippines, and Centre for Information on Low External Input and Sustainable Agriculture, pp 84–88

Zhu, Y., Wang, Y., Chen, H. and Lu, B. (2003) 'Conserving traditional rice varieties through management for crop diversity', *BioScience*, vol 53, no 2, pp158–162

8

The Contribution of Biodiversity to Modern Intensive Farming Systems

Amani A. Omer, Unai Pascual and Noel P. Russell

Agricultural productivity and the sustainability of farming systems both draw heavily on the ecosystem services provided and supported by biodiversity. Further, there is some evidence that the biodiversity-related loss of ecosystem services may matter more in biodiversity-poor or intensive farming systems than in biodiversity-rich, 'wild' or extensive systems. Modern agricultural practices and the intensification often associated therewith have been linked to biodiversity loss and the degradation of ecosystems services (MEA, 2005). In addition, modern intensive agriculture has been criticized for largely ignoring the symbiotic interactions and resource-use complementarities between agricultural and non-agricultural species (Omer et al., 2007).

Although the intensification of agricultural production has resulted in considerable gains in human welfare, it is increasingly unsustainable. The gain in productivity to meet the rising demand for food of a growing and more affluent population has been achieved at significant environmental cost. It has resulted in substantial changes in the biodiversity of agroecosystems, raising a concern that the degradation of ecosystem services could worsen in the first half of this century unless these problems are properly addressed (MEA, 2005). This calls for the development of more sustainable (and highly productive) forms of modern agricultural production.

The prevailing view is that achieving sustainability through biodiversity conservation requires the imposition of heavy restrictions on farming and agriculture as conventionally practised. This chapter, by contrast, argues that when farmers and farming businesses are well-informed about the benefits of conservation and the costs of biodiversity loss they are able to integrate conservation goals into decision-making and achieve conservation through voluntary adjustments to agricultural production practices. However, since these costs and benefits are not reflected in the market, biodiversity policy has an important role to play in correcting market failure by emphasizing the inter-linkages between biodiversity conservation and the sustainability and productivity of agricultural production. In particular, policy has a role in identifying and promoting options to conserve or enhance specific ecosystem services in ways that reduce negative trade-offs or that provide positive synergies with other ecosystem services. Yet the importance of biodiversity in agroecosystems is not being fully reflected in policies or realized at the farm level. The Millennium Ecosystem Assessment (2005) thus suggests that the challenge of reversing the degradation of ecosystems, while meeting increasing demands for their services, will involve significant changes in policies and institutions, alongside changes in agricultural practices.

Here, we draw from this debate and contribute to it by investigating, from an economic perspective, the effects of biodiversity conservation on productivity in the context of an intensive agroecosystem where high productivity has been achieved through increased use of chemical and mechanical inputs and continued human interventions that act as substitutes for ecological services. We specifically address the dynamics of this relationship using a bio-economic model that describes the effect of agrobiodiversity (based on associated on-farm biodiversity) on the marketable supply of crop output. This model is used to derive a hypothesis that is tested using economic and ecological data from a panel of specialized cereal producers in the UK, where there is evidence that agrobiodiversity has been declining over recent decades (Winter, 2000; Stoate et al, 2001).

A dynamic problem

In the absence of economic incentives or policy restrictions for biodiversity protection it is usually assumed that producers' primary objective will be to maximize immediate profit without considering either the impact of their decisions on biodiversity or the effects of biodiversity on production, particularly in the long-term. This is for three broad reasons. First, markets for agricultural commodities do not reflect the impact of biodiversity loss on agricultural productivity or the benefits of its conservation. Second, many of the ecosystems services provided by biodiversity are open-access in nature, meaning that producers are able to benefit from biodiversity protection (provided it occurs somewhere within the landscape) without incurring any cost. Third, the ecosystem services provided by biodiversity are, in effect, public goods and therefore they deliver direct economic benefit to producers collectively rather than to individual producers. Hence, under uncontrolled market conditions, producers would not be expected either to supply the level of conservation that society wants or to consider the full benefits of biodiversity conservation for agricultural productivity in their private decisions. A static model is often used, therefore, to investigate private decision-making that is not constrained by changes in the state of biodiversity. Such models fail, however, to consider the dynamics of agriculture and the underlying processes that are central to agricultural productivity.

In order to address the spatially and temporally dynamic nature of agrobiodiversity and farmer decision-making, this chapter develops a model that is sensitive to changes over time and across space. This model recognizes that agricultural productivity depends on the underlying support and services provided by biodiversity, but that additional incentives may be needed to persuade producers to pursue conservation and changes in agricultural practices over and above the optimum required to directly promote agricultural production. The challenge facing policy makers is to derive a set of policy measures, and institutional frameworks to deliver them, that ensure compatibility between the social and private optima. Such policy measures will be required: (a) to promote conservation activities in the agricultural sector; (b) to promote biodiversity-friendly practices in agricultural production; and (c) to promote consideration of the long-term impacts of private decisions.

For the purposes of this chapter, it is assumed that a well-designed biodiversity policy system is in place that sends the correct signals to producers about the biodiversity costs of unsustainable modern agricultural practices as well as the benefits of biodiversity conservation. Hence, producers are expected to consider both the short- and long-term effects of their economic decisions. Thus, in the presence of adequate information and economic incentives for biodiversity protection, the private decision-maker would consider the biodiversity impacts and implications in their economic decisions. The optimization problem is no longer static as it recognizes the spatial and dynamic nature of the economic and ecological processes that underpin farming activities. Hence, the production decisions and the interrelated issues of biodiversity could be analysed in a dynamic framework, as shown next, which differs from the static one by incorporating a spatial dimension and technological restrictions.

A model of biodiversity conservation in intensive agriculture

The bio-economic model utilized here assumes that economic decisions (e.g. optimal allocation of inputs) for a given area of land are motivated both by levels of crop output and by the agroecosystem's environmental quality, reflected by the state of on-site biodiversity. Further, it is assumed that the decision-maker's objective is the maximization of the discounted present value of net profit derived from both outputs subject to the constraints imposed by the policy system. The theoretical model underlying these assumptions is elaborated in Appendix 6.A. The model setup reflects a subset of economic decisions that would principally affect landuse activities, and the underlying welfare that these activities generate. The objective is to find the optimal trade-off in the allocation of social benefits yielding services: agricultural supply and the biodiversity conservation. The role of economic incentives discussed below following the presentation of results is then to influence producers' decisions and induce them to make decisions that are consistent with social optimality

The model leads to steady state (long run) equilibrium (Figure 8.A1), with two convergent isosectors that depicts the joint evolution of biodiversity and crop output as a saddle-path towards the equilibrium. In the context of the current analysis, attention is focused on low-biodiversity intensive agro-ecosystems notionally represented by points within isosector I in Figure 8.A1.

In this context, the effect on optimal crop output supply of a change in the stock of agrobiodiversity can be investigated from both a static and a dynamic comparative analyses perspective. It can be shown that the optimal supply of marketable output can increase (albeit at a declining rate) along the transition path to the long run equilibrium of output and biodiversity stock when the latter increases in the transition towards the steady state. On a given area of land, this implies that biodiversity and agricultural productivity are positively correlated. It can also be shown that the supply of crop output can be increased either by investing in improving the state of biodiversity-neutral agricultural technology or by enhancing the levels of biodiversity in agricultural landscapes. This means that, in principle, the decision-maker can choose between the two strategies to increase food supply in the long run. These hypotheses and the details of the optimal solution, the properties of the optimal adjustment pathway and an analysis of the impact on agricultural output of biodiversity are derived using a similar approach to the approach undertaken in Omer et al (2007).

Data

The data used in this study come from a panel of approximately 230 cereal producers from the East of England, for the period 1989-2000. The dataset includes information on cereal output, level of input application and socioeconomic characteristics of the farm households. In addition, a variable measuring on-farm functional agrobiodiversity is included. Summary statistics for these variables appear in Table 8.1 and more details on the data and how the biodiversity index is constructed can be found in Omer et al (2007).

Table 8.1. Summary statistics for variables in the stochastic frontier models for cereal farmers in the East of England

Variable	Mean	St. Dev	Minimum	Maximum
Crop output (£/ha/API)	874.85	194.49	261.55	5141.61
Agrobiodiversity index (ABI)	13.63	1.04	9.99	16.22
Fertilizer application (£/ha/API)	87.55	32.78	0.68	571.90
Labour application (£/ha/API)	163.87	92.56	3.34	1093.45
Machinery application (£/ha/API)	208.98	93.51	12.55	1382.01
Pesticide application (£/ha/API)	91.41	27.57	1.99	345.62
Farm area (ha)	178.58	137.21	7.89	1008.18
Farmer's age (years)	50.91	10.52	27	79
Environmental Payments (£/ha/API)	2.77	11.00	0	93.63
Share of hired labour from total labour (0-1)	0.44	0.25	0	1

Source: Omer (2004)
Note: A total of 2788 observations were obtained in an unbalanced panel of approximately 230 different specialist cereal farms over the period 1989-2000.
API: Agricultural Price Index for the relevant inputs (or output) and year.

The data allow estimation of stochastic production frontier (SPF) models that provide an explicit representation of the production surface underlying the theoretical analysis, where it is assumed that farmers are optimally adjusting their production processes so that they are operating along the production frontier (Iráizoz et al, 2003).

The empirical model

In order to test the key proposition from the theoretical model, a reduced form dynamic parametric frontier model is used and fitted to this data. The stochastic production frontier (SPF) approach allows both estimation of the output production frontier that represents best practice among farmers (as assumed in the theoretical model) and the possibility of real deviations from the frontier attributed to the effects of variation in the sampled farmers' level of technical efficiency (TE). After technical inefficiency is controlled for, it is possible to qualify the key relationships derived from the theoretical model along the production frontier as it evolves over time. It should be noted that the frontier provides a closer approximation to the 'optimal path' than a more traditional econometric specification which does not allow for technical inefficiency. Hence, the data on marketed crop output is used to estimate the output optimal path which is reduced to an estimable function $y(x_t, z_t, a_t)$.

The model fitted to the twelve years, $t=1, 2,...,T$, and farm-specific data, i, takes the following form:

$$y_{it} = \beta_0 + \sum_k \beta_k p_{kit} + v_{it} - u_{it} \quad (6.1)$$

where:

y_{it}: natural log of crop marketed output of farm i at time t (x £100 per hectare/Agricultural Price Index);

p_1: natural log of ABI (biodiversity index);

p_2: natural log of fertilizer input value (x £100 per ha/API);

p_3: natural log of labour input value (x £100 per ha/API);

p_4: natural log of machinery input value (x £100 per ha/API);

p_5: natural log of pesticide input value (x £100 per ha/API);

p_6: year of observation where $p_6 = 1, 2,...,$ 12.

Assuming that v_{it}s are independently and identically $N(0,\sigma_v^2)$ distributed random errors independent of the non-negative random error term, u_{it}, associated with technical inefficiency in production, β_k stands for the parameter vector to be estimated using FRONTIER4 (Coelli, 1996). A range of different specifications of this general Cobb-Douglas SFP model were explored and tested (see Omer et al, 2007). These tests supported our choice of the following non-neutral inefficiency model (Battese and Broca, 1997):

$$u_{it} = \delta_0 + \sum_j \delta_j q_{jit} + \sum_j \sum_k \delta_{jk} p_{kit} q_{jit} + w_{it} \quad (6.2c)$$

The δ_j coefficients are associated with the effects of the following inefficiency effects covariates:

q_1: Natural log of farmer's age (years);

q_2: Natural log of the amount of environmental payment (subsidies) obtained by the household;

q_3: Dummy variable, 1 if the farm participates in any agri-environmental scheme introduced in 1992, 0 otherwise;

q_4: Proportion of hired to total labour applied in the farm;

q_5: Dummy variable, 1 if use of hired labour hours, 0 otherwise;

q_6: Year of observation, $t=1,2,...,12$.

This model includes interactions between farm-specific variables and the input variables in the stochastic frontier. This approach is similar to the approach by Pascual (2005) to test the bidirectional effect of soil fertility (also an environmental input) with potential simultaneous effects on frontier output and TE.

Table 8.2 shows the results of various hypothesis tests regarding the specification of this model and the results of the model are given in Table 8.3.

Table 8.2. Generalized Likelihood-Ratio Tests for SPF model for cereal farmers in the East of England (1989-2000)

Null Hypothesis	Log likelihood	LR statistic	CV* (5%)
H_0: $\gamma = \delta_0 = \delta_j = \delta_{jk} = 0$	1007.31	707.65	55.19
$H_0 = \beta_1 = 0, \delta_{1j} = 0, j = 1,....,6$	1352.69	16.87	14.07
$H_0 : \beta_6 = 0, \delta_{6j} = 0, j = 1,....,6$	1177.02	368.23	14.07
$H_0 : \delta_{jk} = 0, k, j = 1,.....6$	1261.79	198.67	43.77
$H_0 : \delta_{6k} = \delta_{k6} = 0, k = 1,...,6$	1318.76	84.73	11.07
$H_0 : \delta_{6j} = \delta_{6j} = 0, j = 1,...,6$	1313.58	95.09	11.07
$H_0 : \delta_{3k} = \delta_{4k} = 0, k = 1,...,6$	1341.35	39.56	19.92

Source: Omer (2004)
*Critical Values are also obtained from Kodde and Palm (1986).
LR: Likelihood Ratio.

Battese and Broca (1997) derive the elasticity of crop output with respect to the kth input variable (c.f. appendix 6.B). The elasticity of mean output with respect to the kth input variable has two components: (1) the elasticity of frontier output with respect to the kth input, given by the estimated β_k-s; and (2) the elasticity of TE with respect to the kth input. The mean output, frontier and efficiency elasticities for each of the variable inputs averaged throughout the 1989-2000 period are presented in Table 8.4.

It can be observed that for the whole period, agrobiodiversity is positively affecting mean output levels even though greater levels of agrobiodiversity appears to have negatively affected TE in the sector. This has also occurred with the application of fertilizers and more dramatically with the use of farm labour. Regarding the latter, the negative effect on efficiency seems to outweigh the positive effect on the frontier, implying an excessive use of labour in cereal farming. By contrast, the use of machinery and pesticides show relatively large mean output elasticity due to their positive effect both on the frontier and on TE.

What is of more interest here is the effect of the evolution of the stock of agrobiodiversity, proxied by ABI (z_t), on the levels of frontier output, as this is more directly associated with optimal marketable crop output as described in the theoretical model (variable y_t). The results are consistent with the second hypothesis from the theoretical model, i.e. that there is a positive, although declining, effect. The frontier elasticities with respect to ABI are positive and have tended to decrease at a rate of 0.06 percent per annum (Figure 8.1). It also appears that the effect of the stock of biodiversity on TE has been different before and after 1996. While there is initially a negative elasticity of TE, after 1996 the elasticity becomes positive reaching 0.15 in 2000. The net effect of biodiversity through the impacts on both frontier output and TE indicates that while, until 1993 (the year after broad environmental payments were introduced in the farming sector), higher levels of agrobiodiversity were associated with declining mean yields (average elasticity of -0.1), after the incorporation of the environmental payments for biodiversity conservation the impact on mean output has reversed with an elasticity in 2000 of 0.26. These results suggest that agrobiodiversity conservation schemes have not undermined the productive performance of the cereal sector.

Incentives and potential policy frameworks to support specific ecosystem services

Concerns about the sustainability of modern intensive agroecosystems are a global issue. Agroecosystems are under pressure to deliver an increasing and sustainable supply of food. Modern intensive agriculture has been the main source of achieving food security in the North and has become central to agricultural development in the South. However, the link between modern agricultural activities and the degradation of ecosystem services and biodiversity is well recognized. The question has been how to design agricultural systems and markets that are capable of providing an increased supply of food without impairing the ecological integrity of production systems. In considering this question, this study has explored the dynamics of interactions between agriculture and biodiversity in terms of the effects of biodiversity conservation on agricultural productivity. It suggests that biodiversity levels in agroecosystems can be enhanced without impairing agricultural productivity; that is, increasing food production from a fixed resource base by simultaneously increasing the provision of ecosystem services.

Table 8.3. MLE parameter estimates of the generalized Cobb-Douglas SPF model

		Model 3	
		Coefficient	t-ratio
	β_0	1.69	12.33
P1: biodiversity	β_1	0.13	2.58
P2: fertilizer	β_2	0.05	4.03
P3: labour	β_3	0.01	2.91
P4: machinery	β_4	0.05	4.16
P5: pesticides	β_5	0.14	11.63
P6: time	β_6	0.04	31.67
Inefficiency model			
Constant	δ_0	-0.60	-3.62
Q1: age	δ_1	-0.05	-2.47
Q2: environmental pay	δ_2	0.10	3.50
Q3: d1	δ_3	-0.68	-0.73
Q4: hired labour	δ_4	0.38	0.42
Q5: d2	δ_5	0.71	0.77
Q6: time	δ_6	0.29	2.16
P1.q1	δ_{11}	0.02	2.78
P1.q2	δ_{12}	-0.04	-3.50
P1.q3	δ_{13}	0.42	1.18
P1.q4	δ_{14}	-0.04	-0.11
P1.q5	δ_{15}	-0.24	-0.70
P1.q6	δ_{16}	-0.08	-1.66
P2.q1	δ_{21}	0.01	4.74
P2.q2	δ_{22}	-0.01	-2.83
P2.q3	δ_{23}	0.75	5.16
P2.q4	δ_{24}	0.22	2.41
P2.q5	δ_{25}	-0.20	-2.62
P2.q6	δ_{26}	-0.04	-6.27
P3.q1	δ_{31}	0.00	3.09
P3.q2	δ_{32}	0.00	1.81
P3.q3	δ_{33}	-0.19	-2.43
P3.q4	δ_{34}	-0.19	-3.33
P3.q5	δ_{35}	-0.05	-1.29
P3.q6	δ_{36}	0.02	4.02
P4.q1	δ_{41}	0.00	1.29
P4.q2	δ_{42}	-0.01	-2.93

P4.q3	δ_{43}	0.11	0.92
P4.q4	δ_{44}	-0.46	-5.14
P4.q5	δ_{45}	0.24	3.76
P4.q6	δ_{46}	0.00	-0.50
P5.q1	δ_{51}	0.01	5.45
P5.q2	δ_{52}	0.00	0.79
P5.q3	δ_{53}	0.10	0.92
P5.q4	δ_{54}	-0.05	-0.58
P5.q5	δ_{55}	-0.38	-5.81
P5.q6	δ_{56}	-0.05	-6.74
P6.q1	δ_{61}	0.00	1.63
P6.q2	δ_{62}	0.00	2.10
P6.q3	δ_{63}	-0.02	-1.59
P6.q4	δ_{64}	-0.05	-5.30
P6.q5	δ_{65}	-0.06	-4.86
P6.q6	δ_{66}	-0.01	-13.34
Variance Parameters			
σ^2		0.08	17.05
γ		0.86	63.98
Log-likelihood		1361.13	

Source: Omer (2004)
Note: D1: Dummy variable for environmental payments received (1 if received, 0 otherwise); D2 dummy variable for hired labour (1, if positive expenditures in hired labour, 0 otherwise)

Table 8.4. Average crop output elasticities with respect to all the inputs in the model (1989-2000)

Variable	Frontier output elasticity	Technical efficiency elasticity	Mean output Elasticity
Agrobiodiversity	0.13	-0.10	0.04
Fertilizer	0.05	-0.02	0.03
Labour	0.01	-0.05	-0.03
Machinery	0.05	0.00	0.05
Pesticides	0.14	0.14	0.28
Time	0.04	0.09	0.13

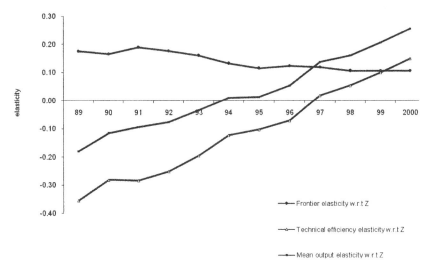

Figure 8.1. Change in elasticity of output with respect to Biodiversity (1989-2000)
Source: Omer (2004)

The results presented here also emphasize the need for an efficient environmental policy framework that integrates environmental and economic goals of biodiversity conservation. Such a framework should ideally correct for the three basic forms of market failure: (1) inadequate information; (2) poorly defined property rights; and (3) pricing of resources below their full economic and environmental cost. Appropriate information should be provided to farmers and stakeholders to raise awareness of the environmental impacts of conventional production patterns and the implications of these impacts for the economic profitability and sustainability of farming businesses. This could be through the use of education channels or other means of information provision. It is also important to recognize the interconnectedness of biodiversity conservation and to provide appropriate incentives that encourage farmers to work in partnership with each other. Furthermore, the policy framework needs to provide incentives that reflect the full economic and environmental costs of resource use.

A combination of incentive measures that emphasize the inter-linkages between biodiversity conservation and the sustainability of modern agricultural production are required to promote the conservation of biodiversity within agroecosystems. These measures should also consider the spatial and temporal aspects of market failures that underpin the externalization of biodiversity loss. These may include: (1) farm level-based measures; (2) landscape-based (club or cooperative) measures; and (3) market-based measures.

Farm-level incentives are required to promote biodiversity-friendly sustainable agricultural technologies and practices and to mitigate the negative impact of biodiversity-degrading agricultural practices; that is, to encourage private producers both to recognize the private benefits derived from biodiversity (i.e. enhanced production frontier) and to provide the public goods and services which are also derived from biodiversity but which are not adequately valued in the market. Farm-level incentives are widely used in OECD countries (OECD, 2004) and within the European Union. In fact, our empirical analysis shows that the expansion of the EU-CAP based biodiversity conservation schemes in the early 1990s have enhanced productivity on the intensive cereal farms in our sample. Farmer participation in EU schemes is considered in more detail by Rosemarie Siebert in Chapter 16.

Landscape-based (club or cooperative) incentives promote collaboration and coordination between different producers within a given landscape. This is needed to achieve ecologically efficient biodiversity conservation with respect to the spatial scale of habitat structure and ecological processes by ensuring that biodiversity policies recognize the connectedness of conservation activities across the landscape. As Omer (1997) argues, activities required for biodiversity conservation and enhancement are not usually under the control of a single decision-maker. Further, due to the open access nature of many of the ecosystem services provided by biodiversity, it is important that incentives encourage as many farmers as possible to participate in individual and cooperative conservation activities. In the absence of such widespread participation, the provision of biodiversity conservation or enhancement may not be socially optimal, since individual producers can enjoy the benefits (in terms of ecosystem services) of biodiversity provided by others without incurring the cost of conservation themselves (Omer 1997; Krawczyk et al, 2005). Examples of this type of incentive scheme are difficult to find but issues related to their design have been investigated by Smith and Wilen (2003) and Shogren et al. (2003).

Market-based incentives attempt to pay private producers to protect or enhance biodiversity at a rate which reflects the true value of ecosystem services provided by biodiversity. Market-based incentives differ from, and complement, other farm and landscape-scale measures in that they attempt to address market failure either through the explicit correction of market failure with respect to existing supply chains, or through the creation of new markets for new ecosystem services. In other words these systems aim to directly harness consumer preferences for biodiversity conservation by providing market structures and information that enable these preferences to be expressed to those who jointly produce food and ecological habitats. Eco-labelling and certification, for example, have been identified by the OECD (2005) as measures to provide information to consumers about biodiversity and to provide a financial reward to those producers capable of supplying biodiversity conservation. Various types of environmental certification and labelling are discussed in more detail in Chapters 10 to 12. Market-based incentives that rely on the creation of new markets for ecosystem services are discussed in Chapters 15 and 17. From an economic perspective, the main difficulty in using market-based mechanisms is valuing biodiversity loss and the services that are enhanced by its conservation (Pascual and Perrings 2007).

All these different incentive measures recognize and capitalize on the principal synergies identified in our analysis between productivity and biodiversity to the extent that they are focused on directly encouraging biodiversity enhancement and/or reducing biodiversity degradation. In contrast, incentives focused more directly on agricultural output, such as output subsidies and policies aimed at extensifying production techniques or setting productive land aside, ignore or even oppose these synergies. However a key lesson here is that all measures should recognize the dynamic nature of biodiversity and consider the time scale that is required to achieve ecologically efficient and economically productive sustainable agricultural systems. This implies a need to develop appropriate policy frameworks that are capable of delivering specific ecosystem services in any given context. The objectives of such frameworks would be enhancing the provision of these services in ways that reduce negative trade-offs or that provide positive synergies with other ecosystem services.

Russell et al (2005) examine the current Common Agricultural Policy of the European Union and conclude that it has a number of elements that encourage farmers to exploit the synergies identified in our analysis. For example, at the farm level, the decoupling of general support payments from current production decisions is an important first step in reducing incentives for continued intensification and the potential overuse of chemicals. At the same time, the introduction of a cross-compliance system linked to these payments has introduced a broad-based system of incentives for many improvements in agricultural practice that include basic conservation activities. Furthermore the multi-level Environmental Stewardship Scheme (ESS) provides a more targeted system of incentives for specific types of conservation activity. However, a much more broad-brush approach is taken in relating incentives to the dynamic and spatial nature of ecological processes. For example, ESS agreements are optional and typically run for five years only, potentially limiting both the temporal and spatial coverage that might be achieved. However, lower (entry) level agreements must cover the whole farm area so some degree of spatial integrity is achievable. At the same time, there are provisions within the higher-level scheme for additional payments to support cross-farm collaboration (thus providing a type of landscape based incentive) but this component is mainly focused on agreements covering common land, or agreements on land where a single archaeological feature extends over more than one farm. The recent CAP reforms and the reduction in direct price supports (a change in market-based incentives) will have moderated incentives for over-intensification, and broadened those for biodiversity conservation, but the current policy system does not provide effective incentives for efficient ecological management over time and space (Russell et al 2005). Furthermore Hodge and Reader (2009) have identified the failure of the current agri-environmental schemes in establishing a framework within which incentives could be used to support the provision of specific benefits.

This analysis has significant implications for the developing economies of the South. The economy of most developing countries is based on agriculture. Development opportunities are thus also based largely on agriculture, making them generally more vulnerable to the impacts of environmental pressures such as climate change and biodiversity loss. In addition, there is an urgent need to increase food production in order to combat hunger, under-nutrition, diseases and poverty. Hence, the challenge facing policy makers in developing countries is to devise policy measures that consider how to utilize the benefits of modern agricultural technologies while combating environmental and social problems.

Conclusion

Modern agricultural landscapes are characterized by the increasing size and homogeneity of crop monocultures. Concerns regarding the potential negative environmental effects of monocultures are well established, but relatively less attention has been paid to the economic effects of agrobiodiversity loss. Further, while ecologists mostly agree that increased intensification is a driver of agrobiodiversity loss, the feedback effects on productivity are less well understood. For example, increasing the number of species on a farm may reduce productivity levels of the main crop in the short run, through greater competition for resources. At the same time, biodiversity, by providing ecological services (e.g. pollination, nutrient enhancement, pest control), can increase agricultural output in the longer run (Jackson et al, 2005).

This chapter has explored one link between the conservation of agrobiodiversity and crop output in specialized intensive farming systems. A behavioural model is used to set out the hypothesis that biodiversity can support increased marketable output in the longer run, through outward shifts in the production frontier. The empirical analysis to test this hypothesis is based on estimating an output distance function using data from cereal farms in England for the period 1989–2000.

The econometric analysis cannot reject our hypothesis. This has important implications for the design of agri-environmental policy as it suggests that the introduction of agrobiodiversity conservation policies can represent a win-win scenario. That is, this study supports the claim that biodiversity in agricultural landscapes can be enhanced without negatively affecting agricultural productivity in already very intensified agricultural systems if the correct incentives are put in place. In one sense, these empirical results complement the findings of other recent studies (e.g. McInerney et al, 2000) that additional conservation investment induced by the agri-environmental policy system can generate additional benefits for farmers and society at large by supporting and enhancing agricultural multifunctionality. This is an area of promising research that clearly needs to expand in interdisciplinary scope to promote the integration between ecologically meaningful biodiversity information and economically consistent data at both the farm and the landscape scale.

References

Altieri, P. (1999) 'The ecological role of biodiversity in agroecosystems', *Agriculture, Ecosystems and Environment*, vol 74, pp19–31

Battese, G.E. and Broca, S. (1997) 'Functional forms of stochastic frontier production functions and models for technical inefficiency effects: A comparative study for wheat farmers in Pakistan', *Journal of Productivity Analysis*, vol 8, pp395–414

Coelli, T. (1996) *A Guide to FRONTIER v.4.1: A Computer Program for Stochastic Frontier Production and Cost Function Estimation*, Working Paper 7/96, Centre for Efficiency and Productivity Analysis, Department of Econometrics, University of New England, Armidale, Australia

Hodge, I. and Reader, M. (in press 2009) 'The introduction of Entry Level Stewardship in England: Extension or dilution in agri-environment policy?', *Land Use Policy*, www.sciencedirect.com/science?_ob=ArticleURL&_udi=B6VB0-4W55T55-1&_user=554534&_coverDate=04%2F26%2F2009&_alid=97343949 8&_rdoc=1&_fmt=high&_orig=search&_cdi=5912&_sort=r&_docanchor=&view =c&_ct=3&_acct=C000028338&_version=1&_urlVersion=0&_userid=554534&m d5=492412767d7d22abce4a57d10173ded8, available online 26 April 2009

Iráizoz, B., Rapún, M. and Zabaleta, I. (2003) 'Assessing the technical efficiency of horticultural production in Navarra', *Agricultural Systems*, vol 78, pp387–403

Jackson, L., Bawa, K., Pascual, U., and Perrings, C. (2005) *Agrobiodiversity: A New Science Agenda for Biodiversity in Support of Sustainable Agroecosystems*, DIVERSITAS Report No. 4, DIVERSITAS, Paris

Kodde, D., Palm, A. (1986) 'Wald criteria for jointly testing equality and inequality restriction', *Econometrica*, vol 54, no 5, pp1243–1248

Krawczyk, J.B., Lifran, R. and Tidball, M. (2005) 'Use of coupled incentives to improve adoption of environmentally friendly technologies', *Journal of Environmental Economics and Management*, vol 49, pp311-329

McInerney, J., Barr D., MacQueen G. and Turner M. (2000) 'What's the damage? A study of farm level costs of managing and maintaining the countryside', *Special Studies in Agricultural Economics No 51*, Agricultural Economics Unit, University of Exeter, Exeter, UK

Millennium Ecosystem Assessment (2005) *Ecosystems and Human Well-being: Synthesis*, Island Press, Washington DC.

OECD (Organisation for Economic Cooperation and Development) (2004) *Handbook of Market Creation for Biodiversity: Issues in Implementation*, OECD, Paris

OECD (Organisation for Economic Cooperation and Development) (2005) *Policy Brief: Preserving Biodiversity and Promoting Biosafety*, OECD, Paris

Omer, A. (1997) 'Economics, ecology, biodiversity and the economic theory of clubs', Master dissertation, The University of Manchester, Manchester

Omer, A. (2004) 'An economic analysis of interactions between agriculture and biodiversity', PhD thesis, The University of Manchester, Manchester

Omer, A., Pascual U. and Russell, N. (2007) 'Biodiversity conservation and productivity in intensive agricultural systems', *Journal of Agricultural Economics*, vol 58, no 2, pp308–329

Pascual, U. (2005) 'Land use intensification potential in slash-and-burn farming through improvements in technical efficiency', *Ecological Economics*, vol 52, no 4, pp497–511

Pascual, U. and Perrings, C. (2007) 'The economics of in-situ biodiversity conservation in agricultural landscapes', *Agriculture, Ecosystems and the Environment*, vol 121, pp 256–268

Russell, N., Yalden, D., Walker, J., Omer, A., Pascual, U. and Wheeler, P. (2005) *Investigating the Potential Role of Sustainable Intensification in Agro-Ecological Systems*, Report on Project 224-25-0095 of Rural Economy and Land Use (RELU) Programme to ESRC, NERC and BBSRC

Shogren, J.F., Parkhurst, G.M., and Settle, C. (2003) 'Integrating economics and ecology to protect nature on private lands: Model, methods and mindsets', *Environmental Science and Policy*, vol 6, pp233–242

Smith, M.D. and Wilen, J.E. (2003) 'Economic impacts of marine reserves: The importance of spatial behaviour', *Journal of Environmental Economics and Management*, vol 46, pp183–206

Stoate, C., Boatman, N.D., Borralho, R.J., Rio Carvalho, C., de Snoo, G.R. and Eden, P. (2001) 'Ecological impacts of arable intensification in Europe', *Journal of Environmental Management*, vol 63, pp337–365

Tscharntke, T. Klein, A.M., Kruess, A., Steffan-Dewenter. I. and Thies, C. (2005) 'Landscape perspectives on agricultural intensification and biodiversity ecosystem service management', *Ecology Letters*, vol 8, no 8, pp857–874

Winter, M. (2000) 'Strong policy or weak policy? The environmental impact of the 1992 reforms to the CAP arable regime in Great Britain', *Journal of Rural Studies*, vol 16, pp47–59

Appendix 6.A: The theoretical model

The model assumes that economic decisions (e.g. optimal allocation of inputs) for a given area of land are motivated both by levels of crop output and by the agro-ecosystem's environmental quality, reflected by the state of on-site biodiversity. Further, it is assumed that the decision-maker's objective is the maximization of the discounted present value of net profit derived from both outputs subject to the constraints imposed by the policy system. The net profit is defined as the difference between the aggregate profit (π) and the social damage (D). Note that D(B) is an exogenous policy parameter, the value of which is chosen through an unspecified policy mechanism to internalize the social cost of biodiversity loss. The profit function (π) is specified as $\pi=\pi\,(y_t,)$, where y_t represents the flow of marketable agricultural output at time t, with $\pi_y>0$, $\pi_{yy}<0$, i.e. the profit function is strictly concave. The damage function (D) is specified as $D = D(b_t)$, where b_t stands for biodiversity loss attributable to intensive use of artificial inputs, x_t, the damage function is an increasing and convex function of biodiversity loss, i.e. $D_b>0$, $D_{bb}>0$. This general formulation allows conservation investment to be interpreted as 'forgone output', either as direct current investment in conservation activities or as reduced output arising from adopting environmentally enhancing production practices. This setup reflects a subset of economic decisions that would principally affect landuse activities, and the underlying welfare that these activities generate. The 'underlying' problem is to find the optimal trade-off in the allocation of social benefits yielding services: agricultural supply and the biodiversity conservation.

Following recent studies (e.g. see Tscharntke et al, 2005), the crop production function is assumed to be positively affected by the stock of biodiversity, z_t, alongside the conventional agricultural input set x_t. In addition, the 'state of the art' of agricultural technology is captured by, a_t, as an exogenous shifter of the production possibility frontier, thus representing neutral technical progress. Normalizing the unit price of crop output, the value production function is represented by $f(x_t,z_t,a_t)$, assumed to exhibit well behaved properties, i.e. $f_i>0$, $f_{ii}<0$ for $i=x_t$, z_t and a_t. We further assume that the stock of z_t can be increased by conservation investment, c_t. In this sense, farmers choose the optimal transitional time paths of y_t and x_t, accounting for the evolution of the stock of agrobiodiversity in the agro-ecosystem. The income flow from $f(x_t, z_t, a_t)$ is then allocated to marketable output and conservation investment. That is:

$$c_t = f(x_t, z_t, a_t) - y_t \quad (6.\text{A}1)$$

By focusing on the functional diversity of species, the effect of a change in z_t, on the marginal product of x_t, is likely to be different at each level or sublevel of z_t. For example, an increase in insect or micro-organism diversity would increase the marginal product of fertilizer since it enhances soil productivity $(f_{xz}\geq0)$. Alternatively, an increase in natural vegetation diversity would decrease the marginal product of fertilizer as it increases the competition against the cultivated crops $(f_{xz}\leq0)$. Similar examples could be stated for other components of biodiversity. For simplification, the production function $f(\bullet)$ is assumed linearly separable in all its arguments.

Similarly, the biodiversity impact (or loss) function which represents social damage is expressed by $b_t=b(x_t, z_t)$. The former effect represents the impact of increasing use of conventional agricultural inputs while the latter is included to reflect the notion that the stock of biodiversity makes a positive contribution to ecological integrity, in the sense that biodiversity can enhance the ability of the agro-ecosystem to tolerate and overcome the potential adverse effects of agricultural landuse activities (Altieri, 1999). It should be noted that while z_t refers to the level (*stock*) of biodiversity in time t, b_t refers to biodiversity 'loss' (a *flow* variable). Additionally, it is assumed that at the margin, biodiversity loss increases (decreases) at an increasing (decreasing) rate due to increases in input intensification (biodiversity stock), i.e. $b_x>0$, $b_{xx}>0$, $b_z<0$, $b_{zz}>0$ and for simplicity $b_t=b(x_t, z_t)$ is assumed to be linearly separable in x_t and z_t.

The decision-maker has to choose the optimal time paths of the control variables y_t and x_t, accounting for the evolution of z_t in the agro-ecosystem. This evolution reflects biodiversity stock, conservation investments, c_t, and artificial input use, x_t, that proxies the level of intensification. This can be expressed as:

$$\dot{z} = g(z_t, c_t, x_t) \quad \text{(6.A2a)}$$

The evolution of agrobiodiversity is captured by equation (6.A2a) which can be written as a linear function since the focus here is on managed agroecosystems that are generally low in biodiversity:

$$\dot{z} = \alpha z_t + \delta c_t - \gamma x_t \quad \text{(6.A2b)}$$

where α, δ and γ are all constant parameters. The natural rate of growth of the biodiversity stock is given by $\alpha > 0$. According to equation (6.A2b), z_t is positively density dependent and it also increases by investments in conservation, δ being the rate of induced growth. The parameter δ also can be interpreted as the marginal degradation in z_t caused by increase in y_t, i.e. the opportunity cost of c_t. The biodiversity stock is also assumed to be negatively affected by input intensification, reflected by the parameter γ. It is worth noting that whilst biodiversity is considered to be natural capital, it is assumed that no depletion in biodiversity occurs as a result of its support to the production process.

The optimization problem is expressed, for a positive discount rate ($\rho>0$) as:

$$\max_{y,x,c} \Pi(y_t, b_t) = \int_{t=0}^{\infty} [\pi(y_t) - D(b_t)]e^{-\rho t} dt \quad \text{(6.A3)}$$

subject to: (1) the environmental conservation investment function (c.f. equation 1); (2) the evolution of z_t, (c.f. equation 6.A2a); (3) the impact function $b(.)$; (4) the initial condition $z(0)=z_0$; and (5) the non-negativity constraints $x \geq 0$ and $b \geq 0$. This yields the current-value Hamiltonian:

$$\tilde{H} = \pi(y_t) - D(b_t) + \varphi(\alpha z + \delta f(.) - \delta y_t - \gamma x_t) \quad \text{(6.A4)}$$

where φ is the current shadow value of biodiversity. The properties of the optimal trajectories for the state and control variables can be deduced after applying the Maximum Principle, and a subset of these properties is illustrated by a phase diagram in the (z_t, y_t) space (Figure 8.A1). The diagram depicts the joint evolution of

$\dot{z} = g(z_t, y_t)$ and $\dot{y} = h(z_t, y_t)$ as a saddle-path towards the steady state (long run) equilibrium with two convergent isosectors (labelled I and III). In the context of the current analyses, attention is focused on low-biodiversity intensive ago-ecosystems notionally represented by points within isosector I.

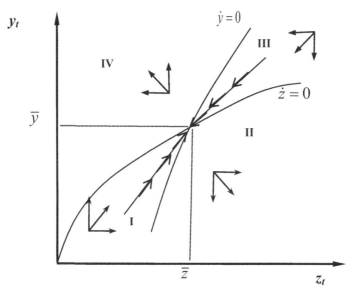

Figure 8.A1. Saddle point equilibrium in the biodiversity–marketable output (z_t, y_t) phase space
Source: Omer (2004)

In this context the effect on optimal crop output supply of a change in the stock of agrobiodiversity z_t, can be investigated from both a static and a dynamic comparative analyses perspective. It can be shown that the optimal supply of marketable output can increase (albeit at a declining rate) along the transition path to the long run equilibrium of output and biodiversity stock when the latter increases in the transition towards the steady state. On a given area of land, this implies that biodiversity and agricultural productivity are positively correlated. It can also be shown that the supply of crop output can be increased either by investing in improving the state of biodiversity-neutral agricultural technology or by enhancing the levels of biodiversity in agricultural landscapes. This means that, in principle, the decision-maker can choose between the two strategies to increase food supply in the long run. These two hypotheses and the details of the optimal solution, the properties of the optimal adjustment pathway and an analysis of the impact on agricultural output of biodiversity can be derived using a similar approach to the approach undertaken in Omer et al (2007).

Appendix 6.B: The empirical model

Under model 3, the elasticity of crop output with respect to the kth input variable can be calculated as:

$$\frac{\partial \ln E(y_{it})}{\partial p_k} = \frac{\partial \beta p}{\partial p_k} - C_{it}\left(\frac{\partial \mu_{it}}{\partial p_k}\right) \quad (6.B1a)$$

where

$$\mu_{it} = \delta_0 + \sum_j \delta_j q_{jit} + \sum_j \sum_k \delta_{jk} p_{kit} q_{jit} \quad (6.B1b)$$

$$C_{it} = 1 - \frac{1}{\sigma}\left\{\frac{\phi(\frac{\mu_{it}}{\sigma} - \sigma)}{\varphi(\frac{\mu_{it}}{\sigma} - \sigma)} - \frac{\phi(\frac{\mu_{it}}{\sigma})}{\varphi(\frac{\mu_{it}}{\sigma})}\right\}_{it} \quad (6.B1c)$$

and ϕ and φ represent the density and distribution functions of the standard normal random variable, respectively.

It follows from Battese and Broca (1997) that the elasticity of *frontier output* with respect to the kth input, $\dfrac{\partial \beta p}{\partial p_k}$, is different from the the elasticity of *TE* with respect to

the kth input: $-C_{it}\left(\dfrac{\partial \mu_{it}}{\partial p_k}\right)$.

9

Genetic Erosion and Degradation of Ecosystem Services of Wetland Rice Fields: A Case Study From Western Ghats, India

Nadesapanicker Anil Kumar, Girigan Gopi and Parameswaran Prajeesh

Lowland valleys throughout the Western Ghats region of India have traditionally been used for rice cultivation due to the availability of water and conducive soil. Kerala is a high rainfall area blessed with two monsoons—southwest and northeast. The entire year's precipitation takes place in a short span of time with heavy downpours. Due to the steep slopes and gravelly loam texture of the uplands most of the water reaches the intervening valleys as surface runoff or as sub-surface flow. The valleys then absorb this water and cushion its flow. After saturation in the valleys, water is released to the lowlands, helping to maintain water tables and enrich water bodies. Paddy is a water loving crop, and as the only crop which can survive the marshy conditions during the monsoon months its cultivation is regarded as the only sustainable agricultural land use. As an agroecosystem, the rice field provides a range of additional tangible and intangible services to the local community. These include food production, providing water for irrigation and for survival, microorganisms essential for soil health and land productivity, checking soil erosion, paving the way to genetic diversity, enhancing associated biodiversity, and sheltering species of food, fodder and medicinal value. The functions and value of a rice field depends upon its location, adjacent environment, water source and quality, biological diversity etc and, most importantly, management. Yet difficulties in converting or finding markets for these services means that the farmers who are instrumental in maintaining ecosystem services do not benefit economically. For the most part, the non-marketable benefits accrued from rice fields are enjoyed by the community as a whole.

The conversion of rice fields and dwindling diversity of rice landraces are the two biggest challenges in conserving the agrobiodiversity of Kerala. Since the mid 1970s, the area under paddy cultivation has declined approximately 70 percent (DES, undated; Nair et al, 1999). In Wayanad district where this research was undertaken, the area under rice cultivation has declined approximately 61 percent since the mid 1980s (DES, undated). Most of this can be accounted for by a shift from rice and subsistence food farming to cash cropping.

Landuse patterns are the outcome of many individual decisions by farmers in a given area. Economic factors such as market conditions, costs of production and the availability of input factors (capital, technology and labour) interact with non-economic factors including existing social structures and value systems, cultures and traditions, tenure relations and family size, to shape decisions about what to plant and how to plant it. Individual farm decisions determine household profit and well-being, landuse, credit requirements and the adoption of new technologies. They also affect issues such as prestige and leadership in the community and the long-term ecological stability of an area. This chapter deals with the particular challenges to sustainability and biodiversity created when shifting economic, technological and demographic conditions bring traditional cultures and practices which promote agrobiodiversity into conflict with pressures to diversify crops, intensify production and lift productivity.

Background: global threats to the ecosystem services provided by paddy fields

There is a conventional wisdom that markets and market economies mostly lead to socially desirable outcomes. Yet it is also well known that economic activity frequently has undesirable social and environmental consequences (Karl-Gustaf Löfgren, 1995). Pearce and Moran 1994 (see also ODA, 1991) identify two major types of failure contributing to biodiversity loss; namely, market failures and intervention failures. Market failures arise from distortion due to 'missing markets' or the inability of existing markets to capture the true value of natural resources. Divergence between the private and social values of biodiversity, and failure to capture the values of biodiversity in market transactions, are among several factors causing biodiversity loss (ODA, 1991; Perrings et al, 1992; Pearce and Moran, 1994; Swanson, 1995; Perrings, 2000). Heavy discounting of environmental goods such as biodiversity accelerates their loss (Ninan et al, 2007).

Intervention failures may be described as market distortions that arise from governmental actions (Pearce and Moran, 1994). Often, such actions are attempts to respond to economic and demographic pressures, market failures, faulty incentives and policy distortions. In developing countries, the goal of securing low food prices for the urban poor is often pursued at the expense of the interests of food producers in an attractive and stable price (Pearce and Moran, 1994). Pressure to improve living conditions and lifestyles is a major threat to biodiversity. It is acknowledged that there are trade-offs between development and biodiversity loss and that some biodiversity will be lost even if development becomes more sustainable.

One of the most substantial interventions, from the perspective of food production, was the Green Revolution, which transformed rice production throughout the world (especially in Asia) from the mid 1960s. This transformation was based on the intensification of irrigated rice production systems; that is, increased use of resources per unit of rice production area (Loevinsohn, 1985). Intensification involved the use of modern high-yielding rice varieties (traditional varieties are often considered to be low yielding in comparison with modern varieties, due largely to the ability of the latter to respond to increased applications of synthetic fertilizers and pesticides, along with increases in the number of crops grown per year enabled by the planting of short duration varieties). Production increases came from: increased land area planted with rice (32%); irrigation and double cropping (25%); fertilizers (22%); and the inherent higher yielding quality of modern varieties (21%) (Pingali and Garpacio, 1997). Increased use of machinery and pesticides were other contributing factors for improved rice productivity.

Broadly speaking, farmers and policy makers considered pesticides a guarantee against crop failure and essential to modern rice production, and chemical insecticides were widely adopted as primary agents of pest control (Pingali and Garpacio, 1997; Loevinsohn, 1985; Thresh, 1989). At the same time, intensive rice monoculture systems created an environment that was conducive to pest growth (Pingali and Garpacio, 1997). Although rice insect outbreaks have been recorded over the last 1300 years, they have become more frequent and the insect pest complexes have changed in the last three decades (Heinrichs, 1994). The long history of rice cultivation in many parts of the world allowed the evolution and maintenance of stable and balanced relationships between rice insect pests and their natural enemies, which include predators and parasitoids (Ooi and Shepard, 1994). However, broad spectrum biocides affected the natural enemies that managed insect pests. Although insecticides are known to have rapid curative action in preventing economic damage (Chelliah and Bharathi, 1994), indiscriminate use has led to the destruction of natural enemies, causing the resurgence of several primary and secondary pest species and the development of insecticide-resistant pest populations (Smith, 1994; Ooi and Shepard, 1994). Other detrimental effects of pesticide misuse include human health impairment due to direct or indirect exposure to hazardous chemicals, contamination of ground and surface waters through runoff and seepage, the transmittal of pesticide residues through the food chain (Pingali and Roger [eds.], 1995), and harmful impacts on other living organisms inhabiting the agroecosystem and surrounding habitats (Bambaradeniya, 2000; Fernando, 1996).

Changes associated with irrigation structures to enhance the efficiency of irrigation water use have also resulted in negative impacts to fauna associated with rice fields. For instance, lining irrigation canals with concrete or replacing them with pipes has resulted in the loss of habitat for a variety of aquatic invertebrate and vertebrate fauna in the rice fields of Central Japan (Fujioko and Lane, 1997; Lane and Fujioko, 1998).

Genetic erosion is a process threatening the genetic integrity of crops (Guarino, 1995). In the past decades, genetic erosion in rice genetic resources has been severe and the necessities of conservation have been emphasized (Chang 1984). A case study from the Terai community of Nepal showed that the erosion and even extinction of rice landraces had increased following ad hoc promotion of modern varieties and changes in landuse. The adoption of modern varieties in this context was based on higher yield potential, better market demand, better pricing and reduced lodging compared with local landraces. However, the loss of local crop diversity threatens local and global food security. Further, such losses are pervasive and will accelerate if no proper initiative is taken to protect them. It is necessary to develop site-specific strategies to conserve local rice diversity and enhance its use to improve the livelihoods of rural farming communities (Chaudhary et al, 2003). The combination of new conditions including rapid population growth, new agricultural techniques and high-yielding modern varieties—alongside economic and cultural changes—have led to the biological impoverishment of rice germplasm in China. In surveys conducted in Thailand between 1983 and 1991, significant erosion of the rice germplasm was reported (Chitrakon et al, 1992). In Italy, comparative surveys from the 1920s to 1950s and from the 1980s to 1990s showed that the genetic erosion rate of wheat had risen from 0.48-4 percent per annum to 13.2 percent per annum. There have been no significant differences in erosion rates between field and garden crops although there has been the impression that garden crops are better preserved over the long run (Hammer and Laghetti, 2005).

The study site: Wayanad District, Kerala, Western Ghats,

Covering an area of 125,548 square kilometres, the Western Ghats is a 1600 kilometre-long mountain chain running along the western edge of the Deccan plateau; separating the plateau from a narrow coastal plain along the Arabian Sea popularly known as the Malabar coast (Figure 9.1). The range starts in the north near the border of Gujarat and Maharashtra, south of the River Tapti, and runs through the states of Maharashtra, Goa, Karnataka, Tamil Nadu and Kerala, ending at Kanyakumari, at the southern tip of India. About sixty percent of the Western Ghats are located in the state of Karnataka. These hills cover 60,000 square kilometres and form the catchment area for a complex of river systems that drain almost 40 percent of India (Vijayan, 2007). The average elevation is around 1200 metres.

At the extreme southwest of the Indian peninsula lies the State of Kerala. Kerala enjoys unique geographical features that have made it one of the most sought after tourist destinations in Asia. Often called 'God's own country', it is bestowed with rich biodiversity and soothing weather. Wayanad district of Kerala is an east sloping, gently undulating, medium elevation plateau abruptly descending in the west to Kerala plains but merging imperceptibly with the Mysore plateau to the east. It is a UN accredited biosphere reserve with an altitude range of 750 to 2100 metres. The district is unique for its rich wealth of flora and diverse ethnic cultures. The tribal population includes ten different tribal groups which constitute 17 percent, of the total population; the highest tribal population in the State of Kerala (ORGCCI, 2001). The five dominant tribal groups are Kurichya, Mullukuruma (Kuruma), Paniya, Adiya and Kattunaikka. Others are Thachinadan Mooppan, Karimbalar, Uralikuruma, Pathiyar and Wayanadan Kadar. Wayanad also has the largest settler population in Kerala. The Jains from the adjacent state of Karnataka are believed to have arrived in the 13th century. The Nairs of adjacent districts made an entry in the 14th century, followed by Muslims. There was large-scale migration from southern Kerala in the early 1940s, most of whom were Christians.

Figure 9.1. Western Ghats and Sri Lanka political boundaries and biodiversity hotspots (Source: Adapted from cepf-stage.industrialmedium.com)

The name Wayanad is said to be derived from *Vayalnadu* meaning land (*Nadu*) of paddy fields (*Vayal*) and sometimes called *Vananadu* meaning land of forest (*Vanam*). Valleys surrounded by low range undulating hills characterize typical paddy fields in Wayanad. This district (approximately 2136 square kilometres in size) contributes significantly to the foreign exchange earnings of the State through cash crops such as pepper, cardamom, coffee, tea, ginger, turmeric, rubber and areca nut (seed of the areca palm used as a mild stimulant). The district has an area of 113,000 hectares of agricultural land, of which 1853 hectares is uncultivable. Horticultural crops cover 16,756 hectares and cash crops 65,469 hectares. The recorded area of cultivation of paddy in 1992 was 21,660 hectares. This area has since shrunk due to the rapid conversion of paddy fields to other uses.

Table 9.1. Species found within wet rice fields of Kerala

Sl No	Category	No of Species
1	Algae	34
2	Rooted and Floating plants	19
3	Zoo planktons	46
4	Birds	45
5	Weeds, Pests and Hoppers	15
6	Predators	18
7	Fishes	4
8	Amphibians	5
9	Reptiles	3
10	Associated plants	~150
	Total	**~339**

Source: Gopikuttan and Kurup, 2004; Narayanan et al, 2004; Reshmi, 2005

The Western Ghats is one of the world's ten hottest 'biodiversity hotspots'. It has over 5000 flowering plant species, 139 mammal species, 508 bird species and 179 amphibian species. At least 325 globally threatened species occur in the area (Myers et al, 2000). Paddy fields within Kerala, more specifically, are known to shelter numerous species of plants and animals of use value (see Table 9.1). The occurrence of medicinal plants is high in certain types of *Vayals* and they are the chief source of several wild food species like Sessile joy weed (*Alternanthera sessilis*), Spiny pig weed (*Amaranthus spinosus*) etc. The faunal diversity associated with paddy fields is also rich and plays a significant role in controlling harmful insects/pests. A total of 16 species of birds associated with paddy fields in Wayanad have been listed. The diversity of fish and its availability is reported to be high in paddy fields. Water-loving species like crabs, frogs and edible snails are also abundantly seen. The tribal people collect several edible greens from paddy fields (Narayanan et al, 2004). Many plants of ethno-botanical use have been listed from rice fields (Reshmi, 2005). Additional ecosystem functions associated with paddy fields in Wayanad include maintenance of fertility and productivity, hydrological cycles and water purification (Gopikuttan and Kurup, 2004).

Traditional management of rice agrobiodiversity

According to Richharia, India was once home to nearly 200,000 varieties of rice (cited in Dogra, 1991). Within Kerala, both natural and artificial selection in the different agro climatic zones have resulted in a large number of traditional varieties suited to each region in terms of traits such as resistance to biotic and abiotic stresses, ability to survive extreme agro-edaphic situations and quality attributes. The enormous variability existing in rice in Kerala consists of several wild species as well as introgressions between wild and cultivated species, primitive cultivars or landraces, commercial types, pure line selections of farmers' varieties etc. Malabar District—located in the northern half of Kerala and some coastal regions of present day Karnataka—is considered as one of the centres of origin of crops like pepper (Willis, 1966) and diversity of rice. Rice cultivation here dates back to 3000 BC (Manilal, 1990). Wayanad was endowed with a number of traditional rice varieties with a wide range of unique characters. A study by M.S. Swaminathan Research Foundation in 2000 showed that there were more than 75 traditional rice varieties cultivated throughout the district. Some of the varieties are believed to have evolved in this place and some were imported during the course of immigration of people from the plains (Tables 9.2 and 9.3).

These traditional varieties provided several kinds of insurance against crop failure. Traditional crops provide more energy in comparison to improved varieties on a per unit basis and the consumption of traditional crops helps to meet the high-energy requirements for carrying out heavy tasks in high elevation areas. Cooking quality, palatability, grain colour, aroma, calorie content, satiety (feeling of stomach fullness), medicinal qualities, high fodder and grain yield are the main attributes that influence the choice of a variety among the *Kurichiya*—a tribal community of traditional rice cultivators. Major agronomic features that influence the choice of variety are resistance to disease and pests, tolerance to flood and drought etc. Traditional varieties are composed of different traits and are better adapted to different conditions or combinations of conditions than others. They have potential for further progress in many agricultural areas, especially in those exhibiting unpredictable and/or unfavourable conditions. Traditional varieties require less external chemical inputs compared to high-yielding varieties, which reduces environmental pollution due to the indiscriminate application of chemical pesticides and fertilizers.

Tribal farmers—especially communities like the *Kurichiya*—conserve a number of traditional rice varieties which are suitable to the land they possess and vary in maturity periods. Each variety possesses unique characteristics and adaptability to biotic and abiotic stresses. The diversity of rice varieties possessed by the communities helps to meet their food, nutritional, cultural and economic requirements.

Table 9.2. Characteristics of rice varieties of Wayanad

Category	Serial no.	Name	Characteristics
Locally adapted varieties for abiotic and biotic stress	1	Veliyan (Mannu Veliyan)	Drought and flood tolerant, source of high calorie energy used in brewing home liquor and the burned husk is used as homemade tooth powder.
	2	Chettuveliyan	Flood resistant, comparatively high yield bold and red colored grain, nutritious and tasty rice, it gives a feeling of fullness when consumed, resistant to various biotic and abiotic stresses, high fodder yield along with good grain yield
	3	Palveliyan	Highly preferred for rice gruel ('Kanji'), white kernel
	4	Thondi	Tasty rice, red kernel
	5	Palthondi	Highly preferred for Kanji, white kernel
	6	Marathondi	Red and stiff rice
	7	Mullanpuncha	Drought resistant
	8	Thonnuran Thondi	Short duration, traditionally treated as famine crop, harvested in emergencies during scarce periods
	9	Kalladiyaryan	Highly drought resistant, suitable for valleys and terrains
	10	Onavattan	Tasty rice, introduced variety
	11	Chempathi	Scented rice
	12	Chomala	Highly tasty rice, white kernel, preferred for breakfast dishes during special occasions
	13	Chenthadi	Highly flood tolerant
	14	Adukkan	Tolerant to pest and disease attack and
	15	Velumbala	comparatively tolerant to drought
Holy and medicinal varieties	16	Chennellu	Used for body rejuvenation, to treat strokes,
	17	Navara	stomach ulcers, vomiting etc, this rice is considered the king among traditional rices
Scented varieties	18	Kaima	Preferred for preparing breakfast dishes and ghee rice
	19	Urunikaima	Preferred for preparing breakfast dishes
	20	Mullankaima	Used during special occasions in the family
	21	Poothadikaima	Strong aroma, preferred for preparing beaten rice
	22	Gandhakasala	Preferred for Biriyani and Payasam in
	23	Jeerakasala	special occasions in the family

Table 9.3. Status of traditional rice varieties cultivated in Wayanad District

Variety	Status		Variety	Status	
	Available	Lost		Available	Lost
Anakkomban		X	Manjuvari		X
Aryan		X	Mannuveliyan	✓	
Aryankali		X	Marathondi	✓	
Athiyan		X	Mullanpuncha	✓	
Bhoothakali		X	Mullanmunda		X
Chembavu		X	Mundon		X
Chempathi	✓		Njavara	✓	
Chenthadi	✓		Onavattan	✓	
Chennellu	✓		Onganpuncha		X
Cheriyakaima		X	Paalathira		X
Cheriyaryan		X	Padukuliyan		X
Cheruvellari		X	Palachemban		X
Chettuveliyan	✓		Palliyat		X
Chitteni		X	Palthondi	✓	
Chomala	✓		Palveliyan	✓	
Chuvannamodan		X	Parambuvattan		X
Gandhakasala	✓		Peruvazha		X
Jeerakasala	✓		Ponnarimala		X
Kaima	✓		Ponnaryan		X
Kakkathondi		X	Poothadikaima	✓	
Kalladiyaran	✓		Poothala		X
Kalluruthi		X	Puncha		X
Kannichennellu		X	Rajani		X
Karavala		X	Thaichoonal		X
Karyamkari		X	Thavalakkannan		X
Karumkaima		X	Thekkencheera		X
Karuthan		X	Thondi	✓	
Kattamodan		X	Thonnooranthondi	✓	
Kochootti		X	Unrunikaima	✓	
Kochuvithu		X	Valichoori		X
Kodaguveliyan		X	Valiyakaima	✓	
Kodiyan		X	Vattan		X
Kothandan		X	Velumbala	✓	
Kozhivalan		X	Veliyan	✓	
Kumbalon		X	Vellari		X
Kuttadan		X	Villi		X
Kuttiveliyan		X	Wayanadan Thondi		X
Morandan		X			

Source: Anon., 2001

Socio-cultural aspects of conservation

According to historical documents and orally transmitted legacies, shifting cultivation (slash and burn) was the first form of cultivation in Wayanad. Millet was the main crop along with upland rice. Later, the popularization of plantation crops and changes in tenure relations paved the way for the gradual disappearance of shifting cultivation.

The Kurichiya were the first agricultural tribe to settle in Wayanad District (Aiyappan and Mahadevan, 1990). Settled agriculture began with rice cultivation in the valleys and swampy areas of the foothills. Flat valleys (relatively scarce) were conventionally used for rice cultivation. Tall and water tolerant varieties were cultivated in the valleys. Swamp and waterlogged areas were largely converted for rice cultivation. Two crops were cultivated per year—*Nancha* (rain crop) and *Puncha* (summer crop) depending on the availability of water.

At present, rice cultivation is confined to mainly tribal dominated areas of the district. Traditional wisdom, value, principle, social structure, family system, taste and preference etc contribute to rice cultivation among them. The Kurichiya and Kuruma are the two major tribal communities practising rice cultivation in the district. They own land and follow traditional methods of cultivation. The Paniya and Adiya are traditionally landless and dependent on rice cultivation for employment.

The Kurichiya and Kuruma are especially focused traditionally on cultivation of paddy to satisfy multiple needs including food and fodder, fuel, thatching material, employment, beliefs and cultural sentiments. Most of the cultural traditions and customs of these tribes were closely associated with paddy fields. They also had depended on paddy fields for a number of other services, collecting green leafy vegetables, fish, trapping of birds and animals for food etc. Rice cultivation is a labour intensive work and the cost of labour can account for a major portion of the total cost of cultivation. Paddy cultivation was thus traditionally a joint occupation with both Kurichiya and Kuruma adopting social structures and norms to share labour (Sasikumar,1996a, 1996b).

Rice is an integral part of the culture and traditions of the tribal communities. According to traditional beliefs, obeying traditions and rituals brings prosperity and well-being for the family; pleasing the deities in order to save crops from natural calamities, wild animals and the outbreak of pest and diseases. Cultivation of certain traditional varieties is central to following the rituals. For example, a rice variety called Chennellu is an inevitable offering to God; Veliyan is for community feasts.

Traditional wisdom is another factor that contributes to rice cultivation. The classification of *Vayals* into three types, namely *Kuni Vayal, Kundu Vayal* and *Koravu Vayal* on basis of soil texture, mud content, percolation and retention of water, fertility of land and location of the field is a fine example of prudent land and water management. Management based on this classification helps the Kurichiya in efficient utilization of physical and human resources. The Kurichiya developed management practices in line with the availability of physical resources in each

Vayal type and cultivated diverse traditional varieties in each of such type. They used drought tolerant, short duration varieties for *Kuni Vayal* since water holding capacity is low there; flood tolerant, medium duration varieties in *Kundu Vayal*; and long duration, flood resistant varieties for *Koravu Vayal*.

In order to utilize maximum available labour, different varieties of traditional rice with different maturity periods were selected. Since transplanting requires more labour, varieties with different durations helped them to adjust days of transplantation. Long duration varieties were sown first, followed by medium duration varieties and then short duration ones last in the season; thereby making maximum utilization of labour and the natural resources of the field throughout the year.

Threats to the survival of rice genetic diversity in Wayanad

Paddy cultivation all over Kerala, but especially in Wayanad, is under tremendous pressure of large-scale conversion to non-food grain cultivation and for other commercial purposes. The ratio between cash crop and food crop in the year 1973 was 30:70. By the end of the 1990s this had reversed to a ratio of 70:30. Low returns are a major cause for conversion. Rice cultivation is taken up now in more and more isolated pockets; mostly by tribal communities like Kurichiya or Kuruma for their own consumption irrespective of the profit or loss. Urbanization, increased demand for land for non-agricultural purposes, and changed dietary preferences have also led to conversion of paddy fields. Indiscriminate conversion of rice fields, in turn, makes continued rice cultivation of remaining lands more difficult—concentrating disturbances from birds, pests and diseases in smaller areas—and paves the way for genetic erosion. As Table 9.3 shows, of the 75 known traditional rice varieties once grown in Wayanad, only 20 are still available to farmers.

Cultural change

As mentioned above, Nairs, early Jain settlers and the tribal communities including Kuichiya, Kuruma and Wayanadan chettys were the main landlords of Wayanad who controlled the paddy fields. The concept of individual property ownership was unknown to tribal communities.

Kurichiya households traditionally did not adopt mechanization or utilize outside labour for paddy cultivation but exclusively depended on unpaid family labour, especially women's labour (Girigan et al, 2004). There prevails a gender-based division of labour in paddy cultivation whereby men do the ploughing and women do the transplanting and weeding (Sasikumar,1996a). It is customary for all the members to take part in agricultural operations, which reduces labour costs considerably. Under the joint family system, property rights are vested in the collective ownership of family members. The chieftain of the family has the right to make decisions in consultation with other members of the family. Since food security is the prime concern of the family, available land is used mainly for the cultivation of food crops, especially rice. This joint family system, however, is being progressively weakened in favour of a nuclear family system, due to interaction with mainstream communities and other reasons. This leads to joint family property being divided among members. Due to fragmentation and uneconomic holdings, family members increasingly prefer cultivation of cash crops for securing more income, paving the way for conversion of rice fields to other less labour intensive, but economically more profitable crops.

The Kuruma traditionally lived in uni-ethnic settlements and shared labour within the community to reduce paid labour costs. However, due to various reasons including the nuclear family set up, increasing cost of living, imitation of more mainstream lifestyles etc, Kuruma in various parts of the district are starting to opt for more profitable alternative crops. The tendency to abandon conventional norms is more prevalent among younger and more educated Kuruma, weakening the tradition of rice cultivation.

They believe the performance of rituals will bring good harvests and ensure food security of the household. Both Kurichiya and Kuruma communities had strictly followed all these customs in the past. However, the new generation among them is generally less interested in the continuance of such traditions. Often, they allocate a small piece of land for rice cultivation for the sake of the rituals and the rest of the land is used for cultivation of cash crops. The size of the land for rice cultivation depends on the decision-making power of the senior members of the family.

Land partition has major implications for biodiversity. In many cases, those farmers still cultivating rice are not able to act as germplasm saviours for traditional varieties due to the small amount of land they have inherited. Naturally, for economic sustainability, they are attracted towards the new generation short duration crops. Moreover, people are attracted to characteristics of the new hybrids such as high yield and disease and pest tolerance, which they regard as major advantages over the comparatively poor yield and profitability of traditional varieties. Another important factor has been the decline of straw roofed huts and consequently the demand for rice straw from tall varieties. Growth of urban areas, changes in cultural and nutritional habits, and increased population have also contributed to biodiversity erosion.

Relative profitability

In Kerala, production of paddy is sufficient to meet only one third of the State's demand (Narayanan, 1994). In an open market, this would lead to high prices and encourage more farmers to cultivate rice. However, prices are kept artificially low by government measures including the public distribution system and the deregulation of rice imports from other parts of the country. This has made rice cultivation uneconomical at the prevailing price.

Increasing costs of production and consequent decline in net profit is another important reason for the decline in area under rice cultivation. Over the past two decades, costs of production, especially labour costs, have risen disproportionately to the price of paddy. While the price of paddy increased by around three times during the period 1970-71 to 1988-89, the cost of labour registered almost a six fold increase (Narayanan 1994). Farmers have been faced with the dual problems of labour scarcity—as potential workers shift to other industries—and demands among remaining workers for higher wages.

Similarly the relative price of rice rose more slowly than the prices for alternative crops. Average farm prices of paddy in Kerala for the period between 1970-71 to 1987-88 registered an increase of 178 percent compared with banana (306%), pepper (615%), ginger (4960%), coconut (394%), Tapioca (474%), cashew nut (683%) and rubber (313%) (DES, undated). Because of the unfavourable relative price, cultivators have shifted to other profitable crops. This has its own significance in the context of Wayanad and other parts of the Western Ghats region, where valleys were mainly converted for banana, areca nut, ginger and coconut cultivation. Cost benefit analysis reveals that banana provides a net income nearly 17 times greater than that of paddy. Despite requiring an investment three times higher than that of paddy, banana returns a profit on that investment of 115 percent compared with only 23 percent for rice cultivation.

New initiatives for rice biodiversity conservation

The Protection of Plant Varieties and Farmers' Rights Authority (PPV&FR authority, Ministry of Agriculture, New Delhi, India), under the provisions of the Gene Fund of the PPV&FR Act 2001, recognized the Kurichya and Kuruma tribal communities of Wayanad for their collective efforts in the conservation of novel rice germplasm. They have been honoured with the Second Plant Genome Savior Community Recognition Award for the year 2008, for their efforts in the conservation of 20 unique rice germplasms (see Table 9.2). The Wayanad District Tribal Development Action Council under the aegis of the Community Agrobiodiversity Centre of M.S. Swaminathan Research Foundation submitted the application for the award. These communities of farmers were identified for the award by the authority through a process of public announcement and examination by an expert committee. In the near future, the Community Agrobiodiversity Centre will be undertaking additional activities to conserve these 20 rice varieties, including selection and purification of quality seed materials, multiplication by farmer participatory action and, finally, elevating market potential for delicious Wayanadan red rices like Veliyan, Adukkan and specialty varieties like Kayama, Gandhakasala, Jeerakasala etc. The Wayanad District Tribal Development Action Council members will be ambassadors for these varieties, facilitating seed distribution and popularizing the cultivation of these treasures.

Conclusion

Kerala is gifted with rich rice diversity. The rural and tribal farmers of Kerala used to cultivate hundreds of traditional rice varieties to satisfy their dietary, economic and other requirements. Most of these varieties have either disappeared or are on the verge of disappearance because of poor profitability, lack of quality seeds, low yields, and a paucity of pragmatic research and extension support. When most of the farmers exploit the resources for immediate benefits only, the sanctity of the agricultural tradition will be in great trouble. Farmers' practical knowledge about local ecosystems was usually reflected in their farming technologies. However, the obligatory shift in economic, technological and demographic conditions demands increasingly rapid adjustments in farming systems. As a result, conventional science based research and extension with high levels of external inputs gained popularity. The emphasis has been on intensification and diversification so as to enhance productivity, without caring for sustainability. Even though such practices lead the way to high economic profitability, the sustainability of natural resources has been fading over the years.

This study suggests it is necessary to bring back the traditions in order to sustainably interact with nature so as to conserve natural resources for future generations. Also, the variability in diversity which assures the stability of the population must be conserved and used in appropriate ways in order to provide source materials to realize future demand for new varieties. It is correctly said that there are no free lunches for diversity. Given our limited resources, preservation of diversity in one context can only be accomplished at some real opportunity cost in terms of well-being forgone in other spheres of life, including, possibly, loss of diversity somewhere else in the system. As Weitzman (1993) points out, the implementation of injunctions to preserve diversity are hampered by the lack of appropriate operational objectives and frameworks for research which respect and capitalize on traditions that enhance sustainability.

References

Aiyappan, A. and Mahadevan, K. (1990) *Ecology, Economy, Matriliny and Fertility of Kurichias*, B.R. Publishing Corporation, Delhi

Anon (2001) *Phase I Completion Report on Conservation, Enhancement and Sustainable and Equitable Use of Biodiversity*, submitted to the Swiss Agency for Development and Co-operation, M.S. Swaminathan Research Foundation, Chennai, New Delhi

Bambaradeniya, C.N.B. (2000) 'Ecology and biodiversity in an irrigated rice field ecosystem in Sri Lanka', PhD Thesis, University of Peradeniya, Sri Lanka

Chang T.T. (1984) 'Conservation of rice genetic resources: Luxury or necessity?', *Science*, vol 224, pp251–256

Chaudhary, P., Gauchan, D. Rana, R.B., Sthapit, B.R. and Jarvis, D.I. (2003) 'Potential loss of rice landraces from a Terai community in Nepal: A case study from Kachorwa, Bara, *Plant Genetic Resources Newsletter*, no 137, pp14–21

Chelliah, S. and Bharathi, M. (1994) 'Insecticide management in rice', in E.A. Heinrichs (ed) *Biology and Management of Rice Insects*, Wiley, New Delhi, India and International Rice Research Institute, Manila, Philippines, pp657–680

Chitrakon, S., Sato, Y.I., Morishima, H. and Shimamoto, Y. (1992) 'Genetic erosion of rice in Thailand', *Rice Genetics Newsletter*, vol 9, pp73–74

DES (Department of Economics and Statistics) (undated), 'Agricultural Statistics, 1970-71 to 1987-89', Government of Kerala, Thiruvananthapuram, India, www.kerala.gov.in/statistical, accessed 14 August 2009

Dogra, B. (1991) *The Life and Work of Dr. R.H. Richharia*, B. Dogra, New Delhi, India

Fernando, C.H. (1996) 'Ecology of rice fields and its bearing on fisheries and fish culture', in S.S. de Silva (ed) *Perspectives in Asian Fisheries*, Asian Fisheries Society, Manila, Philippines, pp217–237

Fujioko, M. and Lane, J.S. (1997) 'The impact of changing irrigation practices in rice fields on frog populations on the Kanto Plain, Central Japan', *Ecological Research*, vol 12, pp101–108

Girigan, G., Kumar, N.A. and Arivudai Nambi, V. (2004) 'Vayals: A traditional classification of agricultural landscapes', *LEISA India*, vol 6, no 4, pp27–28

Gopikuttan, G. and Parameswara Kurup K.N. (2004) *Paddy Land Conversion in Kerala, An Inquiry Into Ecological and Economic Aspects in a Midland Watershed Region*, Final Report, Kerala Research Program on Local Level Development, Centre for Development Studies, Thiruvananthapuram, India

Guarino, L. (1995) 'Assessing the threat of genetic erosion', in L. Guarino, V.R. Rao and R. Reid (eds) *Collecting Plant Genetic Diversity: Technical Guidelines*, CABI Publishing, Wallingford pp67–74

Hammer, K. and Laghetti, G. (2005) 'Genetic erosion: Examples from Italy', *Genetic Resources and Crop Evolution*, vol 52, no 5, pp629–634

Heinrichs, E.A. (1994) 'Rice', in E.A. Heinrichs (ed) *Biology and Management of Rice Insects*, Wiley, New Delhi, India and International Rice Research Institute, Manila, Philippines, pp1–12

Löfgren, K-G. (1995) 'Markets and externalities', in H. Folmer, H.L. Gabel, and H. Opschoor (eds.) *Principles Of Environmental And Resource Economics, A Guide for Students and Decision-Makers*, Edward Elgar, Cheltenham, UK

Lane, J.S. and Fujioko, M. (1998) 'The impact of changing irrigation practices on the distribution of foraging egrets and herons (Ardeidae) in the rice fields of Central Japan', *Biological Conservation*, vol 83, pp221–230

Loevinsohn, M. (1985) 'Agricultural intensification and rice pest ecology: Lessons and implications', Paper presented at the *International Rice Research Conference*, 1–5 June, 1985, International Rice Research Institute, Los Banos, Philippines

Manilal, K.S. (1990) 'Ethnobotany of the rices of Malabar', in S.K. Jain (ed) *Contribution to Indian Ethnobotany*, Scientific Publishers, Jodhpur, pp243–253

Myers, N., Mittermeier, R.A., Mittermeier, C.G., Da Fonseca, G.A.B. and Kent, J. (2000) 'Biodiversity hotspots for conservation priorities', *Nature*, vol 403, pp853–858

Nair, K.N.S, Gopalakrishnan, R., Menon, R.V.G., Kannan, K.P. and Padmakumar, K.G. (1999) *Report of the Expert Committee on Paddy Cultivation in Kerala, Vol 1. Main Report, Government of Kerala, Thiruvananthapuram*, India, pp61–62

Narayanan, N. C. (1994) 'Towards operationalizing the concept of sustainable land use: A micro level study of valley landforms in Thrissur, Kerala', in A. Agarwal (ed) *The Challenge of the Balance*, Centre for Science and Environment, New Delhi

Narayanan Ratheesh, M.K., Swapna, M. P. and Kumar, N.A (2004) *Gender Dimensions of Wild Food Management in Wayanad, Kerala*, M.S. Swaminathan Research Foundation, Chennai, India, www.mssrf.org/bd/ebooks/ebook5.pdf , accessed 14 August 2009

Ninan, K.N., Jyothis, S., Babu, P. and Ramakrishnappa, V. (2007) *The Economics of Biodiversity Conservation: Valuation in Tropical Forest Ecosystems*, Earthscan, London

Ooi, P.A.C. and Shepard, B.M. (1994) 'Predators and parasitoids of rice insects', in E.A. Heinrichs (ed) *Biology and Management of Rice Insects*, Wiley, New Delhi, India and International Rice Research Institute, Manila, pp 613–656.

ORGCCI (Office of the Registrar General and Census Commissioner, India (2001) *Census of India 2001*, Government of India, New Delhi

ODA (Overseas Development Administration) (1991) *Biological Diversity and Developing Countries: Issues and Options*, Natural Resources and Environment Department, Overseas Development Administration, London

Pearce, D. and Moran, D. (1994) *The Economic Value of Biodiversity*, Earthscan, London

Perrings, C. (2000) *The Economics of Biodiversity Conservation in Sub-Saharan Africa: Mending the Ark*, Edward Elgar, Cheltenham

Perrings, C., Folke, C. and Mäler, K.G. (1992) 'The ecology and economics of biodiversity loss: The research agenda', *Ambio*, vol 21, no 3, pp201–211

Pingali, P.L. and Roger, P.A. (eds) (1995) *Impact of Pesticides on Farmer Health and Rice Environment*, Kluwer and International Rice Research Institute, Manila

Pingali, P.L. and Gerpacio, R.V. (1997) 'Living with reduced insecticide use for tropical rice in Asia', *Food Policy*, vol 22, no 2, pp107–118

Reshmi, D. (2005) 'Ethnobotany of flowering plant diversity associated with paddy fields: A case from Wayanad', M.Sc. Dissertation, University of Calicut, India

Sasikumar, M. (1996a) 'Kurichya', in T. Menon and M. Madhava (eds) *The Encyclopedia of Dravidian Tribes*, vol 2, The International School of Dravidian Linguistics, Thiruvananthapuram, India, pp 159–168

Sasikumar, M. (1996b) 'Mullukuruma', in T. Menon and M. Madhava (eds) *The Encyclopedia of Dravidian Tribes*, vol 2, The International School of Dravidian Linguistics, Thiruvananthapuram, India, 276–285

Smith, C.M. (1994) 'Integration of rice insect control strategies and tactics', in E.A. Heinrichs (ed) *Biology and Management of Rice Insects*, Wiley, New Delhi and International Rice Research Institute, Manila, pp681–692.

Swanson, T.M. (ed) (1995) *The Economics and Ecology of Biodiversity Decline: The Forces Driving Global Change*, Cambridge University Press, New York, NY

Thresh, J.M. (1989) 'Insect-borne viruses of rice and the green revolution', *Tropical Pest Management*, vol 35, no 3, pp264–272

Vijayan, V.S. (2007) 'Research needs for the Western Ghats', Ashoka Trust for Research in Ecology and the Environment (ATREE), www.westernghatsforum.org/abstract_12_05.pdf, accessed 30 November 2008

Weitzman, M.L. (1993) '"What to preserve": An application of Diversity Theory to Crane Conservation, *Quarterly Journal of Economics*, vol 108, pp157–183

Willis, J.C. (1966) *A Dictionary of the Flowering Plants and Ferns*, 7th Edn, Revised by H.K. Airy Shaw, Cambridge University Press, Cambridge

10

Environmental Certification: Standardization for Diversity

Tad Mutersbaugh and Dan Klooster

Prompted by ethical concerns, food safety scares and awareness of environmental issues such as biodiversity loss, grassroots organizations, industry coalitions, NGOs, governmental agencies and transnational institutions have contributed to the development of production standards, auditing processes and certification systems. Among the best-known of these are organic certification of agriculture and food processing, Fair Trade, and the Forest Stewardship Council (FSC) approach to the environmental certification of forests. These instruments combine a set of defined social and/or environmental standards, an auditing and certification procedure, and a label indicating that certified products come from fields, forests, fisheries and/or factories where production practices meet the required standards (Mutersbaugh et al, 2005). Certification serves multiple purposes. Environmental NGOs look to certification to influence and regulate global production systems in ways that national governments either can't, or won't. Producers utilize certification to protect their livelihoods against the pressures of global commodity chains.

In this chapter, we examine organic certification and forest certification in Mexico in order to understand how certification systems affect farm and forest-level biodiversity and to clarify the specific impacts of the international standardization of environmental certification procedures. Organic and forest certification have impressive global reach, both geographically and institutionally. Both unite producers in biodiversity-rich areas of the Global South with relatively well-off consumers in the Global North, and both are incorporated, directly and indirectly, into national and transnational governmental regulatory structures and international development strategies. Mexico has come to the fore—along with Costa Rica—as a global centre for certified production. Besides organic and forestry certification, there are also extensive (government mediated) environmental services certifications in watershed protection, carbon sequestration and endemic species conservation, among others. In part, this arises from the close integration of Mexico into the North American Free Trade Agreement (NAFTA) and from Mexico's 'upper middle income' status that, relative to most nations of the Global

South, permits the Mexican government to subsidize costly conservation activities. Another important factor is the high degree of rural organization, with large numbers of semi-collective landholding 'corporate' communities, ejidal authorities, and peasant confederations that provide an institutional basis for administratively-intensive rural product certifications. In this regard, our case study locations reflect a confluence of factors that have made Mexico a global centre of experimentation in certification.

It will be argued that the contribution of certification schemes to producers' livelihoods plays a key role in the uptake of certification, the biodiversity management strategies that producers subsequently employ and, consequently, the coverage and impact of these schemes. First, we outline the matrix ecology perspective which will be used in the chapter to contextualize people and productive land uses within a broader conservation strategy. Next, we examine the biodiversity implications of evolving practice for organic certification of coffee and forest certification in Mexico. Finally, we identify the key limitations of environmental certification as a biodiversity conservation strategy and discuss the implications for improving biodiversity benefits. This will highlight a need for explicit coordination between certification practices and landscape-scale biodiversity conservation strategies.

Conservation beyond protected areas: certification, matrix ecology and biodiversity

Effective protection of biodiversity, including 'wild' biodiversity, requires the extension of conservation efforts beyond the 'territorial' approach of national parks, biosphere reserves and other protected areas (Zimmerer, 2006). Certified production provides a 'non-territorial' complement to protected areas. Quite apart from the importance of biodiversity within and among deliberately cultivated species, this hybrid vision recognizes: first, that landscape-level biodiversity provides important ecosystem services to agriculture and forestry; and second, that fields and forests managed to protect biodiversity serve to complement core protected areas by improving their ecological functioning and providing buffer zones between these areas and environmentally destructive conventional farming and forest management practices. In contrast with 'fortress conservation' (Brockington, 2002), the non-territorial approach of certified agriculture and forestry provides politically, socially and economically feasible options in areas where biodiversity loss is of concern, but vacating people to set up reserves raises issues related to social justice, food security, the capacity of the state to pay for and manage reserves, and so on (Zerner, 2000; Zimmerer and Bassett, 2003).

A managed-production approach to conservation is supported by recent research in matrix ecology (Vandermeer and Perfecto, 2007, 2008). This research examines biodiversity in the context of landscapes comprised of multiple ecologically unique patches (such as a stand of old-growth forest, a wetland or rocky outcrop) embedded within a more generalized matrix of vegetation communities (such as agricultural fields or managed forests). Within this patch-and-matrix landscape, overall landscape biodiversity (gamma biodiversity) arises as the product of several nested forms of biodiversity. These include alpha diversity (the number of distinct species *within* each patch) and beta or 'rollover' diversity (the number of species within a distinct group or genus spread across patches within a specified landscape).

Alpha, beta and gamma biodiversity are all significantly affected by matrix quality, which is defined as a matrix capable of supporting the movement of plants and animals between patches. Modelling studies show that relatively high matrix quality supports high beta and alpha biodiversity by allowing plant and animal populations to interact across space, share gene pools and replenish populations in the event of localized population extinction (Vandermeer and Perfecto, 2007). High-quality matrices also help to foster competition and niche separation between species. To provide an example, a high-quality matrix of organic coffee could support frog biodiversity by providing a supportive habitat that permits frogs to move between riparian zones—thereby allowing them to replenish declining populations—yet also be sufficiently uninviting so as to discourage a single frog species from becoming too dominant. By contrast, low quality matrices dominated by agricultural or forest monocultures form a biologically homogeneous 'sea' that prevents population interaction and results in species extinction even when the patches are relatively large and geographically proximate to extensive reserves (Bhagwat et al, 2005).

A matrix-ecological perspective suggests that patch-and-matrix strategies which retain farmers, foresters (and herders) on the land can provide levels of landscape biodiversity protection and conservation greater than those provided by exclusionary reserve strategies. At the same time, matrix ecology reinforces concerns about the conservation of agrobiodiversity (Brookfield, 2001; Zimmerer, 2006). Recent empirical work has established that a heterogeneous agricultural matrix better supports movement between patches (Perfecto et al, 2005; Philpott et al, 2008). Biodiverse production zones characterized by both a high degree of intra-specific diversity and a high species diversity cultivated as polycultures may, therefore, contribute to the conservation of species in embedded patches and nearby uncultivated areas. In fact, the tendency of traditional farming, forestry and forage practices in use since before the era of agrochemical-based production to generate spatially heterogeneous agroecological landscapes at a number of scales (Padoch and Peters, 1993; Padoch et al, 1998; Zimmerer, 1999) may be responsible for much of the endemic biodiversity that reserves seek to protect.

Is it then possible to create and certify standards of practice or measures of matrix quality that will foster biodiversity conservation? Certainly, it is possible to devise standards based upon agroecological research, and many earlier organic standards included requirements for maintaining biodiversity in, for example, coffee plot shade canopies. However, the increasing involvement of governments and transnational institutions over the last decade or so in the development and international harmonization of standards and certification procedures has raised concerns about the weakening of ecological provisions and the removal of sensitivity to local agroecologies.

Forest certification

Forest certification is the process of evaluating forests or woodlands to determine if they are being managed according to an agreed set of standards. The most influential program is the Forest Stewardship Council; a multi-stakeholder institution that combines environmentalists, social activists and private sector actors involved in forest management and wood product manufacture and retailing. As of 25 May 2009, the FSC had issued 982 certificates in 82 countries, covering nearly 114 million hectares; equivalent to more than 7 percent of the world's productive forests (FSC, 2009a). More than 200 million hectares have been certified by competing industry-led and government-led certification systems, but most environmental groups prefer to endorse the FSC due to questions over the rigor and legitimacy of other forest certification systems.

A brief history of the FSC

The FSC grew out of a 1980s global movement to govern forest management through boycotts of tropical woods and direct action campaigns against wood retailers and logging companies (Cashore et al, 2004; Klooster, 2005). Critics of that strategy noted that policies to discourage logging could perniciously encourage deforestation by giving land managers incentives to convert forests to pasture and export crops that were not the focus of boycotts. Interest grew in environmental certification and labelling programs that consumers could use to identify products from well-managed forests; creating a reverse boycott and rewarding sound forest management (Conroy, 2007). Following the failure of the Rio Earth Summit to produce a binding inter-governmental forest agreement, 130 participants from 26 countries, including wood users, retailers, forest management companies, and social and environmental interest groups came together to establish the FSC and the first iteration of the FSC International Standard was released in 1993 (FSC, 2002).

From its initiation, the FSC developed a transnational scale of operation. The ambition was to become the world's preferred forest management standard and through this to establish a new paradigm for global forest management that is reflected in consumer demand (FSC, 2006). Environmental organizations began pressuring retailers such as Home Depot (self-described as the world's largest home improvement retailer) to make commitments to purchase only certified wood. At the same time, national buyers' groups and industry-based Global Forest and Trade Networks integrated private sector wood users and retailers who pledged to buy and sell FSC-certified wood. As major retailers and wood users committed to buying only certified wood, they pressured their suppliers to certify. Meanwhile, the WWF, the World Bank, and national governmental agencies also promoted forest certification among forest managers and wood processors, sometimes subsidizing the costs of evaluations and forest management improvements. Both the number of forest certificates and the area of certified forests grew rapidly (Klooster, 2005).

The FSC develops principles, criteria and indicators of sound forest management which reflect the multi-stakeholder nature of the organization. The initial set of principles and criteria was developed during three years of internal negotiations, with economic, social, and environmental interests equally represented. Despite the compromises resulting from this multi-stakeholder process, advocates consider this to be the strongest set of standards that could be developed politically (Conroy, 2007, p84). The FSC maintains the principles and criteria for certifiable forest management and oversees an explicitly inclusive process of revising and updating them (Klooster, 2009). The FSC (undated) summarizes its principles and criteria as:

1. Compliance with all applicable laws and international treaties.
2. Demonstrated and uncontested, clearly defined, long-term land tenure and use rights.
3. Recognition and respect of indigenous peoples' rights.
4. Maintenance or enhancement of long-term social and economic well-being of forest workers and local communities and respect of workers' rights in compliance with International Labour Organization (ILO) conventions.
5. Equitable use and sharing of benefits derived from the forest.
6. Reduction of environmental impact of logging activities and maintenance of the ecological functions and integrity of the forest.
7. Appropriate and continuously updated management plan.
8. Appropriate monitoring and assessment activities to assess the condition of the forest, management activities and their social and environmental impacts.
9. Maintenance of High Conservation Value Forests (HCVFs) defined as environmental and social values that are considered to be of outstanding significance or critical importance.
10. In addition to compliance with all of the above, plantations must contribute to reduce the pressures on and promote the restoration and conservation of natural forests.

FSC and biodiversity conservation

Many FSC standards address biodiversity directly or indirectly. Ten core principles and 56 criteria inform FSC management standards, including a growing number of national and regional interpretations (FSC, 2002; FSC, 2008). Basically, the standards prohibit conversion of forests or any other natural habitat, require respect for workers' rights and indigenous peoples, and require that culturally important sites, sacred sites, and high conservation value forests be specifically identified and carefully managed.

Principle 1, Compliance with Laws and FSC Principles, for example, requires forest management operators to respect all applicable national laws in the country in which operations are based together with 'international treaties and agreements to which the country is a signatory' such as the Convention of Biological Diversity (FSC, 2002, p4). According to Principle 6, Environmental Impact:

Forest management shall conserve biological diversity and its associated values, water resources, soils, and unique and fragile ecosystems and landscapes, and, by so doing, maintain the ecological functions and the integrity of the forest (FSC, 2002, p6).

Criteria for this principle include requirements to protect species of special concern by protecting key habitats and establishing conservation areas appropriate to the scale, intensity, and uniqueness of the affected resource. Forest managers must also control hunting and take measures to maintain forest ecological functions such as regeneration, succession, and genetic diversity. Other criteria include the stipulation that forest managers map and protect representative samples of existing ecosystems, appropriate to the scale and intensity of operations and the uniqueness of the affected resources. They must also develop written guidelines to minimize the environmental impact of logging on soils, vegetation, and water resources.

Principle 7 requires a forest management plan. Criteria require the plan to include a profile of adjacent lands, an explicit rationale for logging methods, resource inventories, monitoring of forest response, the identification of rare, threatened, and endangered species, and maps, including maps of protected areas. Principle 9 addresses high conservation value forests. It stipulates that:

> management activities in high conservation value forests shall maintain or enhance the attributes which define such forests. Decisions regarding high conservation value forests shall always be considered in the context of a precautionary approach (FSC, 2002, p.9).

Criteria require the management plan to include measures that maintain or enhance the conservation value of such forests, including a monitoring program.

These standards affect forest management practice through a system of independent inspections and audits. Accreditation Services International, an independent organization, uses FSC principles and criteria to accredit third party inspection and auditing firms. Responding to requests from forest management operations, auditing firms inspect management plans, visit forests, and consult with forest workers, surrounding communities, environmental authorities and other stakeholders to determine if management upholds the FSC principles. Upon certification, forest management companies can sell their wood with a label attesting to its well-managed source. Frequently, auditing firms award certification with conditions—called Corrective Action Requests (CARs)—that specific management improvements be made within a given timeframe. In the Mexican state of Oaxaca, CARs have required forestry operations to modify their forest management plans to take into account the needs of threatened and endangered species, to map priority areas for conserving animal habitat, and to establish procedures to monitor species diversity as logged sites regenerate (see public summaries posted to SmartWood, 2009).

The initial intensive evaluation is the basis for a five year certificate, contingent on annual on-site audits to ensure continued adherence to FSC principles and compliance with any CARs requested during the certification audit. Failure to comply with CARs can eventually result in suspension of the certification. Similarly, sawmills, furniture plants, paper mills and other wood-transforming organizations can request chain-of-custody certification which permits them to attach a label to products manufactured from certified wood. Figure 10.1 illustrates the FSC system of standards, audits, and certification.

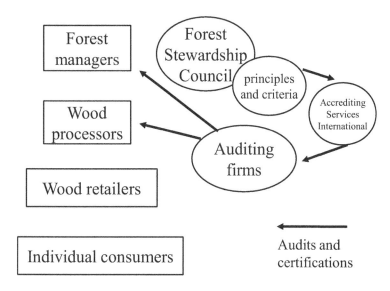

Figure 10.1. How Forest Stewardship Council certification works

The FSC and conservation organizations have recently made efforts to clarify and systematize the process of identifying and managing High Conservation Value Forests as mentioned in Principle 9 (FSC, 2009b). Recent evaluations and audits have consequently resulted in numerous CARs that have required forestry operations to synthesize available information on the conservation values of their forests, consult with specialists, and recruit universities, government agencies and NGOs to identify, map, and develop plans for monitoring the flora and fauna of HCVFs. The community of San Pedro el Alto, for example, responded to the requirements of Principle 9 by contracting a study of HCVFs in its management area to identify and map the distribution of protected species. The auditors noted that:

> other protective measures include[d] the protection of water courses and amphibian habitats, the prohibition of hunting, avoiding the killing of rattlesnakes and scorpions by forest workers, maintaining dead fallen and standing trees to encourage their colonization by species of amphibians, reptiles, and birds [among other measures] (SmartWood, 2008, p7; authors' translation).

Conversely, a community which had been having trouble meeting its CARs for species lists, monitoring the impact of logging and regeneration and the identification and delimitation of HCVF, among other issues, was suspended from certification (SmartWood, 2007).

The limited reach of forest certification

A substantial proportion—perhaps 80 percent—of Mexico's forests are *ejidos* or *comunidades*. Approximately 15,800 communities have at least some forests, of which 2300 conducted logging using federal permits between 1992 and 2002. Only a minority of these communities (especially large communities with commercially valuable forests) have formed logging businesses of one kind or another and only some of these manage their forests in a manner close enough to the principles and criteria of the FSC to have a hope of obtaining certification.

Further, unlike Fair Trade, forest certification does not include any guaranteed minimum prices or subsidies to compensate producers for the costs of getting certified. And unlike organic certification, forest certification does not appear to generate any consistent market premiums that would serve the same function. Although premiums have occasionally been observed for certain certified hardwoods (Morris and Dunne, 2004; Russo and Lobeira, 2006), retailer monopolies (Rametsteiner and Simula, 2003; Klooster, 2005) and a lack of evidence that consumers are willing to pay more for certified wood products (Anderson et al, 2005) appears to limit their spread.

Certification involves costs for evaluations, audits, and required forest management improvements. The cost per hectare of certification varies greatly. However, larger operations generally bear lower costs per unit area (See Table 10.1) and are thereby better placed to absorb these costs (Klooster, 2006). Not surprisingly, the Mexican and global certified forest landscapes are dominated by large forest management operations. The global landscape is further dominated by forestry operations located in the Global North (Rametsteiner and Simula, 2003; Cashore et al, 2006; Stringer, 2006). As of June 2009, only 15 percent of the certified area worldwide was tropical or subtropical, and community forests made up less than five percent of the total certified area (FSC, 2009c). These are troubling statistics given that tropical and subtropical forests shelter higher biodiversity and are more threatened than temperate zone forests, the contributions that community forestry makes to rural development and conservation (Klooster and Masera, 2000), and the initial intent of the FSC to conserve tropical forests in the Global South (Molnar, 2003).

Table 10.1. Forest certification costs in Mexico

State	Number of units	Area (ha)	Evaluation cost per ha (US$)	Cost including yearly audits and costs of CARs
Durango	5	268,078	$0.23	$0.35
Michoacán	1	11,000	$2.87	$3.14
Oaxaca	1	21,901	$0.55	$1.03

Quintana Roo	2	104,200	$0.27	$0.49

Source: Instituto Nacional de Ecología (2004); reported in Barrera (2007).

If increased prices for certified forest products do not exceed the costs of obtaining and maintaining certification, the most obvious and direct incentive for forest managers to seek certification is missing. It may be possible that buyers and sellers of certified wood products downplay the existence of any price premiums and so the existence of higher prices for certified wood is under-reported in the literature (personal communication with Michael Conroy, December 10, 2007). However, even in the absence of price premiums certification may provide producers with a range of benefits including better access to markets (Klooster 2006). The problem for small producers is that—as major retailers commit to purchase wood and wood products only from certified sources—the cost of FSC certification becomes a basic cost of market access. Many researchers raise questions about the ability of certification to reach community forests in the Global South, especially as they face globalized markets dominated by gigantic processing firms and retailers (Morris and Dunne, 2004; Taylor, 2005; Klooster, 2006).

Organic agriculture in the Global South: biodiversity and certified organic coffee

Organic products are those that have been third-party certified as produced, stored, processed, handled and marketed in accordance with product-specific standards designed to maintain the health of soils, ecosystems and people while avoiding inputs with adverse effects. In the USA, the sale of organic products increased from about $1 billion in 1990 to $17.7 billion in 2006. About 2.8 percent of food and beverage sales in the US are organic. Global demand for organics reached $38.6 billion dollars in 2006, double that in 2000 (OTA, 2008).

Coffee is a particularly useful commodity through which to examine how certification of organic production might contribute to biodiversity conservation. Its cultivation covers more than 10 million hectares globally with more than 5 million hectares in Latin America (FAO, 2009). Many of these hectares are located in montane (subalpine or 'cloud forest') areas associated with high rates of biodiversity loss. Elsewhere, coffee plantations form critical habitat buffers around mountain wildlife reserves (Bhagwat et al, 2005; Williams-Guillén et al, 2006; Philpott et al, 2008). Mexican coffee is predominantly located in the Mesoamerican biodiversity hot spot. With respect to vegetation structure, particular forms of coffee (such as small farmer 'rustic' and 'bajo monte' plantation coffee) replicate important aspects of remnant native forest cover including tree diversity, multi-story canopies and high degrees of landscape heterogeneity (Haslem and Bennett, 2008; Perfecto and Vandermeer, 2008).

A brief history of organic standards

Organic standards form the basis by which independent auditors inspect production systems in a process similar to that described for forest certification. From its roots as an alternative agricultural movement, organic has become increasingly codified, standardized and incorporated into governmental and transnational regulatory structures. Until the mid-1990s, organic certification frameworks (including those compliant with basic umbrella standards developed by the International Federation of Organic Agriculture Movements) varied significantly depending upon the specifics of commodity production processes (Guthman, 1998), ideals of quality (Mansfield, 2004), and local cultures of interaction (Mutersbaugh, 2004; Seppanen and Helenius, 2004). State regulation was limited and third-party inspections generally not required (Michelsen, 2001). The Organic Crop Improvement Association certification, for example, developed initially as a peer-based evaluation system organized around local chapters and thorough yearly field surveys (González and Nigh, 2005).

By the late 1990s, a series of parallel national standards and harmonization initiatives were underway; first in Europe and subsequently in the US, Japan and elsewhere. Key players in this movement towards harmonization were transnational institutions including the International Organization for Standardization (ISO) and the World Trade Organization (WTO). In 1996, ISO produced Guide 65 (*General requirements for bodies operating product certification systems*), and later the ISO 9000 series (*Requirements for quality management systems*) which together established the fundamental parameters for harmonized certification processes including the provision that compliance with standards must be monitored by independent (third party) auditors. The dominance of this model may be explained in part by the strategic alliance between ISO and the WTO. Specifically, countries whose standards regimes do not comply with the ISO framework open themselves to challenge under the WTO Agreement on Technical Barriers to Trade, and thus to potential sanctions, for arbitrarily restricting trade.

Organic certification procedures have thus been standardized globally to comply with ISO requirements and facilitate trade. Nations of the Global North have been the leaders in the process, but it has extended to other national contexts as well, particularly in nations whose export sectors are oriented towards EU, US and Japanese consumer markets. In order to export organic produce into the US, for example, Latin American and other producers must comply, and *only* comply, with US standards as established by the US Department of Agriculture's (USDA) National Organic Program (NOP). Mexico's new *ley organica* has embraced ISO and NOP compliance (Gómez Tovar et al, 2005), as has the Chilean organic rule (Martinez and Bañados, 2004).

Harmonization reduces the costs to exporters of complying with multiple national standards. However, the specific production standards included in the USDA's NOP (which are not stipulated by ISO) are less environmentally stringent than those standards developed by major early innovators such as the Organic Crop Improvement Association and Naturland. Although the NOP did include biodiversity in its definition of organic production, specific biodiversity conservation measures (such as requiring a biodiverse stand of native shade trees on organic coffee farms) were excluded from the final version of the NOP standards (Vos, 2000).

Organic certification and biodiversity

As Table 10.2 indicates, certified-organic practices that affect biodiversity may be divided into three groups. This grouping of practices pertains to all organic agriculture certified to USDA, EU or Japanese standards, although this discussion is limited to the case of organic coffee. The first group specifies required practices. Because biodiversity-enhancing standards were dropped in the process of the USDA's codification of NOP, none of these are specifically focused on enhancing biodiversity. Conversely, some organic requirements institute practices that tend to reduce biodiversity. For example, requiring pest, weed, and disease control necessarily introduces cultivation techniques and production inputs that will harm biodiversity. In the ecological sense, pests and weeds are aspects of a biodiverse plantation—their control must reduce biological measures of biodiversity.

The second column considers practices that are regulated by organic norms. Should farmers elect to make use of inputs, organic standards limit farmers to a list of approved chemicals, preventing the use of environmentally persistent biocides and fertilizers. Organic agriculture still promotes soil fertilization—utilizing compost and other 'natural' fertilizers—the use of which may reduce biodiversity (Tillman, 1982). Finally, the third column addresses the many production practices that, though neither restricted nor regulated by the USDA organic rule, are nonetheless often associated with certified organic production. Both the second and third columns contain an array of practices, regulated or not, that farmers find desirable to increase production or improve quality. Given the cost of certification and historically low coffee prices, certified organic farmers are left two possible paths to combat economic marginality: maximize production at the expense of conservation goals or obtain a shade-grown or other biodiversity certification to offset costs.

Table 10.2. Representative coffee cultivation practices affecting agrobiodiversity

Activities required by USDA organic standards	Activities constrained by organic standards	Activities in response to quality premiums
Buffer zones	Composting and compost application	Yield-improving agronomic practices (pruning, replacement)
Elimination of synthetic biocides and fertilizers	Production inputs including biocides and fertilizers	Shade-tree planting and shade regulation
Pest, weed and disease control	Soil fertility maintenance	
Crop rotation (including erosion control)		

If a certified organic coffee farmer pursues the yield-intensification option he or she is likely to implement a number of cultivation practices including: shade tree removal and replacement with nitrogen-fixing Cuajiniquil (*inga* spp) shade trees, multiple brush clearings, organic fertilizer applications, pruning and epiphyte removal from coffee trees, and terracing and planting of vegetative erosion control barriers. Each of these measures may significantly reduce biodiversity within plots; especially where a diversity of native shade trees are replaced with Cuajiniquil which greatly compromises the plot's ability to support a diverse fauna—both resident and transient (Gordon et al, 2007). Numerous studies have found that fauna as diverse as birds, frogs, beetles, butterflies and mantled howling monkeys depend both on habitat heterogeneity and the availability of specific food and habitat trees; especially high-canopy trees (Pineda and Halffter, 2004; Driscoll and Weir, 2005; Williams-Guillén et al, 2006). High rates of biodiversity are thus only consistently found in rustic coffee planted as an understory among existing remnant forest shade trees (Gordon et al, 2007; Perfecto et al, 2005; Philpott et al, 2008; López-Gómez et al, 2008).

The tendency of high-yield organic agriculture to encourage activities such as shade regulation and impose a uniform cultivation style across space remains less damaging to biodiversity than agro-chemically intensive conventional agriculture (Perfecto et al, 2005). Nevertheless, the question remains as to whether organic standards may not do more to stipulate and/or reward superior biodiversity management as practised by many small farmers in developing world contexts. Organic agriculture's lack of specific biodiversity guidelines is not intrinsic to organic certifications. Such guidelines were removed through the processes of standards harmonization that occasioned the rise of state-sponsored organic certifications (USDA Organic, EU 2092/91, Japan's MAS). A push for biodiversity standards at that time met political defeat by agribusiness interests (Vos, 2000). Bringing organic and biodiversity certifications together will require, then, either a political struggle within the context of US organic law (or EU regulations which would occasion a global struggle over definitions and 'trade barriers' within the context of harmonization) or a separate, universal biodiversity certification that attains sufficient consumer and NGO support either to increase the reach of standalone biodiversity certification (such as those administered by the Smithsonian Migratory Bird Council, Conservation International, The Rainforest Alliance, Naturland etc) or to integrate such certification as an additional biodiversity premium under the Fair Trade rubric, as is organic at present.

Discussion

Certified production systems play an important role in making visible the biodiversity value of agricultural areas and managed forests within a conservation matrix. They open a space in which farmers and foresters can engage with ecologists, conservation authorities, and environmental NGOs in the shared goal of biodiversity conservation. That said, as our cases indicate, certified production systems confront challenges of a practical, scientific and economic character.

Certification occurs at the scale of farms and managed forests. These are management units which are essential for conservation strategy but they are not sufficient for it. Matrix ecology suggests the need to manage biodiversity both within patches (alpha diversity) and across patches (beta and gamma diversity), and thus a broader vision and system of territorial management is needed to coordinate the actions of relatively small farms and forest-holdings. Currently, certification has a strong focus on alpha diversity, and it could play a role by adding certified conservation value to broad environmental initiatives ranging from global species conservation to carbon mitigation projects. In the future, however, biodiversity certification needs to be better integrated into a broad conservation matrix that would understand producer-managed environmental conservation as on par with, and essential to, regional and global conservation strategies. Ideally, for example, there should be coordination between forest certification and agricultural certification since both often share the same landscape.

Markets are not very good at providing public goods such as biodiversity conservation. The economics of certified commodity-based environmental conservation rests on the hope that farmers, foresters or other rural producers who comply with conservation standards will be supported by higher prices. During the 1990s, certification movements operated as consumer-driven alternative trade organizations. In the organic case, consumers paid higher prices that were returned to the producers in the form of price premiums. Unfortunately, in some sectors, price premiums failed to keep pace and were no longer sufficient to cover increased conservation and certification costs. Production costs were also driven higher by an increase in production standards and certification requirements necessary to label products as organic (Mutersbaugh, 2005), yet premiums stagnated as organic product distributors were able to obtain cheaper supplies from corporate agribusiness organic producers (Guthman, 2004) or from countries with lower farm incomes (Renard, 2005).

In the forest certification case, certification promoters induced certified supply faster than certified demand, and easily identified price premiums thus developed only in isolated cases. Furthermore, despite the original goals of the forest certification movement to promote biodiversity conservation in the Tropical South, certification has grown much more rapidly in the Global North. At any rate, large retailers dominate markets for environmentally certified agricultural and forest products, and this fundamentally shapes the distribution of income along the commodity chain.

Ironically, then, the tremendous international commercial success of organic agriculture and forest certification has not been matched by economic success of producers in the Global South. Premiums alone have not been sufficient to provide a living wage for producers or to make the instruments attractive to as large a number of land managers as could be hoped. Economically, it seems that even though certification requires substantial outlays for inspections and management improvements, it guarantees little for producers, although it may play an important role in niche creation strategies, in accessing more stable markets, and in providing non-monetary benefits. As an instrument for commodity chain governance, however, there may be no alternative. The instruments can deliver important biodiversity benefits, but because of high up-front costs and the lack of a price guarantee to cover these costs, they don't necessarily provide producers with adequate incentives for adoption; nor do they justly compensate producers for the costs of conserving biodiversity. These problems are especially prevalent among poor Southern producers who manage most of the world's biodiversity.

Where markets don't provision public goods on their own, additional supports are often needed. In the face of uncertain price premiums, farmers and foresters who conserve biodiversity may need direct payments and subsidies to cover the costs of certification and management changes. Fair Trade provides one model where price premiums are not taken for granted, and where explicit redistributive mechanisms channel income to producers to keep prices above the cost of production and to reduce the costs of certification. In many cases, governmental agencies already supplement or replace producer premiums; for example, by providing producers with subsidies for certification and conservation costs and assistance with export commercialization.

As the preceding paragraphs suggest, national governments and transnational institutions have taken an increasingly active role in promoting certification, in developing standards, and in governing certification systems (particularly mechanisms for compliance verification). Governmental involvement has been in part driven by consumer demands, but also by farmer (and corporate agribusiness) requests for regulatory change—part of the reason for the advent of the USDA National Organic Program—in order to assist in gaining access to EU organic markets. Governmental involvement has led to a rationalization of environmental standards to comprise a two-tiered system of *governing institutions* such as standards-setting bodies (e.g. the USDA National Organic Program, the EU 2092/91 standard), accreditation bodies, and certification agencies that administer the *practices* including standards, inspections and seals to ensure that the product conforms to the relevant standard and farmer and inspector accreditation programs.

The rationalization or harmonization of environmental certification—namely the international effort to put standards under the aegis of transnational and governmental institutions—has met with mixed results. On the one hand, the harmonization of standards and certification under transnational norms provides a global system of checks that has eliminated much of the slippage and regulatory incoherence that characterized the unwieldy universe of competing certifications. On the other hand, rationalization can lead to a politicization of certification governing institutions that puts them at risk of stakeholder capture and may work to the detriment of stronger environmental standards.

We have presented the cases of organic agriculture and forestry certification. In the first case, organic agriculture initially championed strong environmental and biodiversity standards, but these standards were compromised as control shifted from NGOs to national governments (Mutersbaugh, 2005). The FSC, on the other hand, emerged as an international multi-stakeholder organization in which the need to protect the label's legitimacy with NGOs and consumers mitigates the economic interests of producers and retailers to make standards as low as possible (Klooster, 2009). In both cases, standards reflect compromises between the need to make certification both stringent—in the sense of leveraging important changes to management practices—and acceptable—in the sense of attracting producers to adopt certification. They also reflect the outcomes of political struggles over who becomes included as a stakeholder and whose voices prevail in the standards-setting process.

Finally, these studies raise the broader question of when and under what conditions a single global standard or standards-setting process would provide a common rule applicable on a global level. The FSC case study demonstrates how over-arching principles and criteria can subsequently be adapted as national or regional interpretations of those global standards. Large corporate actors are able to get some accommodations with the label yet, at least ideally, certification is conducted with sufficient regional variation to allow for local ecological protection and social participation. There is also a degree of flexibility in the application of the standards, although this is increasingly formalized through step-wise and small and low intensity forestry applications. In the organic case, there are no specific biodiversity protections—and no mechanism for adding such protections—and, as a result, nothing to prevent the most biodiverse contemporary forms of coffee production (rustic farms planted under existing forest canopies) from giving way to specialized shade farms favoured by larger and better capitalized producers for their greater coffee-producing capacity. In either case, the question is that of whether it is possible to envision a standardization of (ecological) difference such that standards protect and nurture ecological heterogeneity across space.

Conclusion

Addressing the environmental consequences of consumption is arguably the single most pressing global environmental concern. Whether we speak of a healthy food system, forest conservation, global warming or mass species extinction, certified production linked to acts of consumption provides one such means to address these global ecological crises. For this reason, the types of certification and products certified have mushroomed beyond what seemed possible only a decade ago, and these in turn have contributed greatly to everyday consumer knowledge about the consequences and responsibilities of consumption. We have described the ways certification systems can affect farm and forest-level biodiversity and identified several key concerns that need to be addressed if certified production is to provide a useful solution to global environmental degradation. These include the need for explicit coordination between certification practices and landscape-scale biodiversity conservation strategy, a structure for supporting ecologically-minded producers not wholly reliant upon consumers' willingness to pay and distributors' willingness to pass the premium on to producers, and a continuing engagement by all concerned parties with the politics of harmonization. Given the right standards and better producer incentives, certification can improve biodiversity and producer livelihoods, but this depends on the ability of conservation advocates to develop and defend such standards and certification practices. The risk is that large retailers, producers and certification agencies capture the process and reduce certification to a convenient source of exclusionary rents, with little or no benefits for biodiversity or small communities.

References

Anderson, R.C., Laband, D.N., Hansen, E.N. and Knowles, C.D. (2005) 'Price premiums in the mist', *Forest Products Journal*, vol 55, no 6, pp19–22

Barrera, J.M. (2007) *Certificación y competitividad en ejidos y comunidades forestales de Mexico*, Durango, Mexico, p59

Bhagwat, S.A., Kushalappa, C.G., Williams, P.H. and Brown, N.D. (2005) 'A landscape approach to biodiversity conservation of sacred groves in the Western Ghats of India', *Conservation Biology*, vol 19, no 6, pp1853–1862.

Brockington, D. (2002) *Fortress Conservation: The Preservation of the Mkomazi Game Reserve, Tanzania*, Indiana University Press, Bloomington, IN

Brookfield, H.C. (2001) *Exploring Agrodiversity*, Columbia University Press, New York, NY

Cashore, B., Auld, G. and Newsom, D. (2004) *Governing Through Markets: Regulating Forestry through Non-State Environmental Governance*, Yale University Press, New Haven, CT

Cashore, B., Gale, F., Meidinger, E. and Newsom, D. (eds) (2006) *Confronting Sustainability: Forest Certification in Developing and Transitioning Countries*, Yale School of Forestry and Environmental Studies, New Haven, CT

Conroy, M.E. (2007) *Branded! How the 'certification revolution' is transforming global corporations*, New Society Publishers, Gabriola Island, Canada

Driscoll, D.A. and Weir, T. (2005) 'Beetle responses to habitat fragmentation depend on ecological traits, habitat condition, and remnant size', *Conservation Biology*, vol 19, no 1, pp182–194

Food and Agriculture Organization of the United Nations (FAO) (2009) 'United Nations Food and Agriculture. FAOSTAT', http://faostat.fao.org, accessed 26 July 2009

Forest Stewardship Council (FSC) (2002) *FSC Principles and Criteria for Forest Stewardship*, www.fsc.org/fileadmin/web-data/public/document_center/inter national_FSC_policies/standards/FSC_STD_01_001_V4_0_EN_FSC_Principle s_and_Criteria.pdf, accessed July 31 2009

Forest Stewardship Council (FSC) (2006) *Summary of Responses: FSC Plantation Review Public Consultation July 2006*, www.old.fsc.org/plantations/docs/Res ources%20-%20FSC%20docs%20and%20reports/Summary%20of%20Resp onses%20to%20July%20Plantations%20Review%20Consultation_2006-09%20 (EN).pdf, accessed 18 January, 2009

Forest Stewardship Council (FSC) (2008) 'FSC and Biodiversity-2: High conservation value forests (HCVF)—Taking special care of particularly conservation worthy forests', www.fsc.org/152.html, accessed 31 July 2009

Forest Stewardship Council (FSC) (2009a) 'FSC in numbers: A truly global system', *Forest Stewardship Council. News & Notes*, vol 7, no 5, p2

Forest Stewardship Council (FSC) (2009b) 'New FSC good practice guide focuses on biodiversity in small-scale and low intensity forest operations (SLIMFs)', www.fsc.org/news.html?&no_cache=1&tx_ttnews%5btt_news%5d=171&cHas h=ec42aa3033, accessed 31 July 2009

Forest Stewardship Council (FSC) (2009c) 'Global FSC certificates: Type and distribution', Retrieved from www.fsc.org/fileadmin/web-data/public/docum ent_center/powerpoints_graphs/facts_figures/09-06-15_Global_FSC_certific ates_-_type_and_distribution_-_FINAL.pdf, accessed 5 August 2009

Forest Stewardship Council (FSC) (undated) 'Overview of the FSC principles and criteria', www.fsc.org/pc.html, accessed August 4 2009

Gómez Tovar, L., Martin, L. Gómez Cruz, M.A. and Mutersbaugh, T. (2005) 'Certified organic agriculture in Mexico: Market connections and certification practices in large and small producers', *Journal of Rural Studies*, vol 21, no 4, pp461–474

González, A.A. and Nigh, R. (2005) 'Smallholder participation and certification of organic farm products in Mexico', *Journal of Rural Studies*, vol 21, pp449–460

Gordon, C., Manson, R. Sundberg, J. and Cruz-Angón, A. (2007) 'Biodiversity, profitability, and vegetation structure in a Mexican coffee agroecosystem', *Agriculture, Ecosystems and Environment*, vol 118, pp256–266

Guthman, J. (1998) 'Regulating meaning, appropriating nature: The codification of California organic agriculture', *Antipode*, vol 30, no 2, pp135–154

Guthman, J. (2004) 'The trouble with 'organic lite' in California: A rejoinder to the 'conventionalisation' debate', *Sociologia Ruralis*, vol 44, no 3, pp301–316

Haslem, A., and Bennett, A. F. (2008) 'Birds in agricultural mosaics: The influence of landscape pattern and countryside heterogeneity', *Ecological Applications*, vol 18, no 1, pp185–196

Klooster, D. (2005) 'Environmental certification of forests: The evolution of environmental governance in a commodity network', *Journal of Rural Studies*, vol 21, no 4, pp403–417

Klooster, D. (2006) 'Environmental certification of forests in Mexico: The political ecology of a nongovernmental market intervention', *Annals of the Association of American Geographers*, vol 96, no 3, pp541–565

Klooster, D. (in press 2009) 'Standardizing sustainable development? The Forest Stewardship Council's plantation policy review process', *Geoforum*, http://dx.doi.org/10.1016/j.geoforum.2009.02.006, available online 25 March 2009

Klooster, D. and Masera, O. (2000) 'Community forest management in Mexico: Carbon mitigation and biodiversity conservation through rural development', *Global Environmental Change*, vol 10, no 4, pp43–70

López-Gómez, A.M., Williams-Linera, G. and Manson, R.H. (2008) 'Tree species diversity and vegetation structure in shade coffee farms in Veracruz, Mexico', *Agriculture, Ecosystems and Environment*, vol 124, pp160–172

Mansfield, B. (2004) 'Organic views of nature: The debate over organic certification for aquatic animals', *Sociologia Ruralis*, vol 44, no 2, p216

Martinez, M.G. and Bañados, F. (2004) 'Impact of EU organic product certification legislation on Chile organic exports', *Food Policy*, vol 29, no 1, p1

Michelsen, J. (2001) 'Organic farming in a regulatory perspective: The Danish case', *Sociologia Ruralis*, vol 41, no 1, pp62–84

Molnar, A. (2003) *Forest Certification and Communities: Looking forward to the next decade*, Forest Trends, Washington, DC

Morris, M. and Dunne, N. (2004) 'Driving environmental certification: Its impact on the furniture and timber products value chain in South Africa', *Geoforum*, vol 35, no 2, pp251–266

Mutersbaugh, T. (2004) 'Serve and certify: Paradoxes of service work in organic-coffee certification,' *Environment and Planning D: Society and Space*, vol 22, pp533–552

Mutersbaugh, T. (2005) 'Fighting standards with standards: Harmonization, rents, and social accountability in certified agrofood networks', *Environment and Planning A*, vol 37, pp2033–2051

Mutersbaugh, T., Klooster, D., Renard, M-C. and Taylor, P. (2005) 'Certifying rural spaces: Quality-certified products and rural governance', *Journal of Rural Studies*, vol 21, no 4, pp381–388

OTA (2008) 'Industry statistics and projected growth', www.ota.com/organic/mt/business.html, accessed July 31, 2009.

Padoch, C. and Peters, C. (1993) 'Managed forest gardens in West Kalimantan, Indonesia', in J.I. Cohen, C.S. Potter and D. Janczewski (eds) *Perspectives on Biodiversity: Case studies of Genetic Resource Conservation and Development*, AAAS Press, Washington, DC, pp167–176

Padoch, C., Harwell, E. and Susanto, A. (1998) 'Swidden, sawah, and in-between: Agricultural transformation in Borneo', *Human Ecology*, vol 26, no 1, pp3–20

Perfecto, I. and Vandermeer, J. (2008) 'Spatial pattern and ecological process in the coffee agroforestry system', *Ecology*, vol 89, no 4, pp915–920

Perfecto, I., Vandermeer, J., Mas, A. and Soto Pinto, L. (2005) 'Biodiversity, yield, and shade coffee certification', *Ecological Economics*, vol 54, no 4, pp435–446

Philpott, S.M., Arendt, W.A., Armbrecht, I., Bichier, P., Diestch, T.V., Gordon, C., Greenberg, R., Perfecto, I., Reynoso-Santos, R., Soto-Pinto, L., Tejeda-Cruz, C., Williams-Linera, G., Valenzuela, J. and Zolotoff, J.M. (2008) 'Biodiversity loss in Latin American coffee landscapes: Review of the evidence on ants, birds, and trees', *Conservation Biology*, vol 22, no 5, pp1093–1105

Pineda, E. and Halffter, G. (2004) 'Species diversity and habitat fragmentation: Frogs in a tropical montane landscape in Mexico', *Biological Conservation*, vol 117, pp499–508

Rametsteiner, E. and Simula, M. (2003) 'Forest certification: An instrument to promote sustainable forest management?', *Journal of Environmental Management*, vol 67, pp87–98

Renard, M-C. (2005) 'Quality certification, regulation and power in Fair Trade', *Journal of Rural Studies*, vol 21, no 4, pp419–431

Russo, M.V. and Lobeira, S. (2006, March 1) 'Survey and analysis of the supply chain for Mexican certified wood products', www.ine.gob.mx/dgipea/bosques /madera.html, 14 July, 2006

Seppanen, L. and Helenius, J. (2004) 'Do inspection practices in organic agriculture serve organic values? A case study from Finland', *Agriculture and Human Values*, vol 21, no 1, p1

SmartWood (2007) *Auditoría Anual 2007. Informe para: Comunidad San Miguel Maninaltepec*,www.rainforest-alliance.org/forestry/documents/comsanmiguelmaninaltepecpubsum07spa.pdf, accessed July 31 2009

SmartWood (2008) *Manejo Forestal Auditoría Anual 2008 Informe para: Comunidad de San Pedro el Alto*, www.rainforest-alliance.org/forestry/documents/comunidadsanpedroelaltopubsum08.pdf, accessed 5 August 2009

SmartWood (2009) 'Certified forestry operation summaries (Mexico)', www.rainforest-alliance.org/forestry/public_documents_country.cfm?country=27, accessed 31 July 2009

Stringer, C. (2006) 'Forest certification and changing global commodity chains', *Journal of Economic Geography*, vol 6, no 5, pp701–722

Taylor, P.L. (2005) 'In the market but not of it: Fair Trade coffee and Forest Stewardship Council certification as market-based social change', *World Development*, vol 33, no 1, pp129–147

Tillman, D. (1982) *Resource Competition and Community Structure*, Princeton University Press, Princeton, NJ

Vandermeer, J. and Perfecto, I. (2007) 'The agricultural matrix and a future paradigm for conservation', *Conservation Biology* vol 21, no 1, pp274–277

Vandermeer, J. and Perfecto, I. (2008) 'Biodiversity conservation in tropical agroecosystems: A new conservation paradigm', *Annals of the N.Y. Academy of Sciences*, vol 1134, pp173–200

Vos, T. (2000) 'Visions of the middle landscape: Organic farming and the politics of nature', *Agriculture and Human Values*, vol 17, pp245–256

Williams-Guillén, K., McCann, C., Martínez Sánchez, J.C. and Koontz, F. (2006) 'Resource availability and habitat use by mantled howling monkeys in a Nicaraguan coffee plantation: Can agroforests serve as core habitat for a forest mammal?', *Animal Conservation*, vol 9, no 3, pp331–338

Zerner, C. (2000) *People, Plants & Justice*, Columbia University Press, New York, NY

Zimmerer, K. (1999) 'Overlapping patchworks of mountain agriculture in Peru and Bolivia: Toward a regional-global landscape model', *Human Ecology*, vol 27, no 1, pp135–165

Zimmerer, K.S. (ed) (2006) *Globalization and New Geographies of Conservation*, University of Chicago Press, Chicago, MI

Zimmerer, K.S. and Bassett, T.J. (eds) (2003) *Political Ecology: An Integrative Approach to Geography and Environment-Development Studies*, Guilford Press, New York, NY

11

Challenges of Global Environmental Governance by Non-State Actors in the Coffee Industry: Insights From India, Indonesia and Vietnam

Jeff Neilson, Bustanul Arifin, C.P. Gracy, Tran Ngoc Kham,
Bill Pritchard and Lindsay Soutar

The dynamics of production and trade in today's global coffee sector are virtually unrecognisable when compared with those that prevailed just two decades ago. The 1989 collapse of an international quota system for coffee was coincident with the withdrawal of state support structures within many producer countries. The livelihoods of coffee farmers worldwide have become increasingly dependent on price movements on the major commodity exchanges in London (for Robusta coffee) and New York (for Arabica). The 1990s also witnessed steady corporate consolidation in the sector and a trend towards rising consumer activism in key importing countries. Consuming country interests concentrated in the affluent regions of North America, Western Europe and Northeast Asia are increasingly able to influence the way coffee is produced and traded in remote sites of production across Africa, Latin America and tropical Asia. A nascent regime of 'non-state regulation' is emerging in which quality, environmental and social standards are embedded within a complex array of corporate codes of conduct, systems of product certification, and rules for supplier compliance.

This chapter examines the introduction and influence of non-state regulation in the coffee sectors of Asia's three largest coffee-producing countries—India, Indonesia and Vietnam—with a particular focus on how buyer-driven regulation is changing environmental management within coffee production systems. However, non-state regulation of social and environmental standards is not unique to coffee and the chapter will tease out the wider implications of non-state environmental regulation for poverty alleviation and sustainable resource management in the developing world. The research reported here is the product of a cross-country comparative analysis of non-state regulation in Asia's coffee sector involving: analysis of the specific environmental requirements of major certification schemes/codes currently in use; ascertaining how widespread the various schemes are within each country; and assessing specified code requirements against known environmental practices in each country to evaluate their implications for natural resource management.

Buyer-driven environmental regulation in the global coffee sector

Growth in global coffee production over the last 30 years has inevitably occurred either through the expansion of coffee cultivation into new areas (often into previously uncultivated tropical forests) or the adoption of high input, intensive coffee production (commonly with a corresponding loss of shade cover and on-farm biodiversity). Consequently, coffee-related deforestation has occurred in all major producing regions across Central and South America, Asia and Africa. Figure 11.1 shows the increase of coffee production in the three case-study countries since 1977, and the particularly spectacular increase in production for Vietnam from around 1990.

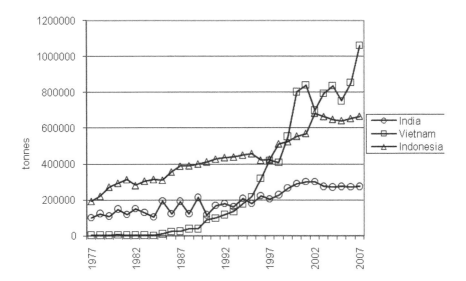

Figure 11.1. Growth in coffee production across India, Indonesia and Vietnam (Data Source: FAOSTAT, 2009)

Originally an understorey species from the East African highlands, coffee is now cultivated within a great diversity of agroecological systems. These range from multi-strata systems where coffee has been introduced as an understorey plant beneath an otherwise 'natural' forest canopy; to coffee planted amongst sparse scatterings of mono-shade (single species of shade tree); to mixed cropping systems where coffee is grown alongside other crops such as cocoa, citrus or pepper; and to systems with a total absence of shade cover (so-called 'sun coffee'). In many instances, coffee agroforests function as buffer zones around protected forest areas, perform important hydrological functions and/or provide wildlife habitat. As a result, land management decisions made by coffee farmers often have important ramifications for conservation outcomes in sensitive upland ecosystems.

Early consumer awareness of the role played by multi-strata coffee agroforests in biodiversity conservation was stimulated by research performed at the Smithsonian Institution in Washington DC, which linked the intensification of coffee production in Latin America—through the removal of shade cover, increases in fertilizer application and sometimes irrigation—with habitat loss for migratory bird species in the US (see Rice and Ward, 1996). This led to efforts to promote environmentally-friendly coffee production in Central America through certification schemes including Smithsonian Bird-Friendly Coffee (shade-grown) and Eco-OK (later Rainforest Alliance) which aimed to provide financial rewards to coffee-growers whose farms contributed positively towards biodiversity conservation.

In the late 1990s, coffees marketed using various 'sustainable coffee' labels were sold within relatively isolated niche markets. However, it was not long before mainstream food and beverage companies including Kraft, McDonalds, UCC and Tchibo recognized the potential of eco-marketing, and codes of practice, certification schemes and green labels began to proliferate. Key coffee industry initiatives now include: the Global Partnership for Good Agricultural Practice protocols (Global-GAP); Utz Kapeh certification (now simply Utz Certified); the Common Code for the Coffee Community (4C); and Starbucks' CAFÉ Practices (Coffee and Farmer Equity) Program. Some independent schemes such as Rainforest Alliance have embraced corporate engagement to the extent that observers have questioned their susceptibility to corporate manipulation (Raynolds et al, 2007). For the most part, these schemes comprise a diversity of partnership models between NGOs and the corporate coffee sector. Conservation International, for example, has played an important role in the Starbucks CAFÉ Practices program and (as of July 2008) 4C counts among its members both Oxfam International and Rainforest Alliance.

Then, there are corporate commitments to purchase third-party certified coffees. In 2006, Nespresso announced an intention to source 50 percent of its coffee from the AAA Sustainable Quality Program by 2010 while, in 2007, McDonalds UK announced that all coffee served in its stores would be from Rainforest-certified farms and Sara Lee committed itself to source 20,000 tonnes of Utz-certified coffee globally in 2008.

Increasingly, producers are finding that conformance to one or more buyer-imposed environmental standards—while ostensibly voluntary—is now a mandatory requirement in order to access most international markets. Yet it remains unclear as to whether producers actually receive tangible financial benefit from their participation in these schemes. In their analysis of 12 different partnerships addressing sustainability in the global coffee sector, Bitzer et al (2008, p282) conclude that 'benefits for producers remain unclear, while lead firms are able to harness the standards as strategic tools for supply chain management'. Similarly, Kilian et al (2006, p325) argue that:

> coffee certification alone does not generate price differentials (with the notable exception of organic coffee sold in Europe). The price is always a function of both quality and certification, where quality can be seen as a more basic prerequisite for a price premium and the certification as a tool to differentiate and to underline the outstanding performance of the product.

Elsewhere, a survey in Northern Nicaragua by Bacon (2005, p508) found that participation in organic and Fair Trade networks did reduce farmers' livelihood vulnerability, but with a note of warning that:

> Certification as a tool for producer empowerment is ... challenged by the proliferation of certfications, such as Rainforest Alliance and Utz Kapeh, which offer lower social standards than Fair Trade and lower environmental criteria than organic certification.

In their evaluation of the impact of fair trade and organic certification in Mexico, Calo and Wise (2005) conclude that given the prevailing cost and price structure for coffee production, certification by itself is not sufficient to make organic coffee profitable for most producers. Yet other studies suggest that certification institutions and standards may in actuality serve simply as new vehicles of corporate control over global food production, trade and consumption (Busch and Bain, 2004). Raynolds et al (2007, p147) argue that:

> The vulnerability of these initiatives to market pressures highlights the need for private regulation to work in tandem with public regulation in enhancing social and environmental sustainability.

Much of the available evidence certainly suggests the increasing influence of private sector actors (namely branded manufacturers) in driving environmental and social accountability along their supply chains, but without a clear consensus on the benefits for producer communities and the environment. Research on the proposed implementation of the 4C coffee code in India has emphasized producer antagonism towards this regime on the basis that it was perceived to execute a shift in audit costs and control over the production process to the detriment of Indian producers (Neilson and Pritchard, 2007).

Table 11.1 summarizes how five major environmental issues are dealt with by five of the most widespread codes. The codes have a variety of aspirations and frameworks that are reflected in highly variable minimum requirements for compliance. Utz Certified, for instance, is premised on a series of 'major musts' and 'minor musts' with which producers must comply. 4C follows a 'Traffic light system' of continuous improvement: 'red light' status indicates that the current practice must be discontinued; 'yellow light' status indicates the practice needs further improvement during a transitional period; and a 'green light' reflects a desirable practice. Starbucks' CAFÉ Practices has a similar philosophy of continuous improvement based on a points system. Organic certification is based on compliance with a minimum set of production standards with which producers must comply. These standards include practices that are expressly forbidden (such as use of proscribed synthetic inputs) and practices that must be used. As there are numerous organic certification bodies active in India, Indonesia and Vietnam we base our analysis solely on the NASAA (National Association for Sustainable Agriculture Australia) standard which offers cross-compliance with standards for most coffee export markets. For the purposes of Table 11.1, and the corresponding analysis in the text, we refer to the most basic level of compliance for each code.

With these points made, attention turns now to specific examples of the implementation of environmental governance in diverse sites of coffee production. Through these examples, we argue that there is a fundamental tension between: the aspirations of these schemes; the globally-consistent requirements they establish for the definition, measurement, monitoring and certification of environmental sustainability; and the embedded circumstances of coffee production within complex agroecological and socio-institutional settings. Whilst specification of certain requirements lend themselves to global standard-setting (prohibition of certain banned chemicals, for instance), there is a propensity of grey areas that harm the efficacy of schemes. For focus and clarity, discussion is limited to three of the five environmental compliance standards listed in Table 11.1 that illustrate these grey areas: limits on forest clearing in Indonesia; on-farm biodiversity and shade cover (which despite the general practice of delinking these indicators for audit purposes, we combine in this analysis due to their relevance to the case study being discussed) in India; and water use in Vietnam. Table 11.2 summarizes the coverage of the various forms of coffee certification within each of these countries.

Table 11.1. Comparison of environmental standards of five main sustainability codes

Environmental compliance standard	Utz Certified (Major musts)	CAFÉ Practices (Criteria requirement)
On-farm biodiversity conservation	No major musts.	There are specific measures that must be implemented to restrict unauthorized hunting and commercial collection of flora and fauna.
Shade requirements	No major musts.	Shade canopy maintained & native trees removed only when constituting a hazard to humans or competing significantly with coffee plants.
Use of Pesticides	Allowed. Not allowed to use products that are banned in the EU, USA or Japan. There are numerous major musts related to record-keeping, storage and use of pesticides.	Allowed. Prohibits use of chemicals listed by the WHO as Type 1A or 1B. Encourages the reduction of agrochemical use and adoption of Integrated Pest Management.
Water use	No major musts.	No Criteria Requirement.
Limits on forest clearing	Must demonstrate no deforestation of primary forest (or secondary forest without compensation) to plant new fields in the 24 months prior to first registration.	No conversion of natural forest to agricultural production since March 2004.
Fertilizer use	Major musts to show competence in fertilizer application, must document all use & must store all fertilizers in line with recommendations.	No specific requirements except in relation to maintaining water quality (fertilizer use should be minimized).

Sources: Utz Certified (2006), Starbucks Coffee Company (2007), NASAA (2008), 4C (2008),

for coffee

Organic (NASAA) standards (minimum requirements that must be met)	Common Code for the Coffee Community (minimum for Yellow light status)	Rainforest Alliance (Critical criterion)
Requires a range of measures to facilitate biodiversity & nature conservation, including setting aside specific areas, planting patterns & management plan.	No hunting of endangered/protected species. A strategy to protect and enhance native flora must be developed.	All existing natural ecosystems must be identified, protected, conserved & restored. Hunting of wild animals prohibited (with exceptions for indigenous peoples).
Except in certain plantations, shade trees & shrubs must be maintained in the production area.	None.	Must establish and maintain shade trees in areas where the agricultural, climatic and ecological conditions permit.
Use of chemical pesticides prohibited.	Allowed. Prohibits use of chemicals listed in the Rotterdam Convention and categorized as Type I and II by the WHO. Also provides a list of other banned chemicals.	Allowed. Prohibits use of substances, including those banned under Stockholm Convention, or by EU or USA regulation.
Must not deplete nor excessively exploit water resources. Must maintain hydrological balances and environmental flows.	Water is not withdrawn beyond replenishment capacity. Water conservation practices implemented.	No critical criterion.
Prohibits clearance of any primary ecosystem for production.	No exploitation of native flora or watersheds designated as protected areas by national legislation is evident.	No cutting of natural forest cover or burning to prepare new production areas.
Use of chemical fertilizers is not allowed.	Fertilizer application is based on standardized prescriptions.	No critical criterion.

Rainforest Alliance (2008).

Table 11.2. Certification scheme coverage in India, Indonesia and Vietnam

	India	Indonesia	Vietnam
Utz Certified	6 large corporate estates covering 10,429 hectares	10 producers certified, covering 12,296 ha.	12 state-owned and private producers covering 12,623 ha.
Starbucks' CAFÉ Practices	Limited. India is not a significant origin for Starbucks although at least 2 estates (including Tata) claim to have been audited.	Widespread influence across the Arabica regions of Sulawesi and northern Sumatra. None in Lampung.	No producers certified
Organic coffee production	One organic cooperative in Andhra Pradesh (non-traditional coffee area).	Numerous organic cooperatives across the Arabica-growing districts only.	Limited (no data available)
4C	Indian coffee board is not a member of 4C. Resistance to adoption exists on range of ecological, social and economic grounds.	Early stages of collaboration. 1 producer member at present.	A founding member of 4C, represented by Vicofa. Program still in introductory stages with some trial projects underway in Central Highland provinces. 1 producer member
Rainforest Alliance	No producers certified	6 certified producers (5 Arabica)	No producers certified

Sources: Utz Certified (undated), Starbucks Coffee Company (undated), 4C (2007), Rainforest Alliance (undated).

Rules on forest clearing: insights from Lampung, Indonesia

It is probably the case that virtually all existing coffee plantations were once tropical forests. Nevertheless, reflecting concerns that continued expansion of coffee cultivation is a significant contributor to tropical forest loss (a form of land-use conversion that branded coffee manufacturers in developed countries certainly do not want to be associated with) all of the codes listed in Table 11.1 contain requirements related to the clearing of forest for conversion to coffee production. The CAFÉ Practices code inserts an end-date clause stating that verified coffee should not be grown on land cleared of forest after March 2004. The Utz Kapeh code states that no deforestation for new plantings should occur in the 24 months prior to first registration; a seemingly weak requirement given that new plantings would presumably require at least two years before producing marketable quantities of beans. The Rainforest Alliance and NASAA codes have general, and apparently outright, prohibitions on the clearing of primary forest for production while the 4C code is more ambiguous. It specifies a prohibition on 'irreversible, destructive exploitation of native flora' and requires that no exploitation of flora is evident that contravenes national legislation. As argued below, this apparent ambiguity may be necessary to take into consideration diverse institutional contexts and local environmental settings at different production sites.

Notwithstanding some very sound reasons to address deforestation within sites of coffee production, the environmental impacts of land-use transformation are rarely straightforward. For example, Verbist et al (2005) have argued that while forest clearing and the subsequent establishment of coffee agroforests in Indonesia has represented a significant landscape transformation it has also had positive hydrological effects for downstream water users (previously a widely-cited reason for evicting farmers from within the catchment). Attempts to construct globally-uniform compliance requirements that recognize this diversity are prone to being either simplistic, or ingenuous. A case in point is the coffee frontier of Lampung, Indonesia.

Lampung Province (Figure 11.2) is Indonesia's largest coffee producing region. The major port in Bandar Lampung was responsible for 65 percent of total Indonesian coffee exports (by volume) during the period 2004-2007 (BPS, 2008) and, together with the northern port at Medan, these Sumatran ports contribute around 85 percent of total exports. Smallholders in Lampung generally cultivate less than two hectares of Robusta coffee, frequently intercropped with cocoa, pepper and corn, and are scattered across upland areas in the western districts of the province. Dry-processed Robusta coffee is then traded along a chain of village collectors, local and regional traders to large warehouses located in Bandar Lampung, some owned by international processing and trading companies, including an instant coffee factory owned by Nestlé. Lampung coffee is generally sold at a quality discount to prices on the London Robusta Exchange, and the ten major destinations for Lampung Robusta (Table 11.3) include many non-traditional coffee importers with little degree of geographical consolidation.

A significant volume of production is also absorbed by local coffee processing companies. Margins along the chain are tight and, reflecting this particularly diverse set of final markets, there have been relatively few attempts by large coffee companies to develop upstream linkages aimed at addressing environmental performance or product quality. When coffee is sold into markets outside of Western Europe and North America, product traceability and buyer-driven environmental regulation are conspicuous in their absence. This is in stark contrast to the situation for high quality Indonesian Arabica, where a variety of product certification schemes have been introduced over the last decade (Neilson, 2008).

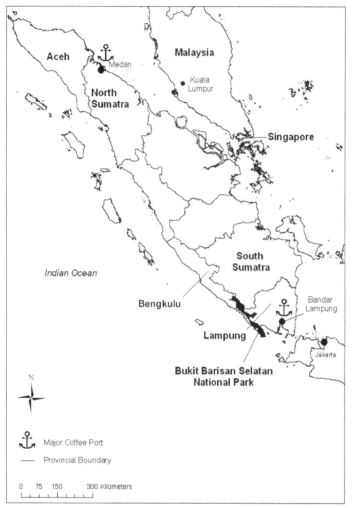

Figure 11.2. Map showing Bukit Barisan Selatan National Park in the coffee-producing province of Lampung, Indonesia (Map source: Authors' own work)

Lampung has been a destination for migrants from Java, Bali and other parts of Sumatra since the Dutch era. The indigenous communities of the province have been severely marginalized by waves of both state-sponsored and spontaneous migration, and today constitute only a small minority of the population. Much of this migration took place in the 1970s, stimulated by the economic opportunities offered by growing coffee on apparently abundant, and cheap, land. Coffee productivity in Lampung is low by international standards at around 600 kg per hectare, with farmers applying low maintenance techniques following initial clearing and planting.[1] This 'frontier' farming approach, born during a time of abundant land resources, continues to permeate the industry today despite a rapidly shrinking area of natural forest in the province.

Table 11.3. Top 10 destinations for South Sumatra Robusta in 2007

	Destination	Share of exports (%)
1	Germany, Fed. Rep. of	16
2	Japan	14
3	United States	13
4	Italy	8
5	Philippines	5
6	India	4
7	Algeria	4
8	Malaysia	4
9	United Kingdom	3
10	Georgia	3
	Others	26

Data Source: BPS (2008). Data is taken as exports of unroasted coffee (HS 090111) from the Panjang port in Bandar Lampung

Remaining natural forest in Lampung is now largely restricted to a slither of land contained mostly within the Bukit Barisan Selatan National Park (BBSNP, Figure 11.2) along the southwest coast and a small area of lowland forest on the east coast located within the Way Kambas National Park. The BBSNP was established in 1982 due to its habitat importance for endangered Sumatran wildlife such as the rhinoceros, elephant and tiger. Encroachment by coffee farmers constitutes a major threat to the continued viability of this park (WWF, 2007). Farmers, many originating from the neighbouring island of Java, are still found along the perimeter of, and within, the park. Despite earlier clearances of these illegal coffee settlers during the Soeharto regime, many re-settled following the socio-political changes of 1998 when forest policing was virtually impossible. During this politically volatile period, the poverty rate across Indonesia increased from around 15 percent in mid-1997 to 33 percent nearing the end of 1998 (Suryahadi et al, 2003). Forest clearing increased significantly during the crisis (Sunderlin et al, 2001), providing a social security safety net for millions of workers laid-off by the dramatic collapse of the manufacturing and service sectors, particularly in Java, during the crisis (Timmer, 2004).

In 1999, a national-level coffee task force (*Tim Kopi*) was established to assess coffee practices in protected areas across the country in light of the economic crisis. One outcome of this taskforce was a more flexible (and politically realistic) policy towards farming in protected areas, including recognition of community-based forestry management. A subsequent Ministerial Decree (No. 31/2001) allowed the possibility for people already farming within a Protection Forest[2] to be allocated temporary use rights conditional on the maintenance of multi-strata agroforestry systems (Arifin, 2005). Application of this principle in the Sumber Jaya District of Lampung appears to have had positive environmental outcomes (Verbist et al, 2005), despite such landscape change potentially violating compliance requirements according to some codes.

A locally-negotiated outcome in Lampung, within a supportive legislative framework at the national level, appears to be offering at least a partial solution to coffee-related deforestation in the province. The Sumber Jaya district, however, is separate from the BBSNP, where intensive conservation efforts on the ground are required to actively protect remaining forest from further encroachment. Research by Sunderlin et al (2001) emphasizes the primacy of forest policing and the effectiveness of adequate social welfare in shaping land management incentives rather than price signals alone. Even if it were logistically possible to trace the origins of all coffee exported from Sumatra to exclude coffee grown within the National Park (and such traceability systems will be difficult to introduce to the bulk commodity trade due to excessively high transaction costs), less environmentally-discerning international and domestic markets would still absorb this production and conservation benefits would be minimal.

Processes of landscape change are ongoing, reversible and complex, and impacts are context-dependent. Even within Lampung, not all forest transformations have equal environmental impacts (Verbist et al, 2005). Clearly, it is unacceptable to promote conversion of world heritage listed rainforest in Sumatra to coffee plantations. However, it is unlikely that an acceptable definition for 'natural' forest could be established that meets the requirement for all production contexts. An exchange between O'Brien and Kinnard (2004) and Dietsch et al (2004) in *Science* exemplifies the potential inadequacies of using narrow definitions of sustainable farm behaviour across production sites (in that case contrasting Latin America with Asia). According to O'Brien and Kinnard (2004), promoting sustainable coffee standards developed in Latin America (notably shade standards) will be insufficient to address conservation problems in Indonesia. Our analysis of the situation for Robusta production in Lampung reiterates this assertion: codes generally lack sensitivity towards the complex institutional drivers of farmer behaviour, including encroachment into protected areas and landuse change, and are unable to recognize the need for trade-offs between local conservation priorities and socio-political realities.

On-farm biodiversity conservation and shade cover in the coffee forests of India

On-farm biodiversity conservation and shade management is a pre-eminent environmental concern within the global coffee industry. As discussed already, wider international environmental concern about coffee cultivation was triggered, to a large extent, by the expansion of 'sun coffees' in Latin America and the publicized impacts for migratory bird habitats. It is not surprising, therefore, that these issues figure strongly in major codes. While two of the codes (Rainforest Alliance and 4C) address biodiversity conservation in terms of prohibiting hunting of native animals on coffee farms, it is the maintenance of a shade cover that probably determines on-farm biodiversity more than any other factor. Indeed, Dietsch et al (2004) argue that shaded coffee agroecosystems can provide habitat at levels comparable to natural forests. As a result, three of the five codes specify a broad requirement for shade trees. Rainforest Alliance (undated) mandates that:

> the program must include the establishment and maintenance of shade trees for those crops traditionally grown with shade, in areas where the agricultural, climatic and ecological conditions permit.

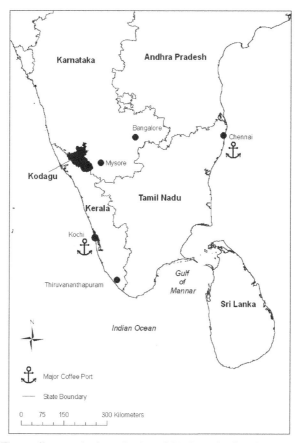

Figure 11.3. The coffee-producing district of Kodagu in South India (Map source: Authors' own work)

CAFÉ Practices requires that 'native trees are removed only when they constitute a human hazard or when they significantly compete with coffee plants'. The specific NASAA standards related to coffee, cocoa and tea production state: 'Except in plantations, shade trees and shrubs must be maintained in the production area to provide nitrogen and shade and help with pest control'. Other coffee certification schemes such as Smithsonian Bird-Friendly Coffee have various, and highly specific, requirements relating to shade tree diversity, crown density and canopy structure.

While this issue reflects a legitimate area of concern for proponents of on-farm biodiversity conservation, its specific incorporation into codes is problematic. This is especially relevant for India's coffee industry, which is located amidst the species-rich tropical forests of the Western Ghats (Figure 11.3). These localities have been designated as an international biodiversity hot-spot (Myers et al, 2000), and attract significant conservation efforts from both national and international organizations. The coffee crop is overwhelmingly planted and cultivated within shaded, multi-crop, ecosystems which support an array of habitat resources (Figure 11.4). On-farm biodiversity can be significant, with the Arehalli smallholder growers' cooperative in the Hassan District of Karnataka claiming that their members cultivate coffee in the midst of more than 100 tree varieties. It is not uncommon for India's coffee estates to provide habitat for tiger, leopard, bison and elephant populations; albeit with considerable human-wildlife conflict (Kulkarni et al, 2007). With deforestation occurring steadily across the Western Ghats (in the state of Karnataka alone, nearly 12% of the forests have been completely lost in the two decades 1980–2000: Ramesh, 2001), remaining forests have become fragmented, and in this context, on-farm conservation efforts in India's coffee districts have taken on key significance. These efforts have largely been focused on maintaining the habitat value of coffee estates by addressing the increasing trend toward removal of diversified shade and the single plantings of the exotic *Grevillea robusta* (also known as silver or silky oak).

According to legend, coffee cultivation was introduced to India during the 16th century by the Muslim saint Baba Budan. However, widespread expansion of the industry occurred only in the mid-19th century, through the vehicle of British colonialism, in the (then) sparsely populated and densely forested hill tracts of the Western Ghats. Today, India is the world's fifth largest producer of coffee, generating 274,000 tonnes of green coffee in 2006. The European Union (EU) absorbs 56 percent of total coffee exports, half of which are sold to Italy (Coffee Board of India, 2009). Karnataka and Kerala account for approximately 59 and 22 percent of India's total coffee growing area respectively. The coffee-growing community in India comprises smallholders (possessing less than 2 ha each), medium-size family 'planters', and a corporate sector including large-scale holdings (Neilson and Pritchard, 2009).

The Kodagu district in Karnataka (the peak production area for lower-priced Robusta output) still has 80 percent of its landscape under tree cover (Moppert, 2000) and is one of the most densely forested districts in India. While it contains three wildlife sanctuaries and one national park, 74 percent of Kodagu's forests lie outside the formal protected area system (Conservation International, 2008). Many of these non-conservation area forests are in fact coffee agroforests, leading to calls for a landscape approach to conservation in Kodagu (Bhagwat et al, 2005a). The heavily-shaded coffee plantations connect remnants of native forest, such that their ecological integrity—within a broader landscape of formal protected areas and sacred (*devarakadu*) groves—is a vital component of wider biodiversity conservation efforts. Kodagu is also a member of the International Model Forest Network and the Critical Ecosystem Partnership Fund, both of which concentrate on incorporating civil society in efforts to preserve habitat connectivity in the district.

Figure 11.4. A multi-strata coffee plantation in Kodagu (Photo source: Authors' own)

In many ways, Kodagu is the perfect exemplar of a coffee production system where maintenance of on-farm shade cover has critical benefits for biodiversity conservation. A survey by Bhagwat et al (2005b) found that tree, bird and fungal diversity in Kodagu was comparable between coffee plantations and adjacent protected forest and sacred groves. At face value then, the prevailing widespread practice of shade maintenance in Kodagu ought to allow most planters to satisfy the minimum shade requirements set out by the coffee codes (and even the stricter requirements set out by the Smithsonian Institution). However, the case of Kodagu also provides another unexpected paradox in the implementation of global certification schemes locally. Indeed, India has been one of the most vociferous critics of industry-wide certification schemes that attempt to make baseline environmental standards a requirement of market entry (Neilson and Pritchard,

2007). With the increasing tendency of codes to be as inclusive as possible, more than 12,000 hectares of, largely unshaded, coffee has been successfully certified by Utz in Vietnam (Utz Certified, 2006). What then, ask the Kodagu planters with their dense and diversified shade cover, does it really mean to have your farm certified as sustainable? Implementation of (certified) Vietnam-style production systems in Kodagu would be an environmental disaster, bringing into question the capacity to fairly benchmark environmental practices across distinct spatial arenas.

Value chain mechanisms designed to create economic incentives for on-farm habitat protection are, in essence, market-driven Payments for Environmental Services (see Chapters 14 to 17). Coffee farmers are paid a price premium for providing an ecosystem service (in this case, habitat protection) valued by coffee consumers in key markets. For example, around 5500 hectares of Bird-Friendly is now certified by the Smithsonian Institution (SMBC, 2009), although the program is not growing nearly as rapidly as more user-friendly models of certification. The program attempts to reward farms that 'provide good, forest-like habitat for birds rather than being grown on land that has been cleared of all other vegetation' (SMBC, 2009).

The success of eco-friendly coffees is premised on a market demand for habitat protection amongst coffee consumers, a clear environmental service provided by coffee producers, and a reliable mechanism (certification) which ensures that price premiums are conditional upon service provision. As noted above, the key export market for Indian coffee is Italy, where sustainable coffee has one of the lowest market shares of all European countries (Giovannucci and Koekoek, 2003). A further 28 percent of Indian production is consumed domestically (Coffee Board of India, 2009) in a highly price-sensitive market where consumers are currently unwilling to pay a price premium for sustainable product. With this domestic market expected to grow rapidly in the coming years (Coffee Board of India, 2009), Indian producers do not have a strong link with environmentally-discerning consumers willing to pay for habitat provision in the Western Ghats.

However, with mainstream international buyers tending towards more user-friendly certification schemes, six large corporate estates in India, covering 10,429 hectares, have obtained Utz Certification (Table 11.2). The Utz program does not demand adherence to rigorous shade requirements (Table 11.1) and certification does nothing to further a conservation agenda in Kodagu. It is difficult, therefore, to envisage the development of supply-chain mechanisms capable of inducing management incentives for habitat provision in Kodagu, as the additional benefits provided by shade are difficult to market. Moreover, the perceived foregone income that accompanies maintenance of diversified shade would be a far more powerful economic driver of behaviour than any possible premium price offered through supply chain certification (see also Gaveau et al, 2009).

Far more important determinants of planter behaviour, it would seem, are the effects of local social institutions. The cultural and institutional context of environmental governance in Kodagu is unique within India, with prevailing family structures and hierarchies, and common property management arrangements, playing a central role in forest and land management. Of particular note are the existence of *devarakadu*, sacred groves and traditional tenure systems affecting on-farm tree rights. The Kodava people of Kogadu practice a form of ancestral worship and reverence for family deities associated with the *devarakadu*. Deep religious reverence for nature rather than resource scarcity tends to be the basis for the long standing commitment to preserving these forests (Ramakrishnan, 1996). A traditional land tenure system, known as *jamma*, maintains hereditary and inalienable rights to land. Whilst restrictions on tree ownership related to *Jamma* tenure are a continuing source of tension in the community (*The Hindu*, 2006), they do appear to have helped protect the biodiversity of trees, birds and other biota on the plantations, and have slowed down the replacement of native trees by exotic fast growing shade trees (Satish et al, 2007). Working with such social institutions and devising local biodiversity management strategies, such as those currently being promoted by the Kodagu Model Forest Trust (Ghazoul et al, 2009), are far more likely to deliver real conservation benefits than are buyer-driven codes based on global benchmarks. Whilst many existing Kodagu plantations would easily satisfy the biodiversity conservation requirements of generic codes such as Utz Certified and 4C, the real challenge for social and environmental sustainability in the region depends on factors wholly outside the scope of these codes.

Water use and extraction: insights from input-intensive coffee production in Vietnam's Central Highlands

Specifications on water use and extraction are limited in the major coffee codes (Table 11.1). Only the NASAA organic standard and 4C contain specific requirements that water extraction should not exceed replenishment capacity, and the 4C specifications are extremely generic. The lack of attention to water management is brought into focus through examination of resource management issues in the coffee regions of Dak Lak Province, in Vietnam's Central Highlands (Figure 11.5), where groundwater depletion has emerged as the pre-eminent environmental concern.

As evident in Figure 11.1, Vietnam exploded onto the world coffee stage from a relatively small export volume of less than 4000 tonnes in 1980 to more than 700,000 tonnes in 2000. Stimulated by the *Doi Moi* economic reforms of 1986, which permitted foreign investment in trade and export, and effectively decollectivized rural production, coffee cultivation expanded rapidly in the Central Highlands, and especially Dak Lak Province (Giovannucci et al, 2004). Government incentives for large-scale migration from the lowlands provided labour while abundant land, fertile basaltic soils and accessible groundwater resources provided the natural base for production. Cultivation of the Robusta species is widespread with average productivity reported to be a staggering 2000 kilograms of green beans per hectare (Giovannucci et al, 2004; ICO, 2005; Marsh, 2007). This has been possible due to high rates of fertilizer use, surplus labour, an absence of shade management, and to intensive field irrigation drawing from high quality basaltic aquifers (D'haeze et al, 2005b, Marsh, 2007).

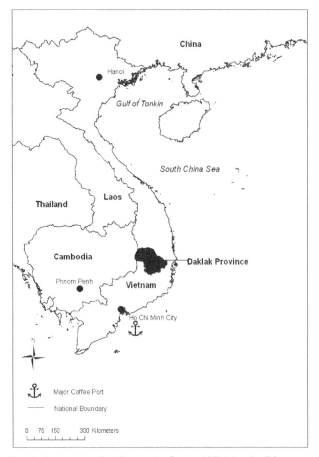

Figure 11.5. Dak Lak province in Vietnam's Central Highlands (Map source: Authors' own work)

The production of coffee in the Central Highlands is dominated by smallholder farmers. At present, an estimated 95 percent of the total area planted to coffee is managed by privately-run smallholders, with the remaining coffee area belonging to state-owned enterprises (Marsh, 2007). These small farmers, however, are relatively well resourced, with a high level of tenure security, good access to finance and high levels of ownership of farm equipment (Rios and Shively, 2006). Vietnamese coffee is sold mainly into the European market, with Germany alone accounting for 15 percent of all exports (perhaps explaining the key position that Vietnam has assumed as a testing site and member of the 4C initiative which was established by the German government with endorsement from the German Coffee Association). Other major markets include the USA, Spain, Italy, and Switzerland (UN Comtrade, 2009).

A supportive policy environment within Vietnam was instrumental in driving the rapid expansion of cultivated area. The Ministry of Agriculture and Rural

Development (MARD) in Vietnam has actively promoted coffee production in the Central Highlands, while the Vietnamese Bank of Agriculture and Rural Development was instrumental in providing access for individual coffee growers to subsidized credit in the Central Highlands for both crop finance and for developing new plantations (Nash et al, 2002). Landuse rights are the primary form of collateral, and the 1988 land reforms (*Resolution 10*) gave farmers 10–15 year usage rights, which were then followed by the 1993 Land Law which granted 50 year usage rights for perennial crops such as coffee and put farmers in control of production decisions (Nguyen and Grote, 2004). The liberalization of fertilizer imports in 1991 resulted in sharply falling retail prices, and subsequent government interventions have generally meant that coffee farmers receive an overall fertilizer subsidy (Nguyen and Grote, 2004). Other supportive policies include investment in research and training, subsidized electricity for farmers, trade reform including the removal of export taxes and quotas, positive interest rates, and the currency devaluation (Nguyen and Grote, 2004).

Deforestation, excessive reliance on agrochemicals and unsustainable groundwater extractions are all key areas of environmental concern in the Central Highlands (Cheesman and Bennett, 2005; D'haeze et al, 2005a; ; ICO, 2005; Lindskog et al, 2005; Bau, 2007; Giungato et al, 2008). It is estimated that anywhere between 235,000 and one million hectares of forest has been cleared for coffee in the Central Highlands since the 1970s (Cheesman and Bennett, 2005; D'haeze et al, 2005a; Lindskog et al, 2005). Farmers have subsequently adopted an unshaded coffee production system quite distinct from the heavily-shaded coffee forests of Kodagu or the community-based agroforestry systems of Sumber Jaya. Application of chemical fertilizers on Vietnam's coffee plantations is high by any standards. Technical guidelines for coffee production issued by MARD (TCN 478-2002) recommend an average of 1525 kilograms of nitrogen fertilizer per hectare. A survey of small farmers undertaken by Rios and Shively (2006) found average rates of NPK fertilizer application of 1387 kilograms per hectare in addition to 323 kilograms per hectare of urea. According to Bau (2007), these amounts are 10–23 percent higher than the actual nutrient demands of the coffee plant.

Water has been considered a free resource or public good in the highlands, with coffee cultivation relying predominantly on irrigation from groundwater and to a lesser extent rivers and streams (Luu, 2002, cited in D'haeze et al, 2005b). According to the MARD guideline, 1650–1980 cubic metres of water per hectare should be applied annually, while Vicofa (ICO, 2005) reports that no less than 650 litres is required per tree very 20 to 25 days during the dry season. Several studies suggest that these levels of extraction are above natural recharge levels (Cheesman and Bennett, 2005), or at least exceed safe aquifer yields during dry years with adverse impacts on downstream water users (D'haeze et al, 2005b). Similarly, other authors have reported that intensive groundwater extraction has lowered the groundwater table under the Dak Lak plateau by up to five metres over the past 20 years (Ha et al, 2001).

While further research is required to gain a proper understanding of local hydrological systems, it is clear that coffee production in Vietnam's Central Highlands faces serious sustainability challenges, particularly in relation to the responsible use of fertilizers and the management of local water (particularly groundwater) resources. Not only do these issues receive only cursory attention in many of the codes summarized in Table 11.1, but the ability of supply chain audit regimes to realistically contribute to appropriate resource management in the Central Highlands is also fundamentally questionable. Taking the case of sustainable water management, the only realistic means by which issues of over-extraction can be addressed is through catchment-wide planning initiatives that rely on substantial technical input and trade-offs between competing users. As exemplified by the protracted process of negotiating water management plans in other places in the world, successful water sharing plans require strong community participation along with hard-nosed negotiating on water allocations. Both the processes and the outcome in this regard will be strongly dependent on, and informed by, the local social, institutional and biophysical environment.

Vietnam's Water Resources Law of 1998 requires a permit for extraction of surface and groundwater resources for agriculture. However, users do not pay any fees and subsequent decrees have essentially exempted individual smallholders. As a result, coffee-related groundwater extraction in the Central Highlands remains largely unregulated (Cheesman and Bennett, 2005; D'haeze et al, 2005b). Catchment-wide water planning initiatives, involving high levels of stakeholder participation, will be an essential first step towards achieving sustainability in Vietnam's coffee sector. Such concerns currently receive minimal attention within current modes of non-state environmental governance (as presented in this chapter) and the capacity of value-chain governance to contribute to inherently localized environmental issues such as these appear to be fundamentally limited.

Conclusion

The wide-ranging intrusion of certification schemes and producer codes of conduct into the global coffee industry reflects a broader trend toward corporate social responsibility globally and an underlying confidence in the ability of market mechanisms to drive the improved ethical performance of industries. Indeed, the emergence of what has been called 'post-sovereign environmental governance' (Karkkainen, 2004) has been presented as a response to the perceived limitations of top-down, territorially defined state structures. However, this chapter has expressed a concern that attempts to reduce the management issues of complex landscape-level processes to a supply chain compliance checklist will do little to address critical sustainability issues in producing regions. We argue that supply chain audit regimes are fundamentally ill-suited to the requirements of natural resource management, which are socially and ecologically embedded within real places in diverse and intricate ways.

Extra-territorial systems of environmental governance, orchestrated by downstream, branded manufacturers under the umbrella of schemes like 4C and Utz Certified risk divorcing environmental management decisions from the place-specific contexts of local agro-ecological problems. The rise of buyer-driven environmental regulation, therefore, has far-reaching implications for global environmental governance more broadly. Corporate social responsibility initiatives are increasingly defining the boundaries of acceptable and unacceptable social and environmental performance in a way which both pre-empts and displaces state intervention. This implies a shift in environmental governance away from the local scale towards globally-defined systems and structures. The challenges of sustainable natural resource management, however, are often environmental externalities that require some kind of institutional intervention from the state.

The need to present clear signals to consumers through standard-setting processes, verification systems and labels necessarily results in a simplification of the environmental challenges being faced in producer regions. Furthermore, the diverse institutional and political structures that underpin environmental decision-making and law enforcement within each region are rarely incorporated within supply chain certification systems. This is due to the inherent difficulties of incorporating local diversity with code structures as well as the widespread prevalence of an oppositional stance taken towards institutional and political actors by many NGOS and corporate interests. As argued by Bitzer et al (2008, p282):

> governments from coffee producing countries remain completely disconnected from partnership-induced change in the coffee chain, whilst governments from coffee consuming countries appear to be incidentally supporting various partnerships without exhibiting a strategic approach to the sustainability challenges of the chain or the situation of the most marginalized producers.

Supply chain traceability systems addressing sustainability issues at sites of production have followed in the wake of similar systems designed to address food safety issues following widely-publicized food scares in the 1980s and 1990s. As such, buyer-driven sustainability schemes are ultimately intended to benefit the same citizenry—consumers—if not for the sake of their physical health, then for their ethical consciences. The argument presented in this chapter holds important implications for development policy in impoverished regions struggling with the complexities of sustainable resource management. Certification schemes, in the coffee sector at least, have been a magnet for donor funding in recent years, promising win-win solutions for the environment and economic development through a mechanism that is relatively cheap and easy to implement, with easily measurable indicators (i.e. number of farmers certified). However, we argue that greater scrutiny is required to ascertain whether such programs are actually delivering the promised environmental benefits on the ground and whether scarce development funds may not be more effectively spent investing in participatory resource management institutions at a local scale.

Notes

[1] Based on a farmer survey by Jeff Neilson and Bustanul Arifin in 2008 of 324 coffee-growing households across Indonesia, including 122 households in Lampung.

[2] The term 'Protection Forest' refers to *Hutan Lindung*, a category of forest protection within Indonesia applied to upper catchments to prevent soil erosion and maintain hydrological functions but without the active protection afforded to formal conservation areas such as National Parks. In contrast, 'Protected Areas' refers to all forest areas (including National Parks and Protection Forest) where any form of forest clearing is legally prohibited.

References

Arifin, B. (2005) 'Institutional Perspectives of Lifescapes Co-Management: Lessons Learned from RUPES Sites in Sumatra Indonesia', in D. Murdiyarsuo, and H. Herawati (eds) *Carbon Forestry: Who will benefit?*, Centre for International Forestry Research, Bogor, Indonesia, pp156–175

Bacon, C. (2005) 'Confronting the coffee crisis: Can Fair Trade, organic, and specialty coffees reduce small-scale farmer vulnerability in Northern Nicaragua?', *World Development*, vol 33, no 3, pp497–511

Badan Pusat Statistik (BPS) (2008) *Indonesian Foreign Trade Statistics: Volume I 2003–2007 Exports*, Badan Pusat Statistik (Central Statistics Agency), Jakarta, Indonesia

Bau, L.N. (2007) 'Current situation of coffee production and measures to coffee sustainable development', in *Measures to Coffee Sustainability*, MARD and Central Extension Centre, Hanoi, Vietnam

Bhagwat, S.A., Kushalappa, C.G., Williams, P.H. and Brown, N.D. (2005a) 'A landscape approach to biodiversity conservation of sacred groves in the Western Ghats of India', *Conservation Biology*, vol 19, no 6, pp1853–1862

Bhagwat, S.A., Kushalappa, C.G., Williams, P.H. and Brown, N.D. (2005b) 'The role of informal protected areas in maintaining biodiversity in the Western Ghats of India', *Ecology and Society*, vol 10, no 1, Article 8

Bitzer, V., Francken, M. and Glasbergen, P. (2008) 'Intersectoral partnerships for a sustainable coffee chain: Really addressing sustainability or just picking (coffee) cherries?', *Global Environmental Change*, vol 18, no 2, pp271–284

Busch, L. and Bain, C. (2004) 'New! Improved? The transformation of the global agrifood system', *Rural Sociology*, vol 69, no 3, pp321–346

Calo, M. and Wise, T.A. (2005) *Revaluing Peasant Coffee Production: Organic and Fair Trade Markets in Mexico*, Global Development and Environmental Institute Medford, MA

4C (2007) *Annual Report*, http://www.4c-coffeeassociation.org/download/2008/4c-annual-report-2007.pdf, accessed 6 August 2009

4C (2008) *Common Code for the Coffee Community, Updated Version February 2008*, www.4c-coffeeassociation.org/download/2008/4C_001_CodeDocument-2008_v1.1_en.pdf, accessed 18 August 2008

Cheesman, J. and Bennett, J. (2005) *Managing Groundwater Access in the Central Highlands (Tay Nguyen)*, Viet Nam Research Report No. 1, Asia Pacific School of Economics and Government, The Australian National University, Canberra

Coffee Board of India (2009) 'Database on Coffee January 2009', Economic and Market Intelligence Unit of the Coffee Board, Bangalore, www.indiacoffee.org, accessed 30 March 2009

Conservation International (2008) 'Biodiversity hotspots', www.biodiversityhotspots.org, accessed 17 July 2008

D'haeze, D., Deckers, J., Rae, D., Phong, T.A. and Loi, H.V. (2005a) 'Environmental and socio-economic impacts of institutional reforms on the agricultural sector of Vietnam: Land suitability assessment for Robusta coffee in Dak Gan region', *Agriculture, Ecosystems and Environment*, vol 105, pp59–76

D'haeze, D., Rae, D., Deckers, J., Phong, T.A. and Loi, H.V. (2005b) 'Groundwater extraction for irrigation of Coffea canephora in Ea Tul watershed, Vietnam: A risk evaluation', *Agricultural Water Management,* vol 73, pp1–19

Dietsch, T., Philpott, S.M., Rice, R., Greenberg, R. and Bichier, P. (2004) 'Conservation policy in coffee landscapes, *Science,* vol 303, pp265–266

FAOSTAT (2009) 'radestat Database, Food and Agricultural Organization of the United Nations', Query: Green beans—export volume tonnes, http://faostat.fao.org/site/406/default.aspx, accessed 31 March 2009

Gaveau, D.L.A., Linkie, M., Suyadi, Levang, P. and Leader-Williams, N. (2009) 'Three decades of deforestation in southwest Sumatra: Effects of coffee prices, law enforcement and rural poverty', *Biological Conservation*, vol 142, no 3, pp597–605

Ghazoul, J., Garcia, C., and Kushalappa, C.G. (2009) 'Landscape labelling: A concept for next-generation payment for ecosystem service schemes', *Forest Ecology and Management*, vol 258, pp1889–1895

Giovannucci, D. and Koekoek, F.J. (2003) *The State of Sustainable Coffee: A study of Twelve Major Markets*, Daniele Giovannucci, Philadelphia, PA

Giovannucci, D., Lewin, B., Swinkels, R. and Varangis, P. (2004) *The Socialist Republic of Vietnam: Coffee Sector Report No. 29358-VN*, Agriculture and Rural Development Department of the World Bank, The World Bank, Washington, DC

Giungato, P., Nardone, E., and Notarnicola, L. (2008) 'Environmental and socio-economic effects of intensive agriculture', *Journal of Commodity Science, Technology and Quality*, vol 47, nos I–IV, pp135–151

Ha, D.T., Phuoc, P.H.D., Nguyen, N.T., Du, L.V., Hung, P.T., Espaldon, V.O. and Magsino, A.O. (2001) 'Impacts of changes in policy and market conditions on land use, land management and livelihood among farmers in central highlands of Vietnam', in A.G. Garcia (ed) *Sustaining Natural Resources Management in Southeast Asia*, SEAMEO Regional Center for Graduate Study and Research in Agriculture (SEARCA), Los Baños, Philippines

Hindu, The (2006) Meeting on tree rights a farce, says committee, *The Hindu*, 12 November, www.hindu.com/2006/11/12/stories/2006111210920300.htm, accessed 6 August 2009

International Coffee Organization (ICO) (2005) *Development of and Prospects for the Vietnamese Coffee Industry*, ED 1957/05, International Coffee Organization, London

Karkkainen, B.C. (2004) 'Post-sovereign environmental governance', *Global Environmental Politics*, vol4, no 1, pp72–96

Kilian, B., Jones, C., Pratt, L. and Villalobos, A. (2006) 'Is sustainable agriculture a viable strategy to improve farm income in Central America?', *Journal of Business Research*, vol 59, pp322–330

Kulkarni, J., Mehta, P., Boominathan, D. and Chaudhuri, S. (2007) *A Study of Man-Elephant Conflict in Nagarhole National Park and Surrounding Areas of Kodagu District in Karnataka, India*, Envirosearch, Pune, India

Lindskog, E., Dow, K., Axberg, G.N., Miller, F. and Hancock, A. (2005) *When rapid changes in Environmental, Social and Economic conditions converge: challenges to sustainable livelihoods in Dak Lak, Vietnam*, Stockholm Environment Institute, Stockholm, Sweden

Luu, N. (2002) *Exploitation Capacity and Recurrent Groundwater Resources in Dak Lak Province (kha nhang khai thac va hien trang tai nguyen nuoc duoi dat tinh Dak Lak)*, Institute of Meteorology and Hydrology, Buon Ma Thuot, Dak Lak, Vietnam

Marsh, A. (2007) *Diversification Smallholder Farmers: Viet Nam Robusta Coffee*. Agricultural Management, Marketing and Finance Working Document No. 19, Food and Agricultural Organization of the United Nations, Rome, www.fao.org/Ag/ags/publications/docs/AGSF_WorkingDocuments/agsfwd19.pdf, accessed 31 March 2009

Moppert, B. (2000) 'The elaboration of the Landscape', in P.S.Ramakrishnan, U.M. Chandrashekara, C. Elouard, C.Z. Guilmoto, R.K. Maikhuri, K.S. Rao, K.G. Saxena and S. Shankar, (eds) *Mountain Biodiversity, Land Use Dynamics and Traditional Ecological Knowledge*, Oxford and India Book House, New Delhi, India

Myers, N., Mittermeier, R.A., Mittermeier, C.G., da Fonseca, G.A.B. and Kent, J. (2000) 'Biodiversity hotspots for conservation priorities', *Nature*, vol 403, pp 853–858

Nash, J., Lewin, B. and Smit, H. (2002) *Vietnam: Agricultural Price Risk Management, Pepper, Rubber, Coffee, Phase I Report*, World Bank, Washington, DC

National Association for Sustainable Agriculture Australia (NASAA) (2008) *The NASAA Organic Standard*, www.nasaa.com.au/data/pdfs/AAAA%20NASAA%20Organic%20Standard%2013%20May%202008.pdf, accessed 28 August 2008

Neilson, J. (2008) 'Global private regulation and value-chain restructuring in Indonesian smallholder coffee systems', *World Development*, vol 36, no 9, pp1607–1622

Neilson, J. and Pritchard, B. (2007) 'Green coffee: The contradictions of global sustainability initiatives from the Indian perspectives', *Development Policy Review*, vol 25, no 3, pp311–331

Neilson, J. and Pritchard, B. (2009) *Value Chain Struggles: Institutions and Governance in the Plantation Districts of South India*, Blackwell, Oxford

Nguyen, H. and Grote, U. (2004) 'Agricultural Policies in Vietnam: Producer Price Estimates, 1986–2002', *MTID Discussion paper No. 79*, Markets, Trade, and

Institutions Division of the International Food Policy Research Institute (IFPRI), Washington, DC

O'Brien, T.G. and Kinnard, M.F. (2004) 'Response to Dietsch, T., Philpott, S.M., Rice, R., Greenberg, R. and Bichier, P. (2004): Conservation policy in coffee landscapes', *Science,* vol 303, pp265–266

Rainforest Alliance (2008) *Sustainable Agriculture Standard*, www.rainforest-alliance.org/agriculture/documents/SAN_Sustainable_Agriculture_Standard_%2 0February2008.pdf, accessed 28 August 2008

Rainforest Alliance (undated) 'Products from Farms Certified by the Rainforest Alliance: Coffee Producers', www.rainforest-alliance.org/agriculture/documents/cert_coffee.pdf

Ramakrishnan, P.S. (1996) 'Conserving the sacred: From species to landscapes', *Nature and Resources*, vol 32, no 1, pp11–19

Ramesh, B.R. (2001) 'Patterns of vegetation, biodiversity and endemism in Western Ghats' in Y. Gunnell and B.P. Radhakrishna (eds) Sahyadri: The Great Escarpment of the Indian Subcontinent, *Memoir*, vol 47, no 2, Geological Society of India, Bangalore, pp 973–981

Raynolds, L.T., Murray, D. and Heller, A. (2007) 'Regulating sustainability in the coffee sector: A comparative analysis of third-party environmental and social certification initiatives', *Agriculture and Human Values*, vol 24, pp147–163

Rice, R.A. and Ward, J.R. (1996) *Coffee, Conservation and Commerce in the Western Hemisphere: How Individuals and Institutions can Promote Ecologically-Sound Farming and Forest Management in Northern Latin America,* Natural Resources Defence Council and Smithsonian Migratory Bird Centre, Washington DC

Rios, A. and Shively, G.E. (2006) 'Farm size and nonparametric efficiency measurements for coffee farms in Vietnam', *Forests, Trees, and Livelihoods*, vol 16, no 4, pp397–412

Satish, B.N., Kushalappa, C.G. and Garcia, C. (2007) 'Land tenure systems: A key to conserve tree diversity in coffee-based agroforestry systems of Kodagu, Central Western Ghats', *Second International Symposium on Multi-strata Agroforestry Systems with Perennial Crops,* September 2007, CATIE, Turrialba, Costa Rica

Smithsonian Migratory Bird Centre (SMBC) (2009) 'Find Bird Friendly® Coffee', Smithsonian Migratory Bird Centre, http://nationalzoo.si.edu/ConservationAnd Science/MigratoryBirds/Coffee, accessed 30 March 2009

Starbucks Coffee Company (2007) *CAFÉ Practices Generic Evaluation Guidelines 2.0*, Starbucks Coffee Company, Seattle, WA www.scscertified.com/csrpurchasing/sbux/docs/CAFEPracticesGenericEvaluati onGuidelinesV2.0_010307.pdf, accessed 18 August 2008

Starbucks Coffee Company (undated) 'CAFÉ Practices, approved verifiers', www.scscertified.com/csr/starbucks_approvedverifiers.html, accessed 6 August 2009

Sunderlin, W.D., Angelsen, A., Resosudarmo, D.P., Dermawan, A. and Rianto, E. (2001) 'Economic crisis, small farmer well-being, and forest cover change in Indonesia', *World Development*, vol 29, no 5, pp767–782

Suryahadi, A. Sumarto, S. and Pritchett, L. (2003) 'Evolution of poverty during the crisis in Indonesia', *Asian Economic Journal*, vol 17, no 3, pp221–241

Timmer, C. P. (2004) 'The road to pro-poor growth: the Indonesian experience in regional perspective', *Bulletin of Indonesian Economic Studies*, vol 40, no 2, pp177–207

UN Comtrade (2009) 'United Nations Commodity Trade Statistics Database', http://comtrade.un.org, accessed 30 March 2009

Utz Certified (2006) 'Certified Code of Conduct', www.utzcertified.org/index.php?pageID=111&showdoc=111_0_14, accessed 18 August 2008

Utz Certified (undated) 'Certified producers', http://utzcertified.org/index.php?pageID=141, accessed 6 August 2009

Verbist, B., Putra, A. E. D. and Budidarsono, S. (2005) 'Factors driving land use change: Effects on watershed functions in a coffee agroforestry system in Lampung, Sumatra', *Agricultural Systems*, vol 85, pp254–270

Worldwide Fund for Nature (WWF) (2007) *Gone in an Instant: How the Trade in Illegally Grown Coffee is Driving the Destruction of Rhino, Tiger and Elephant Habitat. Bukit Barisan Seletan National Park, Sumatra, Indonesia*, WWF—Indonesia, Asian Rhino and Elephant Action Strategy, Bukit Barisan Seletan Program

12

Geographical Indications and Biodiversity

Erik Thévenod-Mottet

A wide number of agro-food products are known for where they come from and the ways in which they are grown or produced. Names such as Basmati, Roquefort and Camembert speak both to the unique agroecological and cultural circumstances that shape the qualities of particular products, and to a sense of place and authenticity that goes beyond their immediate sensory characteristics. Geographical Indications (GIs) provide a legal framework to protect and promote such products. The World Trade Organization's Trade Related Intellectual Property Rights (TRIPS) Agreement, adopted in 1994, defines GIs very broadly as:

> indications which identify a good as originating in the territory of a Member, or a region or locality in that territory, where a given quality, reputation or other characteristic of the good is essentially attributable to its geographical origin.

This definition has become the international reference point for discussion of GIs even though a number of national and international legal definitions pre-existed TRIPS and the implementation of GI protection worldwide remains characterized by considerable diversity. The number of recognized GIs is growing quite quickly around the world. For example, there are currently more than 800 registered agrifood GIs in the EU (excluding wines and spirits, of which there are more than 4000). One hundred and seventeen GIs were registered in India between 2003 and 2009, of which 33 were for agri-food products.

As neither 'quality' nor 'reputation' are explicitly defined by the TRIPS Agreement, it appears that the commercial value enjoyed by GIs is the primary rationale for their legal protection. Nevertheless, protecting the commercial value of GIs may still enable their use to achieve positive impacts on biodiversity, potentially allowing producers who protect traditional varieties or agroecologies associated with particular GIs to benefit from remuneration through the market. Thus public goods may be provided through the market for specific agri-food goods. In order to assess the extent to which this is likely, this chapter examines the complex nature of GIs, the conceptual relationship between GIs and biodiversity, the empirical realities of this relationship, and future prospects for biodiversity-friendly GI protection. A brief description of GIs discussed throughout this chapter is found in Table 12.1.

GIs: a complex market standard and a tool for public policies

The legal concept of GIs emerged in European countries some decades ago; initially taking the form of what are called permissive systems and more latterly moving towards prescriptive systems. The permissive approach is focused on minimal protection of consumers and producers against the use of the geographical designation on products which do not originate from the designated region. It deals with 'indications of source' which are not specifically registered or recognized, but may be considered by courts or tribunals in the case of conflicts. The prescriptive approach, by contrast, links each GI with a product having characteristics that are precisely defined. It considers that deception can occur not only in relation to the geographical origin, but also in relation to the specific qualities of designated products. This led to the creation of a new regulatory tool—the official registration of GIs—which consequently distinguishes between those GIs which are officially recognized as such and all other 'potential' GIs which may be eligible for protection. Thus, whereas early judicial and legal attempts to deal with GIs mainly focused on the delimitation of a geographical area in order to specify the circle of legitimate users, the development of prescriptive systems resulted in detailed mandatory descriptions of the specificity of each product concerned. This is the model of the *appellation d'origine* developed in France and other European countries. These collective mandatory prescriptions may be a powerful tool to direct and ensure some social and biodiversity impacts from the growth and/or manufacture of GI products.

Another trend, at the international level, that has influenced the development and regulation of GIs has been a move from the field of agricultural policies towards the field of intellectual property. Within the TRIPS Agreement, in particular, GIs are rather simply defined as private rights based on the economic value of a geographical name as determined by its reputation in the market. In much the same manner as a patent or a trademark, TRIPS does not explicitly connect GIs to any public concern beyond the recognition and protection of private property.

However contradictory this may appear at first glance, all national and international GI standards are influenced, in various ways, by both the prescriptive trend pioneered in Europe and the more minimalist approach of the TRIPS. The first move justifies the European concept of GI as a quality standard, whereas the second move explains the contrary vision of GI as a private intellectual property right which should not be used for specific public policies nor be defined through a specific coherent system.

Table 12.1. Examples of Geographical Indications

Geographical indication	Product	Location	Production per year	Number of producers
Abricotine	Apricot spirit	Valais, Switzerland	800 hl	4 distilleries, 40 fruit producers
Basmati	Rice	India and Pakistan	> 4 million tonnes	Not available
Camembert de Normandie	Cow cheese	Normandy, France	4300 tonnes	8 cheese-dairies, 1 farm cheese-maker, 1400 milk producers
Cardon épineux de Genève	Cardoon Vegetable	Geneva, Switzerland	130 tonnes	10 producers
Cour-Cheverny	Wine	Loire valley, France	55 ha 1540 hl	30 vine-growers and wine-makers
Damassine	Prune spirit	Jura, Switzerland	Not available	10 distilleries, 150 fruit producers
Gruyère	Cheese	Western Switzerland	30,000 tonnes	180 cheese-dairies, 52 alpine farm cheese-dairies, 2500 milk producers
Livarot	Cow cheese	Normandy, France	1300 tonnes	3 cheese-dairies, 1 farm cheese-maker, 108 milk producers
Neufchâtel	Cow cheese	Normandy, France	1500 tonnes	6 cheese dairies, 24 farm cheese-makers, 70 milk producers
Pico Duarte	Coffee	Dominican Republic	2000 tonnes	550 farmers
Poiré du Domfrontais	Perry (pear cider)	South Normandy, France	1000 hl	30 fruit producers and perry makers
Pont-l'Évêque	Cow cheese	Normandy, France	2800 tonnes	7 cheese dairies, 4 farm cheese-makers, 422 milk producers
Rye Bread from Valais	Rye bread	Valais, Switzerland	500 tonnes	60 bakeries, 2 mills, 50 farmers
Roquefort	Cheese	Southern France	19,000 tonnes	7 cheese-dairies, 2500 milk producers
Single Gloucester	Cheese	Gloucestershire, England	Not available	4 farm-based cheese-dairies
Tequila	Agave spirit	Mexico	2,850,000 hl	120 distilleries, 12000 agave farmers
Tomme de Savoie	Cheese	Savoy, France	6000 tonnes	15 cheese-dairies, 30 farm cheese-makers, 850 milk producers

The common EU prescriptive system for agri-food products other than wines and spirits was established in 1992 with two forms of GI; the Protected Designation of Origin (PDO) and the Protected Geographical Indication (PGI). For a product to be designated a PDO, all production and processing activities must take place in the delimitated area. For processed products to be registered as PGIs, some activities may be undertaken in other regions (generally the production of raw materials) provided that at least one stage of production or processing takes place in the delimited area. The application of this principle demonstrates a certain incoherence, however, with PGIs being assigned to fresh fruit and vegetables (which are obviously cultivated in the designated area) and to processed products which require both the processing and production of raw materials be undertaken within the designated area (e.g. cheeses, like the Tomme de Savoie PDO for which all the stages from the milk production to the ripening must take place in the delimitated area).

In such a framework, the codes of practices for PDO-PGI products are defined through collective responsibility, and increasingly reflect concerns about methods of production in relation to traditional, heritage and environmental values. Given that consumers and marketers place value on product attributes related to the mode of production, there is some opportunity for collective strategies and public policies to enlarge the notion of GI typical quality in order to include practices which, for example, are favourable to biodiversity. GI standards thus have the potential to acquire new dimensions as policy instruments. This is reflected in Europe where policy arguments in favour of GIs have expanded over time to include: (1) the protection of consumers from deception and of producers from unfair competition in relation to unlawful use of the designation for products not originating from the designated area or not having the expected quality; (2) the management of the quantity supplied by an industry; (3) endogenous local development and social cohesion; and (4) biodiversity and cultural heritage protection (Sylvander et al, 2006). All these arguments were found in the preamble of the EU Reg. 2081/92, and they are nowadays inserted in international debates.

Unlike the other main forms of intellectual property right (IPR), the nature of GIs is collective and open (according to the requirements on the products); they protect tradition rather than innovation; and the duration of the protection is unlimited in time. Since the 1990s, however, a similar perspective on IPRs has begun to develop concerning traditional knowledge, folklore and biological resources; in particular, through debates at the World Intellectual Property Organization (WIPO). Relationships between these intellectual property fields were established both in negotiations and scientific research (Roussel and Verdeaux, 2007), reinforcing the environmental and heritage dimension that was already emerging in European GI standards.

Why GIs should be related to biodiversity issues

Among all forms of intellectual property right, GIs are those which are most disputed regarding their nature, coverage and implementation. Trademarks, patents and copyright are generally regarded as neutral tools in the sense that they are intended only to grant limited rights (in terms of both scope and duration) to designated owners in order to encourage people to invent, create and trade. They make no assessment of intrinsic value. Nor are they concerned with quality or the protection of consumers (Hermitte, 2001). Some countries have sought to replicate this neutrality in their approach to GIs; mainly countries of the New World such as the USA and Australia. Neutral GI standards are generally based on the trademark concept and/or regulated through judicial procedures related to unfair competition or the misleading of consumers. In these standards, there is no particular assessment of criteria related to methods of production, biological resources etc, and no mechanism of state arbitration amongst producers. They are free to organize themselves and to formulate agreements regarding the protection of product quality through mandatory codes of practice, or not. Should they reach agreement, codes of practice may be of any kind, focus or level of detail. It is, therefore, likely that neutral GI standards are likely to do no more, and possibly much less, to integrate biodiversity concerns than either less territorial standards such as organic and fair trade or other local and international initiatives supporting ecological production.

Alternatively, GIs are perceived in numerous other countries such as France, Italy and India as a form of recognition of specific products and production systems that can be integrated with public policies that aim to influence territories, communities, environments etc. In addition, the protection conferred to GIs often contributes by itself to the reputation attached to each protected designation by associating it with an official horizontal quality standard identified, as in the European Union, with a common logo.

Concern about public goods—such as cultural heritage, consumer trust in the food system, biodiversity and sustainable agricultural practices and landscapes—has helped to stimulate considerable interest in GIs in non-European countries. This interest is linked, in particular, to the opportunities offered by GIs for local processes of social development. Most policy initiatives have been taken in line with national strategies to ensure WTO TRIPS compliance. Other initiatives stem from local projects or from the influence of extension, research or development activities. While legislation on GIs is not always in real use in developing countries, there is a growing concern and involvement of public policy with the aim of protecting, regulating and enhancing local initiatives for these products, as well as with supporting externally initiated projects with potential benefits for rural communities.

The reputations of geographically distinct products are both the source of commercial value attached to their designation and the grounds for their legal protection. Reputation is based on origin; a concept that denotes more than a point in space. Origin encapsulates a local set of relations between material resources and knowledge; between cultural elements, methods of production and processing, biological resources and landscapes etc. Depending on the type of product in question (from fresh vegetables to processed meat products, from cheeses to coffees), the elements of this set of relations will vary in form and importance.

Importantly, whatever these elements and relations are, it is not possible to capture and document their full complexity and diversity in the product's specification. Just as with other forms of product certification discussed in Chapters 10 and 11, standardization inevitably means that choices must be made about who and what will be included, modified, omitted etc. Nevertheless, as the specificity of GI products is often determined by particular local biological resources (from bacteria to ecosystems), the GI product's specification would logically aim at preserving those biological resources and their use. National GI standards and their doctrine can strongly support this approach. Generally speaking, the GI producers' strategy to distinguish their product from substitutes through links to *terroir* appears to be a key factor for commercial success (Barjolle and Sylvander, 2000).

For GI standards defined according to a strong public doctrine and implemented by state authorities, biodiversity concerns may be directly and indirectly associated with GIs as a public policy tool. From such a perspective, the recognition of a GI results from assessment of the conformity of the GI code of practices with public policies. Two kinds of assessment may be distinguished, corresponding to different levels of complexity. The first of these is the assessment of the GI specification in terms of local genetic resources, traditional methods of production and internal sustainability. This kind of assessment is increasingly applied for European GIs in recognition of growing consumer interest in old local breeds and plant varieties, for organic or 'natural' products and for relief from the pressures of industrialization, delocalization and accelerating change more generally. The second kind of assessment takes a broader territorial or even global perspective with respect to how specification of the GI may impact on biodiversity, sustainability and other values. Such an assessment may conclude that the development of a certain GI product should not be encouraged as it would favour monocultural production of the product in question over more diverse agroecologies, or would place too much pressure on a limited resource. Thus the integration of cultural and environmental heritage concerns in GIs will depend on the degree of fusion between the mere legal protection of IPRs and the role of the standard as a sign that is meaningful to consumers concerned with authenticity and sustainability.

To date, concerns for the environment and biodiversity are not explicitly addressed in any national requirements for recognition of GIs. Further, the possibility of their inclusion is subject to significant debate and contestation. While biodiversity is central to debates about sustainable development and implicit in the originality of many GI products, many stakeholders do not see how or why GIs should be used as policy tools for biodiversity conservation. The basic strategic positioning of these stakeholders is to focus on the product rather than the environment; tangible attributes such as taste rather than ethical values; and opportunities for sales and trade of well-known products rather than local diversity. A further layer of complication is added by the complex games played by numerous local and national actors in the field of quality policies which often result in competition between quality signs, such as organic and GI, rather than an integrative approach.

A new paradigm is emerging, linking gastronomy with social and environmental concerns (as can be illustrated by the philosophy of Slow Food), but in a competitive landscape of quality labels, initiatives and policies. Such a situation explains why the current relations between GIs and biodiversity are so contrasting.

GIs and biodiversity: recognizing the heterogeneity

Whatever the general principles of individual GI standards might be—especially with regard to biodiversity—some points may be underlined at the scale of the agroecological and social systems within which those GI products sit. When applying for the registration of a PDO-like GI it is necessary to formalize and standardize the characteristics of the relevant local systems for the sustainability of the GI. Formalizing standards for the product concerned—in terms of requirements regarding materials, methods and final result—inevitably results in the reduction of both pre-existing and potential diversity in materials, methods and outcomes (for examples, see Bérard and Marchenay, 2004). The aim of this reduction is to ensure a certain specificity of the GI product in a collective and constant way. However, such reduction can be excessive and promote the development of monocultures. By way of example, at the end of the 19th century nine main varieties of agave were used in the production of Tequila, but when the Tequila GI was registered in 1974 its production was limited to a single variety of agave (Valenzuela et al, 2006). Similarly, numerous French GIs for wines have restricted the range of authorized grape varieties, excluding local varieties that were not cultivated in other regions, suffered from negative reputations or had already been neglected by the bigger producers.

Bearing this initial constraint in mind, the codification of a GI product has effects on all three levels of biodiversity (genetic/infraspecific, species/interspecific and ecosystemic), as well as on both domestic and wild biological resources. These effects derive as much from implicit provisions and outright omissions as from explicit specifications. The relative territorial importance of a GI system must also be taken into account.

With regard to genetic diversity, numerous GIs cover products that are uniquely derived from local plant varieties or animal breeds that may otherwise be substituted with more productive improved or modern varieties/breeds, thus reducing genetic erosion. Examples include Cardon épineux de Genève PDO (Geneva thorny cardoon, a very local variety); Cour-Cheverny PDO wine (the only remaining area for the Romorantin grape variety); Abricotine from Valais PDO (spirit made from the Luizet apricot variety); and Single Gloucester PDO cheese (Old Gloucester cattle breed). Larson (2007) thus points to the role that GIs may play in increasing the visibility of rare, underutilized and endemic genetic resources, both wild and domestic, within public policies and for consumers.

Additionally, the prescriptions contained within GIs for the reproduction of biological resources are fundamental to their ultimate impact of genetic diversity. As an example, a conflict emerged among producers over the registration of Damassine, a spirit made from a local variety of prune in the Swiss region of Jura. This conflict concerned the three main techniques used to reproduce the trees; namely, grafting, replanting the stump shoots or growing trees from fruit stones. The Ministry of Agriculture finally decided to allow all three methods in the registered product's specification but provided a special sub-designation for spirit derived from trees grown from fruit stones—which is generally considered to be of the highest quality. In this case, granting a specific labelling for this method of production is likely to have positive impacts on biodiversity since grafts come from a limited number of selected trees and thus diminish infraspecific genetic diversity. Additionally, trees grown from fruit stones are generally standard trees which are more favourable to wildlife than are grafted half-standard trees. A similarly biodiversity-positive example centres on the microbiological diversity of the Gruyère PDO in Switzerland, for which it is mandatory to use permanently reproduced cultures of bacteria specific to each cheese-dairy rather than selected dried bacteria strains that are the standard for industrial cheeses and which would provide greater uniformity of product quality.

With regard to species diversity, product specifications may include explicit provisions that extend diversity considerations beyond the biological resources that are directly used. For example, specifications for the Poiré du Domfrontais PDO cover both the local and traditional varieties of pear used in its manufacture and the manner in which these are grown; namely, in extensive types of orchard that provide habitat for wild flora and fauna (de Sainte-Marie, Bérard, 2005). The GI specification thus includes a particular, species rich, agroecology.

However, the impacts of such provisions related to biodiversity in GI specifications (or their absence) is not easy to assess at the ecosystemic or landscape level. The relative importance of the GI product within a production landscape is perhaps the first issue to consider. This may be assessed in terms of the size of this landscape, the types of agroecologies and other ecosystems within it, or the degree of specialization of producers and processors. As an example, the general trend in mountainous regions is to abandon the production of cereals. But in Valais, Switzerland, as soon as an application was submitted to register the reputed Rye Bread from Valais as a PDO the area of rye cultivation began to increase; nearly doubling from 51 to 94 hectares over five years, after years of decline. GIs may, therefore, help to reverse trends towards simplification with associated benefits for species and landscape biodiversity. The economic success of GI products may contribute to the viability of agricultural activities in marginal and mountainous regions, and thus to the maintenance of humanized ecosystems which are interesting for biodiversity, such as alpine pastures. Conversely, just like any other agricultural activity, cultivation of GIs may place pressures on ecosystem biodiversity, particularly if the market value attached to GI products encourages producers to abandon more diversified agroecosystems in order to increase output of more profitable GI products.

The considerable heterogeneity, both synchronic and diachronic, among GI standards systems and product specifications makes it impossible to propose general principles regarding the relationships between GIs and biodiversity. Among registered GIs—including those GIs that exist within a common regulatory system such as the European one—there are at least two sources of heterogeneity. The first is based on incentives for seeking legal protection, and the second is based on collective and state arbitration of each GI product's specifications.

Broadly speaking, there are two main incentives for seeking GI status. One is to protect the economic interests of producers of well known and largely exported regional products from imitations and usurpations (e.g. Roquefort, Basmati and

Tequila) and the other is to facilitate the development of such an origin-based reputation through the use of the GI as a quality standard (e.g. Pico Duarte Coffee) (see Galtier et al, 2008). The first incentive applies to GIs that encapsulate long-established economic values recognized in remote markets. These were generally the first GIs to be registered. Emphasis is often on the processing methods and on the interests of processors and traders. The second incentive often corresponds with territorial development initiatives; integrating producers and other actors through multidimensional projects that are generally more favourable to environmental and cultural concerns. That said, as GIs registered in response to the first incentive have evolved over time they have often moved towards greater incorporation of heritage and environmental values. This may occur either through modification of the specification or through the initiative of producers inside the system. For example, the PDO cheeses of Normandy were first recognized following applications submitted by processors and no specific requirements were placed on milk production other than its local origin. Cheeses registered as PDOs included Neufchâtel in 1969, Pont l'Évêque in 1972, Livarot in 1975 and Camembert de Normandie in 1983. It was not until the 1990s that milk producers began to be involved in the GI systems. Following several initiatives from cheese factories to give financial incentives to milk producers who bred the local Normande cows, based their production on natural pastures, and so on, the four inter-professional organizations responsible for each PDO have more recently begun to revise their product specifications. The revised Livarot specification was approved in 2007 and requires that, by 2017, milk will be produced only from Normande cows. The new specification also requires cheese makers to use only natural sedges harvested within the delimitated area to ring the cheeses.

Despite the intent of most national regulatory systems to comply with obligations under the TRIPS and other international agreements, diversity among systems comprises another source of heterogeneity. Within the EU, product specifications must also comply with general requirements stipulated by the European Regulation. As mentioned above, there is a distinction in the EU between two types of GIs—PDOs and PGIs—the interpretation of which is left to national authorities. There is no EU directive on how to set up codes of practice which consequently vary considerably between member states and families of products. The implementation modalities of the GI definition—in particular, regarding the concept of linkage between product and *terroir*—are both formal and informal. They are also both general and on a case-by-case basis (for example, through the commissions in charge of evaluating applications for registration). The result is a wide diversity in specifications regarding methods of production and processing, the use of biological resources etc. This diversity is expressed in different levels of detail and comprehensiveness related to modernization, mechanization, local and traditional resources etc. As an example for comparable products, the European GIs for cheeses may have requirements varying from raw to pasteurized milk, from local breeds to any breed, from mandatory grazing to silage, from natural milk to additives etc. In addition, some cheeses are recognized as PDOs and others as PGIs, without corresponding to any clear distinction because in both cases the milk must come from the delimited area. The situation is, of course, even more confused at the international level.

GIs and biodiversity: a systematic perspective

One of the main justifications for the official recognition of GIs is to reduce the asymmetry of information between producers and consumers. Considering the huge growth in the number of registered GIs in recent years—growth that will continue as Southern countries develop and implement their own systems—and the heterogeneity among GI standards and regulatory systems, this information objective will become more and more difficult to reach. This chapter has explained the relevance of evaluating the specificities of each GI system according to the characteristics of the relevant legal and institutional framework (Thévenod-Mottet, 2006). At the international level, this regulatory complexity is multiplied by conflicting understandings between countries regarding what GIs are; conflicts that are rooted in national cultures and histories as much as in different legal systems (Torsen, 2005). The diversity that lies behind regulation of GIs as designations cannot be compared with the regulatory situation facing other IPRs. The subject of the protection is quite clearly delimited for trademarks (generally, a graphical representation and its word description, but there may also be a regulation in the case of collective or certification trademarks), copyrights (the artwork itself) or patents (a material and functional description of the invention). From this perspective, the relationships between GIs and biodiversity are, at a global scale, a question of the very nature of GIs. Either this is a right focused on the product itself through a comprehensive definition of materials, methods, results etc; or it is a right focused on producers through specification of the group of authorized users (possibly only according to the delimitation of a geographical area which would more-or-less correspond to an indication of source). In other words, if GIs are considered only and merely as an intellectual property right, there should be no particular rationale for requiring all of them to have positive impacts on biodiversity or other socially desirable values as there is no such requirement for other IPRs.

Linking GIs to local, and often rare or endangered biological resources, may be interpreted as a way to remunerate the in situ conservation of these resources thanks to the willingness of consumers to pay for products with a particular quality. But the impact of a GI on the preservation of one or even several plant or animal varieties may be accompanied by negative effects on species and ecosystemic biodiversity. The economic success of a GI product may reduce the diversity of production in the relevant territory with related impacts on local biodiversity. Evaluation of the impacts of a GI on biodiversity at this level would require baseline assessment of local biodiversity (genetic, species and ecosystemic) before registration of the product's specification, followed by regular monitoring thereafter. Comprehensive evaluation of the impacts of GI registration on biodiversity, however, would also require consideration of a more global perspective. Such evaluation is far from the norm, either in public policies or scientific research, single GI designations or all GI products within the same GI standard. This is the case in the most mature GI policy frameworks, suggesting that the establishment of comprehensive biodiversity assessment mechanisms at the international level is far from likely at the current time.

At the WTO and WIPO, debates over GIs currently focus on technical legal points and the scope of protection. These negotiations may result in an international legal standard for GIs that includes a register of all specifically protected GIs. But, even so, GIs cannot be considered a genuine international standard if there is no common understanding of what is behind the denomination. Is it a mere trademark and indicator of source? Or does it say something about sensory qualities, tradition, sustainability, biodiversity etc? GIs from two countries implementing the TRIPS definition in very different ways could potentially benefit from the same international legal protection of the IPR aspects of GI designation, but how would consumers interpret the meaning and status of a sign with such different content according to different countries? The risk here is that consumers would lose confidence in GIs and diminish their value. Alternatively, the establishment of an international GI standard based on more explicit and detailed definition would imply, whatever the mechanism, an international assessment of the correspondence between each GI and the global standard. Assuming that such an international GI standard would include more substantial requirements than the present TRIPS definition, some or most of the national GI standards would need to be completed or modified, while a considerable number of currently registered GIs would need to modify their specification or lose their GI status.

Conclusion

The integration of environmental (including biodiversity) and cultural concerns within GI standards will depend on how the international system evolves; either towards a more explicit and prescriptive global standard, or towards a permissive system that treats GIs as little more than indications of source. Under the first scenario, it is likely that the GI standard would echo international debates over traditional knowledge, climatic change, biodiversity preservation etc by incorporating these issues in its requirements. Under the second, the 'greening' of GIs would depend on the initiative of private and collective stakeholders and would probably be pursued through alternative standards.

References

Barjolle, D. and Sylvander, B. (2000) 'Some factors of success for origin labelled products in agri-food supply chains in Europe: Market, internal resources and institutions', in B. Sylvander, D. Barjolle and F. Arfini (eds) *The Socio-Economics of Origin Labelled Products in Agrifood Supply Chains; Spatial, Institutional and Coordination Aspects*, INRA-Economica, Paris

Bérard, L. and Marchenay, P. (2004) *Les produits de terroir, entre cultures et règlements*. CNRS Éditions, Paris

Galtier, F., Belletti, G. and Marescotti, A. (2008) 'Are Geographical Indications a way to "decommodify" the coffee market?', Communication presented at the 12th Congress of the European Association of Agricultural Economists EAAE, Ghent (Belgium), 26–29 August

Hermitte, M.-A. (2001) 'Les appellations d'origine dans la genèse des droits de la propriété intellectuelle', in P. Moity-Maïzi et al. (eds), *Systèmes agroalimentaires localises, Études et Recherches sur les Systèmes Agraires et le Développement*, n°32, INRA-CIRAD-CNEARC, pp195–206.

Larson, J. (2007) *Relevance of Geographical Indications and Designations of Origin for the Sustainable use of Genetic Resources*, Global Facilitation Unit for Underutilized Species, Rome

Roussel, B. and Verdeaux, F. (2007) 'Natural patrimony and local communities in Ethiopia: Advantages and limitations of a system of geographical indications', *Africa*, vol 77, no 1, pp130–150

de Sainte-Marie, C. and Bérard, L. (2005) 'Taking local knowledge into account in the AOC system', in L. Bérard, M. Cegarra, M. Djama, S. Louafi, P. Marchenay, B. Roussel and F. Verdeaux (eds) *Biodiversity and Local Ecological Knowledge in France*. CIRAD, IDDRI, IFB and INRA, Paris, www.iddri.org/Publications/Ouvrages-en-partenariat/Biodivweb_eng.pdf, accessed 17 September 2009

Sylvander, B., Allaire, G., Belletti, G., Marescotti, A., Barjolle, D., Thévenod-Mottet, E. and Tregear A. (2006) 'Qualité, origine et globalisation: Justifications générales et contextes nationaux, le cas des indications géographiques', *Revue Canadienne Des Sciences Régionales*, vol 29, pp43–54

Thévenod-Mottet E. (2006) *Legal and Institutional Issues Related to GIs*. SINER-GI WP1 Report, www.origin-food.org/2005/upload/SIN-WP1-report-131006.pdf, accessed 17 September 2009

Torsen, M. (2005) 'Apples and oranges: French and American models of Geographical Indications policies demonstrate an international lack of consensus', *The Trademark Reporter*, vol 95, no 6, pp1415–1445

Valenzuela, A., Marchenay P., Berard, L. and Foroughbakhch, R. (2006) 'Conservación de la diversidad de cultivos en las regiones con indicaciones geográficas: los ejemplos del Tequila, Mezcal y Calvados', in A. Álvarez Macías, F. Boucher, F. Cervantes Escoto, A. Espinoza, J. Muchnik and D. Requier-Desjardins (eds) *Agroindustria rural y territorio*, Tomo 1, *Los desafíos de los Sistemas Agroalimentarios Localizados*, Universidad Autónoma del Estado de México, Toluca, Mexico

13

Value Chain Coordination for Agrobiodiversity Conservation

Jon Hellin, Sophie Higman and Alder Keleman

While some agriculturally-based rural households are autarkic, most are linked to markets. The focus of research and development efforts has, hence, broadened from a concentration on building up farmers' production capabilities to include facilitating farmers' access to markets (Shepherd, 2007). A component of 'making markets work for the poor' includes interest in how market access can contribute to both agrobiodiversity conservation and to farmers' livelihood security. The focus is more on underutilized plant products (including landraces of commodities such as potatoes and maize) which are locally valued and which also have public value in terms of: (1) their contribution to agricultural agrobiodiversity; (2) the opportunity they provide for future generations to generate income; and (3) the maintenance of tradition and culture (Gruère et al, 2006).

However, in terms of market access, producers and collectors of underutilized products, together with those engaged in value-adding activities such as agro-processing, often face high transaction costs. A good example is non-timber forest products (NTFPs). Harvesting of NTFPs often takes place from wild populations and from isolated locations over which the collector seldom has secure tenure. Many NTFPs are also produced in small volumes making it difficult to meet buyers' requirements for quality, quantity and continuity of production. Furthermore, NTFPs include fresh fruits that are often perishable and require careful storage and handling, along with rapid transport to market or to an agro-processing plant (Belcher and Schreckenberg, 2007).

Using case studies from the developing world, this paper identifies challenges and opportunities in the marketing of underutilized plant products in a way that contributes to agrobiodiversity conservation and farmers' livelihood security. The focus is on the identification and coordination of different value chain actors, and the role of public and private sector service providers.

Market access and service delivery

Market demand for underutilized products can be stimulated by new scientific evidence related to their intrinsic properties or by interest in 'new' nutritious foods such as the Andean grain quinoa. Other products may become popular for cultural or fashion reasons. For example, a soap made with oil extracted from wild laurel has been produced for centuries in Syria and has now become popular in Europe where it is sold in natural products outlets (Gruère et al, 2006).

Analysis and coordination of value chain actors is necessary if market access is to contribute to agrobiodiversity conservation and livelihood security. A value chain has been described as:

> the full range of activities which are required to bring a product or service from conception, through the different phases of production (involving a combination of physical transformation and the input of various producer services), delivery to final customers and final disposal after use (Kaplinsky and Morris, 2000, p4).

A value chain consists of a variety of actors that may include input suppliers, farmers, collectors (in the case, for example, of NTFPs) traders, processors, exporters/importers, retailers and consumers.

Transaction costs arise as a result of the movement of products through the value chain; i.e. through the various stages of production, processing and distribution. These costs include searching for information, negotiation, and monitoring and enforcing an agreement. The level of transaction costs depend upon the frequency of the transaction (volumes, number of transactions each time period); insecurity (political and social risks that lead to increased costs when making the transaction); asset specificity (whether particular investments have been made that can not be used for other activities); and information asymmetry leading to limited judgment. A dearth of information on prices and technologies, absence of social connections to established chain actors, weak input and output markets, and credit constraints often make it difficult for smallholder farmers and other chain actors to take advantage of market opportunities (Kydd, 2002). Consequently, value chain actors require financial and non-financial services (often called business development services or business services) in order establish and maintain their competitiveness. Key services include:

- Input supplies (e.g. seeds supplied by commercial providers and/or neighbouring farmers);
- Financial services (micro-credit);
- Market information (prices, trends, buyers, suppliers);
- Transport services;
- Quality assurance (monitoring and accreditation);
- Technical expertise and business advice;
- Veterinary services; and

- Support for product development and diversification.

The range of services that producers and other value chain actors require depends on the type of market that they are seeking to access. Many farmers and other chain actors require 'newer' services in order to meet the challenges posed by modern retailing. These challenges include meeting private quality and safety standards as well as private enforcement of public standards (Pingali et al, 2005). Ironically, trade liberalization, while leading to growing market opportunities, has also led to a long-term decline in state-funded agricultural support. As a result, meeting these standards may require expensive third party certification which may be a major barrier to smallholder participation (King and Venturini, 2005).

Case studies

Native potatoes and quinoa in the Andes

Andean farmers have over centuries developed more than 4000 native potato varieties. Many of these varieties can be considered underutilized, due to their importance in local production systems but under-representation in the market (Hellin and Higman, 2005). The Papa Andina network was established in 1998. Financed mainly by the Swiss Agency for Development and Cooperation and with about 30 partners in Bolivia, Ecuador and Peru, the network has used collective action processes to help participants in potato value chains develop new market niches for the Andean native potatoes grown by poor farmers in remote highland areas (Devaux et al, 2008).

T'ikapapa is the first brand of high-quality, fresh, native potato sold in major supermarkets in Peru. A national organization, CAPAC-Peru was formed by farmer organizations, NGOs, traders and processors to promote high-quality potato products as well as to reduce transaction costs and add value. An agro-processing company (which is a member of CAPAC-Peru) contracts farmers to supply potatoes to the supermarket and owns the T'ikapapa brand under which they are marketed. CAPAC-Peru helps organize farmers to supply potatoes meeting market requirements.

Tunta is a form of freeze-dried potato produced traditionally from 'bitter potatoes'. Through collective action, farmers' marketing and processing capacities in Peru were strengthened, while quality norms were developed and market studies undertaken. The brand *Tunta Los Aymaras* was developed, and is owned and marketed by a farmers' association, '*Consortium Los Aymaras*'. In Bolivia, similar collective action processes were used in market chains for *tunta* and *chuño* (another freeze-dried potato product). A set of Bolivian Quality Standards for *chuño* and *tunta* were prepared, and cleaned, selected and bagged *chuño* were later marketed under the brand *Chuñoso*.

In the case of Andean potatoes, food quality and safety concerns among consumers have stimulated demand for locally grown, organic foods creating new national market opportunities for indigenous foods including native potatoes. Value chain coordination has lead to innovation which, in turn, has contributed to agrobiodiversity conservation. In summary, increasing farmer returns to crops, such as native potatoes, with a high public value has been an incentive for farmers to maintain agrobiodiversity (Devaux et al, 2008). A similar situation has arisen with the quinoa.

Quinoa is an annual plant that has been cultivated in the Andes for over 7000 years and has long been known and appreciated for its nutritional value. Quinoa is found between sea level and above 4000 metres altitude in the Bolivian altiplano. The grain can be used as flour, toasted, or added to soups. Dried, it can be stored for up to ten years. Although quinoa has played a key role in food security and farmers' livelihoods for centuries, farmers now cultivate fewer varieties on a reduced land area. Quinoa is being substituted by imported foods with lower nutritional values such as rice and pasta. Furthermore, while it is relatively easy to grow quinoa, the harvesting and processing of the grain is labour-intensive (Hellin and Higman, 2005)

If the national and regional consumption of quinoa is to be increased, as well as the potential to export, the issues of quality, processing, image and market access need to be addressed. The *Asociación Nacional de Productores de Quinua* (ANAPQUI) represents about 5000 of approximately 20,000 quinoa producers in Bolivia and has focused on processing organic quinoa and selling it on the export market. Many of the farmers who are affiliated to ANAPQUI have qualified for organic certification, ensuring that approximately 80 percent of the association's production is organic. Increased quinoa production (and consumption) has also been encouraged by government-supported initiatives such as the Peruvian government's national food assistance program, *Programa Nacional de Apoyo Alimentaria* (PRONAA). PRONAA purchases quinoa for use in school breakfasts and for the *Comedores Populares* (popular canteens). Coordination among chain actors has led to a growth in quinoa production and sales. This, in turn, is contributing to the maintenance of crop diversity in many parts of the Andes.

Maize landraces in Mexico

Maize grain is a widely traded commodity with little product differentiation on international markets. Nevertheless, maize produces many locally and regionally valued products, including specialty grain types sought for their culinary characteristics (such as colour, texture, and flavour); husks used for craft production and for wrapping *tamales* (maize-dough cakes); and *huitlacoche*, a fungus considered a delicacy in Mexico. Many of these products originate from maize landraces. In some cases, landraces are considered to produce a higher-quality product. Many maize landraces are grown by smallholder farmers who prefer farmer-saved landrace seed over improved maize seed due to price, environmental hardiness, or other considerations. Hence, particularly in Mexico, the centre of origin and diversity for maize, speciality markets contribute to the in situ conservation of maize landraces.

Representative speciality markets include those for *totomoxtle* (maize husks) and those for blue maize and *pozole* maize in the central highlands surrounding Mexico City (Keleman and Hellin, in preparation). Maize husks, used for wrapping *tamales*, represent a booming alternative market for maize producers in the state of Veracruz, providing as much as nine times per hectare the value of maize grain (King, 2006). Complex value chains have developed around these markets, ranging from small-scale household production to household-based processing which adds value to the husks, to larger-scale operations with significant capital investment which export husks to the Mexican-American markets in the United States. The maize husk market has likely contributed to the continued planting of maize in Veracruz, cushioning producers against the variation in maize grain prices that followed the implementation of the North American Free Trade Agreement (King, 2006).

The blue maize and *pozole* markets in the central highlands of Mexico represent contrasting examples of market-based agrobiodiversity conservation. Blue maize, which may originate as a varietal of any of several landrace types, is used primarily to make *tortillas* (flat maize-dough cakes). Blue maize is widely planted by smallholder farmers who receive a price premium of around 15 percent over the price of white maize. Much of the blue maize feeds into small-scale, urban, informal sector businesses producing maize-based snacks, which are primarily run by women. *Pozole* maize is large-grained, floury, and used primarily as an ingredient in a popular meat-based soup. *Pozole* maize is planted on smaller areas and by fewer farmers than blue maize. The raw product fetches a price premium of around 100 percent over white maize, and with value added can be sold for 200–600 percent the price of white maize. The lucrative value-adding opportunities have contributed to the growth of many family-based cottage industries, as well as farmers' cooperatives. Some of these production units have already established forms of branding, labelling their products with the name of the maize landrace used and its region of origin as an indicator of quality (Keleman and Hellin, in preparation).

The contrasts between blue and *pozole* maize highlight a significant issue in speciality maize value chains, namely that while these markets have the potential to contribute to poverty alleviation, this potential may not be realized if profitability is captured by small groups of relatively better-off farmers and processors. Currently, there is little government or NGO intervention in these value chains, and coordination arises primarily via private-sector initiatives, farmers' cooperatives, and business relationships based on social ties. This raises the question of whether and how strategies could be designed to promote equity in the value chains without inhibiting or distorting the function of speciality markets.

Capers in Syria and minor millets in India

Caper plants are distributed throughout the Mediterranean basin. In Italy, France and Spain capers are extensively cultivated, consumed and traded, representing a valuable commodity. However, caper is an underutilized plant product in Syria.

Producers gather caper buds from wild plants and sort them by size. Local traders collect the capers and sell them to foreign traders for bottling and sale on the European market. Collection from the wild provides an unstable supply, while the harvesting methods may be unsustainable and threaten the conservation of the species.

At a multi-stakeholder workshop to discuss ways of improving the caper market chain, the major problems identified were the lack of transparency in the value chain, lack of information and lack of trust. Cultivation was considered the most important potential way forward for production. This was seen as providing greater benefits for farmers and collectors, improving working conditions and enhancing the quality of the product through increased uniformity and coordinating the timing of harvesting. Among other issues, participants emphasized the need to develop a quality controlled product for export markets (Guiliani et al, 2006).

The caper case emphasizes the difficulties of marketing wild harvested products—lack of uniformity, dispersal and difficulty of timing of harvest. It also points to the need for quality control measures. Cultivation of underutilized species raises some issues for both biodiversity conservation and poverty reduction. In the caper case study, some 70 percent of the collectors do not own any land. Thus, a focus on cultivation might exclude the poorest of the producers. In addition, the search for uniformity of product is likely to reduce the genetic diversity of the cultivars, which could conflict with biodiversity conservation objectives. Clearly, market mechanisms alone cannot be a panacea for conservation and poverty reduction.

The importance of coordination among value chain actors was also a feature of minor millets in India. Minor millets (finger millet, foxtail millet and little millet) are considered underutilized plant species because of the lack of research investment they attract and because of their limited commercial importance. They have generally been grown as a subsistence crop by tribal farming communities in Kolli Hills, Tamil Nadu. Consumption of minor millets has been undermined by the availability of subsidized rice. The M.S. Swaminathan Research Foundation (MSSRF), a leading NGO, initiated a program for the conservation of millet biodiversity through commercialization. Three major objectives were identified: to enhance productivity, improve quality and facilitate processing (Gruère et al, 2007).

The minor millets value chain is operated by community enterprises which coordinate value chain activities. The enterprises carry out procurement from farmers, de-husking and processing, and finally value addition and packaging. The end product is packaged 'ready to cook' grains, flour or malt. Niche markets exist among health conscious consumers in urban areas. To expand demand, MSSRF adopted a branding strategy to promote the product as locally grown and certified organic.

Value chain coordination

The above case studies illustrate some of the challenges and opportunities that producers of underutilized products face in accessing markets and maintaining agrobiodiversity. For example, in each of the above case studies, efforts were directed at establishing quality control procedures and branding (potatoes, quinoa, minor millets, and *pozole* maize) so as to distinguish the product in question from competitors or substitutes. This is particularly important where producers and other chain actors are seeking premiums for biodiversity-friendly products.

Agrobiodiversity conservation is an example of an 'extrinsic' quality. Extrinsic qualities cannot be determined by the consumer from the product itself. This compares to intrinsic qualities such as taste, appearance, or chemical composition that are integral to the product and which may be ascertained by consumers or via downstream product testing. In order to demonstrate that a product provides certain extrinsic qualities, monitoring of production practices may be needed along with independent certification (Mutersbaugh, 2005). Certification costs can be high although there are ways to reduce them. One way is through group certification where a sample of farmers is certified. However, this often requires an internal control system to maintain confidence that other farmers are also pursuing 'certifiable' agronomic practices.

The case studies also illustrate that success depends on promoting the growth and improved functioning/performance (e.g. competitiveness, productivity, contribution to agrobiodiversity, employment, value addition, linkage coordination, efficiency) of value chains in ways that benefit poor small-scale producers. The improved functioning of value chains includes:

- Identification of market opportunities;
- Greater inclusion and empowerment of women;
- Better access to appropriate processing technologies;
- Implementation of effective business organization practices;
- More efficient farm to market channels; and
- Timely access to affordable financial and business development services.

The innovations required by value chains of underutilized products to remain competitive often depend on on-going coordination between the actors involved in the chain (Bernet et al, 2005; Hellin and Higman, 2009). This can be more readily achieved by development practitioners, researchers and chain actors undertaking a participatory analysis of the chains.

Participatory value chain analysis

The potato and caper case studies experimented with approaches that brought different value chain actors together to build trust and jointly seek ways to make the chains work better. In the case of Syria, for example, there was a high mark-up at the end of the value chain, a lack of transparency, and mistrust among actors, and this negatively affected the income share earned by poor collectors. The approach whereby different actors are brought together can be referred to as participatory value chain analysis (PVCA) and it has proved an effective tool to enhance market access for underutilized (and other) products. As the Papa Andina network has shown, it has also proved to be an effective approach that contributed to agrobiodiversity conservation (Devaux et al, 2008).

The PVCA is a method that is designed to stimulate innovation along value chains by enhancing stakeholder collaboration and trust. It has evolved from the experiences of different research and development organizations in different parts of the world. The approach often includes the following activities:

- Bring together the primary actors in the value chain, identify their roles, and interrelationships;
- Identify final sales market(s) and market segments;
- Identify market channels and trends within the value chain;
- Identify constraints and opportunities that are holding back growth and competitiveness; and
- Identify commercially viable solutions that can address value chain constraints.

Bernet et al (2006) and Will (2008) provide practical guidelines on PVCA. Once the potential of a specific market channel (or a number of alternative channels) has been identified the analysis moves into a more detailed consideration of how value accumulates along the chain. By better understanding the contribution each actor brings to the product, the aim is to identify inefficiencies, inequities and losses that could be remedied, and/or identify added value that could be captured by smallholder producers. A comprehensive value chain analysis will explore how the chain is 'governed' since this influences how profit margins are divided up along the chain; i.e. which actors or other institutions define the conditions for participation in the chain, ensure compliance with these rules and provide assistance with meeting them (Hellin et al, 2005).

While many value chains are characterized by inequitable relationships between actors, the PVCA can assist chain actors to realize mutual benefits by improving the 'systemic efficiency' of the chain. The process of mapping the structure of the value chain and the actors, diagnosing the key enabling environment issues and assessing service needs can, if conducted in participation with the chain actors themselves, be a powerful way to build understanding and trust between stakeholders. Helping chain actors become more aware of the functions and processes that are needed along the chain in order to satisfy more lucrative or reliable markets is fundamental to PVCA. Research in Kenya on smallholder cooperation and contract farming in the horticultural sector indicates that even the powerful actors (the contractors) needed to address issues of trust and collaboration, or else they could expect a high rate of default, which increases costs and reduces profit margins (Coulter et al, 1999).

The key to successful PVCA is not to focus on individual value chain actors such as farmers but to analyse the degree to which the chain as a whole is able to compete (Henson, 2007). While successful market access often depends on how value chains are structured, the perishable nature of the products, availability of infrastructure, product certification, and the identification of appropriate markets etc, often a fundamental prerequisite is the improved relationships between value chain actors.

Farmers and collective action

A component of value chain coordination may involve the issue of collective action. This can be defined as 'voluntary action taken by a group to achieve common interests' (Meinzen-Dick and Di Gregorio, 2004). Collective action can therefore exist in either the presence or absence of formalized farmer organization. The potato, minor millets and quinoa case studies include an important element of collective action in order to enable producers to access key financial and business services and achieve economies of scale in their transactions with other value chain actors such as processors and retailers. More generally, much interest has focused around collective action and farmer organizations as a means of enabling farmers to access inputs and extension advice, improve produce quality and quantity, meet the costs of certification (see above) and negotiate more effectively (Shepherd, 2007).

The enthusiasm for collective action and farmer organizations has at times obscured the fact that the process of establishing and maintaining viable organizations is not a simple one. For example, a great deal of public (and private) money has been invested in supporting collective action with mixed results in terms of the number of beneficiaries and the sustainability of the organizations (Berdegué, 2002). It is often a challenge to secure commitments from group members to abide by collectively-agreed rules, and then to monitor and enforce compliance with those rules. Furthermore, successful association requires management and entrepreneurial skills; 'soft' assets that many small producers may not have (Pingali et al, 2005).

In some cases, collective action and the establishment of farmer organizations incurs transaction costs which, if too high, may mean that farmers are better off not organizing. There is evidence, however, to suggest that this applies more to producers of staple crops than to those of underutilized species (which may contribute to agrobiodiversity conservation) and of high value agricultural crops (Kruijssen et al, 2007). This is because the net benefits tend to be higher in quality/niche markets in comparison with bulk, mass commodities even though the transaction costs are often higher (Reardon, 2005).

Roles of outsiders and what it costs

What is clear from the case studies detailed here—along with other examples of market access for underutilized products—is that external input is often needed to facilitate farmers' access. The Papa Andina initiative, for example, is coordinated by the International Potato Center and its partners with funding from the Swiss Agency for Development and Cooperation, the Swiss Centre for International Agriculture and the UK Department for International Development. More often than not, however, little is known about the returns when measured against the costs of the support provided by external agencies (Shepherd, 2007; Hellin et al, 2008). Too often governments, donors and NGOs have supported the development of value chains, only for these initiatives to fail almost immediately after support was removed. As part of new thinking on the roles of the state and private sectors in pro-poor markets and growth, decisions have to be made as to the role of private or public sectors in paying for and supporting value chain coordination and, related to this, their role in providing value chain actors with essential business development services.

In the past, many services were delivered with the support of donors and government. Critics of public provision of Business Development Services (BDS) claimed that such provision distorted market prices (as services were delivered, in most cases, in a highly subsidized manner and therefore at considerably lower prices than those determined by market forces) and undermined the provision of BDS by the private sector. Public interventions were not seen as sustainable because of their costs. The result was the emergence of the 'Washington consensus' in the 1980s and 1990s and the ushering in of 'market-led development'. This signified a shift from subsidized supply-led BDS provision to market-determined demand-driven services. The private sector was seen as the driving force behind service delivery and was deemed to be much more efficient than the public sector:

> the goal of market development interventions is for a large proportion of [small enterprises] to buy the BDS of their choice from a wide selection of products offered (primarily) by unsubsidized private sector suppliers in a competitive and evolving market (Miehlbradt and McVay, 2003 p12).

Often, however, the private sector has proven incapable of replacing previous state services due to high transaction costs, dispersed clientele and low profits; i.e. exactly the conditions faced by producers of underutilized products. This has led some to question whether:

> policy changes of liberalization and withdrawal of the state removed from the policy toolkit critical levers to address problems of high transaction costs and risks inducing market failures (Dorward et al, 2004).

In agriculture, there is a role for both the public and private sectors. Public sector support could be justified on the grounds of the public goods, such as biodiversity conservation, supplied by underutilized plant product markets. The Papa Andina project is a good example of where private sector involvement complements public sector investments.

Although the private sector might be best placed for organizing production, processing and marketing of agricultural products, governments are of central importance in determining how markets should function. Governments, for example, can help ensure that the legal and judicial system supports low-cost contract enforcement (including getting rid of red tape), facilitate the flow of market information through effective communication systems, and make transport, electricity, water and other infrastructure systems widely available in order to help support small enterprises and BDS providers (Marr, 2003). Government also has a key role to play in clarifying and assigning property rights which can be an issue with the wild collection of underutilized products (e.g. laurel (*Laurus nobilis*) in Syria (Gruère et al, 2006)) and NTFPs (Belcher and Schreckenberg, 2007). Government can also, as was the case of the quinoa schools program in Peru, stimulate demand for underutilized crops and by doing so contribute to biodiversity conservation.

Agrobiodiversity conservation and small enterprise development

There are literally thousands of underutilized products and numerous species worthy of conservation efforts. It is seldom an easy decision as to which species to focus on. In order to avoid the danger of agrobiodiversity conservation efforts being subsidized in the long-term—and even then collapsing when external support is withdrawn—private sector involvement in value chain development should be sought as early as possible. It may be the case that public sector support is needed to 'kick start' markets but it is best done in a way that promotes rather than crowds out private sector investment, and that allows the state to withdraw as economic growth proceeds (Diao et al, 2007).

A useful approach in deciding where efforts should be focused is that used in small-enterprise development. Potential underutilized products can be analysed from a pro-poor standpoint in terms of their contribution to improved rural livelihoods and their contribution to agrobiodiversity conservation. Based on Lusby and Panlibuton (2004) the following criteria can be taken into account:

- Unmet market demand and growth potential for existing products;
- Potential increase in income and wealth at all levels of the value chain but particularly at the producer level;
- Opportunities for market linkages that assist the value chain to function more effectively and efficiently;
- Potential for employment generation;
- Value added potential;
- Potential for increases in productivity through technological and management innovation;
- Government or donor interest that translates into linkages with government services and favourable policies and
- Contribution to agrobiodiversity conservation.

An analysis that takes into account the aforementioned criteria will invariably include the question of geographical focus and which types of markets. The case studies outlined in this paper targeted domestic, regional and international markets. There is no hard and fast rule as to which of these markets is more likely to foster greater biodiversity conservation. One of the advantages of focusing on domestic and regional markets is that farmers often face lower transaction costs vis-à-vis quality and standards. In the case of exporting organic produce, such as quinoa, to the European Union the process is complex and knowledge is required concerning the choice of certifier for particular export markets (Hellin and Higman, 2005).

However, Henson (2007) cautions that while domestic and/or regional markets generally have lower standards than many export markets, the situation is changing: the general tendency in all markets is towards stricter food safety, quality and other standards.

Potential pitfalls: 'unsustainable over-utilization' and reduced use of landraces

While market access for underutilized products has great potential to contribute to agrobiodiversity conservation and increased farmers' livelihood security, it is important to acknowledge that market forces alone are not a panacea for addressing these problems. Under some circumstances, market forces may have detrimental impacts on agrobiodiversity. After all, the low private value that producers attribute to underutilized plant products may be the direct consequence of the fact that other crops with higher market values offer them better income opportunities (Gruère et al, 2006). As Lockie and Carpenter note in Chapter 1, this can arise because of policies that provide incentives for non-biodiverse agriculture. It can also arise from the trade-offs necessary to meet market demands for homogenous products.

Increased market access for underutilized plant products also brings with it the danger of over-exploitation, a danger recognized in the case study of capers in Syria. The danger is very real when it comes to NTFP production and trade. One objective of many NTFP projects is to encourage biodiversity conservation through use. However, some successful marketing initiatives involving NTFPs have provided a strong incentive for increased production either through more intensive harvesting (harvesting more per unit area), more extensive harvesting (harvesting from a larger area) or from intensified management (either in the forest or through cultivation) (Belcher and Schreckenberg 2007). Padulosi and Hoeschle-Zeledon (2004) refer to this phenomenon as 'utilization becoming unsustainable over-utilization'.

A related danger is that while market demand may be driven by consumer interest in the conservation or social ethics represented by the product in question, trade-offs in the value chain may be necessary to compete in markets in which consumers are accustomed to particular standards of quality and homogeneity. This concern is illustrated by the case of *Nuestro Maíz*, a chain of *tortillerías* (tortilla stores) linked to a major national farmers' organization in Mexico, whose name and marketing strategy appeal to a socially-conscious, locally-based conservation ethic. This chain represents a successful business model, in that it provides an outlet for local maize production, as well as income and employment for participating farmers. However, although the organization's initial intent was to use only landrace maize in tortilla production, it found that when used as an input into large-scale production processes, landraces lacked characteristics of uniformity and shelf-life that were necessary to make the product acceptable to the consumer. *Nuestro Maíz* resolved this problem by combining hybrid maize with landrace maize in the tortilla-production process (Keleman et al, 2009). In other words, it was necessary to reduce the use of landraces in order to find a successful business strategy.

This case highlights some of the tensions in managing the potential trade-offs between conservation, poverty alleviation, and business success. Flexibility is important for businesses such as *Nuestro Maíz* to emerge, evolve and persist in highly competitive markets. Organizations like *Nuestro Maíz* arguably offer conservation and social benefits simply by existing; they provide a market outlet for landrace maize where one might not otherwise exist, and by raising income for farmers (both through sale of maize grain and sharing of benefits from the value-adding process) they support households in continuing a farming lifestyle without which there would be fewer possibilities for in situ maize conservation. Supporting market-driven agrobiodiversity conservation, as such, may also involve designing strategies to allow producers' organizations to flexibly respond to market demands while still maintaining the greatest possible conservation impacts.

A second point which discussions of these markets bring to light is that, while markets for under utilized plant products can drive the continued cultivation of, for example, potato varieties, maize landraces and caper cultivates, there are no guarantees that the positive in situ conservation impacts will be sustainable over the long-run. King (2006) points out that while maize landrace varieties are currently used for husk production in Mexico, the possibility exists that, as markets grow, larger-scale participants will be able to cut production costs using hybrid varieties, lowering the incentive to use landraces for this market. The example of *pozole* maize, potatoes in the Andes and capers in Syria also demonstrated the danger that farmer-selection to conform to characteristics demanded by the market will lead to a narrowing of the characteristics available among native varieties. In other words, while markets may have positive in situ conservation impacts by providing incentives for farmers to continue planting maize landraces and tendering caper cultivars, the impact of market-oriented processes on the genetic diversity of speciality varieties needs further research.

Conclusion

Market access for underutilized species can contribute to agrobiodiversity conservation and improved livelihood security. All smallholder producers face high transaction costs, but producers of underutilized products face the additional challenges of poorly-defined markets and weak demand precisely because their products are less well known. Weak market demand means that established value chains rarely exist and, even where they do, there is an absence of the types of standards and grades that facilitate long distance and impersonal trade. Case studies from the developing world have shown that these challenges can be overcome.

The case studies illustrate that demand for underutilized plant products can be stimulated and that with judicious effort value chains can be established that operate efficiently and equitably, benefiting both farmers and other chain actors. The ability of value chains to deliver greater agrobiodiversity and livelihood benefits depends on how value chains are structured, the relationships between chain actors, and the role of the private and public sectors in providing financial and non-financial services to value chain actors.

Enhancing market access for underutilized plant products via coordination of value chain actors often requires considerable external support and hard decisions have to be made as to the source of this support—public and/or private sectors? Decisions also have to be made about which underutilized products to focus on; i.e. which ones are likely to contribute more to in situ conservation and livelihood security through the development of viable market access? At times, such a decision may seem as much art as science.

References

Belcher, B. and Schreckenberg, K. (2007) 'Commercialization of non-timber forest products: A reality check', *Development Policy Review*, vol 25, no 3, pp355–377

Berdegué, J. (2002) 'Learning to beat Cochrane's treadmill: Public policy, markets and social learning in Chile's small-scale agriculture', in C. Leeuwis and R. Pyburn, (eds) *Wheelbarrows Full of Frogs: Social Learning in Rural Resource Management*, Koninlijke Van Gorcum, Assen, The Netherlands, pp333–348

Bernet, T. Devaux, A., Ortiz, O. and Thiele, G. (2005) 'Participatory market chain approach', *BeraterInnen News*, 1/2005

Bernet, T., Thiele, G. and Zschocke, T. (2006) *Participatory Market Chain Approach (PMCA): User Guide*, International Potato Center, Papa Andina, Lima, Peru

Coulter, J., Goodland, A., Tallontire, A. and Stringfellow, R. (1999) *Marrying Farmer Cooperation and Contract Farming for Service Provision in a Liberalising Sub-Saharan Africa*, Natural Resource Perspectives 48, Overseas Development Institute, London

Devaux, A., Horton, D., Velasco, C., Thiele, G., Lopez, G., Bernet, T., Reinoso, I. and Ordinola, M. (2008) 'Collective action for market chain innovation in the Andes', *Food Policy*, vol 34, pp31–38

Diao, X., Hazell, P., Resnick, P and Thurlow, J. (2007) *The Role of Agriculture in Development: Implications for Sub-Saharan Africa*, Research Report 153, International Food Policy Research Institute, Washington, DC

Dorward, A., Kydd, J., Morrison, J. and Urey, I. (2004) 'A policy agenda for pro-poor agricultural growth', *World Development*, vol 32, no 1, pp73–89

Gruère, G., Giuliani, A. and Smale, M. (2006) *Marketing Underutilized Plant Species for the Benefit of the Poor: A Conceptual Framework*, EPT Discussion Paper 154, International Food Policy Research Institute, Washington, DC

Gruère, G., Nagarajanm, L., King, O. (2007) *Collective Action and Marketing of Underutilized Plant Species: The Case of Minor Millets in Kolli Hills, Tamil Nadu, India*, CAPRi Working Paper 69, International Food Policy Research Institute, Washington, DC

Guiliani, A., Adbulkarim, N. and Buerli, M. (2006) Case Study Presented at the *Regional Consultation on Linking Farmers to Markets*, Cairo, Egypt

Hellin, J. and Higman, S. (2005) 'Crop diversity and livelihood security in the Andes', *Development in Practice*, vol 15, no 2, pp165–174

Hellin, J. and Higman, S. (2009).'Underutilized plant products and market access: Challenges and opportunities', in H. Jaenicke, J. Ganry, I. Höschle-Zeledon and R. Kahane (eds) *Underutilized Plants for Food, Nutrition, Income and Sustainable Development*, Proceedings of International Symposium held in Arusha, Tanzania, 3–7 March 2008, Acta Horticulturae 806, International Society for Horticultural Science, Leuven, Belgium.

Hellin, J., Griffith, A. and Albu, M. (2005) 'Mapping the market: Market-literacy for agricultural research and policy to tackle rural poverty in Africa', in F.R. Almond and S.D. Hainsworth, (eds), *Beyond Agriculture: Making Markets Work for the Poor*, Natural Resources International Limited and Practical Action, London, pp109–148

Hellin, J., Lundy, M. and Meijer, M. (2008) 'Farmer organization, collective action and market access in Meso-America', *Food Policy*, vol 34, pp16–22

Henson, S. 2007. *New Markets and their Supporting Institutions: Opportunities and Constraints for Demand Growth*, Background paper for the World Development Report 2008, Rimisp-Latin American Center for Rural Development, Santiago, Chile

Kaplinsky, R. and Morris, M. (2000) *A Handbook for Value Chain Research*, International Development Research Centre, Canada

Keleman, A., García Rañó, H.A. and Hellin, J. (2009) 'Maize diversity, poverty, and market access: Lessons from Mexico', *Development In Practice*, vol 19, no 2, pp187–199

Keleman, A. and Hellin, J. (in preparation) 'Specialty maize varieties and in situ conservation in the Mexican central highlands'

King, A. (2006) 'Trade and *Totomoxtle*: Livelihood strategies in the Totonacan region of Veracruz, Mexico', *Agriculture and Human Values*, vol 24, pp29–40

King, R.P. and Venturini, L. (2005) 'Demand for quality drives changes in food supply chains', in A. Regmi, and M. Gehlhar, (eds) *New Directions in Global Food Markets*, AIB-794, Economic Research Service, United States Department of Agriculture, pp18–31

Kruijssen, F., Keizer, M. and Giuliani, A. (2007) 'Collective action for biodiversity and livelihoods', *LEISA*, vol 23, no 1, pp6–8

Kydd, J. (2002) *Agriculture and Rural Livelihoods: Is Globalization Opening or Blocking Paths out of Rural Poverty?*, Network Paper 121, Agricultural Research and Extension Network, Overseas Development Institute, London

Lusby, F. and Panlibuton, H. (2004) *Promotion of Commercially Viable Solutions to Subsector and Business Constraints*, Report to USAID Office of Microenterprise Development, Action for Enterprise, Arlington, VA, www.mmw4p.org/dyn/bds/docs/307/Promoting%20solutions%20to%20SS-MED%20constraints.pdf, accessed 7 August 2009

Marr, A. (2003) *Institutional Approaches to the Delivery of Business Development Services: A Review of Recent Literature*, Natural Resources Institute, Chatham Maritime, UK

Meinzen-Dick, R. and Di Gregorio, M. (2004) 'Collective action and property rights for sustainable development: Overview', in R. Meinzen-Dick and M. Di

Gregorio (eds) *Collective Action and Property Rights for Sustainable Development*, International Food Policy Research Institute, Washington, DC, pp3–4

Miehlbradt, A.O. and McVay, M. (2003) *Developing Commercial Markets for Business Development Services: BDS Primer*, International Labour Organization, Geneva, Switzerland

Mutersbaugh, T. (2005) 'Just-in-space: Certified rural products, labor of quality, and regulatory spaces', *Journal of Rural Studies*, vol 21, pp389–402

Padulosi, S. and Hoeschle-Zeledon, I. (2004) 'Underutilized plant species: What are they?', *LEISA*, vol 20, no 1, pp5–6

Pingali, P., Khwaja, Y., Meijer, M., (2005) *Commercializing Small Farms: Reducing Transaction Costs*, ESA Working Paper 05-08, Agricultural and Development Economics Division, Food and Agriculture Organization of the United Nations, Rome

Reardon, T. (2005) *Retail Companies as Integrators of Value Chains in Developing Countries: Diffusion, Procurement System Change, and Trade and Development Effects*, GTZ, Eschborn, Germany

Shepherd, A. (2007) *Approaches to Linking Producers to Markets: A Review of Experiences to Date*, Agricultural Management, Marketing and Finance Occasional Paper 13, Food and Agriculture Organization of the United Nations, Rome

Will, M. (2008) *Promoting Value Chains of Neglected and Underutilized Species for Pro-Poor Growth and Biodiversity Conservation: Guidelines and Good Practices*, Global Facilitation Unit for Underutilized Species, Rome

14

Paying for Biodiversity Conservation in Agricultural Landscapes

Sara J. Scherr, Jeffrey C. Milder and Seth Shames

Agricultural landscapes play a central role as habitat for biodiversity. Satellite images have shown that agricultural activities affect 80 to 90 percent of inhabitable terrestrial area worldwide, and that crop production is a dominant ecological influence (i.e., accounting for over 30 percent of land use) in nearly 40 percent of lands (Wood et al, 2000). Of the 100,000 listed public protected areas, 45 percent have over 30 percent of land in annual crops, and an even larger area is used for grazing and forest products (Hassan et al, 2005). Thus, finding ways to conserve natural habitat and biodiversity within agricultural landscapes is a priority concern. In fact, there is now a considerable body of evidence documenting biodiversity-friendly agricultural practices, as well as conservation management strategies in and around farms and ranches (Scherr and McNeely, 2007). In what will be referred to here as 'ecoagriculture landscapes', such mosaics of agricultural and conservation areas are managed by stakeholders to jointly achieve sustainable food production, local livelihoods and biodiversity/ecosystem conservation.

The conservation values resulting from ecoagriculture systems are typically enjoyed by a variety of groups—from local farmers benefiting from wild pollinators, to downstream water users benefiting from natural riparian strips filtering out pollutants, to the entire global community benefiting from protection of rare species. In many cases, biodiversity-friendly practices are actually more profitable for farmers or provide other tangible use or cultural values, and farmer-friendly habitat management enhances the effectiveness of conservation areas. However, in other cases, farmers or conservation managers incur significant costs in making the transition to ecoagriculture practices, or sustaining them over the long-term. When farmers are not adequately compensated for the biodiversity benefits they provide, they are less likely to adopt these practices, especially when the costs exceed the benefits enjoyed by the farmer. Accordingly, if ecoagriculture is to be scaled up worldwide, it is critically important to find ways to compensate such farmers for the off-site environmental benefits they provide.

Payment for ecosystem services (PES) provides a way of doing this. PES programs compensate land stewards for providing ecosystem services of value to external beneficiaries, thus helping to align the individual private interests of farmers and other land stewards with the collective interests of the local, regional, and global communities that benefit from ecosystem services. PES transactions are distinguished by two key features: first, they are always *voluntary*, between a willing buyer and a willing seller; and, second, the payment to land stewards is *conditional* upon the provision of the agreed-upon ecosystem services (or actions believed to provide the services).

PES programs have been developed around four main classes of ecosystem services: carbon sequestration, watershed protection, biodiversity conservation, and recreation and landscape beauty. This chapter focuses mainly on biodiversity PES. The chapter first reviews the current state of biodiversity PES in agricultural landscapes, discussing the supply and demand of such services, and drawing on lessons learned from existing programs worldwide. Next, it explores potential benefits and risks to farmers of this approach to promoting conservation in agricultural landscapes. The chapter concludes by identifying obstacles and recommending actions to enable the widespread use of PES to support biodiversity conservation and rural livelihoods in agricultural landscapes.

Rationale for paying farmers for biodiversity conservation services

Financing and management of natural protected areas was historically perceived as the responsibility of the public sector and non-governmental organizations (NGOs). As of 2008, there were roughly 60,000 designated protected areas covering 12 percent of the Earth's surface (Chape and Spalding, 2008). However, the last few decades have witnessed severe cutbacks in funding from governments and international public and private donors for the creation and management of protected areas (Jenkins et al, 2003). Increasingly, land purchase- and donation-driven models for conservation are proving unsustainable because land acquisition for protected areas and compensation for lost resource-based livelihoods are often prohibitively expensive.

Meanwhile, the location of so many biologically rich areas in agricultural landscapes necessitates that conservation efforts move beyond strictly protected areas. Clearly, biodiversity and ecosystem services cannot adequately be conserved by a relatively small number of strictly protected areas. Instead, conservation is best conceived as part of a landscape or ecosystem management strategy that situates protected areas within a broader matrix of land uses that are compatible with and support biodiversity conservation in situ. Achieving such an outcome will require new, lower-cost mechanisms for promoting biodiversity conservation on private lands.

One possible way to achieve conservation-friendly land uses on private lands is through regulation. This approach, known as the 'polluter pays' principle, assumes that ecosystem services are public goods, and that the public's right to protect these goods trumps the rights of private land users to manage their land as they see fit. In reality, though, there has been little political will to mandate, much less enforce, strict regulation on private land management throughout much of the world.

In the absence of regulation, land managers will tend to pursue the most profitable land-use practices, ignoring the economic and non-economic values of ecosystem services except to the extent that these services benefit them directly. Because conservation-friendly management is often more expensive or less profitable than conventional agricultural management—at least in the short to medium-term—farmers will tend to overexploit natural resources and undersupply ecosystem services. PES changes the economic equation for farmers by giving them a financial incentive for conservation-friendly management, thus improving the profitability of these practices and encouraging their adoption. Furthermore, experience with similar market-based instruments in biodiversity and other sectors has shown that they may achieve environmental goals at much lower overall cost than regulatory approaches (Bräuer et al, 2006).

A final rationale for paying farmers for biodiversity conservation is to contribute to rural development and poverty reduction. Most obviously, farmers can benefit from an additional income stream that may be less variable than income from agricultural goods. In addition, payments from external beneficiaries can help subsidize the conservation and restoration of ecosystem services that provide important local benefits to farming communities. For example, many low-income farming and pastoral communities are dependent upon forest, freshwater, and aquatic biodiversity for wild foods, medicines, fuels, and farming inputs. Finally, PES programs can improve human capital through associated training and education efforts and through investment in local cooperative institutions (Scherr et al, 2004).

Who are the buyers of biodiversity services in agricultural landscapes?

Five basic types of buyers participate in PES markets and programs, each with distinct motivations:

1. Public sector agencies (national, state or municipal) who seek to secure 'public goods' on behalf of their constituencies;
2. Private sector companies who are under regulatory obligation to offset biodiversity impacts and may do so by purchasing biodiversity credits from land stewards who protect or restore the same or similar species or ecological communities in the same ecosystem;
3. Private businesses or organizations who seek to secure ecosystem services for their use values or for other business benefits;

4. Philanthropic buyers, such as conservation organizations and charitable individuals, who are motivated by the nonuse values of ecosystem services; and,
5. Consumers of ecocertified products who seek to purchase goods produced in ways consistent with their environmental values.

This section discusses the scale of demand from each buyer type and provides some examples of biodiversity PES programs in each category. Data are drawn largely from the Forest Trends and Ecosystem Marketplace (FT and EM) publications *Ecosystem Market Matrix* (2008a) and *Ecosystem Services: Market Profiles* (2008b), and from sources reviewed by Milder et al (forthcoming).

Public sector agencies

Public and quasi-public agencies are the largest buyers of biodiversity conservation services from farmers, with payments totaling at least US$3 billion annually, mostly in the United States, Europe, and China (Miller et al, 2008). Public sector buyers include international organizations such as the World Bank and Global Environmental Facility, national governments that enact agri-environmental payment schemes, and local governments, which usually engage in PES to provide watershed protection for public water supplies.

The largest public biodiversity PES programs are the agri-environment payment programs in the US and Europe, which compensate farmers for providing a variety of conservation-friendly land-use and management practices. Roughly 20 percent of farmland in the EU is under some form of agri-environment program to reduce the negative impacts of modern agriculture on the environment, at a cost of about US$1.5 billion (although much of this land is managed for other ecosystem services, not specifically for biodiversity conservation). In Switzerland, 'ecological compensation areas' using farming systems more compatible with native biodiversity have expanded to include more than 120,000 ha (Biodiversity Monitoring Switzerland, 2006). In the US, programs authorized under the Farm Bill encourage habitat conservation on private lands through payments for protection and restoration, or for the presence of wildlife on farms. In 2009, these payments will total roughly US$4.2 billion (NSAC, 2009).

Outside the US and Europe, Mexico's public watershed payment program has incorporated biodiversity benefits (CONAFOR, 2007), whereas Costa Rica's national PES program compensates landowners for the conservation and restoration of forests, which may be on or adjacent to farms. The World Bank's BioCarbon Fund is one of the largest biodiversity PES programs from quasi-public international organizations, mobilizing US$92 million (WBCFU 2009). This program aims to sequester carbon in forests and agroecosystems while promoting biodiversity conservation and poverty alleviation co-benefits. The Global Environment Facility has greatly expanded its investment in biodiversity payments in agricultural landscapes, including payments for conservation of wild relatives of agricultural crops (GEF, 2007).

Private parties under regulatory obligation

Regulation-driven PES markets result from laws that limit the aggregate level of environmental damage and require parties who exceed their allotted impact to buy compliance credits from other parties (ten Kate et al, 2004). In 2008, transactions from these markets totaled at least US$3.4 billion worldwide, much of this in the US (Carroll, 2008). For example, the US has operated a wetland mitigation program since the early 1980s in which developers seeking to destroy a wetland must buy wetland offsets conserved or developed elsewhere. Such systems, often referred to as 'cap and trade' programs, have also been successfully established for sulphur dioxide emissions, farm nutrient pollution, and carbon emissions. However, developing such markets for biodiversity is more complicated because it is difficult to establish equivalency units for biodiversity.

To date, regulation-driven biodiversity PES has been limited to developed countries; primarily, the US, Australia and the EU (Carroll, 2008). In the US, at least US$370 million was spent annually on endangered species mitigation between 2003 and 2006 (ELI, 2007). In addition, wetland mitigation banking and tradable development rights programs often include biodiversity conservation as one of their objectives. In New South Wales, Australia, for example, a salinity control trading scheme led an irrigators' association to pay landowners to plant trees that combat rising saline water tables while also helping to restore habitat. Legislation in Australia also allows private landholders who conserve biodiversity values on their land to sell the resulting 'credits' to a common pool, while creating obligations for land developers and others to purchase those credits (Brand, 2002).

In the developing world, where regulated markets are still scarce, signs of biodiversity market development are growing, particularly in Brazil, Colombia, South Africa and Uganda (Carroll, 2008). This potential will grow if more countries pass regulations to require corporate real estate and natural resource developers to offset their environmental impacts.

Private parties for other business reasons

Private companies may purchase biodiversity conservation services to demonstrate corporate environmental responsibility, seek to retain their social 'license to operate' or to secure use values from biodiversity—such as chemical compounds and genetic resources sought by pharmaceutical companies through bioprospecting arrangements. Many agribusiness and food industries are seeking to brand their products as biodiversity-friendly, developing internal standards or participating in multi-stakeholder forums to develop industry-wide standards such as the biodiversity standards of the Roundtable on Sustainable Palm Oil (Millard, 2007; IFC, 2009). Chiquita is developing projects in several of their banana-growing landscapes in Central America, that pay farmers to plant native trees in and around their farms to provide biological corridors between protected areas (Chiquita, 2004).

In all these cases, companies invest in biodiversity conservation because of the business case; that is, the expected benefit for immediate or long-term profitability. In addition to business reputation, motivations of private businesses for purchasing biodiversity services include: compliance with existing environmental regulation and policy; influencing emerging environmental regulation and policy; maintaining a 'social license to operate'; securing ecosystem services critical for the quality or efficiency of a product the business is selling; embracing strategic opportunities in new PES markets and business; and pursuing new business opportunities related to their core business (Mulder et al, 2005).

Despite the potential, biodiversity payments from private businesses for business reasons are still nascent markets. Biodiversity offsets are conservation activities intended to compensate for the residual, unavoidable harm to biodiversity caused by development projects. Voluntary biodiversity offset transactions now total between US$2–5 million annually; half in developing countries (ten Kate and Maguire, 2008). While these have tended to focus on extractive industries, models are beginning to be explored for agribusiness contexts, particularly in Brazil. In addition to the one-off voluntary biodiversity offsets, 51 banks subscribe to the Equator Principles. The clients of these banks, on occasion, are required to invest in conservation as part of their loan conditions. The volume of these conservation investments are difficult to track. They are estimated to be roughly US$17 million per year (ten Kate and Maguire, 2008). Incorporating biodiversity offsets into large-scale development projects by private and public actors—road building, mining, oil and gas extraction, agribusiness (including biofuels) and urban development— could bring significant funding to this market, and high visibility and the right standards could encourage projects with high social co-benefits.

Philanthropic buyers

Philanthropic buyers—especially large conservation NGOs such as The Nature Conservancy—are increasing the use of conservation payments and conservation easements as the establishment of new nature reserves becomes more contentious in many regions. Where farmers control land in biodiverse areas they are logical beneficiaries of such payments (FT and EM, 2008b). However, only a small portion of the funds invested by philanthropic buyers in conservation are used specifically to conserve biodiversity on agricultural lands. Within the conservation community there remains considerable debate about whether conservation funds should be expended in agricultural settings where native biodiversity may be significantly degraded, or whether investment should focus on lands in a more pristine natural condition. The outcome of this debate will strongly influence the scale of the philanthropic payments to farmers for biodiversity conservation.

A rapidly growing segment of philanthropic buyers are those in the voluntary carbon offset market who are seeking high-quality credits that not only offset their carbon emissions, but also contribute to biodiversity conservation and local livelihoods (Hamilton et al, 2009). For example, the international NGO Conservation International has developed carbon offset projects that use philanthropic resources to avoid deforestation of high-biodiversity value forests, or restore habitat (CI, 2009).

Consumers of eco-certified products

Markets for eco-certified agricultural products, such as shade-grown coffee, 'conservation beef' and organics, are now valued at approximately 2.5 percent (or US$4.2 billion) of the global food and beverage market and have sustained high growth during the past two decades (Andersson and Oberthur, 2008). Of course, most of value of eco-certified farm products is for the products themselves, with a relatively small and non-specific premium paid by the consumer for the eco-friendly production practices. Although consumers purchase eco-certified products for a host of reasons (including health, social justice, as well as environmental concerns), biodiversity conservation is the ecosystem service addressed in most eco-certification schemes.   Facilitating the expansion of eco-certification for biodiversity production will require better documentation that the farm practices typically required by certification systems do deliver their purported benefits for biodiversity. Efforts now underway by the Rainforest Alliance and others to remedy this situation by developing certification standards that are more rigorously linked to conservation outcomes at the landscape scale are a critical step in solidifying the integrity of eco-certification (see Chapter 11).

What types of biodiversity conservation services can farmers provide?

Farmers and agricultural communities can provide biodiversity conservation through a variety of practices. These range from specific plot-level farming practices such as conservation tillage, no-till cropping and organic agriculture to changes in land-use allocations within farms and across entire landscapes to incorporate extensive grazing systems, agroforestry, extractive reserves and patches or corridors of natural habitat. Although a large and growing literature explores the conservation implications of many such practices (e.g. Buck et al, 2007; Harvey et al, 2005; Harvey and Saenz, 2008; Neely and Hatfield, 2007; Schroth et al, 2004), this section briefly identifies some practices that may be especially conducive to biodiversity PES in agricultural areas. These are divided into three categories: (1) restricting agricultural use; (2) promoting biodiversity-conserving agricultural management; and (3) adopting practices to provide other ecosystem services that incidentally or intentionally also help to conserve biodiversity. See Table 14.1 for a summary of key practices.

Table 14.1. Farm and landscape management practices that can provide biodiversity

Management focus	Ecosystem service provided
Restrict agricultural use	Protect native ecosystems
Conservation-friendly agricultural management	Improve landscape connectivity for mobile species
	Protect habitat for native aquatic species
	Protect habitat for native terrestrial species
	Protect agricultural and livestock genetic diversity
Management for other ecosystem services, with biodiversity conservation co-benefits	Carbon emission reduction (biodiversity co-benefit: avoid deforestation)
	Carbon sequestration in perennial plants (biodiversity co-benefit: improve habitat quality on farms)
	Carbon sequestration in soil (biodiversity co-benefit: improve habitat quality on farms)
	Maintain water quality (biodiversity co-benefit: conserve aquatic biodiversity)
	Salinization reduction (biodiversity co-benefit: reforestation)
	Flood control (biodiversity co-benefit: conserve wetlands)
	Landscape beauty (biodiversity co-benefit: improved habitat)
	Recreational access to wild animals for hunting, fishing, and viewing (biodiversity co-benefit: conservation of critical native species)
	Pollinator protection (biodiversity co-benefit: conservation of insects and the species that feed on them)

conservation services (Scherr et al, 2007, pp. 385-6)

Farm production practices	Landscape management practices
Protect or restore patches and corridors of natural habitat on the farm, such as wetlands, forests, and prairies	Maintain corridors of natural land among farms and between farms and natural areas; establish protected areas on lands of high conservation value or lands less suitable for agriculture
Retain or install hedgerows, windbreaks, and live fences; remove impenetrable barriers	Create networks of natural and seminatural areas in and around farms
Manage crop and livestock wastes; reduce agrichemical usage	Maintain or establish natural vegetation along stream banks
Protect breeding areas, pure water sources, and wild food sources in and around farm plots; adjust the timing of cultivation activities to avoid interference with species' life cycles; increase the diversity of crop varieties and species on the farm	Create networks of natural and seminatural areas in and around farms; establish community forests, extractive reserves, or other low-intensity multiuse areas
Maintain the use of underutilized and threatened crop and livestock species	Maintain networks of farms utilizing these species to create sufficient supply for market
Reduce the use of burning to clear forests or manage crop residues	Reduce unsustainable slash-and-burn practices
Increase the use of perennial crops and tree crops on farms; manage forested areas of farms for conservation and production values	Reforest degraded lands or lands less suitable for agriculture; increased use of agroforestry practices; lengthen fallow periods
Reduce tillage intensity; increase perennial crops and cover crops; leave crop residue on fields	Increase perennial vegetation, and reduce land clearing
Reduce agrochemicals, filter agricultural runoff, soil conservation and runoff management; perennial soil cover	Maintain perennial vegetative filters, road, path, and settlement construction methods
Plant appropriate salinity-reducing tree species on farms	Reforest strategic areas of the landscape
Protect or restore wetlands on farms; retain tree cover; manage soils and ground cover to encourage infiltration of rainwater	Protect or restore wetlands and other riparian areas
Establish live fences; plant attractive native species; revegetate land to hide buildings and farm infrastructure	Revegetation in visible areas of the landscape
Restore fishing streams and ponds; maintain salt licks or vegetation attracting wild species	Protect core habitat areas; establish rules for sustainable harvest in natural areas and on communal lands
Maintain pollinator habitat areas on farm; reduce the use of pesticides	Maintain patches of natural pollinator habitat in the landscape

Restricting agricultural use

Farmers can help conserve biodiversity by maintaining or restoring natural and seminatural habitat patches in the landscape instead of using these areas for agricultural production. This practice is especially important in landscapes where extensive agricultural systems retain a significant amount of biodiversity, but where there are economic pressures to intensify these systems, as is the case in much of Europe (Reidsma et al, 2006) and Central America (Harvey et al, 2005). Restricting agricultural use is also an important strategy at the agricultural frontier in order to protect the world's last large-scale intact forest and grassland ecosystems.

Governments and environmental NGOs can pay farmers to restrict agricultural activities by purchasing permanent conservation easements to keep land out of production or by making recurring conservation payments, including conservation concessions (Rice, 2003). Because restricting agricultural use by definition involves a trade-off between agricultural production and conservation, payment to farmers needs to compensate them for the opportunity cost of production, making this a relatively expensive approach to biodiversity PES (Scherr et al, 2007).

Biodiversity-conserving agricultural management

A lower-cost approach to securing conservation benefits is to pay farmers to manage their land so as to achieve some biodiversity conservation benefits while still allowing for agricultural production. This can be accomplished by switching to more environmentally benign agricultural land uses (such as agroforestry or extensive grazing systems instead of intensive cropping systems), or by adopting agricultural best practices within a given agricultural land use (see Chapter 2). Where land degradation currently limits both the productivity and the conservation value of agricultural areas, PES can be used to encourage and subsidize restoration; potentially a win-win situation.

A wide variety of payment schemes promote biodiversity-conserving agricultural practices. Payments from both public and nonprofit buyers seek to facilitate wildlife movement across agricultural landscapes by encouraging farmers to establish riparian buffers, create or retain hedgerows and live fences, and establish agroforestry systems.

While payments to farmers for biodiversity management tend to be linked to species that are not directly related to production systems (with the exception of pollination and pest control services), the concept of payments for crop and livestock genetic diversity is now also being explored. A Bioversity International project on Payment for Agrobiodiversity Conservation Services is identifying valuation tools, exploring market opportunities in pilot sites and working to promote the nascent concept among policy makers (Bioversity International, 2008).

Management for other ecosystem services, with biodiversity conservation co-benefits

Payments to farmers for other ecosystem services—such as carbon sequestration or storage, watershed services, landscape beauty and salinity control—often provide biodiversity co-benefits, either deliberate or incidental. The biodiversity co-benefits provided by agricultural practices—such as planting trees, increasing soil organic matter, adopting agroforestry systems and refraining from burning forests and crop residues—can explicitly be encouraged through program design (Smith et al, 2007; Lal, 2008; Swingland, 2002). There are currently few opportunities for farmers to receive payments for carbon sequestration under the Clean Development Mechanism (CDM) of the Kyoto Protocol, the program by which carbon emitters in industrialized countries can offset their emissions by investing in projects in developing countries. At present, forest restoration and regeneration projects are the only land-use changes eligible for generating carbon credits under the CDM, and even these have proven difficult to implement (Capoor and Ambrosi 2009). Land use is excluded from the European Union Greenhouse Gas Emissions Trading Scheme as well as the Australia and New Zealand systems (Cooper and Ambrosi, 2009). As most regulatory systems exclude or seriously constrain land-use-related payments, at this time most such payments are made through the voluntary carbon market. This market is growing rapidly and often places a premium on biodiversity and livelihood co-benefits (Hamiliton et al, 2009). A number of voluntary market certification programs have been developed that explicitly evaluate biodiversity benefits, such as the Climate, Community and Biodiversity Alliance (CCBA, 2008).

Contracts for watershed PES aimed at providing hydrological services to downstream users can be designed so as also to protect biodiversity and restore natural habitat (Albrecht and Kandji, 2003). Incentives for maintaining pollination and pest control services also contribute directly to biodiversity conservation. The huge loss of these services globally (MEA, 2005), has motivated a handful of PES projects to pay for pollinator habitat protection (Scherr et al, 2007). Since the benefits of pollination and pest control services are mainly experienced locally, farmers are generally addressing threats through self-organized arrangements among groups of adjacent landowners. Nonetheless, responding to the US pollinator crisis, the 2008 US Farm Bill authorized the Conservation Reserve Program to include public payments for pollinator habitat.

Potential benefits and risks to farmers

Depending on their context, objectives, and design, biodiversity PES programs can involve both benefits and risks to farmers and farming communities.

Potential benefits

Biodiversity payments can benefit farmers by providing additional sources of income, subsidizing transitions to sustainable production, diversifying farm and forestry portfolios, and providing non-income livelihood and community social benefits. Direct payments can improve the reliability of income streams given that other farm income is typically quite variable from season to season and/or year to year. However, most ecosystem service payments provide only supplemental income to farmers (Scherr et al, 2007); thus they should be considered as providing a catalyst or enabling mechanism to transition to ecoagriculture practices, not as a replacement for farm product-based income. Even a modest level of payment, reliably paid over many years, can provide the increment that makes sustainable resource management viable.

Protecting or restoring ecosystem services for outside buyers can also provide non-income benefits to farmers, such as improved local water supplies and new forest-based resources including fuel, medicines and wild game. Restoration of native vegetation may also help to reduce landslides and control soil erosion and sedimentation. In addition, payments may spur the formalization of resource tenure and the clarification of property rights over ecosystem services. Finally, payments made to community and farmer organizations can be used as a social investment and to build local capacity for enterprise management and development, marketing and social organization. The PES program in Antioquia, Colombia, provides an example where PES has provided farmers with a range of non-monetary benefits in addition to cash payments (See Box 14.1).

Box 14.1: Integrating biodiversity in carbon payments in Antioquia, Colombia

In the Antioquia region of northwest Colombia, intensive land use and violent conflict have caused the deterioration in living conditions among local people. As a result, the nearby watershed has been seriously degraded and much of its hydrological properties and biodiversity lost. In addition, prices for wood processing and demand for local wood products, such as banana boxes and handicrafts, have declined.

A project financed by the International Tropical Timber Organization, Swiss Federal Laboratories for Material Testing and Research and Corporación Autonoma Regional de las Cuencas de los Rios Negro y Nare has sought to restore the critical biodiversity of this region by paying small-scale farmers for the carbon sequestered by better land management practices in the watershed. By its fortieth year, the project is expected to have offset 750,000 tons of carbon and has already catalyzed a shift to the sustainable extraction of timber and nontimber forest products, connected biological corridors and trained communities in forest extension, business ventures and forest ecology. Payments are managed by the San Nicolas Forests Corporation, a coalition of governmental organizations, and benefit 10,000 families in the area. The shift to sustainable agricultural and forest management practices has already restored critical habitat for biodiversity, controlled erosion, and protected the ecological services of the watershed. The methodology developed for this project was approved by the CDM in 2008, and the World Bank's BioCarbon Fund will be purchasing all emissions reductions until 2012.

Source: Robledo and Tobón, 2006; Robledo and Ok, 2009

Potential synergies between agricultural production and biodiversity conservation

A critical question—especially in regions where food security is of concern—is whether managing agricultural systems for ecosystem service provision changes the level of agricultural output and its distribution across space and time. In the long-term, and often even in the short-term, managing for ecosystem services can increase the production potential of farms by maintaining and enhancing the soil, nutrients, water and other resources upon which agriculture depends. In other situations, though, managing for ecosystem services requires taking land out of production or reducing the intensity of production, creating a short-term decrease in farm output.

An analysis conducted by the PES project Rewarding the Upland Poor for Ecosystem Services—a project undertaken by the World Agroforestry Centre in Indonesia, Nepal and the Philippines—identified five types of ecosystem service payments that were especially likely to promote production-environment synergies. These included: maintaining water quality; protecting conservation areas; maintaining biological corridors; restoring tree cover for carbon sequestration; and maintaining landscape beauty for ecotourism (van Noordwijk, 2005). This analysis was conducted for landscape settings where farmers tend to be undercapitalized, lack access to external farm inputs and are often labour constrained. In settings where the opposite is true—such as in many parts of the developed world—the synergy/trade-off equation will be different. Synergies also tend to be more common in ecologically degraded landscapes where biodiversity-conserving activities often help restore soil fertility and natural hydrological cycling, thereby benefiting farm productivity and sustainability (Milder et al, forthcoming; see also Chapter 3).

Potential risks

One risk, already discussed, is that biodiversity PES could reduce food production on farms. A related risk is that biodiversity PES programs could cause farmers or rural communities to lose the use or access rights to natural habitats that previously provided them with subsistence or commercial products. Where local people have secure and recognized property rights over natural resources, PES should benefit local people provided that the transaction is truly voluntary and that all users of the resource are represented. But in many landscapes with large remaining areas of natural habitat, local people's rights are customary or poorly defined, so that buyers of biodiversity services may exclude them (intentionally or not) from receiving fair payment. This may lead to a situation where PES becomes a tool for local or external elites to capture the monetary value of important community assets, and even to exclude local people from use of these assets (Smith and Scherr, 2003).

Farmers, particularly small-holders, selling ecosystem services, can help to mitigate these risks and protect themselves by demanding certain conditions are met before a deal is agreed. For instance, agreements should provide ample opportunity for communities to: have input into the design of the deal; build on a prior local self-assessment of ecosystem service needs; allow for the re-negotiation of contracts after specified time periods to reduce risk for sellers; ensure local livelihood and environmental co-benefits; contain eligibility criteria that include poor households; acknowledge well-established community organizations in planning processes; require social impact assessments; and support independent capacity building and advisory services for farmers. If these conditions are met, then PES holds the possibility of real livelihood benefits for some small-holders (Milder et al, forthcoming).

Barriers to effective widespread use of biodiversity payments

Although examples of biodiversity payments have emerged around the world, they have not yet evolved on a scale that makes a globally significant impact on biodiversity conservation and rural livelihoods. Several technical, economic, political, and cultural factors pose barriers to the use of PES at a larger scale. For PES to be globally significant, innovative, and systematic, solutions must be developed to address such barriers.

Technical constraints

Buyers of biodiversity conservation services will be willing to pay farmers only if they can be reasonably certain that the services are actually being provided. Yet, at present, there is insufficient knowledge about how to measure biodiversity, and lack of consensus on how to develop a currency for valuing biodiversity for PES transactions. Such technical limitations constrain the development of market values for biodiversity.

The challenge in measuring and valuing biodiversity lies in the complex nature of biodiversity itself. Whether examined on the genetic, species, or habitat level, biodiversity is an inherently complex unit to define and quantify. Efforts to quantify biodiversity benefits have typically taken two different approaches. First, when specific conservation benefits can be measured directly and immediately in the field, payments can be made for delivery of these services (for example, where farmers are paid a set amount for every breeding pair of an endangered species found on their land). Second, when the effects of specific land uses and management practices on biodiversity conservation are well understood, the adoption of those uses and practices may be accepted as a proxy and a trigger for payments (for example, farmers may be paid by the linear metre for revegetating stream banks for water quality and freshwater biodiversity where this relationship has been demonstrated).

To date, a variety of systems have been proposed or implemented for quantifying biodiversity services for the purpose of PES transactions. Metrics include simple land area, habitat hectares, environmental benefit indexes, landuse point systems, and landscape equivalency analysis (Scherr et al, 2007). Eco-certification programs are developing their own biodiversity criteria and measurement protocols. Determining cost-effective sampling and measurement methods for large-scale PES or eco-certification initiatives will remain a challenge until far more field studies are undertaken in agricultural landscapes comparing metrics against scientific study results.

Implementation constraints

At the implementation level, perhaps the greatest barrier to biodiversity PES is high transaction costs which can dramatically reduce the proportion of the buyer's price that the seller actually receives. Transaction costs include the cost of providing information about biodiversity benefits to potential buyers, costs of identifying, negotiating and building capacity of project partners, and costs of ensuring that parties fulfill their obligations (including auditing, certification and legal costs). Transaction costs tend to increase as the number of individual sellers increases. Thus, especially in the developing world, small farmers and farming communities have been at a serious disadvantage in terms of participating in biodiversity PES, resulting in fewer benefits for them as well as less effective PES programs. This challenge points to the need for intermediary institutions that can coordinate the efforts of many small farmers (Bracer et al, 2007).

A second challenge is that biodiversity conservation usually requires efforts that span multiple landholdings, up to the scale of landscapes or entire ecoregions. Thus, a farmer's ability to provide services may depend to a significant degree on how nearby lands are being used and managed. A number of examples are emerging where land is managed and institutionally supported at a landscape scale. One promising example is the Australian auction system in the Southern Desert Uplands that takes bids from private landowners to contribute to the establishment of habitat corridors (see Chapter 17). The auction format accounts for the interdependence of bids from neighboring properties, meaning that the value of alternative vegetation corridors will depend on strategic cooperation between landholders. The Biodiversity and Wine Initiative of South Africa rewards farmers with higher product prices for compliance with area-wide biodiversity conservation strategies (Biodiversity and Wine, 2009).

A final implementation constraint is the general lack of accessible information about potential buyers and sellers, business models, prices and 'rules of the game'. Typically, information is more available to ecosystem service buyers such as governments and corporations than to farmers, resulting in information asymmetries that can reduce sellers' bargaining power with buyers (Bracer et al, 2007). At the policy level, farmers in the developing world tend to be poorly represented in establishing basic policy foundations for PES including protections for land and resource rights (Bracer et al, 2009). Most existing PES programs do not reflect the flexible, locally adapted arrangements required for sustainable and equitable participation by low-income farmers and farming communities (Bracer et al, 2007).

Cultural constraints

The PES concept has also encountered cultural resistance from some environmental organizations, indigenous rights groups and others concerned about the use of market instruments for managing ecosystem services (e.g. Lovera, 2005). Common objections are that biodiversity has important non-economic values and that societies—including agriculturalists, pastoralists and fisherfolk—have a basic obligation to conserve biodiversity. The concept of selling species or habitats may also be culturally unacceptable to those who do not accept the ownership of nature. For PES to be widely acceptable, it will be critical to frame the approach not as payment for biodiversity itself but as payment for stewardship services that compensate farmers, on behalf of all beneficiaries, for the benefits they provide and the costs they incur in providing those benefits.

Potential scale of biodiversity payments to low-income producers

Milder et al (forthcoming) examine current and projected future trends in markets for biodiversity conservation globally, and the comparative advantage of low-income landowners, and conclude that such markets could benefit 10–15 million poor people annually by 2030. Biodiversity conservation services are highly location-specific and buyers are generally interested in conserving only those habitats and species that are rare, endangered, or in excellent condition (Wunder, 2008). Throughout the developing world, low-income and indigenous communities occupy many of the most biodiverse and threatened lands (Molnar et al, 2004). Thus, the poor may be the suppliers of choice simply by virtue of their location, particularly in voluntary biodiversity markets where buyers such as conservation NGOs and bioprospecters are likely to use strict resource-based targeting.

Historically, government agencies responsible for agriculture and wildlife conservation have been among the largest buyers of biodiversity conservation services. However, the vast majority of these payments have been in developed countries, and most have been allocated to non-poor farmers who agree to scale back or cease agricultural operations on their land (FT and EM, 2008a). It is unlikely that comparably large public-sector payment schemes will emerge in poor developing countries simply because of budget constraints. However, Milder et al (forthcoming) predict that a growing number of middle-income countries will establish and expand government PES for biodiversity or multiple objectives, as has already occurred in South Africa and Costa Rica (Turpie et al, 2008).

The enactment of environmental regulations could allow developing country governments to stimulate the creation of biodiversity markets without spending large sums of money. For example, flexible land-use regulations to limit forest clearance, if enforced, could lead to the establishment of habitat banks or systems of tradable development rights, as has occurred in the US (Jenkins et al, 2004). Similarly, governments or industry guidelines could require biodiversity offsets for large development projects such as mines, pipelines, plantations and dams (ten Kate et al, 2004). Presently, most biodiversity offsets are supplied by large landowners or firms who have the skills and financing to establish marketable habitat banks (Milder et al, 2009). However, in developing countries, low-income communities could be competitive suppliers of biodiversity offsets to the extent that they control land in biodiverse areas and have moderate to low opportunity costs. All such regulated biodiversity markets, however, are contingent on the enactment and enforcement of appropriate laws.

Consumer-driven markets and institutional buyers for eco-certified agricultural and forestry products offer the greatest potential for low-income producers to benefit monetarily from biodiversity-friendly stewardship. For example, the Biodiversity and Agricultural Commodities Project of the International Finance Corporation and the Global Environment Facility has a stated ten year goal that ten percent of all cocoa traded internationally (most of which is produced by smallholders) will be certified as biodiversity-friendly (IFC 2009).[1] The Ecosystem Marketplace considers that of 25 million small-scale producers worldwide who currently grow coffee, it is conceivable that 20 percent could participate in eco-certified production by 2030 (FT and EM, 2008b). Participation of small farmers in eco-certified agriculture remains a challenge due to the relatively high certification and monitoring costs of working with small landowners. However group certification systems and other protocols have been and are being created to address this issue (see Chapter 11).

Scaling up biodiversity PES in agricultural landscapes: challenges and solutions

If biodiversity PES is to have a significant impact in agricultural landscapes, the barriers described above must be addressed. In particular, action is needed to mobilize and organize buyers, establish supportive policy frameworks and institutions, engage and support community and farmer organizations and reduce transaction costs.

Mobilizing buyers for biodiversity services

Markets for ecosystem services cannot exist unless beneficiaries of these services are willing to pay for their provision. Beneficiaries are hesitant to pay for ecosystem services previously considered free, especially when service providers are unable to exclude beneficiaries from using the services, thus creating a strong incentive to free-ride. Three approaches are likely to be most effective in motivating the private sector to pay for biodiversity conservation services in general, including those that can be provided by farmers. First, new regulations can be enacted requiring private actors to minimize or offset their impacts on biodiversity by purchasing credits or engaging in conservation or restoration activities. Second, pressure from a variety of sources can encourage the private sector to take responsibility for conserving biodiversity, again by paying for on-site or off-site conservation and restoration efforts. For example, social advertising, activist movements targeting corporate behaviour, and pressure from investors are beginning to influence some firms to avoid investments and activities that harm biodiversity, and to offset impacts that are unavoidable. Pressure from consumers, in the form of purchasing preferences or boycotts, is also motivating corporate social responsibility as well as the proliferation of ecolabeled products that may be produced in a more biodiversity-friendly manner (Mulder et al 2006).

Third, the most powerful drivers potentially would be regulatory biodiversity offsets for major development investments and the full incorporation of terrestrial carbon into carbon trading markets (The Terrestrial Carbon Group, 2008). Carbon emission offsets are already one of the largest commodity markets in the world and growing. Political momentum is building to include more land-use carbon sequestration possibilities in the post-Kyoto climate change agreement that is slated to begin in 2012. A new wave of payments for Reduced Emissions from Deforestation and Degradation are beginning to flow that reward parties, including farmers, for leaving threatened forests intact. Payments to farmers to sequester carbon through agriculture, forestry and other landuses are also being promoted (Baalman and Schlamadinger 2008; VCS 2008). The extent to which these land-based carbon opportunities materialize will depend largely on the post-2012 climate change framework that will be discussed in Copenhagen in December 2009, and US national climate legislation under discussion at the time of writing.

Strengthening farmer engagement in PES market development

Farmers' organizations, indigenous groups, rural communities and their representatives have an important role to play in shaping future ecosystem service markets. Because new rules may fundamentally change the distribution of rights and responsibilities for essential ecosystem services, it is critical to ensure that rules support the public interest and favour social equity. In addition, international experience suggests that engaging local communities and local governments more fully in PES design and implementation will significantly improve the equity and efficiency of PES programs (e.g. Smith and Scherr, 2003).

A challenging issue in the design of PES programs relates to the targeting of payments, especially to low-income, rural land stewards. On the one hand, PES could function as a powerful tool for rural development and for advancing several of the Millennium Development Goals by rewarding rural communities that have historically provided good stewardship for ecosystem services of national or international value. Similarly, payments could be targeted to encourage the adoption of sustainable agriculture practices or to make them more economically viable. On the other hand, cost-effectiveness considerations may tend to favour payments to land stewards who have historically been bad actors (to encourage improvements in their practices), or for land under a high degree of threat of being converted to less environmentally benign uses. Thus, rural communities that have been practising conservation-friendly land management on a sustained basis may be excluded from receiving payments unless they threaten to switch to more environmentally damaging practices. Design of PES programs must, therefore, balance the goals of economic efficiency and fairness, using payments to reinforce landowners' stewardship ethic while avoiding perverse incentives that can lead to environmental blackmail.

Reducing transaction costs

Transaction costs greatly affect the degree to which demand for ecosystem services translates into actual payments at the level of farms and communities. Proactive efforts are needed to reduce the costs associated with obtaining market information, brokering and managing deals between buyers and sellers, and monitoring the provision of ecosystem services. Market information is critical to reduce uncertainties and risks for market actors due to unfamiliarity with PES, rapid changes in 'rules of the game', and difficulties in connecting buyers and sellers. Available tools include the Ecosystem Marketplace clearinghouse for information on biodiversity credits (speciesbanking.com), and Ecoagriculture Partners' new e-newsletter on PES in Agricultural Landscapes.

Transaction costs can also be reduced by creating new institutions and financial instruments that package ecosystem services for transaction in the marketplace; for example, by bundling biodiversity services provided by large numbers of local producers or by creating investment vehicles that have a diverse portfolio of projects in order to manage risks (Scherr et al, 2004). To convince beneficiaries of biodiversity services to pay for them, better methods of measuring and assessing biodiversity in working landscapes must be developed along with the institutional capacity to put these methods into practice. Overall, looking to the future, ecosystem service markets will need to be supported by a wide network of knowledge services, exchanges, financial instruments and advisers, as is now found in other commodity markets.

Conclusion

PES can provide incentives to farmers to shift to more biodiversity friendly practices, to restore degraded lands and generally to enhance the sustainability of their production systems. Current opportunities for farmers to benefit from PES schemes, particularly for biodiversity, are scattered but critical barriers are falling. Systems of valuation and monitoring are developing quickly, institutional innovations are reducing transaction costs and political momentum is growing throughout the world to support PES efforts. By building on past work and continuing to address key technical and institutional design challenges, farmers and their supporters can seize this moment as PES schemes scale up throughout the world to carve out an appropriate niche for themselves that will provide additional income and achieve the conservation benefits necessary for biodiversity and agriculture to thrive far into the future.

Notes

[1] The BACP has similar goals for palm oil, soy and sugar, but most of these commodities are not supplied by smallholders.

References

Albrecht, A. and Kandji, S. (2003) 'Carbon sequestration in tropical agroforestry ecosystems', *Agriculture, Ecosystems, and Environment*, vol 99, pp15–17

Andersson, M. and Oberthur, T. (2008) 'Certified agricultural products', in FT and EM (ed) *Payments for Ecosystem Services: Market Profiles*, Forest Trends and Ecosystem Marketplace, Washington DC, pp29–31

Baalman, P. and Schlamadinger, B. (2008) *Scaling Up AFOLU Mitigation Activities in Non-Annex Countries: A Report by Climate Strategies and GHG Offset Services for the Eliasch Review*, Climate Strategies, Cambridge, UK, http://climatestrategies.org/reportfiles/ukocc_afolu_mitgation_final_report_final .pdf, accessed 7 September 2009

Biodiversity and Wine Initiative (2009) http://www.bwi.co.za/, accessed 28 August 2009

Bioversity International (2008) 'Economics—On-going and Pipeline projects, Payments for Agrobiodiversity Conservation Services', www.bioversityinter national.org/scientific_information/themes/economics/on_going_and_pipeline_ projects.html, accessed 23 March 2009

Biodiversity Monitoring Switzerland (2006) 'Ecological compensation areas (M4)', www.biodiversitymonitoring.ch/english/indikatoren/m4.php, accessed 13 August 2009

Bracer, C., Scherr, S.J., Molnar, A., Sekher, M., Ochieng, B.O., and Sriskanthan, G. (2007) *Organizations and Governance for Fostering Pro-Poor Compensation for Environmental Services*, ICRAF Working Paper 39, World Agroforestry Centre, Nairobi

Bracer, C., Scherr, S.J., Molnar, A., Sekher, M., Ochieng, B.O. and Sriskanthan, G. (forthcoming) Organizations, institutions and governance for compensation for ecosystem services, *Ecology and Society*

Brand, D. (2002) 'Investing in the environmental services of the Australian forests', in S. Pagiola, J. Bishop and N. Landell-Mills (eds) *Selling Forest Environmental Services: Market-Based Mechanisms for Conservation and Development*, Earthscan, London

Bräuer, I., Oosterhuis, F., Rayment, M., Miller, C. and Dodoková, A. (2006) *The Use of Market Incentives to Preserve Biodiversity*, EcoLogic Institute, Berlin

Buck, L., Gavin, T., Uphoff, N. and Lee, D. (2007) 'Scientific assessment of ecoagriculture systems', in S. Scherr and J. McNeely (eds) *Farming with Nature: The Science and Practice of Ecoagriculture*, Island Press, Washington, DC

Capoor, K. and Ambrosi, P. (2009) *State and Trends of the Carbon Market 2009*, World Bank, Washington, DC

Carroll, N. (2008) 'Compliant biodiversity offsets', in FT and EM (ed) *Payments for Ecosystem Services: Market Profiles*, Forest Trends and Ecosystem Marketplace, Washington DC, pp18–20

CI (Conservation International) (2009) 'Our carbon projects', www.conservation.org/learn/climate/Pages/projects.aspx, accessed 24 March 2009

CCBA (Climate, Community and Biodiversity Alliance) (2008) *Climate, Community and Biodiversity Project Design Standards, Second Edition*, CCBA, Arlington, VA, http://climate-standards.org/standards/pdf/ccb_standards_second_edition_december_2008.pdf, accessed 13 August 2009

Chape, S., and Spalding, M. eds. (2008) *The World's Protected Areas: Status, Values, and Prospects in the Twenty-First Century*, University of California Press, Berkeley, CA

Chiquita (2004) 'Chiquita and Migros establish nature reserve in Costa Rica', www.chiquita.com/chiquita/announcements/releases/pr040614a.asp, accessed 24 March 2009

CONAFOR (Comisión Nacional Forestal) (2007) 'Environmental compensation for biodiversity and development: Towards a sufficient compensation', Presentation to Instituto Nacional de Ecologia, Mexico City, Mexico, February 15–16

ELI (Environmental Law Institute) (2007) *Mitigation of Impacts to Fish and Wildlife Habitat: Estimating Costs and Identifying Opportunities*, ELI, Washington, DC, www.elistore.org/reports_detail.asp?ID=11248, accessed 12 August 2009

FT and EM (Forest Trends and Ecosystem Marketplace) (2008a) *Ecosystem Marketplace Matrix*, Forest Trends and Ecosystem Marketplace, Washington DC http://ecosystemmarketplace.com/documents/acrobat/PES_MATRIX_06-16-08_oritented.pdf, accessed 12 August 2009

FT and EM (Forest Trends and Ecosystem Marketplace) (2008b) *Payments for Ecosystem Services: Market Profiles*, Forest Trends and Ecosystem Marketplace, Washington DC, http://ecosystemmarketplace.com/documents/acrobat/PES_Matrix_Profiles_PROFOR.pdf, accessed 12 August 2009

GEF (Global Environment Facility) (2007) *Biodiversity Focal Area Strategy and Strategic Programming for GEF-4*, www.gefweb.org/uploadedFiles/Focal_Areas/Biodiversity/GEF-4%20strategy%20BD%20Oct%202007.pdf, accessed 12 August 2009

Hamilton, K., Sjardin, M., Shapiro, A., Marcella, T. (2009) *Fortifying the Foundation: State of the Voluntary Carbon Markets 2009,* Ecosystem Marketplace and New Carbon Finance, Washington, DC http://ecosystemmarketplace.com/documents/cms_documents/StateOfTheVoluntaryCarbonMarkets_2009.pdf, accessed 28 August 2009

Harvey, C., Alpizar, F., Chacon, M. and Madrigal, R. (2005) *Assessing Linkages between Agriculture and Biodiversity in Central America: Historical Overview and Future Perspectives*, The Nature Conservancy, San Jose, Costa Rica, www.efdinitiative.org/research/publications/publications-repository/assessing-linkages-between-agriculture-and-biodiversity-in-central-america-historical-overview-and-future-perspectives, accessed 13 August 2009

Harvey, C. and Saenz, J. (eds) (2008) *Evaluación y Conservación de Biodiversidad en Paisajes Fragmentados de Mesoamérica*. INBio (Instituto Nacional de Biodiversidad), Santo Domingo de Heredia, Costa Rica

Hassan, R., Scholes, R. and Ash, N. (eds) (2005) *Ecosystems and Human Well-Being: Current State and Trends*, Volume 1, Island Press, Washington, DC

IFC (Internacional Finance Corporation) (2009) 'The Biodiversity and Agricultural Commodities Program', www.ifc.org/ifcext/sustainability.nsf/Content/Biodiv ersity_BACP, accessed 24 March 2009

Jenkins, M., Scherr, S.J. and Inbar, M. (2004) 'Markets for biodiversity services', *Environment*, vol 46, no 6, pp32–42

Lal, R. (2008) 'Carbon sequestration,' *Philosophical Transactions of the Royal Society B: Biological Sciences*, vol 363, no 1492, pp815–830

Lovera, S. (2005) 'Guest editorial: Environmental markets impoverish the poor', The Ecosystem Marketplace, http://ecosystemmarketplace.com/pages/article. opinion.php?component_id=2268&component_version_id=6448&language_id= 12, accessed 13 August 2009

MEA (Millennium Ecosystem Assessment) (2005) *Ecosystems and Human Well-Being: Synthesis*, World Resources Institute, Washington, DC

Milder, J., Scherr, S.J. and Bracer, B. (forthcoming) 'Trends and future potential of payment for ecosystem services to alleviate rural poverty in developing countries', *Ecology and Society*

Millard, E. (2007) 'Restructuring the supply chain', in S. Scherr and J. McNeely (eds) *Farming with Nature: The Science and Practice of Ecoagriculture*, Island Press, Washington, DC

Molnar, A., S. J. Scherr, and A. Khare. (2004) *Current Status and Future Potential of Markets for Ecosystem Services of Tropical Forests: An Overview*, Forest Trends, Washington, DC

Mulder, I., ten Kate, K. and Scherr, S. (2005) *Private Sector Demand in Markets for Ecosystem Services: Current Status of Involvement, Motivations to Become Involved, and Barriers and Opportunities to Upscale Involvement*, Report to UNDP/GEF on Institutionalizing Payments for Ecosystem Services, Forest Trends and Ecoagriculture Partners, Washington, DC.

Mulder, I., ten Kate, K. and Scherr, S. (2006) *Private Sector Demand in Markets for Ecosystem Services: Preliminary Findings*, Forest Trends, Washington, DC

NSAC (National Sustainable Agriculture Coalition) (2009) 'Agriculture Appropriations Chart: Fiscal Year 2009', National Sustainable Agriculture Coalition, Washington, DC

Neely, C. and Hatfield, R. (2007) 'Livestock Systems', in S. Scherr and J. McNeely (eds) *Farming with Nature: The Science and Practice of Ecoagriculture*, Island Press, Washington, DC

Reidsma, P., Tekelenburg, T., Van den Berg, M. and Alkemade, R. (2006) 'Impacts of land-use change on biodiversity: An assessment of agricultural biodiversity in the European Union', *Agriculture, Ecosystems, and Environment*, vol 114, pp86–102

Rice, R. (2003) 'Conservation concessions: Concept description', Presented to the Fifth World Parks Congress, Durban, South Africa, September 2003, http://conservationfinance.org/Workshops_Conferences/WPC/WPC_documents /Apps_09_Rice_v2.pdf, accessed 13 August 2009

Robledo, C. and Ok, H. (2009) 'Why there are so few forestry products under the clean development mechanism', Forest Carbon Portal, www.forestcarbonportal.com/article.php?item=285, accessed 13 August 2009

Robledo, C. and Tobón, P. (2006) *Alternative Financing Model for Sustainable Management in the San Nicolas Forest: A Participatory and Holistic Approach in Forestry*, The Rights and Resources Initiative, www.rightsandresources.org/ documents/files/doc_279.pdf, accessed 13 August 2009

Scherr, S.J., Bennett, M., Loughney, M. and Canby, K. (2007) *Developing Future Ecosystem Service Payments: Lessons Learned from International Experience*, Report for the China Council for International Cooperation on Environment and Development Taskforce for Ecocompensation, Forest Trends, Ecoagriculture Partners, Peking University, Washington, DC

Scherr, S. and McNeely, J. (eds) (2007) *Farming with Nature: The Science and Practice of Ecoagriculture*, Island Press, Washington, DC

Scherr, S.J., Milder, J. and Inbar, M. (2007) 'Paying farmers for stewardship', in S.J. Scherr and J.A. McNeely (eds) *Farming with Nature: The Science and Practice of Ecoagriculture*, Island Press, Washington, DC

Scherr, S.J., Milder, J. Lipper, L. and Zurik, M. (forthcoming), PSEAL Brief 1, FAO and Ecoagriculture Partners, Rome and Washington, DC

Scherr, S.J., White, A. and Kaimowitz, D. (2004) *A New Agenda for Forest Conservation and Poverty Reduction: Making Markets Work for Low-Income Communities,* Forest Trends, Center for International Forestry Research and World Conservation Union, Washington, DC

Schroth, G., da Fonseca, G.A.B., Harvey, C., Gascon, C., Vasconcelos, H.L. and Izac, A-M.N. (eds) (2004) *Agroforestry and Biodiversity Conservation in Tropical Landscapes*, Island Press, Washington, DC

Smith, J. and Scherr, S. (2003) 'Capturing the vale of forest carbon for local livelihoods', *World Development*, vol 31, no 12, pp2143–2160

Smith, P., Martino, D., Cai, Z., Gwary, D., Janzen, H., Kumar, P., McCarl, B., Ogle, S., O'Mara, F., Rice, C., Scholes, B. and Sirotenko, O. (2007) 'Agriculture', in B. Metz, O.R. Davidson, P.R. Bosch, R. Dave and L.A. Meyer (eds) *Climate Change 2007: Mitigation*, Contribution of Working Group III to the *Fourth Assessment Report of the Intergovernmental Panel on Climate Change*, Cambridge University Press, Cambridge

Swingland, I. (ed) (2002) *Capturing Carbon and Conserving Biodiversity: The Market Approach*, Earthscan, Sterling, VA

ten Kate, K., Bishop, J. and Bayon, R. (2004) Biodiversity Offsets: Views, Experience, and the Business Case, World Conservation Union, Gland,

Switzerland, and Cambridge, UK, and Insight Investment, London, www.forest-trends.org/documents/files/doc_660.pdf, accessed 13 August 2009

ten Kate, K. and Maguire, P (2008) 'Voluntary biodiversity offsets', in FT and EM (ed) *Payments for Ecosystem Services: Market Profiles*, Forest Trends and Ecosystem Marketplace, Washington DC, pp21–22

The Terrestrial Carbon Group. (2008) *How to Include Terrestrial Carbon in Developing Nations in the Overall Climate Change Solution*, www.terrestrialcarbon.org/site/DefaultSite/filesystem/documents/Terrestrial%2 0Carbon%20Group%20080808.pdf, accessed 13 August 2009

Turpie, J.K., Marais, C. and Blignaut, J.N. (2008) 'The working for water programme: Evolution of a payments for ecosystem services mechanism that addresses both poverty and ecosystem service delivery in South Africa', *Ecological Economics*, vol 65, pp788–98

van Noordwijk, M. (2005) *RUPES Typology of Environmental Services Worthy of Reward*, World Agroforestry Centre, Bogor, Indonesia, www.worldagroforestry centre.org/sea/Networks/RUPES/download/Working%20Paper/RUPES_Typolo gy.pdf, accessed 13 August 2009

VCS (Voluntary Carbon Standard) (2008) Voluntary Carbon Standard Guidance for Agriculture, Forestry and Other Land Use Projects, 18 November 2008, Voluntary Carbon Standard, Washington, DC, www.v-c-s.org/docs/Guidance %20for%20AFOLU%20Projects.pdf, accessed 7 September 2009

Wood, S., Sebastian, K. and Scherr, S. (2000) *Pilot Analysis of Global Ecosystems: Agroecosystems*, Report prepared for the Millennium Assessment of the State of the World's Ecosystems, International Food Policy Research Institute and the World Resources Institute, Washington, DC.

WBCFU (The World Bank Carbon Finance Unit) (2009) 'BioCarbon fund', http://wbcarbonfinance.org, accessed 12 August 2009

Wunder, S. (2008) 'Payments for environmental services and the poor: Concepts and preliminary evidence', *Environment and Development Economics*, vol 13, pp279–297

15

Targeting Payments for Ecosystem Services

Edward Stone and JunJie Wu

There is widespread consensus and concern that many anthropogenic activities are unsustainable. In other words, our consumption of resources and generation of waste exceed the regenerative and assimilative capacities of ecosystems globally. Thus, we run the risk of altering these ecosystems. In many cases, such as biodiversity loss, these alterations are irreversible. But why do we care and how should we respond? We care because we rely on ecosystems for a variety of goods and services that form the foundation of any economy. We may respond by enacting policies that enhance the provision of these goods and services. However, the effective design of such policies requires significant care as there is great potential for perverse or unforeseen impacts. Furthermore, the high level of public investment in environmental and conservation programs justifies examination of how to effectively utilize those funds. This chapter explores issues associated with policies targeting the provision of ecosystem services, particularly those targeting agricultural lands and agrobiodiversity.

The term ecosystem services has increased in prominence lately, largely due to the Millennium Ecosystem Assessment (MEA), a global effort undertaken by the UN to further understanding of ecosystem changes, their effects on humans, and the possibilities for mitigation. Ecosystem services are broadly defined as the benefits people receive from ecosystems. The MEA explicitly breaks down ecosystem services into four categories: provisioning services, such as food, fuel, fibre, water, and genetic resources; regulating services, such as climate, water, and disease regulation, water purification, flood control, and pollination; cultural services, such as spiritual and religious ties, recreation, and aesthetic values; and supporting services, such as soil formation, nutrient cycling, and habitat provision (MEA, 2005). Essentially, there is an ongoing paradigm shift toward studying and managing ecosystems in terms of the services they generate. In discussing this shift, there is an important distinction between ecosystem functions or features and ecosystem services. One clear explanation states that 'ecosystem services are the outcomes of ecosystem functions that yield value to people' (Boyd et al, 2005, p9).

From this perspective, the level of a service depends upon the level of ecosystem function and the economic context. For example, one of the values of flood control is the avoided damage, which depends in large part upon the proximity to population centres and structures. When benefits accrue globally, we can largely ignore this distinction; when they are local, we must account for the spatial distribution of ecosystems and human activities in quantifying the levels of services provided. In both the global and local case, threshold effects may be important, with a small change in the level of ecosystem function resulting in a relatively large change in the level of the associated ecosystem service.

Given the goal of enhancing ecosystem service provision on a large scale, we must consider the services provided by private lands and agricultural lands in particular. Farmland constitutes half of the land area of the EU (ECDGA, 2003). In the US, in 2002, cropland accounted for 23.3 percent of the land area, while grassland pasture and range accounted for an additional 30.8 percent, though much of this land is not privately owned (ERS, 2006). Globally, 15 percent of useable land is devoted to intensive crop production, while an additional 30 percent is grassland used for livestock production (Tilman and Polasky, 2005). The large share of agricultural land and the negative effects on ecosystem function often associated with agriculture justify policies targeting these lands. Payments for ecosystem services (PES) are an emerging strategy to encourage service provision, whereby farmers receive payment in return for adopting service-enhancing management practices.

Within the broad family of PES schemes, there is the potential for payments targeting agrobiodiversity directly. There is ample reason to pay for heightened agrobiodiversity as the diversity of species within an ecosystem directly affects the provision of a number of ecosystem services (Tilman and Polasky, 2005). For example, primary production of biomass—and thus carbon sequestration as well—in grasslands is strongly positively correlated with the number of plant species (Tilman et al, 1996, 2001; Hector et al, 1999), as is water quality (Tilman et al, 1996). Additionally, biodiversity has been linked to heightened stability and reliability of service flows (Tilman and Downing 1994; Naeem and Li, 1997; McGrady-Steed et al, 1997). While the case for targeting agrobiodiversity is clear, the appropriate design of these payments should vary greatly depending on the nature of the agrobiodiversity they are intended to foster. For example, if the desired outcome is to enhance the in situ preservation of landraces or crop varieties, the payment scheme might look very different compared to a scheme intended to enhance the variety of the full range of wild species (beyond crop varieties) on the farm. In the former case, the design of the policy would be fairly simple: pay farmers based on the number of varieties they grow. Given that the genetic diversity of plant species is distributed very unevenly across the globe (Vavilov, 1926; Harlan, 1971; Boyce, 2004), policies targeting in situ conservation might be best suited to centres of genetic diversity, sometimes referred to as Vavilov centres. In the latter case, appropriate design of a payment system is less obvious. What management practices lead to enhanced diversity of wild species on the farm? For the purposes of this chapter, we assume that land retirement programs and those promoting adoption of environmental 'best-practices' enhance this second sort of agrobiodiversity, though this assumption warrants further investigation—particularly if enhanced agrobiodiversity is the primary program objective.

Even once we have settled on which management practices to encourage, there remain a host of targeting issues we must consider in designing effective PES programs. Firstly, we must determine the appropriate criteria for deciding which lands to enrol. Should we target lands with low costs of enrolment, those which yield high benefits, or those that maximize some hybrid benefit-cost ratio? Alternative selection criteria can lead to perverse effects and drastically different outcomes for ecosystem service provision and particular interest groups (Wu et al, 2001). Additionally, the presence of threshold effects further complicates optimal targeting with a finite budget. Finally, the spatial nature of service-generating processes has implications for the effectiveness of PES programs. If the survival of a species depends on contiguity and/or proximity of suitable habitats, non-spatial targeting may be ineffective.

The remainder of this chapter is organized as follows. The following section presents the rationale behind PES schemes and the PES approaches adopted by governments in the US and EU. Subsequently, we discuss alternative targeting strategies and their implications for ecosystem services and different stakeholder groups. The next section investigates the potential pitfalls of threshold and spatial effects. Finally, concluding remarks are offered.

PES: rationale and recent context

The economic argument for PES schemes is straightforward. Because farmers are unable to capture the full rents of enhanced ecosystem service provision, the private and social values of management practices that foster service provision diverge. Thus farmers lack incentives to adopt beneficial practices, and the resulting provision of services is below the socially optimal level. By offering compensation, PES programs increase the probability of adoption and thereby the level of service provision. The PES programs of interest in our context are agri-environmental policies; these seek to achieve environmental benefits by altering behaviour in the agricultural sector. Though long-standing examples of agri-environmental policies exist, the scale and scope of these programs within larger farm policy has greatly increased since the 1980s (Bernstein et al, 2004). The negative side effects associated with traditional production-based agricultural policies (Claasen et al, 2001), combined with the difficulty of effectively coordinating environmental and agricultural policies (Just and Antle, 1990), led to the development of agri-environmental PES schemes. While PES schemes may share the goal of farm income support with more traditional agricultural policies, they differ from their predecessors in that payments are 'decoupled' from production. The remainder of this section details the perverse effects of traditional agricultural policy on ecosystem services, particularly agrobiodiversity, and discusses the development and current state of agri-environmental programs in the US and EU.

Traditional agricultural policies seeking to promote production and stabilize farm incomes tend to have negative side effects for ecosystem service provision (ERS, 2006). In the case of agrobiodiversity, there are several effects of concern. First, policy can affect agrobiodiversity by changing individual farmers' optimal planting decisions even in a simple framework of risk-neutrality. However, farmers are not simply risk-neutral profit-maximizers. They also manage risk, sometimes by planting a diverse set of crops or varieties. Thus, agricultural policies that alter the set of risk management tools available to farmers may also impact agrobiodiversity by allowing substitution away from diverse crop choice. Finally, agricultural policy can indirectly affect agrobiodiversity by influencing the size of farms.

Farmers take agricultural policy into account when making planting decisions. Agricultural policies promoting production of particular crops, specifically price supports and subsidies, tend to cause negative environmental outcomes by promoting intensification. Ignoring risk here for simplicity, rational farmers respond to the support of specific crops by shifting to more intense production of the most favoured crops. The intensification of agriculture can result, for example, in increased soil loss and groundwater pollution, degraded wildlife habitat, species decline, wetland loss, and reduced genetic diversity of crops planted (Claasen et al, 2001; see also Chapter 2 for more discussion of the ecological ramifications of agricultural intensification). In other words, intensive or conventional agriculture typically has negative impacts on agrobiodiversity both in terms of the diversity of crops and the diversity of wild species on the farm. The notion that encouraging production has negative effects on ecosystem service provision has gained acceptance and driven some policy reform globally over the past few decades. However, the simple effect described above is not the only channel through which conventional agricultural policy negatively impacts agrobiodiversity.

The incorporation of risk leads to another avenue by which agricultural policies impact agrobiodiversity. With no government intervention, risk-averse farmers limit the risk of losses due to uncertain conditions (land, weather, disease, prices etc) by diversifying their crop choice. However, government supports for farmers—in a wide variety of forms—constitute alternative methods of controlling risk, allowing farmers to abandon diverse production. DiFalco and Perrings (2005) provide a theoretical model of this effect, and their empirical results confirm the substitutability of crop diversity and participation in support programs as risk management tools in southern Italy, a Vavilov centre for cereal grains (Boyce, 2004).

Policies promoting production—and thus intensification—also negatively impact agrobiodiversity indirectly by affecting farm size. Typically, intensive agriculture means monoculture, high levels of input use (e.g. fertilizers and pesticides), and mechanization. This sort of agriculture favours large farms, which can take advantage of economies of scale, and governments seeking to 'modernize' the agricultural sector have historically favoured an intensive production system (Boyce, 2004). High-diversity agriculture tends to be labour intensive (Boyce, 2004) and is thus most appropriately practiced on small farms which have a comparative advantage in labour-intensive activities largely due to the availability of non-wage labour from the extended family (Sen, 1975). Thus, policies which make large-scale farming more attractive may in effect displace diverse agricultural production on small farms. This effect is of particular concern in regions where great diversity of crops and varieties coincides with small scale farming. For example, the Vavilov centres for maize and rice in Central America and the Bengal delta, respectively, may be vulnerable to this variety of agrobiodiversity loss (Boyce, 2004).

PES schemes targeting agricultural lands offer an alternative to traditional agricultural policies that have been taken up by a number of non-governmental agencies and private actors as well as by governments. For example, the World Bank has provided loans to finance direct payments for biodiversity conservation in Latin America and elsewhere, gaining experience in designing effective contracts and monitoring systems. One such program, the Regional Integrated Silvopastoral Ecosystem Management Project, targets agrobiodiversity and carbon sequestration in Costa Rica, Nicaragua, and Colombia (Pagiola et al, 2004). The World Bank has also established several projects promoting shade-grown coffee as a biodiversity conservation tool in Mesoamerica. However, in these cases, the focus is not on paying for enhanced agrobiodiversity directly but, rather, on inducing First World consumers to pay a premium for responsibly grown coffee (Pagiola and Ruthenberg, 2002). While this is an interesting approach, it relies on potentially cumbersome and opaque certification schemes as well as consumer willingness to pay, which can be fleeting. In another example of non-governmental PES schemes targeting agrobiodiversity, the Nature Conservancy purchases conservation easements detailing management practices, often on agricultural lands. One common feature of all of these example programs is their attempt to tip the scales in favour of socially beneficial management practices by providing often marginal monetary incentives to receptive farmers.

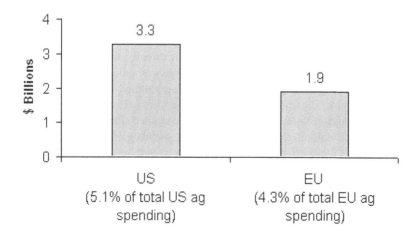

Figure 15.1. 2002 US and EU PES expenditures (Source: USDA, European Commission)

While there have been a number of non-governmental PES schemes, these programs are dwarfed in scale and scope by government programs, particularly those in the US and the EU. While more traditional policies still dominate agricultural budgets, both the US and the EU spend billions annually on agri-environmental programs (see Figure 15.1). Furthermore, there is an upward trend in agri-environmental expenditures in both blocs (see Figure 15.2 and ECDGA, 2003), and both increasingly foster PES policies as a method to continue supporting farm incomes while mitigating the negative externalities associated with production supports (ECDGA, 2003; Bernstein et al, 2004). Despite similar trends in budgets, the US and EU programs differ in the level of federal control and the sorts of ecosystem services they target.

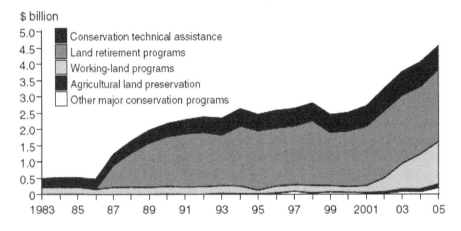

Figure 15.2. Historical US agri-environmental expenditures (Source: ERS, 2006)

In general, US agri-environmental programs aim to reduce the negative environmental impacts associated with agriculture, with the additional goals of supporting farm incomes and preserving agricultural land. While these US programs generally do not target agrobiodiversity directly, the reduction of negative outcomes associated with more traditional policy should enhance this service. Programs promoting amenities associated with agriculture, such as open space and rural aesthetic amenities, are largely left to the states (Bernstein et al, 2004). In 2004, federal agri-environmental programs accounted for 17 percent of $32.7 billion in federal natural resource conservation spending (ERS, 2006). Table 15.1 provides a list of these programs. Historically, land retirement programs account for the largest share of expenditures, approximately 50 percent of spending (ERS, 2006), but in recent years the share of the budget allocated to programs targeting working lands has increased (see Figure 15.2). Working land programs seek to improve environmental performance on land devoted to production. By far the single largest program is the Conservation Reserve Program (CRP), which in the late 1990s had enrolled over 36 million acres, or roughly 10 percent of US cropland (Claasen et al, 2001). The CRP offers farmers payments for the establishment of vegetative cover, such as native grasses, trees, or filter strips that conserve resources and provide habitat on environmentally sensitive land. In its early years, the CRP focused mainly on reducing soil erosion, but following the 1990 Farm Bill, the enrolment criteria were expanded to consider air quality, water quality, and habitat benefits (Claasen et al, 2001). The details of the CRP selection criteria are discussed in more depth in the next section on targeting strategies.

Table 15.1. Agri-environmental programs in the 2008 US farm bill

Primary focus	Programs
Land Retirement	Conservation Reserve Program
	Wetlands Reserve Program
Working Land	Conservation Security Program
	Environmental Quality Incentives Program
	Wildlife Habitat Incentives Program
Agricultural Land Preservation	Farm and Ranch Lands Protection Program
Other	Grassland Reserve Program

Source: ERS, 2006

The US federal government administers a wide range of agri-environmental programs. In general, enrolment eligibility is contingent upon the adoption of certain conservation practices and the avoidance of others. This mechanism, known as cross-compliance, provides a regulatory 'stick' approach to bolster the 'carrot' approach of offering incentive payments through PES schemes and helps to ensure a baseline level of conservation across most agricultural lands. For example, farmers who cultivate highly erodible land or convert wetlands for production are ineligible for government commodity programs (Bernstein et al, 2004). The notion of cross compliance carries over to the EU case as well.

In many ways, EU agri-environmental programs resemble their US counterparts. For example, the timeline of program development is similar, and the decoupling of farmers' income supports from production has figured prominently in reforms of the EU's Common Agricultural Policy dating back to 1992 (ECDGA, 2003). Like the US, the EU has seen a marked upward trend in enrolment and expenditures as agri-environmental programs displace more traditional agricultural supports (Bernstein et al, 2004). The share of agricultural lands enrolled in PES programs climbed from 15 percent in 1998 to 27 percent in 2001 (ECDGA, 2008). In an additional similarity with the US approach, cross-compliance figures prominently in EU agricultural PES schemes, with farmers expected to maintain some baseline of 'good farming practices' as a pre-condition for eligibility.

The scope of EU program goals is however broader than in the US. EU program goals fall into three categories: environmentally beneficial productive farming, non-productive land management, and socio-economic measures and impacts. While the first two categories roughly correspond to working land and land retirement programs in the US, the final category focuses on maintenance of rural lifestyles, communities, and landscapes, which does not figure prominently in US programs

(Bernstein et al, 2004). In addition, EU policy refers specifically to the maintenance of agrobiodiversity as a program goal (EC, 2001), though how this translates to implementation at the member state level is unclear. The degree of federal control is also substantially lower in the EU than in the US. While the European Commission sets program goals and distributes funding, individual member states have latitude in determining baseline eligibility and selection criteria. Each member state enumerates which conservation actions constitute 'good farming practices' and determines which parcels or farms to enrol.

Agri-environmental programs are an economically sensible response to the socially detrimental side effects of agriculture. Specifically, they correct a disincentive for farmers to adopt beneficial management practices. The perverse incentives created by traditional agricultural policy heighten the attractiveness of PES as an alternative form of farm income support. As a result, agricultural PES programs have increased in prominence in both the developing and the developed world, as illustrated by the examples provided above. Despite the apparent potential of PES programs as economically efficient policy tools, there are a number of targeting concerns that may hinder their effectiveness if overlooked. We examine these targeting concerns in the subsequent sections.

Alternative targeting criteria

One relevant question in the design of any PES program is that of targeting: given a finite budget, which resources should be enrolled, or, in other words, which farmers should receive payments in return for adopting specified management practices? From an economic perspective, it seems clear that the ecosystem service benefits of the program will be maximized when those farms that offer high benefits relative to costs are enrolled first. In reality, however, political considerations may trump economics. Furthermore, maximizing the benefits in terms of ecosystem services may not be the sole program goal which may include, for example, providing farm income support, preserving the cultural heritage values of farmland, and so on. Given the large investment in agricultural PES programs, it is important to understand the implications of alternative targeting criteria.

In this section, we present four common alternative targeting strategies and investigate their implications for ecosystem service provision. We also evaluate the distributional impacts and the outcomes from the perspective of resource owners, consumers of agricultural goods and environmentalists. Finally, we provide real world policy examples of these targeting regimes. For a more complete presentation of the theoretical construct underlying the results below, please see the paper by Wu, Zilberman, and Babcock entitled 'Environmental and distributional impacts of conservation targeting strategies' (2001). At the heart of this paper is the characterization of cropland in terms of the potential agricultural output and the potential environmental benefits of retiring that land. Assuming a known joint distribution of output and environmental benefit, the authors are able to solve the social planner's maximization problem and rigorously compare alternative targeting strategies. These results apply to the case where ecosystem benefits are attained by retiring land, and a wide range of other management practices exist which could enhance ecosystem or agrobiodiversity benefits. However, the illustration of different outcomes stemming from alternative targets in the land retirement case yields lessons which apply more generally.

With no policy intervention, all profitable land should be in production. Since environmental considerations do not factor into the decision, this landuse is not socially optimal and action is warranted. With complete information, a regulator could determine an optimal landuse pattern and retire the necessary lands. However, policy makers often lack such information, and allocation of budgets is determined politically, with conservation funds then distributed according to some targeting strategy. Four targeting regimes are described below.

- Cost targeting: enrolling resources with lowest per-unit cost. Early CRP enrolments were consistent with this strategy due to a Congressionally-mandated minimum enrollment acreage.
- Benefit targeting: enrolling resources with highest per-unit benefit. The US Fish and Wildlife service follows this strategy, conserving lands with high levels of ecosystem function. This strategy is also common in the designation of national parks or world heritage sites. The most beautiful or highest benefit lands are typically selected with relatively less emphasis on cost.
- Benefit-cost targeting: enrolling resources with the highest benefit per dollar expended. Beginning in the early 1990s, the CRP began to move toward this criterion. The CRP determines enrolment using the Environmental Benefits Index (EBI). While the EBI is not strictly a ratio of costs to benefits, it does consider costs. Specifically, 150 out of 545 possible points are scored based on cost, with the rest being scored on environmental benefits (ERS, 2006).
- Benefit-maximizing targeting: enrolling those resources that provide the highest total level of environmental benefits. If output demand is perfectly elastic, benefit-maximizing and benefit-cost targeting are equivalent. If however, output demand is not perfectly elastic, then benefit-maximizing targeting yields higher total benefits for a given budget.

The difference between benefit-cost and benefit-maximizing targeting in the case of elastic output demand is attributable to the fact that, in response to the policy intervention, some previously preserved land enters into production. Essentially, land retirement decreases total output, resulting in a higher output price. This new, higher price induces farmers to cultivate some previously unprofitable land. This is known as the slippage effect and may erode the benefits of conservation programs if not considered. The policy intervention has the potential to impact price and cause slippage when demand is not perfectly elastic and the scale of the intervention is large. For example, Wu (2000) shows significant slippage effects in the CRP. In the worst cases, slippage could render a land retirement program counter-productive.

With elastic output demand, benefit-maximizing targeting out-performs benefit-cost targeting because the policy maker behaves like a monopolist. In other words, the policy maker considers the potential price effect and adjusts the enrollment decision accordingly, leading to the enrolment of relatively more high-benefit, high-output land. High-output land has a larger profit margin and thus higher enrolment costs. So, for a given budget, the output effect grows smaller as more high-output land is enrolled. A smaller output effect mitigates the price effect and slippage, allowing benefit-maximizing targeting to outperform benefit-cost targeting in terms of environmental benefits under a fixed budget. Benefit-cost targeting is more efficient (i.e. maximizes the sum of consumer and producer surplus); benefit-maximizing targeting sacrifices market efficiency for higher environmental benefits.

Each targeting strategy results in different price effects and different subsets of the available land being activated and retired. We can compare the outcomes associated with our alternatives using a variety of performance measures. Table 15.2 summarizes the relative performance of our four targeting regimes. For the rigorous development of these results, see Wu et al (2001).

Table 15.2. Comparing targeting strategies

Total Land in Conservation	$Q(U_i)$	$Q(U_2) \geq Q(U_4) \geq Q(U_3) \geq Q(U_1)$
Total Output	Y_i	$Y_2 \geq Y_4 \geq Y_3 \geq Y_1$
Output Price	p_i	$p_1 \geq p_3 \geq p_4 \geq p_2$
Consumer Surplus	CS_i	$CS_2 \geq CS_4 \geq CS_3 \geq CS_1$
Producer Surplus	PS_i	$PS_1 \geq PS_3 \geq PS_4 \geq PS_2$
Environmental Benefit	B_i	$B_4 \geq B_3 \geq B_1 , B_4 \geq B_2$

1=cost targeting; 2=benefit targeting; 3=benefit-cost targeting; 4=benefit-maximizing targeting (Source: Wu et al, 2001)

Based on the results in Table 15.2, cost targeting results in the lowest output and highest price. It is also the preferred strategy of landowners since it provides the largest producer surplus. From an equity standpoint, cost targeting is the most pro-poor strategy if the poor own the land. Conversely, it is the least pro-poor strategy if the poor are consumers. Benefit targeting, on the other hand, results in the highest output and lowest prices. Thus it maximizes consumer surplus and is preferred by buyers of agricultural products and not by landowners. Benefit-cost targeting generates an efficient outcome but when output price responds to quantity it fails to maximize benefits for a given budget and is not the preferred strategy of any group. Benefit-maximizing targeting provides the highest level of environmental benefits and is the preferred strategy of conservationists.

Market forces drive the slippage effect with real implications for the relative performance of different targeting regimes. This section presented the different outcomes associated with four targets and explained some of those differences in terms of the slippage effect. The theoretical model behind these results provides an ideal framework for illustration; however, it does make some strong assumptions. Among others, that land retirement generates environmental benefits in a known fashion and that the benefits of preserving a parcel do not depend on the status of other parcels. In fact, the benefits of a management action on one parcel may depend quite heavily on actions taken elsewhere, a problem which manifests itself in the form of both threshold and spatial effects.

A note on threshold and spatial effects

Just as failure to consider market forces can reduce the effectiveness of a PES program, so too can the omission of relevant features of ecosystem processes. Specifically, threshold and spatial effects often characterize service-generating processes. This section briefly explores the nature of these effects and consequences of ignoring them.

Generally, threshold or cumulative effects exist in a system when, over some interval, small changes in one variable are associated with major changes in the state of the system. We can imagine both point thresholds, where the state jumps discretely in response to a variable change, and zone thresholds, where the state quickly but continuously adjusts (see Figure 15.3). In any case, threshold effects imply a non-linear relationship between a state variable and a choice variable. In the context of PES programs, thresholds are present when significant improvements in the provision of ecosystem services are realized only once program participation reaches a certain level. For example, groundwater may become drinkable or a wild species may survive only if a certain minimum level of cropland is retired and reverts to a natural state. Threshold effects have been documented in a variety of conservation applications, particularly those involving wild flora and fauna (Hugget, 2005; Wu and Boggess, 1999).

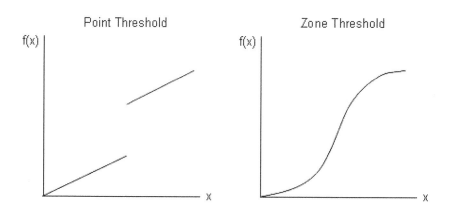

Figure 15.3. Illustrations of threshold effects

Wu and Boggess (1999) illustrate the targeting implications of threshold effects by considering two identical watersheds. There is a limited budget for conservation across both watersheds. Thresholds are present in each watershed, meaning that there is some level of conservation below which benefits are quite low. Above this threshold, conservation benefits increase rapidly. If the conservation budget is small and conservation funds are distributed equally across watersheds, as may be politically expedient, the benefits of conservation may actually be minimized under strong threshold effects. When an equally divided budget fails to achieve the threshold level of conservation in either watershed, we would be better off concentrating efforts in a single watershed. By concentrating effort, we take funds that were generating relatively low benefits in one watershed and use them to surpass the threshold and achieve high benefits in the second watershed. Using a fairly general theoretical model, Wu and Boggess (1999) demonstrate the potentially perverse effects of targeting without considering threshold effects and develop a decision rule for allocating budgets.

In addition to threshold effects, service-generating processes often exhibit spatial dependence. That is, the level of services generated in one location depends on the conditions in surrounding locations. In fact, this may be the rule rather than the exception in natural systems, where, at least on some scale, nearby conditions affect outcomes. Consider the problem of habitat fragmentation and species loss. Species may require particular spatial patterns, such as continuity or proximity of suitable habitats, for success. This realization has given rise to a rich literature on reserve site selection in both terrestrial and marine ecosystems. For example, in a seminal 1975 paper, Diamond addressed the question of whether a single large or several small reserves maximize benefits. A number of papers have built on this question, generalizing the ecological model and incorporating economics (e.g. Etienne and Heesterbeek, 2000; Groeneveld, 2005). The simple truth that location and surroundings matter presents tough modeling challenges and vastly increases data requirements. However, spatially explicit models capture a central feature of natural systems, and economists and ecologists alike have made strong cases in favour of incorporating spatial processes in research (e.g. Bockstael, 1996).

As with thresholds, failure to consider spatial dependence when targeting conservation spending may result in perverse effects. Suppose our goal is to maximize the benefits of conservation given a fixed budget. Treating benefits as spatially independent, our previous analysis indicates that we should opt for the benefit-maximizing targeting strategy. The resulting landuse pattern considers conservation costs and benefits as well as the market slippage effect. If, in fact, the benefits of conservation are spatially dependent, our previous land-use pattern may be suboptimal. If continuity, proximity, or concentration of conservation affects benefits, we could improve our landuse pattern on the margin by dropping some of our previously conserved land and replacing it with land that helps us achieve some desirable spatial pattern. While the newly conserved land is not an attractive conservation investment when considered in isolation, it is attractive when we account for the positive effect on the benefits generated from nearby land. In the extreme case, aspatial targeting could result in highly dispersed conservation when much more concentration is optimal.

Conclusion

Ultimately, we rely on ecosystem services as the basis of every economy. Ecosystem processes provide us with primary raw materials for production and consumption, not to mention regulatory and supporting services that keep the natural world on an even keel. Globally, population pressures, environmental degradation, and even rising food prices and severe weather have people worried that our current track is not sustainable. To that end, interest in policies to stabilize or enhance the provision of ecosystem services has grown, with much attention focused on agriculture. In the heavily subsidized world of US and EU agriculture, agri-environmental PES programs are particularly attractive since they correct a market failure to provide adequate levels of ecosystem services while displacing traditional agricultural policies associated with negative environmental outcomes. Elsewhere—for example, in the case of product certification schemes—PES programs help create a market for beneficial management practices that farmers previously could not pass along the value chain. Furthermore, agriculture accounts for a large portion of global landuse, so small improvements in management practices could translate to large global increases in service provision. The large and increasing level of public and private expenditure on PES programs warrants investigation into efficient and effective policy design.

Despite the strong case for agri-environmental PES programs, they require careful design to avoid perverse effects. First, the price effect of conserving a resource may lead to slippage, whereby some of the conservation benefits are offset by exploitation of previously unused resources. In the extreme case, slippage can even render a program counter-productive. Second, when threshold effects characterize the service-generating process, failure to account for them may result in suboptimal or even minimized conservation benefits for a given budget. When an identifiable threshold exists, spending should be concentrated to achieve the threshold level in one or a few areas rather than dispersed at levels below the threshold across many areas. Finally, the omission of spatial dependence in the service-generation process also results in suboptimal conservation benefits. When benefits are spatially dependent, we cannot compare alternatives by aggregating the benefits from each resource unit considered in isolation. Rather, we must compare alternatives based on the benefits of the resource-use pattern as a whole. In order to maximize the benefits of agri-environmental PES programs, targeting strategies must account for the economic incentives of resource owners as well as the relevant features of the ecosystem service-generating process.

References

Bernstein, J., Cooper, J. and Claasen, R. (2004) *Agriculture and the Environment in the United States and EU*, ERS Report WRS-04-04, US Department of Agriculture, pp66–77

Bockstael, N. (1996) 'Modeling economics and ecology: The importance of a spatial perspective', *American Journal of Agricultural Economics*, vol 78, no 5, pp1168–1180

Boyce, J. K. (2004) A *Future for Small Farms? Biodiversity and Sustainable Agriculture*, Working Paper 86, Political Economy Research Institute, University of Massachusetts, Amherst, MA

Boyd, J., Sanchirico, J. and Shabman, L. (2005) *Habitat Benefit Assessment and Decisionmaking: A Report to the National Marine Fisheries Service*, Discussion Paper 04-09, Resources for the Future, Washington, DC, www.rff.org/Docum ents/RFF-DP-04-09.pdf, accessed 21 August 2009

Claassen, R., Hansen, L., Peters, M., Breneman, V., Weinberg, M., Cattaneo, A., Feather, P., Gadsby, D., Hellerstein, D., Hopkins, J., Johnston, P., Morehart, M. and Smith, M. (2001) *Agri-Environmental Policy at the Crossroads: Guideposts on a Changing Landscape*, US Department of Agriculture, Economic Research Service, AER-794

Diamond, J. (1975) 'The island dilemma: Lessons of modern biogeographic studies for the design of nature reserves', *Biological Conservation*, vol 7, no 2, pp129–146

DiFalco, S. and Perrings, C. (2005) 'Crop biodiversity, risk management, and the implications of agricultural assistance', *Ecological Economics*, vol 55, no 4, pp459–466

EC (European Commission) (2001) *Biodiversity Action Plan for Agriculture*, Brussels, Belgium

ECDGA (European Commission Directorate-General for Agriculture) (2003) *Agriculture and the Environment Factsheet*, http://ec.europa.eu/agriculture/publi /fact/envir/2003_en.pdf, accessed 30 Nov 2008

ECDGA (European Commission Directorate-General for Agriculture) (2008) 'Agriculture and the Environment', http://ec.europa.eu/agriculture/envir/index _en.htm, accessed 30 Nov 2008

ERS (Economic Research Service) (2006) *Agricultural Resources and Environmental Indicators*, US Department of Agriculture, Economic Information Bulletin 16, www.ers.usda.gov/publications/arei/eib16/eib16.pdf, accessed 30 Nov 2008

Etienne, R. and Heesterbeek, J. (2000) 'On optimal size and number of reserves for metapopulation persistence', *Journal of Theoretical Biology*, vol 203, no 1, pp33–50

Groeneveld, R. (2005) 'Economic considerations in the size and number of reserve sites', *Ecological Economics*, vol 52, no 2, pp219–228

Harlan, J.R. (1971) 'Agricultural Origins: Centers and Noncenters', *Science*, vol 174, no 4008, pp468–474

Hector, A., Schmid, B., Beierkuhnlein, C., Caldeira, M., Diemer, M., Dimitrakopoulos, P., Finn, J., Freitas, H., Giller, P., Good, J., Harris, R., Hogberg, P., Huss-Daniel, K., Joshi, J., Jumponen, A., Korner, C., Leadley, P., Loreau, M., Minns, A., Mulder, C., O'Donovan, G., Otway, S., Pereira, J., Prinz, A., Read, D., Scherer-Lorenzen, M., Schulze, E., Siamantziouras, A., Spehn, E., Terry, A., Troumbis, A., Woodward, F., Yahci, S. and Lawton, J. (1999) 'Plant diversity and productivity experiments in European grasslands', *Science*, vol 286, no 5442, pp1123–1127

Hugget, A.J. (2005) 'The concept and utility of ecological thresholds in biodiversity conservation', *Biological Conservation*, vol 124, no 3, pp301–310

Just, R.E. and Antle, J.M. (1990) 'Interactions between agricultural and environmental policies: A conceptual framework', *American Economic Review*, vol 80, no 2, pp197–202

McGrady-Steed, J., Harris, P.M. and Morin, P.J. (1997) 'Biodiversity regulates ecosystem predictability', *Nature*, vol 390, no 6656, pp162–165

MEA (Millennium Ecosystem Assessment) (2005) *Ecosystems and Human Well-Being: Current State and Trends: Findings of the Condition and Trends Working Group*, Island Press, Washington, DC

Naaem, S. and Li, S. (1997) 'Biodiversity enhances ecosystem reliability', *Nature*, vol 390, no 6659, pp507–509

Normille, M.A., Effland, A.B.W., Young, C.E. (2004) *US and EU Farm Policy – How Similar?* ERS Report WRS-04-04, US Department of Agriculture, pp14–27

Pagiola, S., Agostini, P., Gobbi, J., de Haan, C., Ibrahim, M., Murgueitio, E., Ramirez, E., Rosales, M. and Ruiz, J.P. (2004) *Paying for Biodiversity Conservation Services In Agricultural Landscapes*, Environmental Economics Series, Paper 96, World Bank Environment Department, Washington, DC

Pagiola, S. and Ruthenberg, I.A. (2002) 'Selling biodiversity in a coffee cup: Shade-grown coffee and conservation in Mesoamerica', in S. Pagiola, J. Bishop and N. Landell-Mills (eds) *Selling Forest Environmental Services: Market-based Mechanisms for Conservation and Development*, Earthscan, London

Sen, A. (1975) *Employment, Technology and Development*, Clarendon, Oxford

Tilman, D. and Downing, J.A. (1994) 'Biodiversity and stability in grasslands', *Nature*, vol 367, no 6461, pp363–365

Tilman, D. and Polasky, S. (2005) 'Ecosystem goods and services and their limits: The roles of biological diversity and management practices', in R.D. Simpson, M.A. Toman and R.U. Ayres (eds) *Scarcity and Growth Revisited: Natural Resources and the Environment in the New Millennium*, Resources for the Future, Washington, DC

Tilman, D., Wedin, D. and Knops, J. (1996) 'Productivity and sustainability influenced by biodiversity in grassland ecosystems', *Nature*, vol 379, no 6567, pp718–720

Tilman, D., Reich, P. B., Knops, J., Wedin, D., Mielke, T. and Lehman, C. (2001) 'Diversity and productivity in a long-term grassland experiment', *Science*, vol 294, no 5543, pp843–845

Wu, J. (2000) 'Slippage effects of the Conservation Reserve Program', *American Journal of Agricultural Economics*, vol 82, no 4, pp979–992

Wu, J. and Boggess, W.G. (1999) 'The optimal allocation of conservation funds', *Journal of Environmental Economics and Management*, vol 38, no 3, pp302–321

Wu, J., Zilberman, D. and Babcock, B.A. (2001) 'Environmental and distributional impacts of conservation targeting strategies', *Journal of Environmental Economics and Management*, vol 41, no 3, pp333–350

Vavilov, N.I. (1992 [1926]) *Origin and Geography of Cultivated Plants*, Cambridge University Press, Cambridge, UK

16

The 'Green Box': Multifunctionality and Biodiversity Conservation in Europe

Rosemarie Siebert

Over the last 20 years, considerations concerning the protection and sustainable management of biodiversity have become more important in European agricultural practice. European Union (EU) and national agricultural policies emphasize the need for nature-friendly agriculture. It is widely acknowledged that farmers' participation in undertaking conservation activities has a significant impact on the success of biodiversity policies. National and international conservation laws and policies frequently extend to farmland. In some areas, the production or safeguarding of natural values becomes a main task of the agricultural sector next to the production of livestock and crops. This represents a major shift in the EU's Common Agricultural Policy (CAP) that over decades had focused on food production as the main, if not only, task for agriculture. Until the 1980s, EU mainstream policies directed virtually all agricultural measures, and most of the expenditures, to food production. This approach had substantial negative consequences for the environment (Janke, 2002; Sattler, 2008).

> Modern agriculture provides a good example: it has been very successful at increasing food output. But these improvements also came at considerable cost. In the process of increasing output with greater use of renewable inputs, we have lost natural habitats and wildlife; soils have been depleted; water polluted with pesticides and fertilizers; human health damaged by pesticides (Pretty, 2000, p326).

Part of the negative consequences in the biosphere is a loss of biodiversity due to destruction, homogenization, fragmentation, and genetic isolation of habitats (Sattler, 2008). With the emerging awareness of environmental problems caused by agricultural practices during the 1980s, the EU policy focus widened. Accordingly, environmental protective goals as well as structural support for rural areas were incorporated by means of so-called accompanying measures (regulation (EEC) No 2078/92). This shift was accompanied by the development of the concept of multifunctional agriculture which was adopted—albeit with differing accents and perspectives—by several international institutions including the Food and Agriculture Organization of the United Nations (FAO), the Organization for Economic Cooperation and Development (OECD) and the EU (Council Regulation (EC) No 1257/99) (Helming and Wiggering, 2003).

Multifunctional agriculture is a political concept used to identify and value the environmental and landscape services provided by farmers to society. The OECD conceptualizes multifunctionality from an economic perspective concerned with the provision of multiple goods through agriculture (Wüstemann et al, 2008). There are two key elements of multifunctionality from this perspective: first, the existence of multiple commodity and non-commodity outputs that are jointly produced by agriculture; and second, the fact that some of the non-commodity outputs exhibit the characteristics of externalities or public goods for which markets either do not exist or function poorly (OECD, 2001). This perspective accepts that most economic activities will have a range of often unintended outputs and effects in addition to their intended output (OECD, 2001). However, it may also be considered narrow in the sense that it does not explicitly identify outputs such as the social services provided by agriculture and other land uses to sustainable regional development (Barkmann et al, 2004). In contrast, the FAO argues that land provides a basis for multifunctionality both in concert with agriculture and in its own right (FAO, 2000).

From the EU viewpoint, the concept of multifunctionality fits two purposes: first, its application supports negotiations at the WTO level where subsidies to users of agricultural land have to be justified; and second, it legitimizes these financial transfers at the national level with regard to taxpayers. Apart from the production of food and fibre, agriculture is seen to encompass a range of functions including the preservation, management and enhancement of the rural landscape, and the protection of the environment. These functions are not viewed simply as externalities of the agricultural production function (i.e. undirected side-effects disembedded from any specific institutional and political context). Instead, in recognition that much of European society cares about the multiple functions of agriculture, explicit policies to ensure their supply have been established (European Commission, 1999). One of the services eligible for financial support to farmers is the maintenance and enhancement of biodiversity in the landscape as part of the ecological functions carried out by agriculture.

Agri-environmental programs in the 'green box'

The CAP contains two main premises regarding nature protection and multifunctionality: first, farmers have to fulfil certain minimum norms regarding the protection of the environment if they want to receive the full amount of direct EU subsidies (cross-compliance); and second, if society wants farmers to carry out environmental services that go beyond best agricultural practice, it will have to pay for such services through programs aimed at nature protection in agricultural areas (European Commission, 2009). Agri-environmental programs are obligatory components of programs for rural development in all EU countries. They are viewed as important instruments for the implementation of the Habitats Directive (Matzdorf et al, 2006) and as the national/regional implementation of Council Regulation (EEC) No 2078/92. Characteristics of such policies are voluntariness, time limits, and a bonus payment as compensation and incentive for farmers to introduce or maintain: (1) the desired agricultural production practices that are compatible with the environment; and (2) any natural protection policies deemed important. The nature protection services provided by farmers within this framework are viewed as a public good that is unlikely to be provided by the market in an optimal quantity. For that reason, state intervention to increase the supply of this good is considered justified (Bromley, 1997). In order to obtain the bonus, the environmental services have to exceed the standards set by law.

At the end of the 1980s, EU agricultural policies introduced agri-environmental programs as instruments in support of special production procedures that would contribute to natural protection and landscape conservation. In 1987, then European Community (EC) member countries were given the option to provide agricultural businesses located in areas with an endangered environment with an EC co-financing of 25 percent for activities in support of the environment. The CAP reform of 1992 introduced agri-environmental programs according to Council Regulation (EEC) No 2078/92 in support of the previous environmental measures as an accompanying measure. In contrast to the previous EC extensification program, this reform made it possible to subsidize and support the maintenance of desired landuse practices. The co-financing instrument was increased to 75 percent of the cost of environmental activities in less prosperous Objective One regions and to 50 percent elsewhere. The higher financial support of the EU helped broaden the scope for member countries to implement agricultural nature conservation programs, because a larger part of the program cost was paid for by the EU. In Germany, for example, new agri-environmental programs were introduced and existing programs transferred to the new support framework in order to take advantage of the higher limits for co-financing. As a result, co-financing of agri-environmental programs provided by the EU increased about 60 percent by the end of the 1990s in Germany, when compared to the situation prior to the introduction of Council Regulation (EEC) No 2078/92 (Osterburg and Stratmann, 2002). The CAP reform of 2003 retained the obligations of the agri-environmental programs for member states, but those programs remained optional for farmers. The 2003 reform raised the EU co-financing limit to 85 percent in Objective One areas and to 60 percent in other areas. The reform also specified that farmers who, for a five year period, commit themselves to apply production techniques that are compatible with environmental conservation and surpass usual best practices procedures will receive payments to compensate for their additional costs and loss of income. Examples include:

- Environmentally compatible extensification of agriculture;
- Extensive grazing;
- Integrated agricultural business management and organic farming;
- Maintenance of the landscape and historically evolved landscape characteristics such as hedges, ditches, and underbrush; and,
- Maintenance of ecologically valuable habitats and the related diversity of species.

More than a third of EU expenditures for the development of rural areas between 2000 and 2002 were spent on agri-environmental programs. Further, the amount of land under cultivation that was covered by agri-environmental measures, as share of total agricultural land in the EU, increased from 15 percent in 1998 to 27 percent in 2001. The data for 2001 contain all newly signed contracts from the years 2000 and 2001 according to Council Regulation (EC) No 1257/1999—covering some 16 million hectares—as well as ongoing obligations according to the former EU Regulation (EEC) No 2078/92 that converted an additional 18 million hectares (European Commission, 2009).

In view of the various EU programs, how do farmers interpret and respond to these measures? Farmers with roughly 20 percent of the EU-utilized agricultural area (the equivalent of 900,000 EU25 holdings) participate in agri-environmental programs. Nevertheless, the level and quality of farmers' cooperation with policies designed to bring about greater levels of agricultural biodiversity protection and enhancement differs from country to country, regionally, and from one specific context to another across the EU. As a heterogeneous group, farmers cannot be assumed to willingly and automatically cooperate with such policies and instruments. Nor can it be assumed that their attempts at cooperation will be free of implementation difficulties. The willingness and ability of farmers to cooperate in biodiversity conservation is not reducible to the location of their holding or their attitudes towards nature and authority. Neither is their cooperation a simple function of economic factors (Siebert et al, 2006). Rather, the conservation of European biodiversity depends on the interplay of a much more complex set of locality and context specific issues—including agronomic, cultural, social and psychological factors—that, in turn, affect individual farmers' responses to biodiversity-promoting policies for agriculture.

Factors influencing farmers' decision-making

This section discusses those factors that are known to influence farmers' decision-making in relation to participation in agri-environmental programs. It is based both on a review of the literature regarding biodiversity conservation in agriculture (see Siebert et al, 2006) and on expert interviews with 30 representatives from government agencies and associations concerned with biodiversity conservation in Germany (see Siebert et al, 2005).

Economic incentives

For the past 20 years, research results have shown that economic interest is the most important or most frequently mentioned reason for the participation of farmers in agri-environmental measures (OECD, 1998; Drake et al, 1999; Schramek et al, 1999a, b; Deffuant, 2001). These finding are not surprising because farmers need to operate in an economically sound way. The economic interests manifest themselves in many ways including profit maximization, long-term business viability, and/or minimization of risks. At the beginning of the 1990s, mostly smaller and economically weaker farm businesses facing the possibility of dissolution participated in agri-environmental programs in North Rhine-Westphalia, Germany (Nolten, 1997). By the end of the 1990s, the opposite situation prevailed, when mostly large and economically strong businesses participated in agri-environmental measures (Kazenwadel et al, 1998; Weis et al, 2000). Osterburg (2001) showed in a representative longitudinal analysis that forage crop-producing farms which participated in agri-environmental programs achieved a higher business income than did their non-participating counterparts, even though they reduced their production intensity. It has been found, in general, that farmers regard biodiversity conservation and enhancement as a substitute for other activities. This also holds for some less profitable farmers for whom specific measures can have positive effects on farm incomes.

In studies of motivations to participate in agri-environmental measures, research findings increasingly show that economic reasoning is not the only factor guiding farmers' action. The research literature in Finland, the United Kingdom and Germany includes many studies that emphasize non-economic influences. For example, Silvasti (2001) demonstrates in the case of Finland that if the utilization of land by farmers is not endangered, a farmer may make a conscious decision to protect nature voluntarily; but when such utilization is believed to be threatened, the farmer is likely to use his or her land with little consideration for nature. Thus, economic interests in conservation programs appear to have a close connection to values concerning farmers' self-determination and independence.

Some studies show that when farmers are given the opportunity to elaborate on their answers, they often verbalize a combination of economic, social, and ecological interests as reasons for their participation in agri-environmental measures. According to Lettmann (1995), of 100 farmers participating in extensification measures, 55 stated that a contribution to the protection of the environment is the main reason for participation in such programs, and another 33 listed that reason as somewhat important. In second place was the maintenance of their farm organization; in third place an increase in income; and in fourth place a reduction in labour (see also Drake et al, 1999; Schramek et al, 1999a, b). Additionally, social reasons such as maintenance of the farm for future generations, having a satisfactory job and recapturing legitimacy in society play a role in farmers' decision-making regarding agri-environmental measures (Velde et al, 2002).

Two thirds of the experts interviewed in Germany agreed with the statement that financial advantage is the main motivation for farmers to participate in biodiversity protection measures. Some experts elaborated in commentaries, however, that this is an important but not sole reason. Others added that the issue is not profit per se but, rather, compensation for costs and unrealized use of land. Seventeen experts stated that farmers cannot realistically be expected to participate in biodiversity protection measures without financial compensation although, notably, 13 farmers voiced the opposite opinion.

Farmers' individual characteristics

Some, but not all, individual characteristics of farmers affect their decision-making. A general, albeit not uniform, pattern exists according to which younger and better educated farmers are more likely to participate in agri-environmental measures than older and less educated farmers. While there is some variation in the effect of age on participation among the various studies, the significance of education for participation persists throughout. The significance of the variable experience, measured by the proxy indicators of length of active farm management and residency, appears to be low, while former participation in a similar scheme is a strong predictor for participation (Potter and Lobley, 1992; Wilson, 1996; Wilson and Hart, 2000, 2001). A noticeable research deficit is the neglect of gender as a possible determinant, with some notable exceptions (Little and Panelli, 2003).

In the expert interviews, respondents attributed great importance to education as a predictor of participation, whereas they downplayed the importance of age, marital status, farm succession, and gender. Experts view previous participation in similar programs as the most important determinant of participation, even above education. These results are consistent with findings from international comparative studies (Schramek et al, 1999a, b).

Characteristics of the farms

Several farm characteristics, the natural conditions themselves and geographical location, landscape and environmental conditions influence farmers' ability to participate in agri-environmental programs. An important aspect of the farm environment is how the environmental characteristics of the farm compare to those of the scheme itself. As many investigators report, farmers with more extensive farms are more likely to participate in measures aimed to enhance biodiversity

(Buller, 2000; Osterburg, 2001). The results regarding the influence of structural firm characteristics such as business size or the type of business (main source of income or secondary source) differ among the existing studies. Nolten (1997) did not find any significant difference between full-time and part-time farmers regarding participation in various environmental programs. Yet Weis et al (2000) showed that the proportion of part-time farmers was higher among those who did not participate in programs providing benefits for ecological services than it was among those who did participate. Similarly, Kazenwadel et al (1998) reported that 79 percent of farms not participating in agri-environmental programs had off-farm income, far exceeding the proportion of participating farms with off-farm income (51%). Farm organization also plays a role in farmers' participation in agri-environmental programs. There is evidence for fodder crop farms in Germany (Osterburg, 2001) and for dairy farms in The Netherlands that participation in agri-environmental measures yields economic benefits (van den Ham, 1998). Land tenure also influences participation in the UK, where landowners show a greater degree of involvement than do tenant farmers (Walford, 2002). These findings, however, cannot be confirmed for EU countries in general.

Farmers' socio-cultural factors

The existing research findings show that private, informal and formal communication and interaction between farmers have a considerable influence on their decision-making. This applies to the influence of colleagues, family and, especially, advisors. This influence, however, cannot be quantified. In the study of Wehinger et al (2002), farmers pointed to other family members as the most important factor for their decision-making. The same study showed further that a positive participation decision by other farming colleagues also influenced farmers in their own decision-making. A network analysis at the village level revealed that discussion of agricultural topics among family members and friends was declining in importance while such conversations were becoming more frequent among colleagues (Retter et al, 2002). This finding is supported by Prager (2002), who showed that conversations among colleagues are often an important support in the decision-making process regarding the adoption of innovation in agri-environment and nature conservation. According to Vehkala and Vainio (2000), the influence of neighbouring farmers is important both with regard to opposition to a measure and to the decision to start negotiations. Long-term, informal conversations among peers can promote a shared understanding at the local level of particular biodiversity-friendly agricultural practices against which the behaviour of farmers is then measured and evaluated (Retter et al, 2002).

Agricultural advisors have also consistently been shown to exert a positive influence on the decision-making of farmers. This depends on three conditions:

- Trust and mutual understanding between advisors and farmers (Weis et al, 2000);

- Ability to translate the goals of protection measures into applicable and economically reasonable measures (Luz, 1994; Oppermann et al, 1997; Lütz and Bastian, 2000; Holst, 2001); and,
- Ability to adjust information and measures to the business-specific requirements and characteristics (Nolten, 1997; Weis et al, 2000).

The existence of such proactive link-persons to farmers is a question of policy design and seems to be highly relevant in terms of the broad dissemination of information and high acceptance rates (Morris et al, 2000; Winter et al, 2000; Juntti and Potter, 2002). At the same time though, advisors may have a negative effect on farmers' decision-making if they show knowledge deficits and a weak connection to agricultural practice, or if they exhibit paternalistic behaviour. This applies especially to interaction with the representatives of environmental agencies which often leads to negative decisions by farmers regarding participation in agri-environment measures (Mährlein, 1993; Harrison et al, 1998; Heiland, 1999). Several studies at the regional level show that a top-down approach to nature protection leads to a focal point for resistance and protests among land users (Siebert and Knierim, 1999; Stoll, 1999).

The expert interviews clearly showed a positive influence of conversations with experts on the willingness of farmers to participate in biodiversity measures, with 23 of the 30 experts pointing to this influence. Although no expert respondent reported any negative effect on the willingness to participate, four representatives from associations and research groups stated that active engagement of experts in the decision-making process is non-existent. Questions aimed directly at the role of agricultural advisors yielded contradictory responses. Fourteen experts viewed the advice as a factor that helps farmers make a decision to participate in environmental programs, but six experts considered consultancy as contributing to non-participation and five concluded that it has no effect on participation. The qualitative elaborations of the expert respondents reflect the heterogeneous nature of the German agricultural advising system. While some experts considered the influence of advisors to be mostly insignificant, others believed that advisory services had substantial influence on the decision-making of farmers. Some experts judged the system of advice as being mostly production oriented, containing little knowledge and without any active mandate, and thus as being counter-productive for the implementation of biodiversity measures. Yet others identified a three-fold function of farm advising: sensitizing and raising awareness of complex relationships, explaining complicated programs and measures and transmitting specific information.

The role of policy design

This chapter showed at the beginning that, in recent years, biodiversity protection through agriculturally-oriented measures has gained in importance in politics and in public discourse. This increased importance is reflected in changes in the legal framework for such measures. These changing conditions raise the question: does the substantive formulation of programs which aim to improve the environmental situation in agriculture, as well as policy design and implementation, influence the participation of farmers in agri-environment programs for the protection of biodiversity?

If one considers the participation of German farmers in agri-environmental measures to be a meaningful indicator of the acceptance of environmentally-friendly landuse, then one can argue for a reasonably high level of acceptance. In fact, 310,000 of 388,500 agricultural business managers have applied for financial support for almost 30 percent of the total farm land (BMVEL, 2004). However, studies have shown that this broad acceptance is largely restricted to categories of horizontal measures with broad-range goals (Schramek et al, 1999a, b; Osterburg, 2001). In other words, farmers implement mostly those measures that require few changes in their agricultural practices. For example, measures such as green manuring or mulch seed could be implemented by farms with intensive cultivation without a costly change in their business organization (Osterburg, 2001). One cannot, therefore, conclude that high levels of participation in environmentally relevant measures are necessarily indicative of an active acceptance of environmentally-friendly landuse (cf. Ahrens et al, 2000).

Policy design has a substantial influence on program participation. Farmers tend to support voluntary measures (e.g. agri-environment measures, nature protection by agreements etc) (Lettmann, 1995; Schramek et al, 1999a, b; Kaljonen, 2002; Kröger, 2002). Conversely, they tend to resist legal requirements for nature protection for both substantive and for procedural reasons (Mährlein, 1993; Stoll, 1999; Hofinger, 2000). Examples of policy measures that implement a cooperative governance approach include the *Blümleswiesen* (meadow flowers) program in Baden-Württemberg in Germany (cf. Briemle and Oppermann, 2003), the program for biodiversity protection in the Canton Grisons in Switzerland (cf. Baumgärtner and Hartmann, 2001) and the demonstration project *Blühendes Steinburg* (Blooming Steinburg) (Groth, 2008). All three programs combine economic incentives with a system of advice and assumption of responsibility on the part of the agricultural business. This combination has resulted in a high level of acceptance and identification with the measures on the part of participating farmers.

Council Regulation (EC) No 1698/2005 established the European Agricultural Fund for Rural Development which has, since January 2007, provided funding to improve the competitiveness of agriculture and forestry, the environment and countryside, and the quality of life and management of economic activity in rural areas. This has made it possible to implement proposals to support the provision of environmental services by farmers. The *Blühendes Steinburg* demonstration project was part of a measure to support the biodiversity of plants. All full-time and part-time farmers in the county of Steinburg were eligible to participate in this demonstration project provided they had grassland that they used throughout the year for agricultural purposes.

Blühendes Steinburg represents a form of outcome-oriented support for environmental services. In other words, payments to farmers depend directly on concrete and measurable environmental outputs and/or ecological services produced by them. An essential prerequisite for the implementation of goal-oriented remuneration is that reliable indicators are used to determine the amount of financial support. To that end, the project developed an inventory of plants existing on the grasslands in the model region. That inventory formed the basis for remuneration. It is up to the farmer to decide how he or she cultivates the grassland, as long as the selected method accomplishes the desired environmental result. Thus, the farmer may choose from a range of implementation approaches, the accomplishment of the intended environmental service checked directly using the plant inventory, and the reward then based exclusively on the accomplishment of the agri-environmental goal. The financial reward provided by *Blühendes Steinburg* is defined explicitly according to environmental objectives. The existence of these environmental services on agricultural land can demonstrate the protection and promotion of plant biodiversity. In that way, the linkage of rewards for the farmers with the environmental services rendered by them provides the basis for an effective and cost-efficient deployment of public funds.

According to the judgment of many experts, plant biodiversity is well suited for outcome-oriented remuneration, since it is clearly definable and easy to check and can be allocated to individual farm businesses (Groth, 2008). Some experts, however, point to substantial bureaucratic obstacles for the implementation of such programs (Osterburg, 2006). Further, many farmers would like to be more directly involved in the formulation of programs for environmentally-friendly landuse (Matzdorf et al, 2003). This would promote farmer identification with measures since farmers would experience a greater recognition of their interests. Yet when asked about this possibility, only 10 of the 30 experts interviewed stated that the design of agri-environment programs takes the interests of farmers into consideration. Fifteen stated a total disregard for farmers' interests in this process and five had no opinion.

Little research has been done on the issue of a general societal influence on farmers' decision-making. Two studies from the early 1990s about the environmental consciousness of farmers reveal a multi-layered and partly contradictory understanding among farmers about their role in society. Pongratz (1992) and Schur (1990) identified a broad spectrum of attitudes and knowledge of farmers with regard to environmental issues, with the following emerging as key findings:

- Insecurity and inconsistency in their discourse about ecological problems;
- Defensiveness towards criticisms of agriculture regarding the environment; and,
- An openness towards environmental protection and alternative agricultural practices.

Two later studies in Hesse and Lower Saxony in Germany yielded similar results. Farmers viewed themselves simultaneously as the 'best guardians of the environment' and as public scapegoats regarding the environment (Oberbeck and Oppermann, 1994). They understood their main role as producers of food, although they also recognized approval of their (location-specific) extensification strategies in the current agricultural policies (Retter et al, 2002). In all this, a defensive self-perception dominated. This perception was accounted for by public criticism of agriculture and manifested itself in fear of losing one's livelihood. From this vantage point, farmers connected nature and environmental protection mostly with regulations, bans and constraints on their autonomy.

In contrast, representatives of public agencies and associations interviewed as experts viewed farmers predominantly as active landscape managers. According to the views of 23 of the 30 experts, the concept of multifunctional agriculture offers huge potential to advance environmental protection by agriculture. Almost all experts agreed that improvements in biodiversity are a task for farmers to carry out. Thus, a contradiction exists between the ambivalent self-perception of farmers regarding their obligations towards biodiversity and the tasks ascribed to farmers by the interviewed experts.

Conclusion

A review of recent German and European research on factors influencing farmers' positions with respect to environmental-friendly landuse substantiates the existence of a wide range of factors and their interaction. Which of these appear most important? Certainly, most support exists for the importance of economic interests which represent—in varying manifestations including profit maximization, long-term stability and/or risk minimization—a critical factor influencing the decision-making process of farmers. But it is also evident that ecological and social interests play a part in the decision-making process. Moreover, personal values and norms also influence the behaviour of farmers.

Research findings do not support a general influence of personal characteristics of farmers on decision-making, with one exception: previous experience with environmental protection measures. If those experiences were positive, farmers are more likely to participate in new environmental programs. On the other hand, negative experiences, both personally and among peers, reduce the likelihood of participation. For this reason, some experts promote programs with few obligations in order to facilitate the participation of farmers in measures that would alter traditional land-use practices. Such experiences—provided they are positive—may help to increase acceptance of more rigorous programs.

Farm business characteristics have a clear short-term influence on the decision parameters for farmers, but since they can be altered by the farmer medium- to long-term, those characteristics should not be overemphasized for the decision-making process.

The influence of social communication and interaction on the behaviour of farmers is widely supported by research findings. The role-model function of colleagues and the part played by advisors are especially important. The influence of policy design on farmers' decision-making is a function of both program content and the way the policy was formulated and implemented. In contrast, the importance of the position of agriculture in society and of the general political parameters for farmers' decision-making remains unclear. Traditional self-image and perception of the role of the farmer do not correspond with contemporary societal expectations for agriculture as an engaged actor in biodiversity measures.

The research results suggest that one should not understand the promotion of environmentally-conscious actions as a situation influenced by a static set of determining factors but rather as a dynamic process shaped by interactions. In this process, financial compensation or incentives are a necessary but clearly not sufficient condition. Examples of programs that implement a multi-factorial and interactive understanding of governance demonstrate that guidance for and change of behaviour must be conceptualized as a mid- to long-term process. Those examples also show that the design of a policy that is based on the aim to achieve citizen acceptance through active citizen participation (Zilleßen, 2003) is also possible for the realm of ecological landuse. Those forms of policy design, however, also entail greater requirements for the various agencies and stakeholders regarding communication and cooperation with farmers than is the case, for example, with the existing agri-environmental programs (Council Regulations (EEC) No 2078/92 and (EC) No 1257/99). These challenges are clearly supported by the expert interviews which identified high administrative costs and bureaucratic procedures of agencies as important obstacles to the participation of farmers in agri-environmental programs.

References

Ahrens, H., Lippert, C. and Rittershofer, M. (2000) 'Überlegungen zu Umwelt- und Einkommenswirkungen von Agrarumweltprogrammen nach VO (EWG) Nr. 2078/92 in der Landwirtschaft', *Agrarwirtschaft*, vol 49, no 2, pp99–115

Barkmann, J., Helming, K., Müller, K. and Wiggering, H. (2004) *MultiLand. Multifunctional Landscapes: Towards an Analytical Framework for Sustainability Assessment of Agriculture and Forestry in Europe*, Fifth Framework Programme 1998–2002, Thematic Programme: Environment and Sustainable Development, Final Report, EVK2-CT-2002-80023, Leibniz Centre for Agricultural Landscape and Land Use Research (ZALF), Müncheberg, Germany

Baumgärtner, J. and Hartmann, J. (2001) 'The design and implementation of a sustainable plant diversity conservation program for alpine meadows and pastures', *Journal of Agricultural and Environmental Ethics*, vol 14, no 1, pp67–83

Bundesministerium für Verbraucherschutz, Ernährung und Landwirtschaft (BMVEL) (2004) *Statistisches Jahrbuch über Ernährung, Landwirtschaft und Forsten*, Landwirtschaftsverlag, Münster-Hiltrup, Germany

Briemle, G. and R. Oppermann (2003) 'Von der Idee zum Programm—die Förderung des artenreichen Grünlandes in MEKAII', in R. Oppermann and H.U. Gujer (eds) *Artenreiches Grünland bewerten und fördern—MEKA und ÖQV in der Praxis*, Eugen Ulmer, Stuttgart, Germany, pp26–32

Bromley, D.W. (1997) 'Environmental benefits of agriculture: Concepts', in OECD (ed) *Environmental Benefits from Agriculture: Issues and Policies—The Helsinki Seminar*, OECD Proceedings, OECD, Paris, pp35–53

Buller, H. (2000) 'Regulation 2078: Patterns of implementation', in H. Buller, G.A. Wilson and A. Höll (eds) *Agri-Environmental Policy in the European Union*, Ashgate Publishing Limited, Aldershot, pp219–253

Council of the European Communities (1992) *Council Regulation (EEC) No 2078/92* of 30 June 1992 on Agricultural Production Methods Compatible With the Requirements of the Protection of the Environment and the Maintenance of the Countryside, Official Journal L 215, 30 July 1992, pp85–90, http://faolex.fao.org/docs/texts/eur18641.doc, accessed 20 April 2009

Council of the European Union (1999) *Council Regulation (EC) No 1257/99* of 17 May 1999 on Support for Rural Development From the European Agricultural Guidance and Guarantee Fund (EAGGF) and Amending and Repealing Certain Regulations,
Official Journal L 160, 26 July 1999, pp80–102 http://faolex.fao.org/docs/pdf/eur34868.pdf, accessed 20 April 2009

Council of the European Union (2005) *Council Regulation (EC) No 1698/2005* of 20 September 2005 on Support for Rural Development by the European Agricultural Fund for Rural Development (EAFRD), http://eur-lex.europa.eu/LexUriServ/LexUriServ.do?uri=OJ:L:2005:277:0001:0040:EN:P DF, accessed 04 May2009

Deffuant, G. (ed) (2001) *Improving Agri-Environmental Policies: A Simulation Approach to the Cognitive Properties of Farmers and Institutions*, Final Report of the FAIR3 CT 2092 project, wwwlisc.clermont.cemagref.fr/ImagesProject /freport.pdf, accessed 20 April 2009

Drake, L., Bergström, P. and Svedsäter, H. (1999) 'Farmers' attitude and uptake', in G.V. Huylenbroeck and M. Whitby (eds) *Countryside Stewardship: Farmers, Policies and Markets*, Elsevier Science, Oxford, UK, pp89–111

European Commission (1999) *Contribution of the European Community on the Multifunctional Character of Agriculture*, Infopaper, http://ec.europa.eu/agri culture/external/wto/document/ip2_en.pdf, accessed 20 April 2009

European Commission (2009) 'Landwirtschaft und Umwelt', http://ec.europa.eu/agriculture/envir/index_de.htm, accessed 20 April 2009

FAO (Food and Agriculture Organization of the United Nations) (2000) *Cultivating our Futures. Taking Stock of the Multifunctional Character of Agriculture and Land*, www.fao.org/docrep/x2775e/X2775E00.htm, accessed 20 April 2009

Groth, M. (2008) *Kosteneffizienter und effektiver Biodiversitätsschutz durch Ausschreibungen und eine ergebnisorientierte Honorierung: das Modellprojekt "Blühendes Steinburg"*, University of Lüneburg, Working Paper Series in Economics No 105, Leuphana Universität Lüneburg, Lüneburg, Germany, www.uni-lueneburg.de/vwl/papers/wp_105_Upload.pdf, accessed 3 May 2009

Ham, A. van den, Daatselaar, C.H.G., de Haan, T. and Janssens, S.R.M. (1998) *Landbouwers Met Natuur: Hoe Zien Die Eruit? (Farmers with Nature: How do we Perceive Outside?)*, Landbouw-Economisch Instituut, The Hague, Netherlands

Harrison, C.M., Burgess, J. and Clark, J. (1998) 'Discounted knowledges: Farmers' and residents' understandings of nature conservation goals and policies, *Journal of Environmental Management*, vol 54, no 4, pp305–320

Heiland, S. (1999) *Voraussetzungen erfolgreichen Naturschutzes: Individuelle und gesellschaftliche Bedingungen umweltgerechten Verhaltens, ihre Bedeutung für den Naturschutz und die Durchsetzbarkeit seiner Ziele*, Ecomed-Verlag, Landsberg am Lech, Germany

Helming, K. and Wiggering, H. (eds) (2003) *Sustainable Development of Multifunctional Landscapes*, Springer-Verlag, Berlin, Germany

Hofinger, G. (2000) 'Zwischen "Verhinderungsbehörde" und "Biosphäre", Ergebnisse zur Akzeptanz des Biosphärenreservats Schorfheide-Chorin', in A. Grewer, E. Knödler-Bunte, K. Pape and A. Vogel (eds) *Umweltkommunikation. Öffentlichkeitsarbeit und Umweltbildung in Großschutzgebieten*, Luisenauer Gespräche, Band 1, PR Kolleg, Berlin, Germany, pp119–142

Holst, H. (2001) 'Naturschutz- und Landschaftspflegeberatung—dieIintegration von Naturschutz und Landschaftspflege in die "gute fachliche Praxis" als Zukunftsaufgabe', *Berichte über Landwirtschaft*, vol 79, no 4, pp552–564

Janke, R.R. (2002) 'Composing a landscape', in D.L. Jackson and L.L. Jackson (eds) *The Farm as a Natural Habitat. Reconnecting Food Systems with Ecosystems*, Island Press, Washington, pp209–219

Juntti, M. and Potter, C. (2002) 'Interpreting and reinterpreting agri-environmental policy: Communication, trust and knowledge in the implementation process', *Sociologia Ruralis*, vol 42, no 3, pp215–232

Kaljonen, M. (2002) *Maatalouden ympäristötuen paikallisia sovellutuksia (Local Dynamics of Agri-Environmental Policy)*, The West Finland Regional Environment Centre, Vaasa

Kazenwadel, G., van der Ploeg, B., Badoux, P. and Häring, G. (1998) 'Sociological and economic factors influencing farmers' participation in agri-environmental schemes', in S. Dabbert, A. Dubgaard, M. Whitby and L. Slangen (eds) *The Economics of Landscape and Wildlife Conservation* CABI Publishing, Wallingford, pp187–203

Kröger, L. (2002) *Osallistuva Suunnittelu Maatalouden Ympäristöpolitiikass: Viljelijöiden Näkemyksiä Osallistumisesta, Vaikuttamismahdollisuuksista ja Ympäristönhoidosta (Participatory Planning and Decision-making in Agri-environmental Policy: Farmers' Views on Participation and Production of Environmental Goods)*, MTT Agrifood Research Finland, Helsinki

Lettmann, A. (1995) *Akzeptanz von Extensivierungsstrategien. Eine empirische Untersuchung bei Landwirten in Nordrhein-Westfalen*, M. Wehle, Witterschlick/Bonn, Germany

Little, J. and R. Panelli (2003) 'Gender research in rural geography', *Gender, Place and Culture: A Journal of Feminist Geography*', vol 10, no 3, pp281–289

Lütz, M. and Bastian O. (2000) 'Vom Landschaftsplan zum Bewirtschaftungsentwurf (From the landscape plan to the working conception)', *Zeitschrift für Kulturtechnik und Landentwicklung*, vol 41, no 6, pp259–266

Luz, F. (1994) *Zur Akzeptanz landschaftsplanerischer Projekte: Determinanten lokaler Akzeptanz und Umsetzbarkeit von landschaftsplanerischen Projekten zur Extensivierung, Biotopvernetzung und anderen Maßnahmen des Natur- und Umweltschutzes*, Peter Lang, Frankfurt, Germany

Mährlein, A. (1993) *Einzelwirtschaftliche Auswirkungen von Naturschutzauflagen: Eine Theoretische und Empirische Analyse unter besonderer Berücksichtigung Niedersachsens*, Wissenschaftsverlag Vauk, Kiel, Germany

Matzdorf, B., Piorr, A. and Sattler, C. (2003) *Halbzeitbewertung des Plans zur Entwicklung des ländlichen Raums gemäß VO (EG) Nr. 1257/99 des Landes Brandenburg*, Leibniz-Zentrum für Agrarlandschaftsforschung (ZALF) e.V., Müncheberg, Germany, www.zalf.de/home_zalf/download/soz/KULAP1_end bericht_brandenburg.pdf, accessed 20 April 2009

Matzdorf, B., Kaiser, Th., Rohner, M.-S. and Becker, N. (2006) 'Vorschlag für ergebnisorientierte Agrarumweltmaßnahmen im Rahmen des Brandenburger Agrarumweltprogramms *NNA-Berichte*, vol 1, pp244–254

Morris, J., Mills, J. and Crawford, I.M. (2000) 'Promoting farmer uptake of agri-environment schemes: The Countryside Stewardship Arable Options Scheme', *Land Use Policy*, vol 17, no 3, pp241–254

Nolten, R. (1997) *Implementation von Naturschutzsonderprogrammen. Eine empirische Untersuchung in Nordrhein-Westfalen*, Verlag M. Wehle, Witterschlick/Bonn, Germany

Oberbeck, H. and Oppermann, R. (1994) 'Agrarwirtschaft und Dörfer am Scheideweg: Erfahrungen von Landwirten mit dem Wandel gesellschaftlicher Akzeptanz der landwirtschaftlichen Intensivproduktion', *Soziale Welt*, vol 45, no 3, pp259–278

Oppermann, B., Luz, F. and Kaule, G. (1997) Der 'Runde Tisch' als Mittel der Landschaftsplanung. Chancen und Grenzen der Anwendung eines kooperativen Planungsmodells mit der Landwirtschaft, *Angewandte Landschaftsökologie*, Heft 11, Bundesamt für Naturschutz, Bonn-Bad Godesberg, Germany

Organisation for Economic Cooperation and Development (OECD) (ed) (1998) *Co-operative Approaches to sustainable Agriculture*, OECD, Paris

Organisation for Economic Cooperation and Development (OECD) (ed) (2001) *Multifunctionality: Towards an Analytical Framework*, OECD, Paris

Osterburg, B. (2001) 'Umsetzung der VO (EWG 2078/92) in Deutschland—Wirkungen auf Umwelt, landwirtschaftliche Produktion und Einkommen', in B. Osterburg and H. Nieberg (eds) *Agrarumweltprogramme—Konzepte, Entwicklungen, künftige Ausgestaltung*, Sonderheft 231, Landbauforschung Völkenrode, Braunschweig, Germany, pp13–24

Osterburg, B. (2006) 'Ansätze zur Verbesserung der Wirksamkeit von Agrarumweltmassnahmen', in U. Hampicke (ed) *Anreiz—Ökonomie der Honorierung ökologischer Leistungen*, Workshopreihe, Naturschutz und Ökonomie Teil I. BfN-Skripten 179, Bundesamt für Naturschutz, Bonn-Bad Godesberg, Germany, pp19–29, www.bfn.de/fileadmin/MDB/documents/service/skript179.pdf, accessed 4 May 2009

Osterburg, B. and Stratmann, U. (2002) 'Die regionale Agrarumweltpolitik in Deutschland unter dem Einfluss der Förderangebote der Europäischen Union', *Agrarwirtschaft*, vol 51, no 5, pp259–279

Pongratz, H. (1992) *Die Bauern und der ökologische Diskurs*, Profil Verlag, München, Germany

Potter, C. and M. Lobley (1992) 'Ageing and succession on family farms', *Sociologia Ruralis*, vol 32, nos 2/3, pp317–334

Prager, K. (2002) *Akzeptanz von Maßnahmen zur Umsetzung einer umweltschonenden Landbewirtschaftung bei Landwirten und Beratern in Brandenburg*, Kommunikation und Beratung 48, Margraf, Weikersheim, Germany

Pretty, J. (2000) 'Conditions for successful implementation of sustainable agriculture', in M. Härdtlein, M. Kaltschmitt, I. Lewandowski and H.N. Wurl (eds) *Nachhaltigkeit in der Landwirtschaft — Landwirtschaft im Spannungsfeld zwischen Ökologie, Ökonomie und Sozialwissenschaften*, Erich Schmidt Verlag, Berlin, Germany, pp323–343

Retter, C., Stahr, K. and Boland, H. (2002) 'Zur Rolle von Landwirten in dörflichen Kommunikationsnetzwerken', *Berichte über Landwirtschaft*, vol 80, no 3, pp446–467

Sattler, C. (2008) 'Ökologische Bewertung und Akzeptanzanalyse pflanzenbaulicher Produktionsverfahren', PhD Thesis, Humboldt Universität zu Berlin, Berlin, Germany.

Schramek, J., Biehl, D., Buller, H. and Wilson, G.A. (eds) (1999a) *Implementation and Effectiveness of Agri-Environmental Schemes Established under Regulation 2078/92*, vol 1, Main Report, Institut für ländliche Strukturforschung, Frankfurt, Germany

Schramek, J., Biehl, D., Buller, H. and Wilson, G.A. (eds) (1999b) *Implementation and effectiveness of agri-environmental schemes established under Regulation 2078/92*, vol 2, Annexis, Institut für ländliche Strukturforschung, Frankfurt, Germany

Schur, G. (1990) *Umweltverhalten von Landwirten*, Campus Forschung 652, Campus-Verlag, Frankfurt, Germany

Siebert R., Toogood, M. and Knierim, A. (2006) 'Factors affecting European farmers' participation in biodiversity policies', *Sociologia Ruralis*, vol 46, no 4, pp318–340

Siebert, R. and Knierim, A. (1999) 'Divergierende Nutzungsinteressen in Schutzgebieten—Konflikte und Lösungsansätze in Brandenburg', *Zeitschrift für Kulturtechnik und Landentwicklung*, vol 40, no 4, pp181–186

Siebert, R., Knierim, A. and Müller, K. (2005) 'Zur Akzeptanz von umweltschonender Landnutzung durch Landwirte', in U. Hampicke, B. Litterski and W. Wichtmann (eds) *Ackerlandschaften: Nachhaltigkeit und Naturschutz auf ertragsschwachen Standorten*, Springer, Berlin, German, pp89–102

Silvasti, T. (2001) *Talonpojan Elämä: Tutkimus Elämäntapaa Jäsentävistä Kulttuurisista Malleista (Peasant's Life. Research on the Cultural Models Shaping Lifestyle)*, Suomalaisen Kirjallisuuden Seura, Helsinki, Finland

Stoll, S. (1999) *Akzeptanzprobleme bei der Ausweisung von Großschutzgebieten. Ursachenanalyse und Ansätze zu Handlungsstrategien*, Lang, Frankfurt, Germany

Vehkala, M. and Vainio, A. (2000) *Luonnonsuojelun Yhteiskunnallinen Ulottuvuus (The Social Dimension of Nature Conservation)*, Research Institute at the University of Vaasa, Vaasa, Finland

Velde, H.T., Aarts, N. and van Woerkum, C. (2002) 'Dealing with ambivalence: Farmers' and consumers' perception of animal welfare in livestock breeding', *Journal of Agricultural and Environmental Ethics'*, vol 15, no 2, pp203–219

Walford, N. (2002) 'Agricultural adjustment: Adoption of and adaptation to policy reform measures by large-scale commercial farmers', *Land Use Policy*, vol 19, no 3, pp243–257

Wehinger, T., Freye, B. and Hoffmann, V. (2002) 'Zur Bedeutung der sozial-ökonomischen Umwelt für den Wissenstransfer', in K. Müller, A. Dosch, E. Mohrbach, T. Aenis, E. Baranek, T. Boeckmann, R. Siebert and V. Toussaint (eds) *Wissenschaft und Praxis der Landschaftsnutzung*, Margraf, Weikersheim, Germany, pp184–195

Weis, J., Muchow, T. and Schumacher, W. (2000) 'Akzeptanz von Programmen zur Honorierung ökologischer Leistungen der Landwirtschaft', in B. Schweppe-Kraft (ed) *Innovativer Naturschutz: Partizipative und marktwirtschaftliche Instrumente*, Angewandte Landschaftsökologie 34, Bundesamt für Naturschutz, Bonn-Bad Godesberg, Germany, pp107–120

Wilson, G. (1996) 'Farmer environmental attitudes and ESA participation', *Geoforum*, vol 27, no 2, pp115–131

Wilson, G. and Hart, K. (2000) 'Financial imperative or conservation concern? EU farmers' motivations for participation in voluntary agri-environmental schemes', *Environment and Planning A*, vol 32, no 12, pp2161–2185

Wilson, G. and Hart, K. (2001) 'Farmer participation in agri-environmental schemes: Towards conservation-orientated thinking?', *Sociologia Ruralis*, vol 41, no 2, pp254–274

Winter, M., Mills, J. and Wragg, A. (2000) *Practical Delivery of Farm Conservation Management in England*, English Nature Research Report 393, English Nature, Peterborough, UK

Wüstemann, H., Mann, S. and Müller, K. (eds) (2008) *Multifunktionalität. Von der Wohlfahrtsökonomie zu neuen Ufern*, oekom-Verlag, München, Germany

Zilleßen, H. (2003) 'Mediation als Form der Partizipation in der Zivilgesellschaft', in G. Metha and K. Rückert (eds) *Mediation und Demokratie*, Carl-Auer-Verlag, Heidelberg, Germany, pp52–65

17

Market Instruments and Collective Obligations for On-Farm Biodiversity Conservation

Stewart Lockie and Rebeka Tennent

From a policy perspective, it has been suggested that traditional approaches to natural resource conservation—whether based on regulation, public participation or the establishment of reserves—are inflexible, costly and economically inefficient (Elliot, 1994; Whitten et al, 2003). Market-based instruments (MBIs) have been put forward as alternatives that offer governments and resource users the opportunity not only to add to their selection of policy tools, but to address what is considered by proponents the root cause of environmental degradation, market failure. By allowing market mechanisms to determine conservation outcomes it is argued that these may be achieved at significantly lower cost than traditional approaches while simultaneously promoting productivity and innovation. MBIs are designed to help resource users absorb the costs of environmental protection at the same time as providing more cost effective and targeted delivery of government funding. In light of trends towards 'shrinking government funding and reductions in many of the services traditionally provided by government' (Morgans, 1996, p100)—not to mention the sheer temporal and spatial magnitude of many environmental problems—any potential for cost-effective intervention must be considered attractive. MBIs are thus seen by many governments and government agencies as the 'policy frontier' (e.g. Cutbush, 2006) and they have been applied to issues as diverse as greenhouse gas abatement, salinity mitigation, catchment protection, water allocation, native vegetation management and, importantly, biodiversity.

However, MBIs have also been criticized for being applied over-enthusiastically and/or prematurely; failing, as a consequence, to deliver promised outcomes (Whitten and Shelton, 2005). Additionally, we will argue here, MBIs are based on a number of potentially problematic assumptions about the nature of property or resource access rights; the duty of care that is associated with those rights; the relationships between biodiversity, ecosystem services and agricultural production; the distribution of public and private benefits that arise from biodiversity conservation in agriculture; and, perhaps most importantly, the ways in which each of these matters are understood, valued and contested by farmers and other resource users. While MBIs offer an elegant theoretical solution to the problem of market failure it is necessary to examine how, in practice, the introduction of market mechanisms to resource management programs actually does influence farmers' decision-making and management. This chapter will begin by outlining in more detail the logic and characteristics of MBIs as used in the management of natural resources before turning to a case study of two attempts to apply MBIs to conserve biodiversity in Queensland, Australia.

Market-based instruments

The starting point for arguments in support of MBIs is the conceptualization of environmental degradation as an outcome of market failure. Given that a healthy stock of natural resources is an essential condition for long-term production and profitability, producers ought, in a properly functioning market, to be able to absorb and pass on to consumers the costs of protecting and enhancing that stock of resources. Market failure, however, arises from at least three sources. First, inadequate understanding of the long-term impact of resource-use practices may lead to unintended resource degradation. Second, open access property rights regimes encourage resource users to externalize the costs of environmental protection since those producers who do attempt to internalize environmental costs have limited capacity either to exclude other producers from use of the resource or to seek compensation through the market. Third, even when access to resources in not open, natural resource inputs such as water are often priced below their full economic and environmental cost (Scott, 1998).

Biodiversity conservation is vulnerable to all three forms of market failure. The relationships between individual resource-use practices, intended and unintended biodiversity, ecosystem processes and functions, ecosystem services, and agricultural productivity are complex and poorly understood. The impact on ecosystem services and agricultural productivity of farming practices that degrade (or conserve) biodiversity may be felt either off-farm or so far into the future as to encourage their discounting by producers. Further, for many components of biodiversity no markets exist and no values are consequently placed on access, use, conservation or production of those components.

Policy instruments to address market failure may take four broad forms; suasive, regulatory, public and market-based (Whitten and Shelton, 2005). Suasive measures seek to educate producers about the environmental impacts of resource-use and the public and private benefits of ecosystem services. Such measures may go beyond the provision of information and technical assistance to include training in resource planning and management, support to form self-help farmers' groups and associations, and so on. Regulatory measures attempt to mandate the internalization of environmental costs through controls over resource access and/or use. Both suasive and regulatory measures are based on the premise that the conservation of natural resources such as biodiversity is a primarily private good. Public provision, on the other hand, treats resource conservation as a primarily public good which may be provided directly through measures such as the establishment of reserves and/or government funded breeding programs, or indirectly through measures that subsidize the conservation of resources by individuals.

Market-based measures include a variety of trading mechanisms, auctions and price signals designed to influence the behaviour of people in pursuit of policy objectives (Scott, 1998; Farber and Tietenberg, 2006). Markets for natural resources can be created through a range of interventions depending on existing markets and legislative frameworks, the nature of the desired ecosystem services, the reasons for their under-provision, whether they are considered private and/or public goods, and the potential market participants (Whitten and Shelton, 2005). Table 17.1 summarizes the main types of market-based instrument, their characteristics and the types of intervention to which proponents believe they are suited.

Table 17.1. Classification of market-based instruments (sources: Whitten and Shelton, 2005; NMBIWG, 2005)

Classification	Market intervention	Examples	Suited to:
Market friction	Improving efficiency of existing markets by removing obstacles to recognition of ecosystem services	Product differentiation (e.g. ecolabelling), provision of information	Outcomes that can be improved through reduced transaction costs or increased information such as green labelling or web based water entitlement exchanges
Price-based	Setting or modifying prices to incorporate the cost of ecosystem services	Auctions, tenders, grants, rebates, eco-taxes (e.g. pollution taxes)	Diffuse source environmental outcomes such as terrestrial biodiversity, salinity mitigation, water quality etc
Quantity-based	Setting targets to achieve or maintain ecosystem services	Cap and trade mechanisms, offsets	Measurable point source activities such as carbon emissions, water extraction etc

Arguments for the use of MBIs to address market failure, in preference to other policy instruments, are both theoretical and technical. Theoretically, it is argued that the costs of conservation are a cost of production that in a properly functioning market should be internalized and passed on to consumers. Subsidizing the conservation activities of producers is seen as mostly inappropriate due to the potential to distort markets and act as de facto barriers to trade. Further, direct subsidies deny the 'duty of care' to the environment that inheres in private property rights. In other words, users of natural resources have a responsibility, or obligation, to protect not only those resources that directly support their own production but to avoid resource-use practices that undermine the ability of other resource users (such as neighbouring farmers or future generations) to exercise their own property rights due to resource degradation.

Technically, it is argued that MBIs are simply more effective and efficient than other policy instruments; that they can be more targeted in their pursuit of desired outcomes while allowing maximum flexibility to individuals to choose the optimum amount and means of conservation depending on their own circumstances (Farber and Tietenberg, 2006). This encourages change amongst those who can most readily achieve it and provides continuing incentives to find innovative ways to further reduce environmental impacts (Whitten et al, 2007). As a consequence, it is argued that MBIs offer the least-cost path to overall environmental outcome. It follows that MBIs should be the policy instruments of choice regardless of whether the particular policy objective is to address market failure and encourage producers to internalize environmental costs or, alternatively, to pay producers on behalf of the wider community for the provision of distinctly public good outcomes.

Australian experiments in the application of MBIs to on-farm biodiversity

The historic emphasis of agri-environmental policy in Australia has been on suasive measures to address the so-called 'brown' issues—soil erosion, salinization, water quality decline etc. Few regulatory mechanisms have been established in relation to these issues and those that have been established have seldom been used (Lockie, 2000). Over the last 20 years, in particular, Australia has developed an international reputation for innovation in various forms of community-based natural resource management. Initiatives such as the National Landcare Program and National Property Management Planning Program placed considerable emphasis on the development of farmers' own capacity to assess the state of natural resources, to integrate business and natural resource planning at the farm level, and to work cooperatively with their neighbours to plan and address environmental problems at the watershed or district scale (Lockie, 2006). This was viewed as critical in addressing both understandings of the impacts of resource-use and the externalization of the costs of resource-use by landholders. However, while these programs have contributed to significant improvements in natural resource management at the field and farm scales they have struggled to replicate this at the landscape scale (see Lockie, 2006) and Australia's biodiversity remains in serious decline (ASEC, 2006). Not surprisingly, questions have subsequently been raised regarding the extent to which previous measures have been able to address serious and complex environmental problems (NMBIWG, 2005).

The most notable responses, to date, to the perceived shortcomings of the 'Landcare model' have been the regionalization of natural resource planning and experimentation with various forms of financial incentive for improved resource management (see Lockie, 2009; Lockie and Higgins, 2007). However, it must be noted that Australian governments regard agri-environmental programs such as those implemented in the European Union under the rubric of 'multifunctionality' (see Chapter 16) as little more than thinly veiled production subsidies (Lockie, 2006; Dibden and Cocklin, 2009). Whether or not this argument is justified will not be debated here. The critical point is that the strong bias towards free trade and minimal government intervention evinced by Australian governments has had at least two consequences in relation to payments for environmental services. First, comparatively small sums of money have been devoted to financial incentives and those that have been devoted to this purpose have been directed mostly through pilot projects rather than through widespread programs. Second, the preferred mechanisms for financial incentives have been market-based rather than formula-based as with EU co-financing arrangements (see Chapter 16).

Two national MBI pilot programs and a national MBI capacity building project have been supported in Australia since 2003 which have in turn supported five biodiversity projects on agricultural lands, all of which used auction systems (NMBIWG, 2005). Through two funding rounds, the pilot program sought to increase the knowledge base of regional planning organizations in the use of MBIs to manage natural resource issues, in particular for salinity and water quality issues. The official evaluation of Round 1 projects concluded that MBIs were capable of engaging landholders, encouraging voluntary change, effectively targeting public expenditure through appropriate metrics, and thereby delivering ecosystem services at significantly lower cost than grants programs and other measures (NMBIWG, 2005). The evaluation also found that to generate cost savings MBIs require adequate testing and adaptation prior to implementation, well-developed communication strategies to maximize participation by landholders, and adaptation to the particular circumstances of specific environmental problems (NMBIWG, 2005). The focus of Round 2 projects was consequently the refinement of auction and offset instruments in order to improve cost-effectiveness, increase participation, deal better with uncertainty and ensure compliance. As elegant, therefore, as theoretical arguments in support of MBIs may appear it is quite clear that realization of their promise to technical superiority over other policy instruments is dependent on significant investment in the technical capacity of institutions and individuals to utilize them.

This chapter now turns to a more detailed consideration of two of the pilot projects funded under the national program and related funding streams. Data were collected by the authors via face-to-face interviews with 13 landholders and resource management agency staff who participated in the implementation of the projects (see Freckleton and Lockie, 2009). The Biodiversity Incentive Scheme and Landscape Linkages project were price-based MBIs that explicitly targeted the conservation of biodiversity through sanctioning tracks of land. Both used auction systems to direct resources to those landholders who undertook to protect biodiversity at least-cost. While the auction system provided a mechanism to incorporate landholder views on the location and relative significance of valuable ecosystems, it also provided a mechanism to ensure that only those bids which corresponded with official assessments of significance as defined by regional ecosystems maps were seriously considered (Lockie, 2009).

Landscape Linkages

Landscape Linkages was undertaken by the North Queensland Dry Tropics Natural Resource Management Group (NQ Dry Tropics) in the Desert Uplands region of Central Queensland (Figure 17.1). This area was predominately eucalypt and acacia woodlands that have been subject to significant land clearing to increase beef cattle productivity. Landscape Linkages was designed to provide a continuous wildlife habitat of good quality across the southern Desert Uplands, protecting remnant vegetation and areas of biodiversity significance and to manage areas of Ironbark range, and Gidgee and Box woodlands.

Landholders participated in a competitive tender process, indicating how they would manage the land under consideration, as well as the remuneration required to do so. To be rated highly, the area under consideration had to be in reasonable condition for wildlife with a good cover of native grasses and connectivity to other land areas under consideration in the scheme (Rolfe et al, 2005). Successful bidders were offered a two-year non-binding agreement with NQ Dry Tropics through their partner organization in the region, the Desert Uplands Group, to maintain or improve the areas under agreement. Once successful, land areas were graded, and landholders were required to ensure the land under contract was maintained to at least the level it was initially graded. Pasture biomass was used as a proxy measure of biodiversity, meaning landholders had to maintain a minimum level of grasses (around 1500 kg per hectare) to enable at least the minimum amount of pasture biomass to be maintained. Landholders were required to keep a diary and take photos for submission to the Desert Uplands Group. Payments to landholders were staggered at 40 percent upon finalising the agreement, 30 percent after 12 months and the final 30 percent upon completion of the agreement.

Biodiversity Incentive Scheme

The Biodiversity Incentive Scheme was established by the Fitzroy Basin Association (FBA) in Central Queensland (Figure 17.1). The Fitzroy Basin has traditionally encompassed some of the highest land clearing rates in the country with remnant vegetation rates within some sub-catchments now as low as 35 percent. For the FBA, protecting remnant vegetation was of great importance due to the high biodiversity value contained within some regional ecosystems as well as the flow-on benefits to water quality, erosion control and nutrient conservation. The FBA identified priority catchments within the Fitzroy Basin for urgent action, using the Biodiversity Incentive Scheme as a partial means to deliver funding to landholders situated within these catchments.

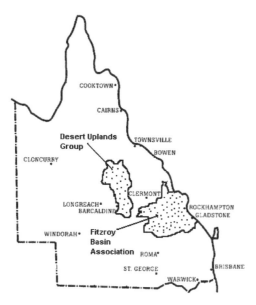

Figure 17.1. Selected Queensland regional natural resource management groups

Through the Biodiversity Incentive Scheme, funding was delivered to targeted catchments with the Fitzroy Basin; predominantly 'endangered' and 'of concern' regional ecosystems, wetlands, and riparian zones in grazing areas. FBA staff conducted property visits for landholders, all of whom were predominantly beef cattle producers, and who had submitted an expression of interest to assess and document existing land condition. This was translated into a land health score which landholders used in their Biodiversity Incentive Scheme application. The applications were then ranked and the highest biodiversity value projects were funded. Landholders were initially required to sign a non-binding agreement of up to two years, although funding was recently recommitted to the program for another year. Pasture biomass was used as a measure of biodiversity. Funding was delivered at a set rate based on Department of Primary Industries land type classification and agistment rates. Payments were staggered at 40 percent on the initial signing of the agreement, 30 percent at the end of the first year, and 30 percent at the completion of the agreement. To secure payment at each of these intervals landholders were either assessed by FBA staff or required to supply photographic evidence of the land condition.

Cost savings and targeted funding

Official evaluations claim that both Landscape Linkages and the Biodiversity Incentive Scheme were able to deliver significant cost savings for government agencies when compared with the cost of public provision through the establishment and maintenance of reserves. Under Landscape Linkages, the cost per hectare protected was around two Australian dollars per year while under the

Biodiversity Incentive Scheme the average cost was AUS$6.40 per hectare per year (Windle and Rolfe, 2006). At face value, this is considerably more cost effective than the expansion of National Parks which, between 1996 and 2006, in Queensland cost the Commonwealth an average of AUS$23.71 per hectare (WWF, 2006) or the resumption of land for conservation purposes, thus meeting a key goal for government in the application of MBIs in terms of cost effective delivery of funding. The question is whether the cost of protecting lands through National Parks or other reserves offers the most relevant unit of comparison. This assumes that the only viable policy alternative to MBIs is to strip farmers of their land; an assumption that is clearly not true. Other policy mechanisms have not, however, been costed.

A second goal in the implementation of MBIs was to achieve more targeted government expenditure. While regulatory instruments (such as the Queensland Vegetation Management Act) have been very specific regarding the ecosystems they sought to protect, they have been largely indiscriminate in terms both of the criteria they apply to assess the condition and significance of ecosystems, and in terms of the management conditions they impose on landholders (Lockie, 2009). Suasive instruments have been even less targeted. MBIs promise to address this issue, but their ability to do so depends on the willingness of relevant resource users to engage themselves in MBI projects. Under Landscape Linkages, specific land types and linkages were targeted. While the primary goal was to establish a continuous wildlife habitat across the Desert Uplands, it was hoped that the main land type under agreement would be Box and Gidgee woodlands. The program targeted these land types by rating them more highly than others in application assessments. Properties that would enable the establishment of a wildlife corridor were also rated more highly than properties without linkages to neighbouring tracks of land under submission. In the end, it was possible to establish a wildlife corridor. However the predominant land type under agreement was Ironbark woodland. Landscape Linkages was unsuccessful in simultaneously targeting land areas and land types.

Similarly, the Biodiversity Incentive Scheme targeted specific catchments by only funding projects that fell within those catchments. A secondary aim was to contract 150,000 hectares within a 10 year period. While the landholders funded were located within target catchments, a smaller land area was contracted than initially anticipated. Between 2006 and 2008, almost 85,000 hectares of remnant vegetation was protected through agreements with 15 landholders. Seventy seven percent of the total bid area formed a corridor, and all of the land placed under agreement had special biodiversity values (Windle et al, 2007). Specifically, of the areas placed under agreement, 1286 hectares included high value endangered, vulnerable and/or rare species, 2916 hectares had high ecosystem value and 8484 hectares had very high ecosystem diversity (Windle et al, 2007).

Raising awareness of the relationships between productivity and biodiversity

Through educative programs required to receive MBI funding, field days, resource management agency staff visits and other program associated activities, these programs assisted in raising landholders' awareness of the relationships between productivity and native biodiversity. Also valuable was the formal interaction between resource management agencies and landholders required throughout MBI programs in forming, maintaining and reinvigorating relationships between landholders and agency staff. Photographs taken of the areas under agreement and diaries of land condition further promoted an understanding of these relationships, helping landholders to identify land areas that required further attention by providing a benchmark against which they could assess land areas not under agreement.

These benefits were not limited to those landholders who signed MBI agreements, and neighbours of landholders who were participating in these programs were often informed or aware of the programs. Exposure to information about MBI projects through meetings and information sessions also encouraged landholders who did not participate to consider their own management practices. For example, information sessions for Landscape Linkages and the Biodiversity Incentive Scheme showed photographs of high value land as well as land that would not be at the level required to participate. In some cases, landholders were advised by agency staff that their land or practices would not meet requirements for funding. This had led to some landholders committing to improving practices to enable future participation in MBI projects.

Environmental outcomes

To date, no measurement and reporting of the biodiversity outcomes of either Landscape Linkages or the Biodiversity Incentive Scheme has been undertaken. The experiences of landholders and agency staff working in each program, however, provide some indication of the likely impacts. Significant land areas under agreement within these programs were described by landholders as essentially unproductive. Management of these areas prior to agreement, therefore, focused on little more than weed and pest control (unproductive lands that were not managed for weeds and pests would not qualify for inclusion on the basis of biodiversity degradation) and few additional environmental outcomes were likely to be attained by placing them under agreement. Land areas that were productive also tended to require few changes to meet the requirements for agreements. Where fencing projects were undertaken, there were clear environmental benefits such as riparian (streambank) restoration and increased use of rotational grazing practices that increase pasture biodiversity (see Chapter 3).

A key issue, however, in determining the biodiversity outcomes of these projects is that each relied on a proxy measure of biodiversity to monitor and report on landholder progress. Agency staff highlighted concerns about using potentially imprecise estimates of land condition that might differ between assessors as a means of determining payments to landholders. Within resource management agencies, reporting on the progress or outcomes of these projects was limited to, for example, hectares of specific land types under agreement, kilometres of fencing and so on. While this reflected the limited practicality and cost-effectiveness of undertaking individual property-level biodiversity assessments, it should be recognized nevertheless that reporting of this type relies on probable rather than determined biodiversity outcomes.

Economic impacts

Despite the current levels of government enthusiasm for MBI projects, the lack of surety of funding to the agencies that implement them through political cycles meant that incentive agreements under Landscape Linkages and the Biodiversity Incentive Scheme were necessarily short-term. Importantly, neither program (nor any of the other MBI Pilot Projects) included an adjustment function to pass the true costs of environment conservation on to consumers. With government the sole buyer, and no means through which alternative buyers for ecosystem services are able to engage in this market, it is unlikely that further environmental services will be provided over and above what government is purchasing or what landholders would have provided anyway. As all participating landholders stressed, tight terms of trade for agricultural commodities limited their capacity to provide services requiring significant capital investment.

Landholders engaged in Landscape Linkages and the Biodiversity Incentive Scheme either reduced stocking rates to meet program requirements—meaning that payments compensated them for lost income rather than providing additional income—or placed unproductive land under agreement and therefore did receive additional income. This had two implications for the outcomes and usefulness of market-based incentives for the provision of ecosystem services. First, where landholders had reduced their stocking rates and, therefore, accrued no additional income, they remained constrained by financial resources and were limited in their capacity to undertake proactive conservation work. Second, with no mechanism through which the cost of providing ecosystem services may be passed on to consumers, it is likely that additional ecosystem services provided through these programs will only continue to be provided as long as the programs themselves run unless it can be demonstrated that the activities necessary to provide ecosystem services also boost productivity and/or profitability within a reasonable timeframe. Some activities, such as the introduction of rotation grazing, may in fact prove to be economically sustainable and thus justify the short-term use of MBIs to promote their adoption. Others, such as de-stocking and the fencing of sensitive lands may be increasingly recognized by landholders as important in securing the ecosystem services essential to productivity in the longer-term. However, experience with other programs has shown that increased awareness of such conservation practices does not lead to an increase in their application when landholders lack the financial resources to do so (Lockie, 1999, 2006). Any long-term provision of the ecosystem services targeted by these projects (again, over and above what landholders would have provided anyway) will require more sustained funding commitments from government.

Discussion

The move towards the inclusion of MBIs in resource management policy in Australia is underpinned by concerns about the continuing decline of Australia's biodiversity, the assumption that biodiversity decline can be curtailed by addressing market failure, and that MBIs can be applied to a number of environmental problems to achieve an economically efficient and targeted approach to conservation. This study found that targeted short-term biodiversity conservation had been achieved through price-based MBIs, and that MBI projects had assisted in building landholder understanding of the relationships between productivity and biodiversity. However, the study also revealed a number of ways in which these projects did not live up to the theoretical and technical arguments in favour of market-based approaches.

First, MBIs did not provide a means through which landholders were able to absorb or pass on the costs of environmental protection. The use of a market mechanism to direct government expenditure may certainly be justified if it can be shown that this offers efficiency and/or effectiveness benefits over alternative mechanisms for investment. However, the only ways in which these projects actually addressed market failure was through the education of landholders regarding relationships between biodiversity and agricultural production. In other words, the MBI projects had some impact as suasive measures alerting landholders to unintended resource degradation but little as agents of market reform. Given that one of the main criticisms of other suasive measures used in Australia such as the National Landcare and Property Management Planning programs has been that they are extremely effective in raising awareness, but not in addressing the tight terms of trade that make it difficult for farmers to implement practices with long-term and/or off-site benefits, the apparent inability of MBIs to address market failure raises significant questions regarding their likely environmental impact over and above other resource management programs.

Second, both MBI projects showed that targeting government expenditure on specific objectives (in this case, the protection of particular ecosystem types) was possible, but that the more criteria for targeting were introduced the less successful they were in meeting these criteria. The manner in which MBIs are represented by their proponents as a highly targeted alternative to supposedly 'blunt' and 'inflexible' regulation and public provision (as if these were the only alternatives) belies the considerable technical complexity involved in applying MBIs to multiple and complex objectives and the new forms of rigidity that any form of targeted policy intervention establishes. Asserting the theoretical and/or technical superiority of any one type of policy instrument is at odds with the inherently complex, multi-objective and multiple stakeholder nature of natural resource management.

Third, in seeking to target government expenditure more effectively the two MBI projects focused on the protection of representative samples of endangered and/or unique native ecosystems. In the selection of priority ecosystem types no consideration was given to the agroecology of on-farm biodiversity; that is, to relationships between the biodiversity of ecosystem types, the ecological functions this biodiversity performed, and the ecosystem services and financial benefits it delivered to agriculture. While farmers and agency field staff involved in the projects had some awareness of these relationships and used them to assess the costs and benefits of participation in the projects, the projects themselves were not designed to improve management of biodiversity on agricultural lands that did not support what were defined by resource management agencies as particularly valuable native ecosystems. The protection of such ecosystems is undoubtedly an important public good—irrespective of any private benefits it may also provide—that warrants public policy attention. However, the dimensions of on-farm biodiversity that provide services to agriculture and to society at large encompass much more than remnants of endangered or unique native vegetation. Policy interventions are required both to address more dimensions of on-farm biodiversity and to ensure that farmers who do not manage remnants of rare or unique native vegetation are not inadvertently sent the message that biodiversity is not their concern.

Fourth, MBI payments made through the two case studies rarely covered the full cost to landholders of biodiversity conservation. According to the economic theory underpinning MBIs this is not in itself a problem since we would not expect that MBIs would necessarily cover the full cost of conservation. One of the arguments in favour of auctions and similar MBIs in fact is that they allow resource users to calculate for themselves the value of an ecosystem service and the cost of providing it. Those that place a high value on services—or can provide them at minimum cost—will require little additional incentive. However, farmers involved in this and other studies (see Cocklin et al, 2006) report difficulty in quantifying the respective value to society and to themselves of environmental care, and in differentiating between what might reasonably be subsidized as a public good and what they should protect anyway as part of the duty of care associated with resource access rights. Some farmers feel it important to demonstrate to the wider community that they are capable of protecting the environment without financial assistance. Many who do accept payments report that since these do not cover the full cost of conservation they offer only a small incentive for activities that would have been undertaken anyway.

Leaving individuals to decide for themselves where and how much conservation to implement does not resolve questions regarding the value of ecosystem services, the public and private distribution of benefits arising from those services, the opportunity costs of particular conservation strategies or uncertainty regarding the effectiveness of those strategies in protecting environmental values in the long-term (Parker, 2005). Nor does it resolve questions regarding how much responsibility individuals should be expected to take for the delivery of ecosystem services to neighbouring farmers, future land users or the wider community as a condition of resource access. Scientific and moral uncertainties are simply hidden behind a theoretical argument for technical efficiency. It is taken for granted that some farmers will assume a greater duty of care than others and offer to deliver public goods at lower cost. Consequently, unlike cap and trade mechanisms that place a cost on resource access, auction mechanisms run the risk of placing a cost on resource protection and offering new opportunities for free-riding by those resource users who do not assume for themselves a high duty of care.

Fifth, the reported cost effectiveness of MBI projects relative to the establishment of public reserves has not been based on adequate consideration of either the probable durability of biodiversity outcomes in the longer-term or the extent to which these outcomes could be achieved through different means. Clearly, the benefits of these programs should be considered on a long-term basis that stretches beyond government funding cycles. Reporting on hectares placed under agreement is of little relevance if those land tracts and their associated biodiversity are conserved for only a short period of time. Similarly, government expenditure through MBI programs cannot be considered efficient and effective if it cannot be shown that landholders participating in those programs provided ecosystem services that were additional both to what they were already providing without specific financial incentives and to what they ought to be expected to provide as a condition of resource access.

Conclusion

The research discussed in this chapter does not suggest that market instruments are unsuitable as tools either for devolving funding to landholders for conservation outcomes or for regulating resource access. Only price-based MBIs were examined in detail (specifically, auctions for the provision of a particular ecosystem service) and proponents of MBIs will acknowledge circumstances in which quantity-based and market friction approaches are more relevant. Nevertheless, the research discussed here does support the argument that the current enthusiasm for MBIs among natural resource policy makers needs to be tempered by a more realistic assessment of their potential and a less dismissive attitude to their alternatives. The reasons for market failure in the provision of ecosystem services from agricultural biodiversity are complex and will not be solved through the allocation of limited government funding through market-based or any other means. No matter how technically proficient agencies become in their administration, it will remain the case that market mechanisms will work most effectively when focused on a small number of objectives. Some aspects of biodiversity such as conservation of specific high-value ecosystem types may lend themselves to this provided a large number of landholders are in a position to supply the required service and derive genuine financial benefit from doing so. However, the relationships between biodiversity, agroecology and farm productivity are seldom clearly specifiable and measurable. Nor are the boundaries between private and public benefit or between resource user rights and responsibilities. The spatial and temporal complexity of agrobiodiversity calls for robust and participatory processes of deliberation and debate over the management of uncertainty and the responsibilities of all resource users.

Acknowledgements

This chapter draws on research undertaken at CQUniversity Australia with financial support from the Australian Research Council (Project No. DP0664599).

References

ASEC (Australian State of the Environment Committee) (2006) *Australian State of the Environment 2006: Independent Report to the Commonwealth Minister for the Environment and Heritage*, CSIRO Publishing on behalf of the Department of Environment and Heritage, Canberra, Australia

Cocklin, C., J. Dibden, and N. Mautner (2006), 'From market to multifunctionality? Land stewardship in Australia', *The Geographical Journal*, vol 172, no 3, pp197–205

Cutbush, G. (2006) *Incentives for Natural and Cultural Heritage Conservation: Paper prepared for the 2006 Australian State of the Environment Committee*, CSIRO Publishing on behalf of the Department of Environment and Heritage, Canberra, Australia

Dibden, J. and Cocklin, C. (2009) '"Multifunctionality": Trade protectionism or a new way forward?', *Environment and Planning A*, vol 41, pp163–182

Elliott, E.D. (1994) 'Environmental TQM: Anatomy of a pollution control program that works!', *Michigan Law Review*, vol 92, no 6, pp1840–1854

Farber, S. and Tietenberg, T. (2006) 'Market-based instruments', in C.J. Cleveland (ed) *Encyclopedia of Earth*, National Council for Science and the Environment, Washington, DC

Freckleton, R. and Lockie, S. (2009) *Market-Based Instruments and the Conservation of Biodiversity on Private Land: An Independent Evaluation of Three Pilot Projects Undertaken by Regional Natural Resource Management Groups in Queensland, Australia*, Institute for Health and Social Science Research, CQUniversity Australia, Rockhampton, Queensland

Lockie, S. (1999) 'The state, rural environments, and globalisation: "Action at a distance" via the Australian Landcare program', *Environment and Planning A*, vol 31, pp597–611

Lockie, S. (2000) 'Environmental governance and legitimation: State-community interactions and agricultural land degradation in Australia', *Capitalism, Nature, Socialism*, vol 11, no 2, pp41–56

Lockie, S. (2006) 'Networks of agri-environmental action: Temporality, spatiality and identity in agricultural environments', *Sociologia Ruralis*, vol 46, no 1, pp22–39

Lockie, S. and Higgins, V. (2007) 'Roll-out neoliberalism and hybrid practices of regulation in Australian agri-environmental governance', *Journal of Rural Studies*, vol 23, no 1, pp1–11

Lockie, S. (2009) 'Agricultural biodiversity and neoliberal regimes of agri-environmental governance in Australia', *Current Sociology*, vol 57, no 3, pp407–426

Morgans, D. (1996) 'Commercialising protected areas: Lessons from the USA', in T. Charters, M. Gabriel and S. Prasser (eds) *National Parks: Private sector's Role*, USQ Press, Toowoomba, Queensland, Australia

NMBIWG (National Market-Based Instrument Working Group) (2005) *National Market-Based Instruments Pilot Program: Round One. An Interim Report*, National Action Plan for Salinity and Water Quality, Canberra, Australia

Parker, W. (2005) 'Do ecosystem service markets have a role in agriculture?', *Farm Policy Journal*, vol 2, pp11–19

Rolfe, J., McCosker, J. and Windle, J. (2005) *Establishing an East-West Landscape Linkage in the Southern Desert Uplands: Final Report for MBI Project 18*, CQUniversity Australia, Rockhampton, Queensland

Scott, F. (1998) 'Market-based approaches for sustainability', in F. Scott, G. Kaine, R. Stringer and K. Anderson (eds) *Sustainability in a Commercial Context: Market-Based Approaches*, Land and Water Resources Research and Development Corporation, Canberra, Australia, pp33–59

Whitten, S., Reeson, A.F., Windle, J. and Rolfe, J. (2007) *Barriers and Opportunities for Increasing Participation in Conservation Auctions*, Land and Water Australia, Canberra, Australia

Whitten, S. and Shelton, D. (2005) *Markets for Ecosystem Services in Australia: Practical Design and Case Studies*, CSIRO, Canberra, Australia

Whitten, S., van Bueren, M. and Collins, D. (2003) 'An overview of market-based instruments and environmental policy in Australia', *Proceedings of the sixth Annual AARES National Symposium*, Rural Industries Research and Development Corporation, Canberra, Australia, pp. 6–23

Windle, J. and Rolfe, J. (2006) *Fitzroy Basin Association's Biodiversity Tender: An Outline and Evaluation*, CQUniversity Australia, Rockhampton, Queensland

Windle, J., Rolfe, J., McCosker, J. and Lingard, A. (2007) *Desert Uplands Committee Landscape Linkage Main Report*, Desert Uplands Committee, Emerald, Queensland, Australia

WWF (Worldwide Fund for Nature, Australia) (2006) *Submission to the Senate Inquiry into Australia's National Parks, Conservation Reserves and Marine Protected Areas*, Supplementary Submission to the Senate Environment, Information Technology and the Arts Committee, Canberra, Australia

18

Agrobiodiversity and Sustainable Farm Livelihoods: Policy Implications and Imperatives

Stewart Lockie and David Carpenter

Our objective in this chapter is to distil some of the broad policy implications of research into the relationships between agriculture, biodiversity and markets. To place these observations in some sort of context, it is important to note that quite apart from the variance in social, political, economic and agroecological conditions faced by relevant policy-making and regulatory institutions around the world (variance that would make highly specific policy recommendations largely redundant), prior to the 1980s the terms biological diversity and biodiversity were largely unheard of. Before the early 1990s, they were not on the international political radar—agricultural biodiversity even less so (see Hannigan, 1995; Escobar, 1998). This is not to say that declines in biodiversity prior to the 1990s were too insignificant to generate either awareness or action. Nor that various aspects of biodiversity were not subject to intentional management by farmers and rural communities, investigation by scientific agencies, campaigning by NGOs and/or intervention by governments. In fact, unlike other global environmental issues such as ozone depletion and anthropogenically-induced climate change that were largely unknown before the late 20th century, considerable efforts had been made for some time to protect native species and ecosystems, to farm in ways that enhance soil biota, and to conserve and exploit the genetic diversity of important food plants and animals.

So what changed? Why did awareness and concern over biodiversity loss escalate to the point that it became one of only two major issues dealt with at the 1992 United Nations Conference on Environment and Development? Accelerating rates of species loss certainly played a major role (Lockie, 2009). So too did the growth of research in conservation biology, the emergence of new biotechnology industries dependent on access to genetic resources, and the establishment of multilateral institutions and legal frameworks through the United Nations capable of coordinating international debate and agreements (Hannigan, 1995). Just as critical, however, was the simplicity and elegance of the concept itself. As a term, 'biodiversity' captures something of the complexity of ecosystem processes, the contribution these make to human social and economic well-being, and the moral charge of ecosystem and species protection (see also Hannigan, 1995). Intuitively, 'biodiversity' makes sense. It takes complex and potentially disparate issues, sums them up, and makes them amenable to political recognition and coordinated policy intervention across a plethora of jurisdictions and scales.

The flip side to this, of course, is that the policy solutions to species decline and other aspects of biodiversity management are unlikely to be as simple and elegant as the term itself. Biodiversity invokes multiple levels of biological organization and interaction across space and time. It invokes multiple levels of human organization and interaction across space and time. Uncertainty and conflict in biodiversity management are not functions solely of ecological complexity and the need to deepen our understanding of ecosystem processes but of humans' conflicting goals, interests, values and aspirations. Nowhere is this more apparent than in agriculture.

Biodiversity, ecosystem services and agriculture

The contribution of biodiversity to agriculture is conceptualized in terms of ecosystem functions and services that provide resources, support productivity, regulate ecological processes and meet social and cultural needs. Such services range from crop adaptability and growth to pest control and flood mitigation. As several of the case studies discussed in this book demonstrate, these services provide tangible economic benefits to farmers as well as helping them to manage risk and underwriting the sustainability of farms in the longer-term. For example, farmers utilizing cell, or controlled-time, grazing in Central Queensland to maximize pasture growth, quality and diversity reported a doubling of pasture yield and greater beef production at lower cost (Dumaresq et al, Chapter 3).

Diversity itself, however, is seldom responsible for the performance of the ecosystem functions that deliver services to agriculture. In general terms, ecosystem services do not depend on diversity per se but on specific groups of organisms and the interactions among and between these groups. Further, often we think of biodiversity comprising cultivated or domesticated species and wild or native species. Putting aside the question of protecting native ecosystems for their own intrinsic value, a more useful division for the purposes of agroecosystem management is between planned biodiversity and associated biodiversity. This recognizes that farmers purposefully manage both domesticated and non-domesticated species using a variety of husbandry practices, and that farms are ecologically embedded within their surrounding environments (including their soil environments) (Altieri, 1999; Chapter 2). Given that species exhibit highly variable levels of spatial and temporal mobility, the delivery of specific ecosystem services through biodiversity is very much scale-dependent.

With this in mind, it is possible to reorganize and add to Altieri and Rogé's (Chapter 2) principles of agroecological design to more explicitly demonstrate the importance and practicality of considering scale in agrobiodiversity management. At the same time, this demonstrates the increasing complexity associated with operationalization of each principle at higher levels of biological and social organization. Agroecological principles of genetic, or infraspecific, diversity, for example, appear relatively straightforward. Utilization of more than one variety of important plants and animals provides insurance against pests, diseases and climatic variability while also providing for more varied dietary and livelihood opportunities (see, for example, Kumar et al's summary of the agronomic, gastronomic and cultural characteristics of different rice varieties utilized in the Western Ghats region of India, Table 9.2). Utilization of genetically heterogeneous landraces, particularly in marginal environments and/or resource-poor communities, provides similar services. The human ecology of genetic diversity, however, is considerably more complicated, a theme we will return to below.

Remembering that diversity per se does not ensure all essential ecosystem processes and services are provided, agroecological principles related to species diversity focus: (1) on functional relationships between species; and (2) feeding biological activity. Increasing the functional diversity of species utilized within a field and/or farm promotes more efficient use of resources such as nutrients, solar radiation, water, etc and provides for better pest protection and compensatory growth. Utilizing practices that promote the growth and accumulation of organic matter (e.g. green manures, cover crops, stubble retention etc) and minimizing practices that destroy soil organic matter (e.g. cultivation) or inhibit biological activity (e.g. agrichemical use) supports soil biota and other aspects of associated biodiversity. A temporal element can be added to these principles. Ensuring that species diversity includes perennial plants within fields, as well as on field margins, provides habitat permanence for pest-enemy complexes, makes use of more ecological niches and improves nutrient and water cycling. Legume-based rotations and fallow periods inhibit pest and disease lifecycles and restore soil fertility.

However, with so many potential combinations of species it is critical that considerable research effort be devoted both to designing and evaluating various spatial and temporal combinations and to documenting and testing those combinations used in traditional farming systems. Further, this research should not be restricted to predominantly cultivated agroecosystems in which the question is essentially what to plant, but should include predominantly grazed ecosystems in which the question is how to manipulate plant populations using livestock.

Spatial and temporal heterogeneity at the landscape level has been highlighted by numerous researchers, a mosaic of ecosystems providing different types of habitat for associated biodiversity and a mosaic of agroecosystems, more specifically, at various stages of succession providing insurance against pests and climatic variability (see also Mutersbaugh and Klooster, Chapter 10). Further, connectivity between habitat types provides for species migration and increases the capacity of predator populations to respond to increases in pest numbers.

Operationalizing the principle of landscape heterogeneity, however, raises important questions about the optimal mix of farmed agroecologies relative to comparatively natural ecosystems within a landscape. These questions are complicated by the increasing number of resource users implicated in the management of resources at a landscape scale (each with their own property rights and responsibilities, production goals, family and cultural responsibilities, beliefs and knowledge etc) and the different goals that landscape scale management of biodiversity may be oriented to. Management for the protection of endemic biodiversity within farmed landscapes is not necessarily contrary to management for the sustainability of the agroecosystems within those landscapes, but neither does it suggest the same ordering of priorities in defining optimal mixes of land use. A clearly under-explored area of research is the contribution of relatively natural ecosystems to various agricultural production landscapes and the degree to which endemic biodiversity may purposefully be built into those landscapes without compromising productivity or, in fact, while lifting it. It may well be true that the financial and risk-mitigation benefits of managing agroecosystems specifically to maximize biodiversity are likely to be greatest in marginal landscapes characterized by both low fertility/rainfall and/or comparatively high spatial and temporal variability (see Chapters 2 and 3). However, as Omer et al demonstrate in Chapter 8, even highly intensive industrialized farms benefit from the ecosystem services provided by biodiversity. The challenge is to find practical ways of building various types of endemic biodiversity into different types of landscape in order to support different kinds of agroecology. The benefits of doing so will extend beyond the obvious 'win-win' for otherwise potentially conflicting environmental and production goals to include the maintenance of political support for farmers to access natural resources.

The erosion of agrobiodiversity as 'market failure'

According to economists, degradation of natural resources such as biodiversity is an outcome of market failure induced by inadequate understanding of the ecosystem services provided by those resources; open-access property rights regimes that limit the incentive individual users have to protect resources; and/or the under-pricing of resources even where they are recognized by some sort of market (see Lockie and Tennant, Chapter 17). Measures to address market failure may take a variety of forms including education and capacity building, regulation, and market-based incentives (MBIs). Reflecting the contents of this book, we are most concerned in this chapter with regulatory frameworks and MBIs, the latter of which may include measures designed both to encourage existing markets to internalize the cost of resource protection and measures which create new markets for ecosystem services.

While some might baulk at the suggestion that market failure explains all resource degradation, there are at least three reasons as to why this understanding provides a useful lens through which to examine some of the common themes to emerge through this book. First, and most important, for the vast majority of farmers it is impossible to divorce agrobiodiversity management from market exchange and associated livelihood activities (see Hellin et al, Chapter 13). Second, theories of market failure, market reform and market-based instruments provide the conceptual framework for an increasing number of public and private sector interventions to redress agrobiodiversity decline. Third, as Lockie and Tennant (Chapter 17) argue, as a complex and diffuse resource biodiversity is particularly vulnerable to market failure. The corollary of this is that biodiversity is also particularly difficult to manage effectively using centralized measures such as command-and-control regulatory instruments.

Regulatory issues

Regulatory frameworks for agrobiodiversity are characterized by two main features. First, they are overwhelmingly concentrated on access to plant genetic resources and, to a lesser extent, biosecurity and the protection of endemic biodiversity from agriculture. Second, they are incredibly controversial due their perceived impacts on the livelihoods of farmers—particularly small resource-poor farmers in the very parts of the world from which most biodiversity is sourced.

Clearly, we have a regulatory blind spot in relation to functional relationships between landscape diversity, the role of agriculture in maintaining that diversity, and the services it provides to agriculture. Explicit legislation, policy and programs for biodiversity are concentrated on cultivated and wild biodiversity as opposed to intended and unintended biodiversity. This is not to say that legislation and programs are not in place in various jurisdictions that lead to positive outcomes for landscape diversity and the delivery of services to agriculture. In Australia, for example, agri-environmental initiatives such as the National Landcare Program and National Property Management Planning Program (see Lockie, 2006) did a great deal to promote widespread use of native shelter belts along field margins, planting of perennial pasture species etc. Reports to the Convention on Biological Diversity acknowledge that these are likely to have had a major impact on the protection of biodiversity but say nothing about the contribution of biodiversity or landscape heterogeneity to agriculture or farm livelihoods (Lockie, 2009). Biodiversity incentive programs (Chapter 17 and below), meanwhile, purposefully leave questions regarding the balance of public and private benefits from endemic species and ecosystem diversity to 'the market'. In practice, what this means is that biodiversity incentive programs leave private landholders to determine for themselves the benefit they derive from, and the responsibility they have to protect, endemic biodiversity. As argued above, a more explicit research and policy focus on the relationships between agricultural production, landscape heterogeneity and endemic species biodiversity is likely to lead to more optimal outcomes for both agroecosystem and endemic diversity.

None of this is to suggest that plant genetic resources are not deserving of considerable policy and legislative attention. As Moore points out in Chapter 4, international food security rests on a small number of commercially grown crops and the management of infraspecific diversity for each of these species. One of the consistent themes running through the chapters of this book that deal with infraspecific diversity is the problematic nature of political debates that frame improved varieties and ex situ conservation efforts as the industrialized, commercialized, centralized and globalized enemy of farmer-friendly, in situ conservation of traditional, genetically heterogeneous varieties and landraces. This is not a division that farmers themselves necessarily recognize or respect. On the Philippine island of Bohol (Carpenter, Chapter 7) and in numerous other contexts (see Zimmerer, 2003), farmers who are actively engaged in in situ conservation also make considerable effort to access fresh genetic material through exchange of traditional, modern and creolized farmer varieties. These farmers do not reject modern seedstock or breeding and conservation techniques. What they reject is the intellectual property rights regimes that have emerged at the same time to protect the rights of breeders; regimes they believe are skewed to the interests of large breeding institutions and agribusiness firms at the expense of small farmers. Concerns focus on a number of issues including recognition of the role that farmers have played in the conservation and development of genetic resources which form the basis for modern plant breeding, the negative impacts on biodiversity and lack of adaptability of genetically uniform modern varieties, and the negative impacts on farmers' livelihoods of restrictions on the acquisition, use, reproduction and further development through their own breeding programs of modern varieties (Srinivasan, Chapter 5).

Here again, though, things are not entirely straightforward. There is no arguing that intellectual property rights regimes are designed to encourage innovation by enabling breeders to assert monopoly control over the commercial exploitation of their products; nor that large institutional and corporate breeders are best able to assert these rights. Further, under the aegis of the World Trade Organization, implementation and enforcement of intellectual property rights regimes has been defined as a trade issue. Signatory counties that fail to implement and enforce acceptable protection for plant varieties open themselves to challenge and potential sanctions for restricting trade. At the same time, however, the international regulatory framework for genetic resources very much reinforces national sovereignty over those resources and allows national regulatory regimes to accommodate provisions for benefit sharing, farmers' rights, scientific access etc (Moore, Chapter 4). Almost all developing countries with plant variety protection legislation in place thus allow farmers the right, for example, to use, save and exchange the seeds of protected varieties without making payment to the owners of those varieties (Srinivasan, Chapter 5).

In contrast with those who see the international regulatory regime as nothing more than a vehicle for corporate enclosure of the genetic commons, Moore (Chapter 4) presents this regime as an enabling framework that must be used more effectively at the national level if the world is going to manage genetic resources successfully in the face of climate change and other challenges. Srinivasan (Chapter 5) elaborates on a number of the issues that must be resolved at the national level, particularly in developing countries. He argues that concerns about the exclusion of small farmers, erosion of genetic diversity, dependence on multinational companies, and so on, are well founded, but that the measures put in place to preserve farmers' rights and researchers' access have failed to reward on-farm conservation and innovation at the same time that they have diluted incentives for innovation among institutional and corporate breeders. Both Moore and Srinivasan agree that a key issue here is institutional, legal and scientific capacity and infrastructure to develop and implement effective national regulatory systems. Black and Kireeva (Chapter 6) add that international and national intellectual property rights regimes are yet to come to terms with the biosecurity implications of genetic resource protection and exploitation. Without significant attention to the capacity issues identified by Moore and Srinivasan we foresee little likelihood that phytosanitary measures such as quarantine and risk assessment will be integrated with intellectual property rights regimes and other strategies to conserve and exploit genetic resources.

Recognizing biodiversity values in agricultural commodity markets

As Scherr et al (Chapter 14) point out, biodiversity-friendly practices are often more profitable for farmers, or provide them with other tangible benefits. The cell grazing case study referred to above is just one example; however, it is an example which shows that increasing profitability is not necessarily sufficient to stimulate rapid adoption of new practices. Information alone does not resolve market failure. It is not enough to know that an alternative farming system may be more profitable. The system itself must be understood, it must be consistent with other personal and cultural values, and farmers must have the resources to implement it. The more complex the system, the more time farmers must invest in learning how to manage it, the more risky its adoption, and the more technical, financial and emotional support they will require (Vanclay, 2004). Biodiversity-friendly farming systems often depend on sophisticated agroecological understanding that makes them significantly more complex than 'conventional' farming systems, while their implementation imposes opportunity costs in terms of labour and capital that could be devoted to other, seemingly less risky, income earning activities.

Complicating this further, unless biodiversity-friendly management practices do boost productivity and/or lower costs, their profitability will depend on some sort of market recognition of biodiversity-friendly produce. Recognition may be based on the contribution of the management system to biodiversity conservation, but it may also be based on more general environmental claims, the unique character of the product, and/or its perceived quality attributes. In turn, recognition may lead to the sale of previously underutilized products; it may lead to price premiums over competing produce; or it may lead simply to more stable market access. Certified organic quinoa, for example (see Hellin, Chapter 13), is marketed as a product that is unique, environmentally-friendly and nutritious. While its continued cultivation may contribute to the biodiversity of Andean agriculture and the livelihoods and food security of the farmers who grow it, these attributes are not particularly visible in the product as marketed for export. Similarly, in the case of food products certified with Geographical Indications (products such as Roquefort or Camembert cheeses), the unique contributions of the agroecological and cultural milieus in which the products were produced to their sensory characteristics and quality are foregrounded, but contributions to biodiversity remain unclear and potentially contradictory (see Thévenod-Mottet and Allaire, Chapter 12). Bird-friendly coffee, by contrast (see Neilson et al, Chapter 11), competes in the mass commodity market for coffee by making explicit biodiversity claims in relation to habitat protection. Alternative eco-certification schemes for coffee tend to make more generalized environmental and, in some cases, social claims. However, all depend on a range of implicit and explicit criteria to simultaneously improve or guarantee product quality. As Neilson et al (Chapter 11) point out, environmental and social claims are not generally sufficient by themselves to maintain access to premium coffee markets. Even in the case of Fair Trade—one of the few schemes to guarantee minimum price premiums—coffee that does not meet high quality standards is usually diverted to other markets including the uncertified and unbranded mass market (Lockie, 2008).

The common thread running through experiences with the marketing of underutilized and/or unique products such as quinoa and eco-friendly certification of otherwise mass market commodities like coffee is the need to construct and coordinate entire value chains. Certification is best understood, in fact, as a tool for value chain coordination; a tool that raises important questions about the purpose of coordination and who benefits from it. Both Mutersbaugh and Klooster (Chapter 10) and Neilson et al (Chapter 11) conclude that certification schemes are generally imposed on producers from above; often by environmental NGOs but increasingly by retailers and other buyers looking to increase their capacity for vertical supply chain coordination and risk management. This is certainly more true of some certification schemes than others and some have made impressive attempts to democratize standards-setting procedures. Nevertheless, the critical point here is that standardized compliance checklists are not, by themselves, sufficiently sophisticated to address complex sustainability issues (Neilson et al, Chapter 11). They do not, for example, link to landscape-scale biodiversity management strategies (Mutersbaugh and Klooster, Chapter 10). Nor do they engage with the local and national institutional and political structures necessary to coordinate and ensure compliance with such strategies (Neilson et al, Chapter 11).

Standards-setting, auditing, certification and labelling are certainly useful tools in the process of encouraging recognition of biodiversity values in agricultural commodity markets. However, government and NGO policy measures need to extend beyond the provision of assistance to farmers to pursue certification. Consideration must be given to who ought to be able to participate, and in what capacity, at every link in the value chain. Tools such as participatory value chain analysis and farmer organization are a step in the right direction, but capacity and willingness must also be developed in the government sector to facilitate market information, regulate transactions, provide infrastructure, clarify property rights, support research and development, monitor ecosystem health etc (Hellin, Chapter 13). Experience to date, in other words, suggests that continued public intervention (albeit not necessarily regulatory intervention) is necessary if farmers are to be able to internalize and then pass on the costs of environmental protection.

Payments for ecosystem services (PES)

Certification and labelling schemes aim to resolve market failure induced by inadequate information and pricing of natural resources by making the otherwise intangible environmental, social and quality attributes of agricultural commodities more visible throughout the value chain. PES, in contrast, do not aim to resolve failures within commodity markets themselves but to construct new markets for ecosystem services. Numerous arguments have been made in favour of PES, some of which relate to property rights and responsibilities and others to the effectiveness and efficiency of expenditure to address environmental degradation. It is widely accepted that access to a natural resource (i.e. a property right) to undertake production also confers a duty of care, or responsibility, to look after that resource and to avoid using it in such as way as to compromise the property rights of others (Reeve, 2001). Farmers do not have a right, under any form of land tenure, to simply do whatever they like with no regard either for the environment or their neighbours. However, the socially optimal level of environmental protection provided by farmers may still be above and beyond what is deemed reasonable as a condition of resource access. Some sort of payment for what is generally understood, therefore, as a public good environmental service is likely to increase provision of that service to a more socially optimal level (Stone and Wu, Chapter 15).

In an ideal world, PES would only ever be directed to unambiguously public goods. However, proponents argue that where market failure means farmers are not able to recoup the costs of environmental protection, PES and other MBIs offer more effective and efficient mechanisms for the investment of public money than alternatives such as legislative intervention or the establishment of reserves (see Lockie and Tennant, Chapter 17). Even where activities such as the protection of endemic biodiversity provide ecosystem services to the farmer, the benefits of these services are likely to be subtle, long-term, and shared with neighbouring resource users who may or may not absorb the cost of protecting endemic biodiversity themselves. Such activities are therefore particularly unlikely to be adopted if they incur significant upfront or maintenance costs (Scherr et al, Chapter 14).

As with all forms of external intervention, however, PES schemes carry the risk of creating perverse incentives and outcomes. Stone and Wu (Chapter 15) identify three categories of risk. First, slippage may occur when the focus of exploitative activities simply shifts from newly protected to previously unused resources. Second, environmental goals may be undermined if PES schemes are insensitive to the non-linear relationships between resource management activities, ecosystem processes and environmental outcomes. Payments that are dispersed over too large an area may fail to generate sufficient critical mass of activity to make a significant difference to service provision. Third, similarly, environmental goals may not be achieved efficiently if PES schemes are insensitive to the spatial interdependence of ecosystem processes. Preservation of particular components of endemic biodiversity, for example, may depend both on a minimum total habitat area and the relative continuity or proximity of habitat fragments depending on specific species requirements. The efficiency of PES thus depends on effective targeting as spreading payments too far, or too randomly, may undermine service provision.

However, as Lockie and Tennant suggest in Chapter 17, the more sophisticated the targeting criteria used for PES, the more difficult it is to achieve this targeting within the framework of a market-based approach. The more targeting is attempted through criteria for PES payments, the less latitude there actually is for resource users to make their own decisions about whether and under what conditions to provide a particular service, potentially undermining the direction of incentives to those resource users willing and able to provide them at least cost. Further, Stone and Wu agree with Lockie and Tennant that many existing PES schemes offer incentives that are not sufficient to fully cover the cost of service provision and are most likely to be taken up, therefore, by farmers who are particularly receptive to the environmental goals of these schemes; that is, farmers who accept they have a duty of care to provide particular services and are willing and able to do so for no or minimal monetary reward. The lesson here is that—like certification schemes and other market-based approaches—PES are not a panacea for biodiversity management but a useful tool that must be carefully targeted and complemented by measures to build the capacity of farmers, NGOs and governments alike to plan and manage natural resources to achieve environmental and production goals.

Conclusion

The importance of effective agrobiodiversity management is only likely to increase in light of existing and predicted trends in climate change (Moore, Chapter 4). Rising mean temperatures, changing rainfall patterns and, perhaps most importantly, increased variability and uncertainty in relation to both, will increase pressure on resource managers and policy makers to find new and creative ways of building adaptability and resilience into agricultural and relatively natural landscapes alike while, at the same time, continuing to lift agricultural productivity. Much of the innovation in environmental policy at the present time is focused on experimentation with various forms of market-based instrument. The use of MBIs recognizes that the vast majority of the world's farmers engage in some sort of market exchange; that commodity markets seldom provide direct and timely rewards for sound environmental management; and that natural resources such as agrobiodiversity are too complex and diffuse to be effectively managed through centralized and/or regulatory measures alone. Some MBIs, including a number of eco-certification schemes, have been developed by civil society and environmental NGOs as a challenge to market relations that exploit and disadvantage especially small farmers. However, there is a danger that in the enthusiasm to develop and test MBIs every social and environmental issue will come to be conceptualized first and foremost as an example of market failure, blinkering us to alternative ways of understanding and addressing those issues. As has been argued at various points throughout this chapter, MBIs do not obviate the continuing and pressing need for research into more biodiversity-friendly and sustainable agroecologies, for resource user and institutional capacity building, or for more effective market regulation.

Policy measures must also recognize that the need for innovation is not driven solely by environmental change. Farm households may have many aspirations including, critically, involvement in the economic and cultural transformations of modernity (Kumar et al, Chapter 9). Respect for these aspirations requires more than incremental improvements in the incomes, food security, or other indicators of well-being for farm households. In the face of social, cultural and economic change, sustainable agroecologies and custodianship of the biodiversity on which adaptation to climate change depends must be linked to economic justice and genuine livelihood options for those who provide these services.

References

Altieri, M. (1999) 'The ecological role of biodiversity in agroecosystems', *Agriculture, Ecosystems and Environment*, vol 74, pp19–31

Escobar, A. (1998) 'Whose knowledge, whose nature? Biodiversity, conservation and the political ecology of social movements', *Journal of Political Ecology*, vol 5, pp53–82

Hannigan, J. (1995) *Environmental Sociology: A Social Constructionist Perspective*, Routledge, London

Lockie, S. (2006) 'Networks of agri-environmental action: Temporality, spatiality and identity within agricultural environments', *Sociologia Ruralis*, vol 46, no 1, pp22–39

Lockie, S. (2008) 'Conversion or co-option? the implications of "mainstreaming" for producer and consumer agency within Fair Trade networks', in C. Farnworth, J. Jiggins, and E. Thomas (eds) *Creating Food Futures: Trade, Ethics and the Environment*, Gower, Aldershot, UK

Lockie, S. (2009) 'Agricultural biodiversity and neoliberal regimes of agri-environmental governance in Australia', *Current Sociology*, vol 57, no 3, pp407–426

Reeve, I. (2001) 'Property rights and natural resource management: Tiptoeing round the slumbering dragon', in S. Lockie and L. Bourke (eds) *Rurality Bites: The Social and Environmental Transformation of Rural Australia*, Pluto Press, Sydney

Vanclay, F. (2004) 'Social principles for agricultural extension to assist in the promotion of natural resource management', *Australian Journal of Experimental Agriculture*, vol 44, pp213–222

Zimmerer, K. (2003) 'Just small potatoes (and ulluco)? The use of seed-size variation in "native commercialized" agriculture and agrobiodiversity conservation among Peruvian farmers', *Agriculture and Human Values*, vol 20, pp107–123

Index

For Product Safety Concerns and Information please contact our EU
representative GPSR@taylorandfrancis.com Taylor & Francis Verlag GmbH,
Kaufingerstraße 24, 80331 München, Germany

Printed and bound by CPI Group (UK) Ltd, Croydon, CR0 4YY
08/05/2025
01864425-0003